BORN OF LAKES AND PLAINS

ALSO BY ANNE F. HYDE

Empires, Nations, and Families:
A New History of the North American West, 1800–1860

An American Vision:
Far Western Landscape and National Culture, 1820–1920

Shaped by the West: A History of North America
(co-authored with William Deverell)

Frémont's First Impressions:
The Original Report of His Exploring Expeditions
of 1842–1844 (editor)

The West in the History of the Nation
(co-authored with William Deverell)

BORN OF LAKES AND PLAINS

Mixed-Descent Peoples and the
Making of the American West

Anne F. Hyde

W. W. NORTON & COMPANY
Independent Publishers Since 1923

For information about permission to reproduce selections from this book, write to
Permissions, W. W. Norton & Company, Inc., 500 Fifth Avenue, New York, NY 10110

For information about special discounts for bulk purchases, please contact
W. W. Norton Special Sales at specialsales@wwnorton.com or 800-233-4830

Manufacturing by LSC Harrisonburg
Book design by Brooke Koven
Production manager: Anna Oler

Library of Congress Cataloging-in-Publication Data

Names: Hyde, Anne Farrar, 1960– author.
Title: Born of lakes and plains : mixed-descent peoples and the making
of the American West / Anne F. Hyde.
Description: First edition. | New York, NY : W. W. Norton & Company, [2022] |
Includes bibliographical references and index.
Identifiers: LCCN 2021037131 | ISBN 9780393634099 (hardcover) |
ISBN 9780393634105 (epub)
Subjects: LCSH: West (U.S.)—History—19th century. | Racially mixed people—
West (U.S.)—History—19th century. | Indians of North America—West (U.S.)—
History—19th century. | Fur traders—West (U.S.)—History. | Whites—
Relations with Indians.
Classification: LCC F591 .H993 2022 | DDC 978/.02—dc23
LC record available at https://lccn.loc.gov/2021037131

W. W. Norton & Company, Inc., 500 Fifth Avenue, New York, N.Y. 10110
www.wwnorton.com

W. W. Norton & Company Ltd., 15 Carlisle Street, London W1D 3BS

1 2 3 4 5 6 7 8 9 0

CONTENTS

MAPS

A NOTE ON TERMS

THIS BOOK is about Indigenous Americans and the new peoples with whom they traded, fought, and made families. Those traders and settlers came mainly from Europe but also from Latin America and Africa. Race and language have thorny histories. Every term that describes racial mixing can hurt, especially words appearing in the historical record and in federal, state, and territorial law. For the people I track through the past, I've chosen *mixed-descent* because it avoids the language of blood or race. It suggests how families draw different past heritages together.

Words linked to race science and eugenics, like *mixed-breed* and *half-breed*, only appear when quoted from the historical record. *Metis, mixed-race, mixed-blood*, or *mixed-ancestry* appear in the book but lightly.

As Europeans, Euro-Americans, European immigrants, and Latin Americans evolved into U.S. residents, they lumped themselves together into a category they called White, to distinguish themselves from Blacks or Native Americans. Whites lumped all Indigenous people together as *Indians* or *Natives*, terms still used today to describe Indigenous peoples collectively. When Indigenous people reclaimed governments, language, and land—a process still unfolding—they used *American Indian* and *Native American* as collective terms with power. Along with specific tribal names, this book uses *Indian, Native,* and *Indigenous* interchangeably. I never put racial terms, Native languages, or names in quotes unless, of course, I'm quoting someone in the past who used those words.

PREFACE

In the winter of 1790, a courtship blossomed between an Irish fur trader and an Ojibwe woman on a lonely island off Lake Superior's southern shore, a place haunted by Ojibwe ghosts. The eight children born to this couple would negotiate treaties, send sons to die in the Civil War, and publish poetry in Ojibwe and English.

Cree uncles and fathers, living and hunting north of Winnipeg in the 1770s, allowed a Swiss immigrant to marry into their band. The child of that union, Cree and Swiss, chose to marry two different men in a life that took her from the dry plains of the Canadian Shield to the Douglas fir forests of the Pacific Northwest.

A mixed Otoe-American family welcomed a baby during a summer fur trade rendezvous. Born in 1832 amid thousands of hunters, traders, and their families gathered high in the Rocky Mountains, that daughter later sued the Otoe and U.S. nations for the right to homestead on the Great Plains.

These family stories are scenes in a long-hidden history of Native Americans and Europeans mixing blood and blending families. It begins in 1600 with the fur trade on the Great Lakes and Hudson's Bay, extends through the colonial violence of the eighteenth century, carries on through the hacksaw of nineteenth-century U.S. expansion to the Pacific Coast and the Native response, and ends in the twentieth century in a new Indian Country, on reservations and in cities across the U.S. West and Canada.

At the heart of this book are acts personal and passionate, violent and loving, familiar and familial. When warm bodies lay close

in winter, they created new hearts beating by summer. Too often
only one body was willing and the other was captive, raped, or abandoned. But sex has stunning generative power, and that power to
make kin, blend villages, and build clans anchors this account of
mixed-descent families and how war, trade, and love extended them
across North America.

A narrative of our past with shared blood at its heart puts Indigenous people at the center of the history and fills in a dimension
missing in other accounts. Generations of scholars have now shown
the astonishing violence that European conquerors, U.S. officials,
armies, missionaries, and encroaching settlers visited on Native peoples. But if we understand early America only as a tale of unending
violence, we miss the families and relationships that enabled Native
peoples to survive into the present. Indigenous people were not
simply victims. Mixing heritage and blending families was often a
Native choice. They showed creativity and resourcefulness in using
family making to secure their lives and heritage.[1]

To TRACK this American tale, I chose five mixed-descent families
as guides. Whether they lived on Canadian lakes, in summer bison-
hunting camps on the Plains, or around reservation schoolhouses,
these families show the deep and varied roots of mixed-heritage
history. They were not average folk—they had the status to create
and preserve a trove of letters, account books, photographs, deeds,
diaries, invoices, bills, memoirs, poems, and drawings. The McKays
married Crees, Chinooks, and Cayuses from what is now Canada,
Washington, and Idaho. In search of fur, and guided by Cree explorers, Alexander McKay would find the Arctic Sea and, accompanied
by his Cree-Scots son Thomas, sail around the tip of South America. Crane clan Ojibwes made families with Johnstons and Schoolcrafts in Michigan, New York, and Ontario. Ozhaguscodaywayquay,
married to John Johnston, would prevent U.S. diplomats from being
killed when they insulted Ojibwe leaders in 1820. Her future son-
in-law, Henry Schoolcraft, was part of that nearly fatal mission. He

would become an architect of the U.S. Indian policy that replaced fur trading with Indian removal in the 1830s.

Farther west and south, young fur traders Andrew Drips and Lucien Fontenelle worked in Otoe and Omaha villages along the Platte and Missouri rivers. They succeeded by marrying Native women. By the 1830s, along with their wives, Macompemay and Mehubane, Drips and Fontenelle supplied a new fur trade in the Rocky Mountains. The Hairy Rope Cheyennes convinced St. Louisans William and Charles Bent to open a trading post on the U.S.-Mexico border. A diplomatic marriage between William Bent and three Cheyenne sisters allowed that fort to stand for decades, part of a Great Peace orchestrated by southern Plains Native nations. The records that all these families left behind show the fear, love, and hate swirling around them but also reveal how people managed to recover and rebuild, again and again—a fuller, truer version of frontier life.[2]

I also chose these families because they experienced violence and heartbreak. The Johnstons' Michigan business and home were burned to the ground by U.S. troops in 1812. The Cheyenne Bents lost dozens of family members at the Sand Creek and Washita massacres in the 1860s but made new lives on dry plains in Oklahoma. Louise Drips lost her land in Nebraska and sought help from Dakota relations on the Great Sioux Reservation. She didn't survive, but seven of her eleven children did. Sometimes people and records disappear entirely, because war and migration made life so chaotic, or because people chose to disappear. This history ends early in the twentieth century because detailed census records end after 1940, and families protected decisions made by those still living.

These family stories are bound by a focus on sex and marriage. When John Johnston appeared in an Ojibwe winter lodge on Lake Superior's southern shore with frostbitten feet, he needed help. The Ojibwe clan that saved him and made him kin by marriage had intermarried with French traders for several generations. In sixteenth- and seventeenth-century North America, long before European trade developed, Native peoples used sex and marriage with other Native groups as a means of managing diplomacy, business, and war.

Marriage was more about linking clans or nations through children than about love, and it could be temporary. Women and men married to bring resources to their households. Sometimes casual, sometimes not, sex carried people across racial and cultural borders by making strangers into kin.[3]

When fur traders and the Catholic church used intermarriage to conquer new places or grow a labor force, they trod familiar paths laid out by Indigenous practice. Because Europeans could obtain essential knowledge about animals, hunting, geography, and climate only by building relationships with Indigenous communities, through women and then children, the fur trade braided lives.

This history of frontier mingling, however, also had a violent edge. A seventeenth-century slave trade brought Indigenous people and Europeans together as both captors and captives. In the aftermath of the American Revolution, the nation claimed its new backcountry by giving land to White settlers and driving Native people west, destroying any earlier practical and peaceful alliances. For fur trade families like the McKays, Johnstons, and their Cree and Ojibwe kin, much of the violence came from competition in the fur trade. The Cree and Swiss Marguerite McKay's earliest memories were of her father's murder by another fur trader. The fur trade, and its family core, turned murderous when London investors decided there was too much money in the trade to leave it to Canadians. Thomas McKay shot British immigrants in 1816 when a war over pemmican got out of hand. Those corporate battles moved south and west with the trade.

The great hinge in the story is the nineteenth century. Just as Andrew Drips and Lucien Fontenelle arrived in St. Louis in 1819 to begin lives in the Missouri River fur trade, and as the Chinook Timmee married the Cree-Canadian Thomas McKay along the Columbia River, waves of settlers swept west into Indian Country, powered by a lust for land and justified by emerging ideologies of manifest destiny and White supremacy. By the early nineteenth century, many White families on the frontier itched to exterminate "Indians," but not local neighbors they hunted with and married. Federal and state governments passed removal legislation to force both Native and mixed-descent people from their eastern homelands. President

Andrew Jackson justified such action by arguing that Indians were but "a few wandering savages . . . unwilling to submit to the laws of the States and mingle with their population." In fact, Native peoples had long owned slaves, paid taxes, organized quilting bees, and married into local White, Black, and mixed families.[4]

As U.S. officials built the administrative structures required to remove eastern Indigenous people and to make war on western nations, marrying and mixing continued as a business strategy in the western fur trade. In the 1820s, young men like Andrew Drips married into Otoe communities who had been pushed from Iowa to Nebraska and now hunted and raised families along the Missouri. In the 1830s, other families—Bents and St. Vrains—went south to the Arkansas River to trap fur, hunt bison, and trade for horses with Cheyenne, Comanche, and Arapaho partners.

By the 1830s, federal and state law, enforced by the U.S. Army, had cleared the eastern United States of much of its Native and mixed-race populations. Now the problem of encroaching settlement spread westward. By the 1840s, several generations of mixed-descent families had spread into Indian Country onto western land not yet open for White settlement. As officials and land speculators in Missouri, then Kansas and Nebraska, tried to open up land for White Americans clamoring for opportunity, they faced a world already created by the fur trade. The legislation, diplomacy, and businesses required to make U.S. territories into states required an army of federal agents: supervisors, surveyors, trading post operators, licensing officials, and missionaries. Because of the job requirements and location, many of these officials had mixed-descent families or were themselves White and Native.

When White settlers repeatedly violated treaties that Native nations had negotiated with the U.S. government, and when Indian nations protested or took action to protect their borders, the result was three decades of Indian war. Between 1848 and 1878, war spread from Minnesota to Oregon and from the Dakotas to Texas. War tore apart families created by the fur trade. William McKay and his brothers served as scouts and translators in the Pacific Northwest's decade-long war, an era when defining who was and wasn't an Indian became essential both for military officials and for Indian leaders. In the 1860s, Mary Jane Drips and her sisters, Otoe and White, fled their Kansas City home for the Nebraska Great Nemaha Half-Breed Tract—land set aside for mixed-descent families in a removal-era effort to convince such families to move west with their Native kin.

A long, nasty, and still-unresolved debate around race was energized with the abolition of slavery and the effort during Reconstruction to guarantee citizenship to Black Americans. Many White Americans insisted that the color line in the postwar South needed to be policed more fiercely. That reaction bled over into attitudes about Indigenous Americans, their mixed-descent kin, and their places on the racial spectrum. The Cheyenne Bents, who had survived massacres and a removal from Colorado in the 1860s, found themselves in Indian Territory in the 1870s, living on a barren reservation. Mixed-descent people like the Bents—agile traders, cattle ranchers, and translators in the southwestern borderlands—went from being diplomats between nations to being a racial problem that the state had to excise.

In the years after the Civil War, as railroads, homesteaders, and Indian reservations spread over the West, immense federal power and confident Christian reformers threatened to steamroll the Native world. Mixed-descent people, like George and Julia Bent in Oklahoma and Emily Fontenelle on the Omaha reservation, now had to explain to their Native kin the U.S. policies of incarceration on reservations and the "mighty pulverizing machine" of allotment. A strategy of dividing up Indian reservations and their commonly owned land for allotment of tiny farms to individual "Indians," this federal policy would take 500 million acres of land out of Indigenous control. Allotment policy also required assessments of "blood quantum," that measure invented by nineteenth-century scientists to gauge how much "pure" Indian blood someone had. So beginning in the 1890s, hundreds of thousands of people signed up in the allotment rolls as "full-bloods," "mixed-bloods," "half-breeds," one-quarter, one-eighth, or "mostly white," a false precision that empowered racism as federal law.[5]

By the late nineteenth century, mixed-descent families found themselves in the crosshairs of federal and state laws that made intermarriage illegal. Their own Native kin often saw them as race traitors, aspiring to profit from Indian land loss. Faced with such danger, mixed-descent people hid, passed as members of other races, and denied their family heritage. By recovering those stories, and a history that has been largely erased, we gain a new vision of the past. A history of blending families across centuries of violence and war has vital significance today as Indigenous Americans navigate the racist yoke of blood quantum and as every American struggles to understand heritage and race.[6]

To grasp this history, we need more supple understandings of both marriage and family. Early on most of these relationships involved White men and Native women, making it easy to naturalize men's power and women's weakness. But when the Otoe Macompemay or the Cree Marguerite Waddens married White traders, they understood that marriage could be temporary and easily dissolved. Marriage could involve one man marrying many women to increase household power and influence, as Omaha leaders Big Elk and Joseph La Flesche did. When women needed resources for their families, as a young Cayuse woman did when she met Thomas McKay, she was among many women who married many men, one at a time. Women created households of women to protect their property and children, as the Drips, Barnes, and Geroux families did in Nebraska. Most rarely, marriage meant one man and one woman spending a lifetime together.[7]

Marriage was always a bridge linking individuals to larger communities. When George Bent, White and Cheyenne, was removed from Colorado to Oklahoma, he hoped he could save his world by building those bridges, by making kin among Cheyennes, Utes, and Arapahos. Kinship might carry his family across chasms of danger and loneliness, as it ever has.

BORN OF LAKES AND PLAINS

The Peoples of North America, 1600

Inuit

Inuit

Inuit

Inuit

Kutchin Hare

Tagish Dogrib

Nahane
Tlingit Tahltan Slavey

Haida

Chilcotin Cree

Cree

Cree

Naskapi

Cree

Beothuk

Nootka Squamish Sarcee
Lumni Okanagan

Chinook Spokane Blackfoot Assiniboine Ojibwe

Cayuse Nez Percé

Klamath Shoshone Crow Mandan

Modoc Paiute

Cheyenne

Pomo Shoshone Ute
Miwok

Yokut Paiute

Mission San
Francisco de Oraibi Navajo

Chumash Hopi

Tahue Apache Pueblo

Apache

Nakipa Mission de Cuquiárachi

Concho Apache

Ignacieno Yaqui Toboso

Tahue

Pericu Cora

Tecual Cazcan

Tamazultec

Pampuchin

Quebec (1608) Micmac

Abenaki Port Royal
(1605)

Odawa Cataraqui

Menominee Huron Fort Orange

Nakota Dakota Wampanoag

Lakota Ho-Chunk Fox Iroquois Villages Pequot

Omaha Iowa Miami Lenni Lenape

Pawnee Otoe Illinois Shawnee Powhatan

Arapaho Kaw Missouria Cahokia (former site)

Kiowa Osage Kaskaskia Tuscarora

Cherokee Waccamaw

Santa Fe (1612) Quapaw Chickasaw

Pueblos Caddo Tunica Coushatta

Comanche Wichita Villages Choctaw Creek Yamasee

Tonkawa Natchez Apalachee St. Augustine (1565)

Chitamacha Timucua

Karankawa Tekesta

Bocalo

Ojibwe

Ojibwe

Huastec

Tepehua

Ixcatec Maya

Mexico City Mixe

Chatino

Quiche

Indigenous Homelands

□ **Indigenous Settlements**

✳ **European Settlements**

N

0 ———— 250 mi

0 ———— 400 km

PROLOGUE

Seasons of Marriage and War

On the northern tier of North America, winter came hard—
life-and-death hard. Swiftly flowing rivers, the passage-
ways into and out of the interior, developed thick crusts of
impenetrable ice. Rushing waterfalls froze in place. Fish slept sus-
pended just beneath the frozen surfaces. Tucked away in caves, some
mammals hibernated, while others prowled through the winter's
cold, protected by luxurious fur coats.

Those distinctive mammals had fur in every color of winter and
summer landscapes. Ermines, hares, and foxes turned white when
the snow fell, and their fur grew in a thicker pattern. A mink's winter
coat concentrated twenty-one thousand hairs in a space the size of a
thumbprint. Animals who lived on and under icy streams had double
coats to insulate them. Beavers—giant rodents found everywhere in
North America—came in a variety of browns, from sandy river bottom to wet wood. Their dense, soft undercoats and coarse outer hair
allowed them to thrive in frozen streams and winter wind.[1]

People who lived in the northern regions of Europe, Asia, and
North America ate animal flesh and bones for calories to fuel life
and work. Animals' winter coats enabled hairless humans to survive
winters. Animal pelts covered their bodies and lined their shelters.

1

Only winter hunters knew where to find these animals and how to turn their fur into garments. They shared that knowledge and those valuable furs only with family and friends, people who were willing to mix blood and share life.

Before 1600

Fur, both beautiful and useful, had been part of an ongoing trade between North American peoples for a thousand years. Caddo chiefs wore gorgeous panther capes, Cree parents diapered babies with beaver skins, Otoe boys ran races in shoes lined with bearskin, and Ojibwe brides decorated their robes with white ermine fur.[2]

Furs formed a small part of a continental exchange of goods, services, and human beings. Feathers from birds in what is now Mexico ended up in ceremonial buildings along the Mississippi River. Shells from the Gulf of Mexico and the Pacific Coast appeared along the Hudson River, and otter pelts from California, ocelot furs from eastern Texas, and beaver and bison skins from Canada and New Mexico showed up everywhere. Trading included necessities but also sacred objects that gave leaders the power to start and end wars.

The continental trade in North America built networks among families, clans, and villages. It was so central to life that no one would risk trading with a stranger. Rituals around trade—eating, drinking, sex, tattooing, and sharing smoke—made strangers or enemies into friends or family. For anyone living in a Haudenosaunee fortress or an Ojibwe lodge, making kin created a cocoon of obligations that carried them through life. Only through trade could people meet their basic obligations to feed and protect relatives.[3]

Trade and family linked people across a continent in communities as different as Inuit igloo villages and the tall adobe buildings of the Pueblo. Best estimates of how many people lived in the Americas before European contact range from 70 to 100 million people. In forbidding deserts and mountains to fertile river bottoms and forests, people used a breathtaking variety of farming techniques and family arrangements to live and prosper. People spoke thousands of languages, and their religions, art, and architecture reflected that cultural richness.

Linguists group Indigenous Americans by language type. Crees, Ojibwes, Odawas, Cheyennes, and Shawnees share an Algonquian language base; the Iroquois, Hurons, Senecas, and Cherokees speak Iroquoian languages. Siouan speakers include Lakotas, Dakotas, Otoes, Assiniboines, Ho-Chunks, Omahas, and Osages. Native people's tribal names indicated where they came from and their family lineage—clans that included many generations of closely related people. Some clans built villages together, and others were subsumed by larger polities or kingdoms. Groups of independent villages could act as confederacies. Names changed to reflect these new combinations. European traders or missionaries gave groups names that they heard people use—like Cree, Sioux, Flathead, Mohawk, and Omaha. These names often stuck even when they were incorrect. No one used the label *Indian* or *Native American* until long after "Europeans" (who didn't call themselves that either) arrived.[4]

Before the arrival of Europeans, great Native empires with splendid cities rose and fell, spawning new religions, accounting systems, and art. That rich history disappears when we view Native America from the perspective of European settlement; from this vantage point, we see nothing but a conquered land littered with Indian bones. A history of North America with mixed-descent families at its core creates a different view of the past, one with resourceful people making families through centuries of contact and war.[5]

The fur trade with Europeans began at a dynamic moment in North American history. By the 1400s, power and wealth had coalesced along the Mississippi River. Thickly settled agricultural villages produced crops, pottery to store food, and beautiful items that celebrated the religious beliefs linking these peoples. Many nations and confederacies paid tribute with crops and labor to build great mound cities like Cahokia and Natchez, which rose around earthen structures that stood at the ceremonial hearts of these cities. The trade in labor, food, and luxury goods fed the rise of kingdoms where hundreds of thousands of people lived, protected by powerful rulers who controlled the Mississippi and the Gulf of Mexico.

We don't know where the cultural ideas that invigorated these kingdoms came from, or why this burst of power dimmed. It may be that by 1500, these kingdoms had become too big and could no longer protect their subjects from famine and warfare. Refugees from the Mississippian world moved east and south. They formed new nations in the late sixteenth century, including the Choctaws, Creeks, and Chickasaws in the south. Others moved north along the Missouri and Ohio rivers.[6]

A powerful and mobile warrior society moved to fill the power vacuum after the Mississippian kingdoms fell. By 1550, a confederation of villages and peoples, calling themselves the Haudenosaunee, dominated power politics in eastern North America. The French would lump them together as Iroquois, but as separate nations the Seneca, Onondaga, Oneida, Cayuga, Mohawk, and Tuscarora built palisaded towns and united as the strongest military force in North America. The Iroquois Confederacy expanded its territory with war and then governed it with a constitution known as the *Gayanashagowa* or "Great Law of Peace." That law was transmitted by wampum—strings of shell beads that carried complex messages and had the power to make people listen.[7]

Power politics pushed many Native Americans to move. Those who endured the Mississippian kingdoms' destructive fall built new confederacies around fields, orchards, and hunting grounds in what is now the U.S. South. Iroquois attacks in what would become New England and southern Canada pushed Hurons and New England Indians north. Others—Ojibwes and Odawas—moved west to Lake Superior and the upper Mississippi River. In new homelands, people settled into regular rounds of seasonal activities, ceremonies, and trade.

Amid that reconfiguration there began a trade in animal skins with Europeans that would unsettle the entire continent. Change began in the 1490s, when fish and then fur drew European sailors to North America. By 1534 the explorer Jacques Cartier arrived on the St. Lawrence River to find boats full of "wild men clothed in beastes skines" who offered animal pelts in trade. Local Native people knew precisely what Europeans wanted. When ships arrived, "Indians rowed out" to "trade beaver skins and other fine furs for red cloth." The first traders didn't stay, hoping to find something more immediately enriching than a few furs.[8]

The fur trade began along the St. Lawrence River and at Hudson's Bay, that giant bite out of North America that fooled ship's captains into thinking they'd found a passage to China. It was named for Henry Hudson, a Dutch explorer who had made that mistake in 1610. Hudson and his sailors had steered into a giant inland body of water that was not a "western sea." They wintered in North American ice while local Cree fed them. When the explorers returned to England with Cree furs, English investors replaced their dreams of Chinese silks with dreams of North American peltry. Now, in a moment of great change for Indian people, Europeans came to stay in those very North American places where wars had disrupted life.[9]

Ojibwe Summers

At this moment, Ojibwe families were starting over. Calling themselves *Anishnaabeg* for more than a thousand years, they had traveled from their homelands in eastern Canada to hunt around the Great Lakes. Now, pushed by Iroquois raiders, they moved there permanently. They settled in a place where a giant otter, an animal that always protected humans, had guided them. There they would plant new gardens, fish in new streams, and make new alliances.[10]

The Ojibwe laid claim to the most strategic sites in North America, Michilimackinac and Baawitigong. These places lay at the heart of water systems that connected nearly all of North America. Michilimackinac was the Indian name for the region around Mackinac Island that links Lakes Huron and Michigan. Baawitigong later became Sault Ste. Marie, where a narrow channel and a great set of rapids guard the entrance to Lake Superior, the largest freshwater body on the planet. The people who lived there called it *Ojibwe Gichigami* or the "Ojibwe's Great Sea." The French named them "Saulteurs" or "people who live by the falls."[11]

No matter how long they lived on a landscape, Ojibwes never con-

NATIVE COMMUNITIES AND EUROPEAN TRADERS, CA. 1650

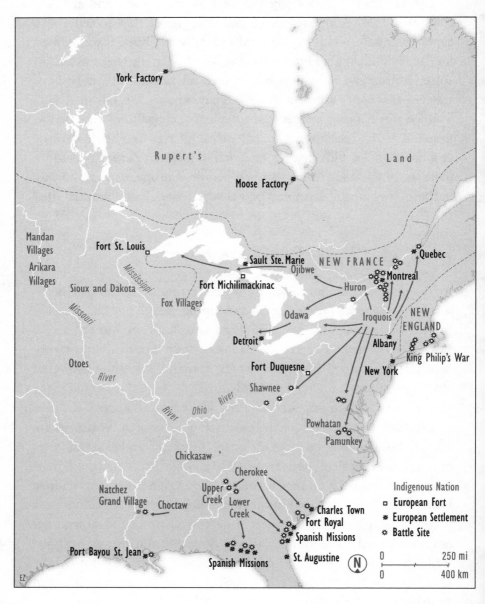

York Factory

Rupert's   Land

Moose Factory

Mandan
Villages   Fort St. Louis
Arikara   Sault Ste. Marie
Villages   Ojibwe   NEW FRANCE   Quebec
         Sioux and Dakota   Fort Michilimackinac   Montreal
                                              Huron
                    Fox Villages
                                        Odawa   Iroquois   NEW
                                                                                  ENGLAND
         Otoes   Detroit   Albany
                  River   King Philip's War
                                        Fort Duquesne   New York
                                    Shawnee

                               River
                         River   Ohio   River
                                                               Powhatan
                                                               Pamunkey

                    Chickasaw

                                   Cherokee
         Natchez   Upper   Indigenous Nation
         Grand Village   Creek   Lower   □ European Fort
                  Choctaw   Creek   Charles Town   * European Settlement
                                              Fort Royal   ✲ Battle Site
         Port Bayou St. Jean   Spanish Missions
                                                                    0   250 mi
                    Spanish Missions   St. Augustine   N   0   400 km
EZ

sidered themselves its owners. They had rights to use resources but also obligations to share them with a wide network of people they considered kin and allies. Even though the Ojibwe moved through different places in different seasons and shifted villages when wood, water, or land ran out, their mobility did not mean that they had no concept of borders. They knew those places like their children's faces. They buried bones, hosted ceremonies, and fought to protect their homes.[12]

Enemies often challenged borders and families. In the early 1600s, Ojibwe warriors waged a naval battle against the Fox nation, who lived on Lake Michigan's southern edge. Some four hundred Fox warriors, hoping to take Ojibwe women and children, raided La Pointe, an Ojibwe stronghold on southern Lake Superior. On a summer morning, hidden by fog, the Fox war party paddled their river canoes silently up to the village and stole four Ojibwe children. They thought they had gotten away, but the Ojibwes heard them and leaped into their large lake canoes. Ojibwe paddlers chased them to a site where the lake had steep walls. Ojibwe warriors waiting above killed every Fox in the party.[13]

Each summer Ojibwe warriors and their families followed the freshet of melting streams down the two hundred rivers feeding Lake Superior to bountiful, carefully protected summer villages. As one Jesuit put it in 1626, "they seem to have as many abodes as the year has seasons . . . but in summer they all gather together." Families reunited with feasts and celebrations, including the *midewiwin* (grand medicine society) ceremonies that initiated young people into adulthood and gave them clan names. Huge gatherings reintroduced long-separated kin, reminded them of their duty to their clans, and created connections to other people. Crees and Assiniboines came south from the fur-rich country that drained Hudson's Bay. Odawas and Hurons came east from villages lining the St. Lawrence. People lingered in the long summer days to plant and harvest corn, gather berries and rice, and trade for things they couldn't grow, gather, or hunt.[14]

People married and made new families in big summer gatherings, building alliances that enabled Ojibwes and other Anishnaabeg speakers to create a prosperous Great Lakes empire. Corn, canoes, wild rice, maple sugar, and fish all became sought-after trade items. To shield that bounty from Dakotas to the west and from Iroquois on the east, Ojibwes became warriors and captors. According to Ojibwe historians, Dakotas did not descend from the same people, shared no language, and had been "mortal enemies from time immemorial." Ojibwes called Dakotas "roasters" for what they did to captives. Ojibwes, in contrast, incorporated captives into their clans via adoption, marriage, and ceremonies, though they killed prisoners who caused trouble. So anyone—Hurons, Potawatomis, and even sometimes Dakotas—could become family to Ojibwes.[15]

Women were essential in creating connections to potential allies. Their unions with men in other villages and nations, bearing children who cemented kinship, made these links personal. Children, whether they came from a marriage or not, were members of their mother's clan, increasing its size and power. Each summer Ojibwes and their new kin strengthened tenuous ties with Feast of the Dead celebrations. The ceremony enabled two separate peoples literally to bury their pasts and to celebrate renewed relationships. When people abandoned a village, they took the bones of their ancestors with them. When they settled a new site with new people, they buried the bones of their ancestors together. When their dead rested together, and families shared children, they became one people.[16]

Marriage, central to alliances, did not mean a lifelong commitment to a single person. For an Ojibwe woman, marriage was only one relationship in a mesh of kin, far less important than her relationships with her father and her brothers. She owed her actual family responsibilities—providing protection, resources, and comfort—to a clan who shared an animal relative, a *nindoodem*. Cranes, bears, catfish, loons, martens, wolves, moose, and a dozen more beings connected the human world to the nonhuman one, connections that were essential for a successful life in North America. A marriage to someone outside one's clan was a strategic relationship. It strengthened ties to other villages and clans and was essential to meeting clan needs for hunters, warriors, or parents.[17]

Marriage, because it was strategic, could be violent. Amid war and turmoil, when clans needed to build population, they captured women. Some marriages started with captivity and rape, but Ojibwe families had ceremonies and traditions to make captives into full community members. Sex was not uniquely tied to marriage. Sex could improve the chances of success for a hunt or maple tree-tapping, or it could simply offer pleasure in the moment. Jesuit priests and French explorers were shocked by young women who offered up sexual favors during hunts and celebrations. To those observers, Indian women seemed "depraved" because they wanted men as "much as men wanted women," then left these temporary liaisons "with scarcely a look behind." Marriage, sex, and trade operated in tandem with war, captivity, and slavery. In periods of war, captives filled villages as adopted family members or as slaves who did the hard work of growing corn, building towns, and carrying water. They could also be tortured and killed to demonstrate Ojibwe strength.[18]

Women had power as objects of captivity and enslavement and as clan members who incorporated new people into village life. Because they created human lives and managed food resources and households, women influenced community decisions about strangers, who always posed risks. A stranger could offer trade goods, new information, and political linkages, or threaten war, disease, or theft. One way to lessen that danger was to make traders or captives into family, giving them a stake in the clan. By the time the French arrived, Ojibwes had generations of experience in making kin with marriage and war.[19]

One summer in the 1590s, long before a priest or literate explorer recorded the events, some Frenchmen arrived at Great Lakes summer gatherings. They came in canoes paddled by Ojibwe clan members. They offered useful metal objects like kettles and axes that Ojibwe traders exchanged for furs. Ojibwe women had their work cut out for them when those Frenchmen arrived. Warned by their non-human spirit guardians that strangers were coming, Ojibwes were shocked by their ugly red faces and unwillingness to bathe. Some people claimed French men were hairless moose. Others insisted they were human, but humans without clans or families, a puzzle indeed.[20]

During late summer hunting and food gathering trips with Ojibwes, young French men found themselves evaluated for their ability to paddle and carry heavy loads. They accompanied young women to harvest rice and berries and to gather firewood. In summer, the lessons were friendly, but as winter approached, French men would be tested further. They had to recognize danger and show bravery. If those men hunted well and learned some Ojibwe, some young women might consider them marriage partners. As Ojibwes packed up their summer villages at the end of the season, young Frenchmen who had joined a family could be invited to spend a winter. The rest would be sent back to Quebec.

By 1608, when the explorer and mapmaker Samuel de Champlain arrived on the St. Lawrence to found a colony, French men already lived in Ojibwe villages as hunters and husbands. Champlain's grander dreams of colonial riches for France failed in the face of local realities. He chose a poor site for his fort. The imposing cliff, where today's Quebec City stands, was a no-man's-land between powerful Native confederacies. Many years later, reflecting on his first years in Canada, Champlain wrote, "The advice I give to all adventurers is to seek a place where they may sleep in safety." During the first winter, half of Champlain's settlers died from Iroquois raiding and from hunger. Local Hurons stepped in to feed and protect Champlain and his settlers, saving the enterprise. To repay that help, Champlain joined hundreds of Huron and Algonquin warriors on a march south from the St. Lawrence to attack the Iroquois. By joining the Hurons in the attack, Champlain and the French made themselves mortal enemies of the Iroquois.[21]

Champlain, now an ally and a kinsman to his Huron neighbors, soon realized that he and his allies could never overpower the Iroquois and that trading furs would be their only business. Facing such dangerous conditions, men left Samuel de Champlain's struggling French settlement along the St. Lawrence for Native villages where they could live and trade in relative safety. Because Champlain, the French leader, had joined the Hurons, that made him an ally to their kin, Ojibwes and Odawas, when they fought the Iroquois together. Building credibility as an ally, Champlain's actions made other Frenchmen welcome in Huron and Ojibwe villages.[22]

Cree Autumns

Crees—Algonquian language-speakers and allies of Ojibwes and Hurons—thrived in the Canadian north. Living in an arctic and subarctic world, they specialized in hunting and using fur. Their successful expansion in the 1600s and 1700s came from access to forest, ocean, and plain, which they used to hunt arctic game in winter and to gather and dry fish and berries in summer. Because they lived too far north to plant crops, the Cree were hunters, traders, and boat builders. To get corn, squash, and tobacco, they built relationships with Huron farmers who lived farther south, traveling as far as the Great Lakes and into present-day Minnesota and North Dakota.[23]

Each autumn Cree families who had spent the summer along Hudson's Bay and its southernmost piece, James Bay, moved inland. As the first ice formed and the cold wind howled across open water, they traveled south or west into forest hunting grounds. They spent the shortening fall days in small family groups, hunting big game and small birds. First came "ye flying of ye geese"—as one Hudson's Bay Company man recalled later about vast flocks of geese that girls and boys netted when they landed. The boreal forests and the forbidding tundra and ice provided a carnivore's cornucopia: moose, caribou, bear, deer, geese, duck, and the many arctic creatures with double pelts. Cree men hunted these animals, and Cree women turned skins and furs into clothing. Everyone told stories about the challenges of storms, starting fires in blizzards, and tracking animals in forest and snow as they smoked fish, duck, deer, and caribou to store in caches for winter.[24]

The abundant beaver, crucial to maintaining diverse ecosystems on streams flowing south from Hudson's Bay, were not as delicious as caribou or moose. But their waterproof pelts became warm robes and rugs. Beaver lodges and dams created places where fish spawned and where animals could drink all winter. Cree hunters viewed beavers as partners in their effort to live in the Canadian north.[25]

In early January, when thick ice had settled in and deep snow made moving easier, Cree camps moved by snowshoe and toboggan to a winter site, where larger Cree kin groups gathered. Now hunters sought beaver, marten, otter, and mink because their furs were thickest and warmest. Cree families made a rich life from their surroundings. Hair, bones, and sinew housed and protected them. A trader described Cree women working caribou sinews, "long fibers as fine and even as fine thread," by moistening and separating a sinew, twisting it, and forming it into a sharp point that could be threaded when dried. Once Cree women discovered the convenience of metal items, like kettles and needles, they became valued household goods.[26]

In 1610 Cree families greeted Henry Hudson and the English traders who followed him to Hudson's Bay, teaching them how to survive winter and find fur. Crees had done a little trading with the earliest French traders, but the poor-quality cloth and worn-out kettles they received didn't encourage them to seek more. They were fortunate in this respect: the isolation that brought the Cree broken pots also insulated them from the growing power of the Haudenosaunee Confederacy and from the first waves of disease that spread north from the St. Lawrence and the Great Lakes.[27]

Crees traveled as far south as Lake Superior (in summer, a paddle of several weeks from James Bay) to trade. Jesuit records from the 1640s describe huge flotillas of Cree canoes that appeared with "their dogs barking" to trade skins for corn and other items. The Jesuits didn't know where they lived, only that they came from the North Sea (Hudson's Bay). The Iroquois, who well knew where they lived, made a raid far north to Cree lands in the 1660s. According to Cree memory, crafty village elders led the invaders to cliffs where they fell to their deaths. According to Iroquois stories, they surprised the Crees and took home some captives. Either way, the raid shows how connected the most remote parts of North America could be.[28]

In 1660 news of a French trader who wanted to meet the Cree reached James Bay villages. A party of Cree families traveled south to see for themselves. Pierre-Esprit Radisson, a French trader and translator, reported that a thousand people came to meet him near Lake Superior. They "feasted well" and "beat drums made of leather kettles covered in staggs skin." Most significant for Radisson, they "brought the finest furres we have ever seen." To capture the potential value of trading with northern hunters, several French expeditions tried to reach Hudson's Bay but failed—the circuitous route to travel a thousand miles north from the St. Lawrence required two hundred portages. It wasn't until 1672 that two Jesuit priests, Charles Albanel and Paul Denys, reached Cree villages on James Bay. Their three canoes were guided and protected by sixteen Montagnais paddlers.[29]

The Jesuits, amazed by the number of people living so far north, began baptizing, while their Native paddlers began trading. But later that year an English ship arrived and broke up the brief French incursion into that region. English sailors captured Albanel and his guides, regarding them as enemies to their Hudson's Bay project. To protect their new trading enterprise, the English took the Jesuits back with them to England, ending the last real effort that New France made to claim that far northern place.[30]

The trade in furs with Europeans unbalanced long-established political relationships between Native nations. The new source of wealth empowered Native people to purchase allies and weapons. Gunpowder and muskets were revolutionizing warfare across the globe in the early 1700s, and North America was no exception. The Iroquois Confederacy, long a power in the northeast, became a superpower with guns it obtained from English traders. For other nations like the Cree, the fur trade brought missionaries, new diseases, and few guns. Intermarriage remained crucial to their efforts to protect power and manage the costs of killing, which had become too easy.[31]

Bitter Winters

Trade with Europeans brought Native peoples another terrible threat. Beads, blankets, and cloth carried germs of smallpox, measles, and mumps. Such diseases—familiar, uncomfortable, and occasionally deadly in Europe—devastated North America because people there had no immunity to them. Illness came in two waves: in summer when traders arrived, and in winter when people made their camps in the few places where water ran year round. Hurons, for example, spent winters in densely populated palisaded towns surrounded by fallow cornfields. When disease came in the 1630s, it overwhelmed them. They ran out of food, places to care for people, and eventually, gravesites. Hungry dogs ate the bodies, a sign of the disaster unfolding in some villages.[32]

Native people knew where disease came from. It came from Jesuit priests, the earliest European arrivals in their communities. The package of early seventeenth-century French colonization and trade included missionaries because the French government had no money to fund expeditions to North America and the Catholic Church did. Traders and priests believed that French success in North America was possible only by converting their powerful Indian neighbors to Christianity. Hundreds of Jesuit priests made the pilgrimage to North America. Not interested in fur or empire, but resolute in their faith in converting Native Americans, the priests who arrived in tiny settlements along the St. Lawrence had little idea of the germs they carried along with their ideas.[33]

Indian people accused priests of hiding illness in their Bibles and traders of carrying evil spirits in their tobacco boxes. And they were right. Priests saw people dying of smallpox on the ships that carried them to New France and in the small communities they traveled through along the St. Lawrence. Sharp traders did resell goods that contained the scabs of smallpox victims, living bits of virus. A Huron leader named Taretande, addressing his people in 1636, accused the Jesuits of sorcery. He declared that if anyone else in his family died, he would "split the head" of the first Frenchman he saw. Rightly suspicious, Hurons murdered traders and Jesuits, even though some Indian leaders and French allies begged them not to.[34]

Epidemic disease took an unimaginable toll on Indigenous America. The loss unrolled over the entire seventeenth century in twenty-year waves. Scholars debate the total loss because priests or officials who reported the death toll saw only a tiny portion of it. The best estimates suggest that in New England and New France, where the fur trade spread fastest and earliest, population loss could have been 50 percent—meaning more than a million people. Some nations lost nearly everyone. Jesuit priests, themselves shocked by the ferocity of the disease, recorded that distraught elders "spoke only in sighs of the enumeration of the dead in their families." Imagine the shock and pain that losing 40 or 60 percent of kin and neighbors would unleash.[35]

Parents buried their dead children, and communities lost their leaders. Such loss made survivors unable to eat or sleep. They couldn't make wise decisions. Grief made them torture captives with particular venom, hit children, and start foolish wars. A Jesuit describing Algonquians in 1636 wrote that "the recollection of the death of their kindred fills them with madness." Life seemed overwhelmingly grim, but new families fed people and helped them recover from their grief. The bereaved could recover only through care and recompense for their dreadful loss. Terrible winters in 1632, 1634, and 1636 required new ideas, bravery, and grit. Families had to be rebuilt so that children without parents and adults without spouses could become part of new households. And in newly blended families, they lived on.[36]

Redemptive Springs

Even in villages filled with rotting dead and staggering survivors, spring arrived. Huron villages, extensive, densely populated, and host to Jesuit missions, were so decimated by disease that they couldn't find enough people or energy to move or plant corn. The few survivors died from hunger if they couldn't find other villages to take them in. In Ojibwe villages, visited by smallpox but with fewer losses, new babies appeared, and people planted and fished to support that new life. They dried bark to repair houses and build new canoes, and in early spring they tapped maple trees for their sap.

As sap filled wooden buckets, women's tears flowed when they considered winter's death. Without enough people, clans and villages were in danger. Women returning from sugar camps demanded wars to avenge lost relatives and capture new ones. Men agreed to attack other communities and bring back people who could be integrated into families, replacing dead relatives. Ojibwe, Huron, and Iroquois raiders hit at all hours of the day and night, but the purpose of these raids wasn't death or military success, it was life. Terrible for the captives and grievous to their mothers, the raiders brought back the living to replace the dead.[37]

In camps where the Ojibwe took in their devastated Huron kin, women assessed captives taken in raids with a harsh calculus. Women and children had more value as child bearers and adoptees. Many older boys and men were executed, but only after grueling ceremonies in which they recounted their life stories and demonstrated their ability to withstand torture, ensuring success in the next world. Captives chosen to become part of Ojibwe clans were first tested with neglect and torture. If they survived that with stoicism, adoption ceremonies made them family. They would be bathed, clothed, and treated with great kindness. Female clan members worked hard to create new kin from strangers.[38]

Captives did become beloved family and even took the names of dead relatives. A few former enemies became great leaders. Others who never adjusted were enslaved or tried to escape. Unending cycles of epidemic disease made the mourning wars larger and longer. By the 1650s, captives, adoptees, and refugees made up perhaps a third to a half of Ojibwe villages. The many newcomers enabled the Ojibwes to repopulate their homeland. In 1659 Jesuit priests reported to their superiors in France that Ojibwe and Odawa villages as large as two thousand people awaited Christian attention.[39]

Seeing opportunities to convert in these calamitous times, Jesuits imagined that they brought peace and salvation. Instead, they stepped into a war zone filled with grieving mothers. While some Indians battled to rebuild populations, an even more powerful Iroquois Confederacy gathered strength. When the Iroquois mounted raids, they could count on material and military support from allies across a vast space that now included the region around the Ohio River. And the Iroquois had guns. The French forbade traders to give Ojibwe, Odawa, and other Algonquian allies guns, but English traders working on the Connecticut River and Dutch traders living along the Hudson offered guns in trade. Guns and grieving mothers unleashed violence on a new scale. Labeled the Beaver Wars because they coincided with the earliest decades of the fur trade, between 1630 and the 1660s, this era of raiding had little to do with beaver but everything to do with rebuilding populations.[40]

Summer, usually the peaceful season of family gatherings and marriage, now became a season of war and captivity. By the 1640s, Ojibwes avoided summer travel on the St. Lawrence. Instead, they cautiously crossed Lake Huron and traveled up the Ottawa River with its more than thirty portages. After ten weeks of travel, they could reach Montreal, a new French outpost on the St. Lawrence. To cement its claim on New France, the French government encouraged settlement by offering land to early settlers, called *habitants*. They weren't rural French peasants but mostly soldiers and fishermen who proved unable to manage the poor soil and short growing season. When Ojibwe canoes arrived each summer brimming with furs, corn, maple sugar, and dried meat, hungry Frenchmen traded eagerly. After successful summer or fall trips, Ojibwe headmen often invited a few French traders to return with them for winter.[41]

In 1654 a literate trader named Médard de Grosseilliers accompanied a group of Great Lakes Indians back to their winter camps near Lake Superior. When Grosseilliers returned with a profitable pile of fur, he wrote enthusiastic letters about hundreds of Indian villages and successful winter hunts where he had been treated with "great kindness." As Iroquois raiding along the St. Lawrence ground on through the 1670s and '80s, French settlers, most of them young and male, had little investment in a pitiful French colony under constant attack. A French priest described the constant danger when the Iroquois "held our French so closely besieged that no one ventured on a ramble without losing his life." Farming, already tricky, failed when the Iroquois burned villages and stole corn stores.[42]

So the prospect of making a living alongside powerful Native residents who had food, weapons, and women held great appeal to French settlers. By 1680, nearly one-quarter of all male French colonists had left farming for the fur trade. Recognizing this reality, a French minister passed an edict encouraging intermarriage between French settlers and Native women. He imagined that these new families would settle in French towns, but instead French men and their

Native families left French villages on the St. Lawrence for Indian towns. Great Lakes villages, eager for allies and kin, welcomed the recruits. *Habitants*—French settlers who farmed New France for their king—thus became *hivernants* who spent their winters (*hiver* in French) hunting and trading with Indians.[43]

With Ojibwes, Odawas, and Hurons having moved to the northern Great Lakes, and the Illinois, Meskwakis, and Potawatomis resettled in the southern Great Lakes country, large villages, surrounded by permanent fields, spread from the Ohio River to the northern Great Lakes. Ojibwes initially had little interest in the fur trade, but Iroquois raiders still came as far west as the Great Lakes, where they took wives and children. In 1662 a great Ojibwe leader named Myingeen (Wolf) led a war party of allied Ojibwe and Odawa clans to challenge a large war party of Iroquois near Sault Ste. Marie. Myingeen's force crushed the Iroquois and took their weapons in a victory that people still recounted hundreds of years later. After the failure of many other raids against Iroquois armed with guns, however, Ojibwes stepped up hunting and processing furs to trade for their own guns. But the long journeys to the St. Lawrence carrying a winter's cache of furs invited Iroquois attacks and left families at home in danger. Now Ojibwes wanted traders to come to them so that they could protect their homeland.[44]

By the 1670s, the French colonial economy depended on an ever-increasing stream of fur pelts flowing to Montreal from the Great Lakes homes of the Odawa, Ojibwe, Winnebago, Potawatomi, and Illinois—all enemies of the Iroquois. The English and the Dutch depended equally on furs brought to Albany by the Iroquois and their allies. France's strategic calculations changed when Ojibwe and Odawa leaders, faced with population losses and an inadequate supply of guns from the French, began trading with the Dutch, who offered guns and safe trading houses. With their Great Lakes alliance at risk, the French responded by opening missions at Michilimackinac, the Great Lakes island stronghold that Ojibwes and Odawas needed to protect. In the 1680s French soldiers built Fort St. Joseph on Lake Huron, Fort de Buade on Lake Michigan, and Fort Crevecoeur on the Illinois River, all to strengthen trade relations and military alliances. The French came on Native terms. If they wanted to trade with Great Lakes peoples, they had to support them in war and peace. Providing ammunition, soldiers, and forts was a start.[45]

A Different Season

Native peoples entered the fur trade to serve their own needs. But when European ships met Native canoes and then sailed out of sight into the Atlantic, they carried North American furs to distant markets with consequences that would upend Indigenous America.

In the first half of the seventeenth century, demand for fur rose in both Europe and Asia. For centuries, sumptuary laws had limited who could wear fur, protecting a limited supply for the rich and royal. But that changed in the early 1600s, with the emergence in Europe of a commercial economy. The ability to pay became all that mattered. Merchants, scholars, and craftsmen—anyone with money—bought fur coats and beaver hats to protect themselves against London fog, Parisian rain, Dutch ice, St. Petersburg snow, and Yangzhou wind. Nothing protected against cold better than fur. Beaver, with its dense undercoat of up to twenty-three thousand hairs per square centimeter, which rendered the fur soft and waterproof, became essential.[46]

As demand exploded, so did prices. North America was still shipping modest quantities of pelts abroad, while the fur-bearing mammals of Eurasia were nearly decimated. By 1661, the London gadabout and diarist Samuel Pepys complained that the cost of his beaver brought him "near to tears when it fell from my head and into the mud by which it was spoiled and I ashamed of it."[47]

By the 1670s, as the fur trade evolved into an international business, large corporate enterprises like the Hudson's Bay Company of London and government entities like France's Compagnie des Indes occidentales demanded more furs from North American suppliers. This was the weak link for shipowners and international traders: getting Native communities to deliver enough pelts to make a trading season and shipping system profitable. With distant corporate investors demanding regular profits, traders hired more and more young European men to hunt with Indian bands each winter. A burgeoning international business was now dependent on fragile human relationships.[48]

Meanwhile, in the heart of the Iroquois Confederacy, New England and New France began fighting each other. In the 1690s, Native warriors initially joined French and English soldiers in ugly extensions of wars on the European continent. With names like King William's War and Queen Anne's War, these European-based battles had colonial agendas that caused divisions between Iroquois people and ate away at their hard-won power. As war spread and divided their communities, Iroquois leaders assessed the damage.[49]

The Iroquois decided to abandon their English allies and instead rebuild their communities. They reached out to lost relatives everywhere—those who had joined the French and the Jesuits and those who had been captured by other Indigenous nations. They even reached out to the Ojibwes and Hurons, longtime Algonquian foes. As wampum belts, returned captives, and baled beaver skins traveled through the forests and down the rivers of eastern North America, a delicate détente emerged. A newly braided Ojibwe, Huron, French, Potawatomi, and Iroquois world developed along the St. Lawrence and deep into the Great Lakes. In these places, French men made livelihoods and families with Native peoples. This was not a New France; it was a powerful Native alliance with blood and marriage binding its members.

=1=

Ozhaguscodaywayquay and John Johnston: Mixing Blood in the Fur Trade, 1670–1790

In 1792 an Irishman got lost in the woods. As he wandered through that winter day on the southern shore of Lake Superior, an Ojibwe boy found him. The boy, Waishkey, brought John Johnston home. As Waishkey's family tended to the Irishman's frozen feet, they learned John's story, and he learned a little Ojibwe. It was a passage in the North American history of mixing blood, begun so long ago when the fur trade started drawing Europeans to Indian lodges.

Johnston, new to the trade, had been abandoned by his French-Canadian and Native American partners. He chose to winter in a spot where no traders came because no Indians lived in that famously haunted place. Ignorant of such details, Johnston, his French and Native paddlers knew, would fail as a trader and would likely freeze and starve on the Lake Superior shore. They cut their losses, got back into their canoes, and paddled away.

The Ojibwe band who found Johnston was led by Waubojeeg or White Fisher, whose daughter was Ozhaguscodaywayquay, or Green Prairie Woman. As can happen with lonely men lost in the woods, John Johnston fell in love with Green Prairie Woman, and they would spend a lifetime together in what became the Upper Peninsula of Michigan.[1] The events that brought them to this fortunate meeting had been unfolding over more than a century.

Founded in War: The Hudson's Bay Company

The Hudson's Bay Company, an English corporation created through royal charter, began operations in 1670 during a war between Ozhaguscodaywayquay's ancestors and their enemies, the Iroquois. The decades-long conflict spread from New England and Upper Canada south to the Appalachian backcountry. French, English, and Native men died in raids, and their children were snatched from their homes. As families mourned dead fathers and stolen children, they turned to European traders for weapons and ammunition to take revenge.

Trading arms for furs brought opportunity to some Dutch, French, and English merchants, but it made life more dangerous for everyone. By the end of the first century of European investment in North America, the hopeful vision of easy profits and overflowing royal coffers had been ruined by war between European nations and with Indians. To save their North American project, European monarchs demanded new strategies from their colonial governors. For example, in 1676, a new English royal governor, Edmund Andros, arrived with orders to stop the wars spreading across the region. Ending war with New England Native nations and with France required Andros to approach Iroquois military leaders and ask for help.[2]

As the power brokers in the region, the Iroquois now added the English to their Covenant Chain, a legal agreement binding Iroquois and their chosen allies as partners in war. An alliance with the English gave the Iroquois military support and better weapons in their attacks on Algonquian nations, but it also brought war into more backcountry communities. Raiding and captivity, now undertaken with guns provided by the English, meant that captives included French, Dutch, and English children living in the midst of a Native world.[3]

In 1690 the New York town of Schenectady (from an Iroquois word meaning "beyond the pines") suffered a raid that would be remembered for generations because so many children were lost. Besieged by continuous war, the entire community huddled in a makeshift fort. On a cold February night, a force of two hundred Iroquois and French fighters attacked the fort. Sixty people—men, women, and children—were instantly murdered. Twenty-seven children were taken captive. So swift and expert was the attack that only two Iroquois lost their lives. Five captives were eventually redeemed when their families paid a ransom for their return. The rest, after being dragged through the snow, tied to horses, and left terrified and hungry for weeks, arrived in a Mohawk town north of Montreal. Those who survived, now clothed and fed by Mohawk families, began new lives. Kind treatment and renaming ceremonies made English and French children into beloved members of the Mohawk nation.[4]

Some Native people avoided recurring war by reminding their neighbors of old kin networks and trade relationships. Traditional techniques, like pipe ceremonies and wampum exchanges, could allow peaceful trade even among enemies. In the Ohio River Valley, apple orchards and cornfields surrounded villages of Miamis, Senecas, Shawnees, and Delawares who integrated French and Spanish traders into their worlds. Far to the west, Lakotas, Dakotas, Omahas, and Mandans developed a new trade centered on horses, corn, and bison robes.[5]

Because of the violence around the St. Lawrence, Hudson, and Connecticut rivers, the Hudson's Bay Company explored the possibilities of trading fur far to the north. In 1667 the English king, Charles II, commissioned a group of French, English, and Dutch investors to assess Hudson's Bay, explored by Henry Hudson in 1611. Fishermen and fur traders knew about the region's wealth of furs but warned about its shocking cold and forbidding residents. English investors, watching French ships bringing furs out of the St. Lawrence, hoped to find a northern path into that trade. King Charles's cousin, Rupert, paid for and then accompanied the expedition. When the ships returned to England after a successful summer of fur trading, they convinced Charles to claim "Rupert's Land" for England and to incorporate the Hudson's Bay Company in 1670.[6]

Rupert's Land and the Hudson's Bay Company seemed unlikely

to succeed. Neither Charles II nor his cousin Rupert had any idea of what they had claimed. The original grant included the "streights, bayes, lakes, creeks, and soundes, that drained into the Baye." That vague language included a whopping hunk of interior North America, more than a third of present-day Canada, stretching from Hudson's Bay to the Rocky Mountains. The French, who didn't know what Rupert's Land included either, vehemently opposed the claim but could do little about it from Montreal. In 1670 the English company set up a temporary trading post at Hudson's Bay and began trading with Cree Indians. Here, far to the north, English ship captains and fur traders avoided Iroquois and French settlements along the St. Lawrence, while creating their own Native allies who would bring a treasure in furs to the edge of Hudson's Bay each summer.[7]

Distant and naïve, investors envisioned a simple system. Traders were to sail into Hudson's Bay in early July, after the ice was gone, and trade with the eager Crees and Assiniboines who gathered along the shoreline. Then they would load up ships with valuable furs, all prepared for shipment and in perfect condition, and sail out of Hudson's Bay before the end of August, when the winds would shift and the ice flows returned. What really happened was quite different. Ships left England in March, when the Atlantic currents carried them most easily northwest. They arrived in the Hudson Strait in late spring to find solid ice. Frustrated ship captains then sailed south along the coast of Newfoundland to fish and to put something of value in their holds. When they returned to Hudson's Bay in late August, local Crees had already headed inland. English traders had to travel to Cree villages only to find a disappointing number of poorly prepared summer-weight furs. Then they faced oncoming winter. Many ships wrecked on ice floes as they tried to sail east, while the lucky ones were frozen into the bay for winter.[8]

Despite this inauspicious start, the English doubled down on Hudson's Bay. They realized that a successful trade required permanent forts where goods and supplies could be stored over long winters when ice and snow sealed off access to the region. Those outposts housed English men who spent winters trading for furs, then processing and packing them for shipment. To cement England's claims to the region, King Charles appointed a royal governor to oversee affairs at Hudson's Bay. That governor reported to the king and a group of investors in London. By 1680, with Cree assistance, English governors and laborers had built York Factory, the center of the business, and four more forts along the southern and western edges of the bay. Several hundred men now wintered there.[9]

The success of this grand and costly effort—papers signed with golden seals, investments made, and bricks laid—depended on one thing: getting Native people to hunt and prepare furs to sell to English companies. Native people would hunt to supply European demand only if that hunting met their own needs and ambitions. If the English wanted Natives to take them to winter hunting grounds, they had to become allies and, more than that, kin. Deep in Canadian boreal forests, Hudson's Bay men forged relationships with Crees and Assiniboines who were interested in trade. Along Hudson's Bay or around the Great Lakes, where young Irish men got lost and then found in winter, the only people who could make English traders, paddlers, and fur workers into Ojibwe or Odawa family were Native women. Mixing blood, building families and clans across language groups and nations, would do what war and colonial policy could not: create islands of peace and profit in the early 1700s. These blended families would eventually link Otoes along the Missouri River and Ojibwes at the Great Lakes to Crees on the edges of Hudson's Bay.[10]

Such families became visible because a global desire for fur created big companies that kept lots of records. Hundreds of small outfits competed with big companies to bring furs to New York, Montreal, London, Canton, and Paris. Operations large and small created work contracts, bills, and lists of names and items bought and sold. Such business detritus, along with diplomatic records kept by French and English officials, left visible traces of human beings who met, married, and sent generations of descendants into the fur trade world of North America.

The Great Peace of 1701

By the end of the seventeenth century, war threatened both family making and the fur business. A combination of long-simmering Native raids and imperial conflicts between European nations and their shifting Indian allies intensified and expanded the violence. The martial culture of Iroquois warriors required young men to launch war parties and avenge slights to their honor. That costly cycle of killing between Iroquois villages reduced the number of men. To stem population decline, Iroquois leaders focused on captivity, rather than killing, to rebuild their numbers. In response, as the Huron and the Ojibwe recovered their strength and found new allies with Great Lakes nations, they raided western Iroquois communities. The violence of the 1680s and '90s elevated many an Iroquois or Ojibwe warrior to the highest level of honors. But the cost was too high, especially when Native people began killing each other with guns supplied by their French and English allies. Native people saw that something had to change. Just as the Thirty Years' War (1618–48) in Europe bankrupted kings and brought famine, decades of warfare in North America served no one. Boasting about war exploits and surviving torture didn't feed families.[11]

At the end of the 1690s, overwhelmed by war, Great Lakes, New England, and eastern Canadian Indians launched a careful diplomatic effort to build peace. After several years of returning captives and giving gifts, the Iroquois Confederacy turned its back on its English allies who had drawn it into war and agreed to attend a great peace meeting with its Algonquian enemies. French governors and traders, facing warehouses full of rotting furs they couldn't move along the St. Lawrence because of raiding, helped orchestrate the meeting. French leaders assured suspicious Iroquois ambassadors that they understood the situation, that they "mourned the dead you have lost" and would "cleanse the earth that has been reddened with their blood."[12]

In the summer of 1701 more than thirteen hundred Native people gathered in Montreal. They hoped to reestablish peace by exchanging gifts and people in displays of mutual generosity. Forty nations, including old allies and bitter enemies, came from the Mississippi Valley, the Great Lakes, Acadia, and New England. They brought wampum belts to help them see past their anger. As canoes carrying Indian families traveled east, they ran into dead bodies floating in the St. Lawrence, victims of a terrible influenza epidemic ravaging the city. A Huron chief from the Great Lakes reported that they "found many of our brothers dead along the river." He and other leaders bravely soldiered on and agreed to enter the palisaded walls of Montreal. With more than rhetoric, he noted the sacrifice others had made when "we made a bridge of all these bodies on which we marched firmly."[13]

Over this horrific bridge, they carried living gifts: returned captives and translators. Representatives of Great Lakes nations, arriving in two hundred canoes, met their Iroquois enemies and forgave them. The translators for these discussions were the children of French fur traders and Native people, or French and English captives taken as children. By 1700 a web of mixed-descent people already connected the fur trade, enabling enemies to begin a conversation. The Great Lakes Odawas and Ojibwes built a temporary village outside Montreal's walls while the Iroquois erected ceremonial longhouses inside the town palisades. The gates of the walled city stayed open night and day. Indian visitors traded in French merchants' stores where "powder, balls, vermillion, kettles, iron and copper pots, and French hats trimmed with fake gold lace" moved briskly.[14]

After weeks of gifts, speeches, and ceremonies, on August 4, 1701, the gathered peoples ratified a treaty with pomp and ritual from both France and Indigenous America. "Native chiefs wearing their fur pelts, painted faces, and feathered head-dresses" joined French officials with "white powdered wigs, silk stockings, golden epaulets." They promised to "gather up all the hatchets and all the other instruments of war," which the French governor would place "in a pit so deep that no one can take them back." The governor gave them peace necklaces to carry back to their people, and he smoked a calumet pipe with them as Native nations signed the document. In turn, each Native leader spoke. While wearing the robes of their old enemies, they promised peace and rebuilt relationships.[15]

Fulfilling these promises rested upon the return of captives, even those who had lived in their new homes for decades and become cherished family. Old enemies could share hunting grounds and the "same dishes" as "brothers and children" only if prisoners could be exchanged and families made whole. Over the next year, the Iroquois brought Great Lakes captives to Detroit and even as far west as Michilimackinac, partly to show they were upholding their bargain but also to see if they could hunt around the Great Lakes. The peace, knit by trade and family, seemed to be holding its shape.[16]

Both the Iroquois and the Great Lakes Indians had built Indigenous heartlands in the interior of the continent in the era of European trade. They created new networks of allies as they exchanged furs, European trade goods, and family members. The peace gave Great Lakes peoples a chance to re-create their former power. It protected the Iroquois zone of influence along the Appalachians with new military allies and trading partners who linked Indian Country with French, English, and Spanish colonial communities. Trade expanded, but on Native terms. Expansion was based in the trade of furs for guns and ammunition, weapons now needed to protect that delicate peace.[17]

Peace allowed both English and French fur companies to expand. Since armed Indians and their French allies now protected the Great Lakes, the English focused on Hudson's Bay and on the backcountry of New England. Expanding trade required thousands of European men to move furs from Native villages in the deep interior of North America. Many of these men entered the fur trade to escape military service or debtor's prison. The seven-year term of service required by the Hudson's Bay Company seemed better than serving as cannon fodder or as a ship captain's whipping boy. Throughout the 1700s, Hudson's Bay Company recruiters took boys from British orphanages. They trolled the docks in Glasgow, London, and Cork with promises of meals and transport to North America. Small local fur companies lured sons of French settlers from Trois Rivières and Montreal, as well as American boys from Albany, Boston, Philadelphia, and Pittsburgh. In 1713 the governor stationed at Hudson's Bay complained about the crop of "poor sorry helpless souls" who arrived in "no ways fitting for the Country."[18]

As tentative peace created conditions for an expanding fur trade in North America, demand for fur exploded in Europe. As a luxury— like coffee, tulips, and spices—the more expensive fur got, the more people wanted it. As prices doubled in both the London and the Paris markets over the eighteenth century, the number of furs cross- ing the Atlantic quadrupled. From just two ports on Hudson's Bay, furs shipped each season increased from 2,000 pelts in 1710 to 50,000 pelts by 1740. Combined with the less recorded but still vast trade from the smaller French companies that operated around the Great Lakes, somewhere between 400,000 and 1 million animal skins left North America each year during most of the eighteenth century. The trade would eventually deplete the supply of animals, but only after another century of steady expansion.[19]

A dense human network evolved to hunt, kill, package, ship, and make clothing from millions of beavers, martens, and minks. Brave or desperate young men left home to live among Native American people who didn't speak French or English. They left from docks along the St. Lawrence or from Hudson's Bay in small canoes filled with Crees, Ojibwes, or Hurons. From the moment they arrived at Hudson's Bay, where large Cree settlements encircled the trading posts, or at the edge of Lake Ontario, where Ojibwe and Odawa vil- lages lined the shore, European men entered a new world. Native people knew that landscape like they knew their own skins, and the fur trade made that knowledge valuable. A young Hudson's Bay Company officer admitted that "we would have starved if we did not send out those Indians that keep constant attendance to shoot geese and hares."[20]

The mixed-descent families made in a Native world were a key component of the global fur trade. Every winter produced a har- vest of furs, new relationships, and babies. Every spring European men filled their canoes with furs and hides, dried and pressed into ninety-pound packs. Their local partners loaded household goods and children to move to summer villages, now located near trad- ing depots like Michilimackinac, where Lakes Huron and Mich- igan come together. In 1763 a British census estimated that more than fifty thousand Native people lived by hunting and growing

THE EIGHTEENTH-CENTURY FUR TRADE IN
NATIVE NORTH AMERICA

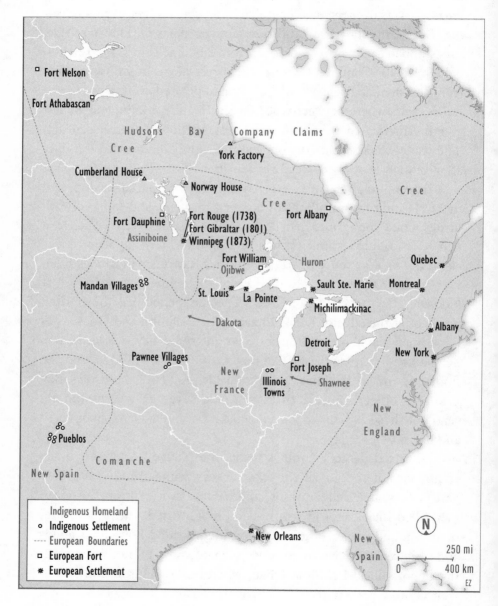

Fort Nelson

Fort Athabascan

Hudsons   Bay   Company   Claims

Cree

York Factory

Cumberland House

Norway House

Cree

Cree

Fort Dauphine   Fort Rouge (1738)   Fort Albany
Fort Gibraltar (1801)
Assiniboine   Winnipeg (1873)

Fort William   Huron   Quebec
Ojibwe

Mandan Villages   St. Louis   Sault Ste. Marie   Montreal
La Pointe
Michilimackinac

Dakota

Detroit   Albany

Pawnee Villages   New   Fort Joseph   New York

France   Illinois   Shawnee
Towns

New

England

Pueblos

Comanche

New Spain

Indigenous Homeland
○ Indigenous Settlement
---- European Boundaries
□ European Fort
✳ European Settlement

New Orleans   New

Spain   0   250 mi

0   400 km

EZ

crops around the Great Lakes. That population overwhelmed the perhaps two thousand European men who lived among them. Irish John Johnston would join Lake Superior Ojibwes in that expanding world. Thousands more Europeans worked farther north where, in the eighteenth century, the Hudson's Bay Company and its competitors built posts and made families among bands of Cree.[21]

Marrying and bearing children together didn't end violence between Indigenous and European Americans. In the 1750s, when colonial wars replaced Indian peace, the means to survive the violence became personal. Indian women, making choices that benefited their families and nations, took risks to weave new families from strangers arriving in their villages and from fur traders who wanted clan business.

Étienne Waddens, Hivernant

Étienne Waddens was one of them. A well-educated Protestant from Berne, Switzerland, he had been hired by the British to fight the French in North America. He arrived in Canada in 1757 at the age of nineteen, as the Seven Years' War was raking across Europe, North America, and the Caribbean. Like many other soldiers, Étienne left the army but chose not to return to Switzerland, which was itself mired in war and religious unrest. Abandoning his past and his Protestant religion, Waddens stayed in Canada as a merchant and a Catholic. By 1761, he felt settled enough to marry a French woman named Marie-Joseph Deguire. They bought property in Montreal and baptized three children in the Catholic Church.[22]

To support his family, Waddens turned to the fur trade. He convinced some Montreal merchants to help him outfit a small contingent of young French men who would travel into Indian Country to trade for furs. The merchants would provide a year's worth of trade goods, supplies, and a canoe to take them into fur country. To repay that loan, the traders had to bring back enough furs to satisfy their sponsors. To protect that investment, Étienne Waddens paddled with them down the St. Lawrence River in 1766, intending to spend the winter around the Great Lakes.[23]

That venture succeeded. By 1770 Waddens had enough money to form his own small partnership, one of many trading outfits that were stealing business away from the Hudson's Bay Company. These smaller fur enterprises—staffed by men willing to travel to the interior and bring trade goods, including guns, ammunition, and alcohol, to Indian settlements—made useful allies for Native people. With advice from tribal leaders, fur traders built a series of inland entrepôts like Michilimackinac, Grand Portage, and Rainy Lake. This trade, run almost exclusively by Native hunters and French-Canadians, rapidly spread north and west after the Treaty of Paris in 1763. As winter trading posts extended farther north, the traders competed directly with the Hudson's Bay Company.[24]

Literate and practical, Waddens rose quickly in that sector of the trade. He had the advantages of being Swiss and not English, and speaking both French and English. In 1772 he received a license to trade at Grand Portage, the connecting point between far northern winter posts and the Great Lakes and St. Lawrence transportation routes. At Grand Portage, the huge canoes built for St. Lawrence and Great Lakes travel, packed with goods from Montreal, were exchanged for lighter, smaller canoes that men paddled up Canadian rivers into Ojibwe and Cree country. Located on the northwestern shore of Lake Superior in what is now northern Minnesota, Grand Portage became Waddens's home.[25]

Étienne Waddens became a *hivernant* or winterer, one of thousands of European men who spent winters with Native people in forts and Indian villages. And during the short days and long nights of winter, Europeans and Native people had sex, sometimes brief or violent, sometimes loving and sustained. Sex often evolved into settled relationships. European men expressed surprise at how quickly the "bewitchen vixens" became their "country" or "fort" wives. Large settlements of Cree and Assiniboine families gathered around Grand Portage every summer. Every fall they took traders like Étienne Waddens with them back to hunting camps. Étienne began a long and stable relationship with a Cree woman whose name we don't know.[26]

A "country wife" offered a trader like Étienne Waddens comfort and economic advantage. If Waddens wanted a band to hunt for him and trade at his post, he had to create a formal family relationship. Like many others in the fur trade, he remained married to his Montreal wife, but he also joined a Cree family. To do so he must have approached the Cree woman's father and brothers in proper ways, bringing gifts, and only then suggesting marriage. He had to meet Cree standards about how husbands should behave and how they should provide for their Cree families. If he failed to recognize his obligations to an entire band, he wouldn't get many furs, and his new wife would leave him.[27]

Often called *mariage à la façon du pays,* or the custom of the country, these unions mixed Indian, French, and British customs. Native people, fur trade companies, and the Canadian government recognized them as legitimate marriages. The Catholic Church also sanctioned such unions, insisting that priests marry people even long after such relationships began.

Though common, such unions involved risks, especially for women. Even European men whose families had lived in North America for generations lacked the survival skills that defined men in these Indigenous societies. Their behavior was unpredictable. Some women were curious enough and attracted enough by the young Europeans to act on their own, but others felt pressure from their families or clans to do so. Either way, it took bravery to be guide and teacher, let alone lover or wife, to a stranger.[28]

To ensure that such relationships served Cree or Algonquian needs, the women taught the *hivernants* how to speak their languages. They taught them how to hunt and trap animals, manage deep snow, and survive on the ice. Sex and relationships kept the *hivernants* in winter camps, but families made them loyal. With sex, whether within or without marriage, came children. The children of these unions helped secure a future for the tribe. A mixed-descent child would become a permanent link to the White trading world but also a member of an Indigenous clan with resources and power.[29]

For Native people, marriage demanded broad reciprocal arrangements that Waddens might not have understood. Husbands and wives provided for and cared about each other, but their marriage was one among many relationships that supported their lives. Marriages didn't have to be lifelong, and people commonly had relationships that were same-sex or polygamous. Women knew that if they kicked out an abusive or lazy partner or if he left, their larger kin networks would support them and provide for their children. Extended families encouraged angry wives and husbands to forgive each other for various transgressions. If they couldn't, unhappy people could try out other partners temporarily or separate permanently.[30]

Étienne Waddens passed the test. His new wife, who spoke Cree, French, and other Indian languages, helped him to negotiate trade and daily life. As he learned Cree, he could convince his new relatives to hunt for him, expanding his business. His Cree family got better access to trade goods because of their relationship with Waddens, and they spread those goods throughout a network of villages. No marriage would be stable or fully recognized until the birth of a child. Marguerite Waddens, born in 1775, bound Étienne to his Cree family.[31]

Marguerite was born at Grand Portage, where the Rainy River links the Canadian forests to the Great Lakes. This spot, on the booming western frontier of the fur trade, drew Indigenous people and others from many regions. The Cree, watching the fierce competition between fur trade companies, operated as crucial middlemen. Spreading south from Hudson's Bay as the fur trade expanded throughout the 1700s, they allied with the Assiniboine, the Ojibwe, and the French. Many Crees became skilled with horses and moved to the Canadian plains to hunt bison. Other Crees, like Marguerite's family, remained farther north and east, hunting large fur-bearing animals and small game in the Canadian forests. They made canoes, built fish weirs, and tapped maple trees. At the end of the eighteenth century, by connecting their lives to Native and European traders and goods, the Cree expanded in numbers and power.[32]

That fur trade world put on its fullest display each summer. Young Marguerite saw the annual celebrations in June and July, when canoes arrived laden with cloth, kettles, guns, food, needles and thread, shoes, tobacco, and rum. Paddled by boatmen singing

French rowing songs, the canoes were greeted with cheers, kisses, and gunshots. After the men unloaded the boats, the paddlers "amused themselves in Good Company at Billiards Drinking Fresh Punch Wine" and sometimes "the more Vulgare were fiteing Each other," according to a 1778 account. Paddlers and clerks alike remembered copious meals of "pork, bread, milk, butter, and liquor," part of the summer plenty.[33]

Farther north similar flotillas of canoes, adorned with flags sewed by Indian women and propelled by specially carved paddles, made their way down the rivers to Hudson's Bay Company forts. The traders on board with their families fired rifles in salute and were welcomed in return by volleys from the forts. Andrew Graham, who headed a large fort on the southwestern edge of Hudson's Bay for many years, remembered this as the high point of summer. Because Graham had a Cree wife and children, he spoke enough Cree to invite the groups formally into the fort or "factory." Cree families set up camp, unloaded furs, and prepared for the greeting ceremony that reflected their traditions of how to meet people and begin trade.

In formal British dress, the European trader who had wintered with the group now introduced the Native leaders, or "captains" as Graham called them. The "most venerable" leader would tell the story of their winter and their journey. That story included crucial information about how many furs Cree bands had with them, how many hunters and how many canoes, but also who had married, had babies, and died. The Cree hunting chief would then ask after the Englishmen's health and declare himself glad to see them. Graham responded by saying that he was happy to see his relatives. Now everyone shared a pipe, eager to trade and renew their bonds of family and friendship. The Crees knew what they were doing. By the mid-1700s, they controlled who hunted where, and their efforts meant higher payments for furs and lower prices for trade goods at Hudson's Bay Company forts.[34]

The business of fur was interrupted by waves of European war and North American imperial struggle but adapted. The Seven Years' War, the longest and fiercest of the colonial wars fought between the French, the British, and dozens of Indian nations, overspread the region north, east, and west of the Ohio Valley. The region was claimed by New France but controlled by Shawnees, Wyandots, Delawares, Miamis, Illinois, Ojibwes, Sacs, and Foxes, who were drawn into the war on every side. When the war ended in 1763, after seasons of battle upset the fur trade along the St. Lawrence and at the Great Lakes, New France no longer existed in North America. Despite that formal change, thousands of French-speaking people, both Native and European, still lived and worked in the fur trade. The British were now in charge, but this had little impact on how the trade worked. Beginning in 1767, the British who took over from French governors in Canada "permitted" traders to winter in villages north of Lake Superior. That policy was simply catching up with how operations actually worked in a business that took European men ever farther into Indian Country.[35]

Marguerite's early life demonstrated how far the fur trade had spread over North America. As forts opened between York Factory on Hudson's Bay and the Great Lakes, she and her parents left Grand Portage to winter in forts far to the northwest. First they stayed near Cree villages in the Saskatchewan Valley, and finally at the southern edge of the Athabasca country, nearly in the Arctic. At 58 degrees north, average daily temperatures in January were −21° Celsius (−6° Fahrenheit), and the sun peered anemically over the horizon only a few hours a day.[36]

At forts like Lac la Ronge, northwest of present-day Winnipeg, the lives of Marguerite and her parents followed long-practiced patterns. Cree women controlled food supplies and cooking fuel and equipment in fur trade forts. Marguerite learned how to smoke meat and fish, and how to make drinking water from snow over an ever-burning fire, facing her mother's wrath if she didn't tend that fire properly. She knew how to skin animals and preserve fur, essential to surviving Canadian winters. Like most traders' children, she spoke Indian languages, French, and English. Also like most mixed-blood girls, she never learned to read or write, skills that would soon become necessary in a world of ledger books and letters.[37]

Cree families with daughters like Marguerite had some advantages in the eighteenth-century fur trade because they had European men who were kin. Intermarriage could bridge chasms between clans, nations, and even fur companies. Like building bridges, however, mixing families also involved risk—bringing strangers and germs into Native communities.

Ozhaguscodaywayquay's Choice

John Johnston was one of many strangers who arrived at Michilimackinac, the site that bridges Lakes Huron and Michigan, in the 1780s. He spent his life on the Great Lakes as husband to an Ojibwe woman named Ozhaguscodaywayquay.

Ozhaguscodaywayquay came from an influential family. Her father, Waubojeeg, was an esteemed warrior and chief of Lake Superior Ojibwe bands. Her mother, Misquobonoquay, came from the Crane clan that lived at Sault Ste. Marie. Her grandfather Ma-Mongazid fought for the French at the Battle of the Plains of Abraham in 1759, the French defeat along the St. Lawrence that doomed its North American empire. With that lineage, Ozhaguscodaywayquay understood the significance of the place she lived. The French called Ojibwes like her family *saulteurs*, referring to their location at the rapids (*sault* in French) between Lake Superior and Lake Huron. By the 1750s, the English were writing the word *Ojibwe* as "Chippewa," trying to approximate what they heard. John Johnston called his family "Chippewa" when he spoke or wrote about them.[38]

During the war, Ojibwes fought valiantly to protect their homes and livelihoods: according to longtime fur trade men, Ojibwes "killed more white men than any other tribe in the North West Country." It was perhaps an exaggeration, but no one would forget the brutal attacks that punctuated the end of the French and Indian War, that piece of a global conflagration fought in North America. After the English defeated the French in 1763, an Indian uprising, organized by an Odawa man named Pontiac, spread from New England to the Great Lakes. Angry at being abandoned by their French allies, Native leaders hated British soldiers and traders whose new policies and poor prices cheated them. Great Lakes Indians showed their military might in an orchestrated plan, unfolding just as British and French diplomats gathered in Paris to sign a treaty. Indigenous military victories reminded North Americans that they lived in an Indian confederacy. Ojibwe, Odawa, Miami, Sac, and Shawnee warriors took all the forts that the French and English had built in the region: Detroit, Pittsburgh, St. Joseph, Sandusky, Miami, and Michilimackinac.[39]

At Michilimackinac, Indian war began with a trick. An influential Ojibwe leader named Minweweh received a wampum belt from Pontiac with details of his plan to take Detroit. To coordinate with Pontiac's attack, the Ojibwe developed an elaborate scheme that depended on the element of surprise to take Fort Michilimackinac, a fortress on an island. On June 2, 1763, a large group of Ojibwes appeared outside the fort and started a game of *baaga'adowe*, a version of lacrosse. The British soldiers inside, warned about Native attacks, should have been alarmed. They weren't. When the guards opened the door and began to play, Ojibwe and Odawa warriors rushed into the fort and killed sixteen soldiers. Indian warriors held the region's forts, including Michilimackinac, for a year or more until British and Native diplomats worked out new relationships and business practices.[40]

Another war that began in 1776 and ended in 1783 shifted imperial control in the region once more. In the aftermath of the American Revolution, the Great Lakes became the border between the United States and British Canada, two new nations amid old Indigenous ones. After the war, thousands of Native and English people from what became the United States fled into Canada. More immediately significant, a series of wars between the Ojibwe and the Dakota Sioux began in 1770, making trade and travel almost impossible between Michilimackinac and the upper Mississippi.

Deadlier even than war, a smallpox epidemic swept through Indian Country in 1781–82, sickening and killing whole villages in a matter of days. People fled, leaving their sick and dead relatives alone, something good Ojibwes never did. According to Indian winter-counts—painted bison hides that kept records—the year 1782 was "small-pox used them up winter." The death toll—at least sixty thousand Great Lakes and upper Missouri people killed—was unrelenting. Three-quarters of the Assiniboine, half the Cree, and a third of the Ojibwe perished with such speed that bones covered villages. The Sioux, because they weren't village dwellers, escaped the worst of the plague and began raiding the now-vulnerable Mississippi and Great Lakes tribes.[41]

In the decades of war and disease that surrounded the American Revolution, the Ojibwes adapted. Initially less interested than the Crees in trading furs, they now participated willingly, in need of guns and allies. As they had with the French a hundred years earlier, they decided to partner with the English in their efforts to rebuild population and power. The Lake Superior Ojibwe war chief Waubojeeg, who had successfully driven the Fox out of Ojibwe country and made a tense peace with the Dakota, settled at La Pointe on the southwestern edge of Lake Superior. Now located on the border between the United States and Canada, that site was safely across the Great Lakes from most Hudson's Bay Company posts. In 1792 La Pointe was Ojibwe country, and both Anglo-Americans and French traders could do business there.[42]

The same geopolitics that changed out who ran the fur trade brought John Johnston to Lake Superior. Johnston was born in Ireland in 1762 to a wealthy landed family who had lost everything in Dublin land speculation schemes when European war upset the British economy. John followed his older brother William to North America in 1790. Without much in his pockets, he headed for Canada hoping for a job in the growing British bureaucracy. After Johnston's ship arrived in New York City, he took another ship up the Hudson River to Lake George, and then up Lake Champlain to Montreal. Unfortunately for his hopes of a government position, few British officials lived in Montreal, still a tough and very French frontier settlement in the 1790s.[43]

Looking for any opportunity, Johnston lodged in Montreal at O'Sullivan's coffee house, a spot run by Irish expatriates where fur traders gathered for gossip and business. There he ran into an acquaintance from Ireland, Andrew Todd. The firm of Todd, McGill had been trading goods in Indian Country west of the Great Lakes for fifteen years. Andrew offered to take John west to Michilimackinac, and with no other options, Johnston took a place in a canoe to the Great Lakes in May 1791.[44]

After weeks of hard paddles and portages, Johnston arrived at Michilimackinac in August, not sure what he had gotten himself into. Todd and McGill had fronted him with supplies for a winter and a canoe full of Indian and French-Canadian voyageurs, but he had little idea how to proceed. He got advice at Michilimackinac to winter south of Lake Superior where fewer traders had headed that year. However, once Johnston's paddlers saw La Pointe, a large island off the southwestern coast of Lake Superior, they had no interest in wintering in such a desolate spot. They also quickly recognized what a greenhorn their new boss was.

Few traders worked at La Pointe because few Ojibwes dared go there. La Pointe was bad luck. Waubojeeg took a huge risk when he brought his Sault Ste. Marie band there. He knew that generations earlier it had been a site of powerful good luck where Ojibwe won battles against Fox and Sioux. But Ojibwes ruined their seventeenth-century luck by sacrificing and eating humans they had bested in war, believing that the practice made them invincible. The ghosts of their cannibalized victims wailed every night, ending the cannibalism and convincing the Ojibwes to leave. Why, indeed, would an important Ojibwe family live in a place haunted by angry ghosts?[45]

Waubojeeg, faced with population loss because of disease and war with the Dakota, gambled on a move to a place that had once been powerful for his people. He made that decision in concert with another local family, the French-Canadian Cadots, who had intermarried with Ojibwe women from Waubojeeg's wife's family for two generations. In the 1780s, Michel Cadot and Waubojeeg left Sault Ste. Marie, and the competitive fur trade there, to settle at La Pointe together with their extended Ojibwe family. As this partnership flourished, linking new families and vanquishing old ghosts, perhaps La Pointe would be safe.[46]

Now, in 1794, hearing those stories and maybe some wailing ghosts, Johnston's paddlers, showing little respect for their untested boss, stole his food and tools and abandoned him. One single boy, a French-Canadian and Cree "translator" named Florentin, stayed with Johnston in his La Pointe winter camp. Johnston turned out to be resourceful and lucky. He later told his son-in-law that he imagined himself to "be like Robinson Crusoe" and was "determined to follow his example." He and Florentin built a rough cabin, though Johnston admitted years later that he was "as helpless as a suckling." They cut enough wood with a homemade ax to keep themselves warm, and Florentin knew how to fish through ice.[47]

His luck became evident one snowy morning when an Ojibwe elder named Ma-Mongazid appeared on Johnston's doorstep with two of his wives and a daughter. Traders had stolen their traveling supplies, leaving them hungry and cold. Because Ma-Mongazid had led Ojibwe people through years of warfare and change, he carried a French medal that recognized his status. Johnston and Florentin invited them in and fed them. Ma-Mongazid invited Johnston to visit his nearby village.[48]

When Florentin abandoned John Johnston in February 1792, Johnston set out to find Ma-Mongazid's village. He got lost and probably would have perished in the cold if Waishkey, Waubojeeg's eldest son, hadn't found him. Johnston ended up in a household that was already obligated to him for his generosity to old Ma-Mongazid. His feet nearly frozen, Johnston spent several weeks recovering. He learned about Native life and learned some Ojibwe from Waubojeeg's daughter, the fifteen-year-old Ozhaguscodaywayquay.[49]

By May, Johnston had developed a powerful personal relationship with Waubojeeg and his family. When the streams opened up and it was time to paddle upriver with the furs he got from Waubojeeg's band, Johnston could imagine a life in the fur trade. He asked Waubojeeg for his daughter's hand. Waubojeeg refused, explaining, "Englishman, my daughter is yet young, and you cannot take her, as white men have too often taken our daughters. If you return to the lake again after this summer, it will be time to think of complying with your request."[50]

Waubojeeg wanted to make sure Johnston understood that marriage meant moving into the Ojibwe world and that Ozhaguscodaywayquay was willing. She knew about the proposal and surely had doubts. Ojibwe parents often arranged marriages for their children, but her worry about marrying John Johnston weighed on her. The summer gatherings of Ojibwe often featured religious ceremonies that encouraged rituals of personal sacrifice and renewal. Anxious about her future that summer of 1792, Ozhaguscodaywayquay made an isolated fast, an *apowa*, and waited for a dream. Years later Ozhaguscodaywayquay described that dream to a visiting English writer. In her dream, a White man approached her with a cup in his hand, saying, "You poor thing, why are you fasting? Here is food for you." The man was accompanied by a dog who "looked up into her face as if he knew her." This dream satisfied Ozhaguscodaywayquay that the Irish stranger was a guardian rather than a threat. Dreams carried power, but even so, a fur trade marriage required personal bravery to leap over the gap in culture.[51]

Johnston, meanwhile, spent that same summer paying off his debts to Todd and McGill. Planning to return to Lake Superior and his future bride, he purchased wedding presents for Waubojeeg's family. He had a ring made of blue enamel with seed pearls that enshrouded a lock of his hair. A ring made with human hair was an unusual gift for an Ojibwe bride. An ornament made of human remains was both bad luck and inconvenient, as she used her hands to gather rice, to fish, or to braid hair. She never wore the ring on her finger but tucked it into a beaded deerskin pocket where she carried other items that kept her safe. But with that ring, John Johnston, an Irish immigrant to Canada, began a life with Ozhaguscodaywayquay, an Ojibwe woman born near Lake Superior.[52]

After their fall marriage in 1792, their first weeks together were not easy. Suddenly sixteen-year-old Ozhaguscodaywayquay was Susan Johnston. Many years later she told her daughter Jane about finding herself in a strange house. After arriving in Johnston's log cabin, she crept into a corner and wept. Hoping to comfort her, John lit a fire in the stove, but the leaping flames and sudden roaring sound terrified her. She ran back to her grandfather's lodge, just across the creek from Johnston's house. She begged her father to end the marriage and to let her stay home. Furious and ashamed, Waubojeeg took her back to Johnston's house. As she told it later, Johnston showed great patience. He allowed her to stay in the corner, covered her with a blanket, and offered her food, just like the man in her dream from the summer before. A few days later she felt able to face her situation. So young Ozhaguscodaywayquay became Susan, pinned her braids back with an ivory comb that Johnston had given her as a wedding present, and went about the ordinary tasks of an Ojibwe woman.[53]

=2=

Wintering Families and Corporate War, 1770–1810

At age seven, Marguerite Waddens witnessed a murder. It probably wasn't her first. Asleep near her mother in a winter camp, she awoke to shouts and gunshots. Raised in fur trading forts, she'd heard those sounds before. Voices speaking loud, fast French and Cree came closer. Usually her mother just reassured her, but this time her mother jumped up as men came out of the trade room and approached the family's lodge. Marguerite heard the men talking about her father. Trouble with Peter Pond, again.

That winter night in 1782, bitter cold in March at Lac la Ronge, a post that Étienne Waddens and his partner Peter Pond built in Canada's far northwest, was Waddens's last. Marguerite could see he'd been shot through the thigh twice. Her mother bound Waddens's bleeding leg and tried to warm her dying husband in a rabbit fur blanket, but he never came to. A French voyageur who'd spent several seasons with Waddens described the argument that had spiraled into shoving, then threats, and finally gunfire. Pond, an American, would murder other men and become a famous explorer and mapmaker in spite of his crimes. Dead of the grievous wound he received from Pond, Étienne left a Cree widow and a mixed Swiss and Cree orphan.[1]

Étienne Waddens's murder was unremarkable in the violent world of eighteenth-century North America. By the 1750s, competition in the fur trade had unraveled the Peace of 1701. Then the French and Indian War, the American Revolution, and backcountry raiding between Natives and Europeans blended into decades-long sieges. Revenge killings unhinged every negotiated peace. The American Revolution did not just redraw borders; it initiated decades of war as Native people effectively resisted efforts to take their lands. In 1784 John Filson, a land speculator and frontier enthusiast, warned of the violence in a treatise he wrote about western lands that was reprinted forty times. He described Kentucky's "promising beginning" but noted that American settlement now faced "hardships and adversity, and was plundered, dispersed, and killed by the Indians." He declared that the newly won land remained "a theatre of war . . . properly denominated the Bloody Grounds."[2]

That theater was the new United States, where Indigenous peoples patrolled their own borders. As in British and French North America, so too now in the United States, cycles of Euro-American encroachment on Indian land, and violent responses from Native people, left white citizens feeling besieged and endangered. A newspaper editorial from 1782 urged White Americans to heed the blood left by victims of Indian violence and called on them to "RETALIATE—and the sound will reverberate from mountain to mountain, RETALIATE, RETALIATE, RETALIATE."[3]

The new American government heightened the conflict by convincing migrants to buy and settle on lands up and down the Appalachians, in the Ohio Valley, and around the Great Lakes. In need of revenue to pay debts and promises to Revolutionary War soldiers, military officials and civil leaders promised to replace the "unending expense of war" with profitable settlement and peaceful trade. But hope of fulfilling that promise was dashed when traders and government officials refused to "coddle" their Indian partners with gifts and diplomacy. When the British took over the fur trade, after the French lost North America, they had faced a huge Native uprising. In 1763 Pontiac's rebellion had forced the British to respect Indigenous borders, to install administrators who married into Native families, and to pay out money and gifts. American officials, hoping to save money and show their independence from the British, refused to follow that model and so turned Indians who had been allies into powerful enemies.[4]

Retaliation, braided into Native and Euro-American life by the end of the American Revolution, had its costs. Daughters like Marguerite Waddens paid the price.

Death and Life of a Swiss Winterer

Étienne Waddens, with his Cree and French fellow winterers, used the disruption of war to build business. In the 1780s, as the American Revolution ground on, Indian hunters and European traders discovered a trove of fur-bearing animals in river systems flowing from the Rocky Mountains and the Arctic Sea. To tap that potential wealth, two fur trade systems evolved.

The Hudson's Bay Company modeled British corporate hierarchy. Operated from London, it employed thousands of people in a distant colony. Getting fur to London required managing an elaborate system of supply stations and food factories staffed by Native people and the families of fur traders. Hundreds of forts, posts, and camps spread out from Hudson's Bay, with winterers working some three thousand miles from English settlements. Teams of French and Native paddlers ferried tons of trade items and food into the distant forts. They then paddled hundreds of thousands of animal skins, processed and packed by Indian women, back to ships in Hudson's Bay. Months later the skins ended up at hatters and furriers in London and New York.[5]

To the south, much smaller outfits of French, British, and American traders built companies that competed with the Hudson's Bay Company. Each small group of investors had personal relationships with hunting bands and family groups of Great Lakes Native nations. Ojibwe leaders, for example, wanted to expand west and south away from Iroquois territory. They partnered with people like John Johnston, who became part of a loose network of French fur traders working around the Great Lakes. Larger than Hudson's Bay in the total number of furs it harvested, the French system, which the British inherited in 1763 when they defeated New France, was less centralized. Its furs still ended up in London hat factories, but its pelts came down many rivers to Montreal, Albany, and New York. The dispersed system allowed for local decisions and a lot of variation, but also made it harder to tax or regulate. Officials complained about not knowing how many traders there were or how to coerce them into paying for licenses. Montreal became the commercial center for that once French and now British fur system.[6]

The sheer scale of the Hudson's Bay Company dictated much about the fur trade. The initials HBC or a shortened title, "the Company," were known worldwide. Local vocabularies demonstrated the Company's dominance. Everywhere in fur country, whether in Sault Ste. Marie or in Hudson's Bay, the value of a prime beaver pelt was one "made beaver" (MB), a unit devised by Company officials. The price of every other item in the fur trade was based on that unit. For example, a marten (a type of mink) was worth 1/3 made beaver, designated 1/3 MB in account books; a blanket cost seven MB, a gallon of brandy four MB, and a yard of cloth three MB. Prices were set at York Factory on Hudson's Bay and spread throughout fur country.[7]

Étienne Waddens and his fellow traders were the leading edge of an organization that would challenge the HBC. For decades the system was a disorganized conglomeration of small companies, but eventually the challengers became the North West Company. In 1779 Étienne Waddens signed on to a proto–North West Company "association." The new outfits went to war with the HBC. They burned forts, stole horses and supplies, destroyed portage routes, and occasionally committed murder, all to best the HBC. That British colossus had no intention of losing any business and vowed to drive the North West Company off the face of the earth.[8]

To avoid such mayhem, Étienne Waddens, his Cree wife, and her band moved to Lac la Ronge, a fort far north of most of its competitors. Waddens's business partner there was the talented and ill-tempered Peter Pond. The two men argued constantly about money and management. During long winters, in close contact, it got personal. After a nasty February 1782 quarrel, Pond threatened to kill Waddens. To make peace a month later, Waddens invited Pond for dinner. After more angry words, Waddens was "shot through the lower part of the thigh" and "buried at 8 the next morning." Peter Pond never went to trial, but the murder ruined his reputation. Waddens had been known as a man of "strict probity," and everyone knew where the blame lay. That crime upended seven-year-old Marguerite Waddens's life.[9]

We don't know what happened to Marguerite immediately after her father's death. No longer part of a European man's life, she and her mother disappeared from the record. Fur trade marriages, the "custom of the country," had their own customs. A father could recognize his Native or mixed-descent wife and children in his will, if he had one. He could set up an account at a company store to care for them. But Waddens left nothing, either to his French Montreal family or to his Cree family. We know this because his Montreal wife sued Peter Pond, unsuccessfully, for damages.[10]

When Étienne Waddens was murdered in 1782, Indian Country and the fur trade were in the midst of a smallpox epidemic. Cree families lost an entire generation of children, their strongest hunters, and mothers who created new life. It is possible that Marguerite lost her mother and joined another band. Remnants of bands gathered together to avoid starving and to provide parents for children. They built new families with new ceremonies but found themselves ever more dependent on the fur trade.[11]

Marguerite's band may have returned south to Rainy Lake, where she had spent her early childhood, seeking out other traders and posts to do business. Throughout the eighteenth century, Rainy Lake was a crucial transit center where paddlers exchanged large Great Lakes canoes, carrying tons of supplies, for smaller, lighter *canots du nord* that deftly managed the icebound smaller rivers in the Northwest. Now the region became even more crucial as a boat-building center. Located in a vast forest and surrounded by rivers that linked most of Canada, Rainy Lake had the raw materials for building canoes. Turning trees into boats required whole communities. Cree and Assiniboine bands settled together with former fur traders. They harvested birch, cedar, and pine trees to build the range of boats essential to a booming fur trade.[12]

Because canoes and their loads of fur packs and trade goods often had to be portaged, or carried around impossible rapids or shallows, they had to be sturdy and light. Long wooden ribs were cut, soaked, stretched, and dried into curved shapes, then covered with a skin of lightweight birchbark—smooth, supple, and waterproof—to make the perfect craft. Men and boys chose the trees best for suited for the boats' ribbed superstructure. Everyone looked for large birch trees that could produce long rolls of supple bark, making the boats seamless. Women and children collected pine and spruce gum to treat, stretch, and seal the bark for canoe skins. The joints of the canoes were sewn together by white pine roots, called *watap,* then sealed with hot pine or spruce resin. Children practiced by making birchbark baskets and toy canoes.[13]

To meet demand for these boats, busy settlements grew around Grand Portage and Fort William, the Lake Superior post that became the North West Company's headquarters. Ex–fur trader Gabriel Franchère described "former Servants of the Company" now "married to Indian women and burdened with heavy family responsibilities; they dare not return to Canada." Instead, Franchère wrote, they "prefer growing a little corn, a few potatoes and living by fishing." These communities provided a labor force for the fur trade: producing food, building canoes, and processing furs.[14]

Marguerite Waddens and Alexander McKay

Marguerite reappears in the records in 1795, when she became connected to another fur trader. By then the deadly competition that had killed her father threatened to ruin everyone. The North West Company, operated by British, Scottish, and Anglo-American loyalists who fled the U.S. colonies during the American Revolution, competed viciously with the Hudson's Bay Company. Marguerite lived with a Cree band in the English River District, a set of posts on the forbidding Canadian Shield, the huge band of eroded rock

Fur Trade Warriors: Hudson's Bay Company and North West Company, 1770–1810

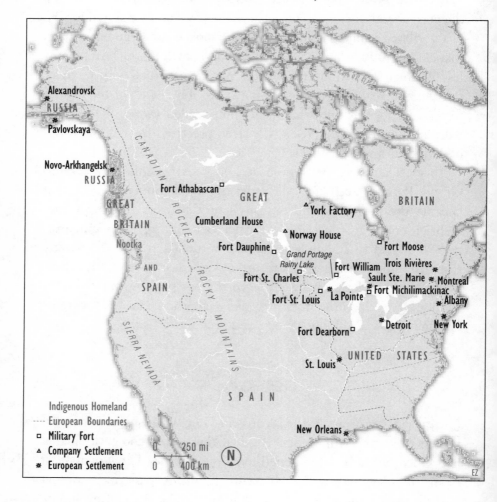

Alexandrovsk
RUSSIA
Pavlovskaya
Novo-Arkhangelsk
RUSSIA
CANADIAN ROCKIES
Fort Athabascan
GREAT
GREAT
BRITAIN
BRITAIN
York Factory
Nootka
Cumberland House
Norway House
AND
Fort Dauphine
Fort Moose
ROCKY
Grand Portage
Rainy Lake
Fort William
Trois Rivières
SPAIN
Fort St. Charles
Sault Ste. Marie
Montreal
MOUNTAINS
Fort St. Louis
La Pointe
Fort Michilimackinac
Albany
SIERRA NEVADA
Fort Dearborn
Detroit
New York
St. Louis
UNITED   STATES

Indigenous Homeland
---- European Boundaries
▫ Military Fort
▲ Company Settlement
✳ European Settlement

SPAIN

New Orleans

0   250 mi
0   400 km
N

EZ

that spreads out from Hudson's Bay. And there she met Alexander McKay, a rising star in the North West Company. Marguerite, young and strong at twenty, offered language abilities and knowledge of both trading posts and Cree bands. She would have been an appealing match for someone like McKay.[15]

Alexander McKay was born in 1770 in New York's Mohawk Valley to Scottish parents. As loyal British citizens, they found revolutionary New York unfriendly in the 1770s. Like many other such families, these bumptious Scottish loyalists moved north to Canada and took up the fur trade. In time, Alexander, along with two of his brothers, Donald and William, joined the rapidly growing North West Company. By 1799, the company employed more than twenty-five hundred people and had dozens of major trading posts spreading west and north.[16]

Alexander's first posting was at Fort Chipewyan, founded in 1788 and as far north and west as you could get. He served well in that isolated post and got the attention of an ambitious Scottish mapmaker and explorer, Alexander Mackenzie. Mackenzie sought a practical route over the Rocky Mountains to the Pacific Coast. His employer, the North West Company, sought new sources of furs and Native allies in a region not already patrolled by the Hudson's Bay Company. Convinced that a water route connected Great Slave Lake, a huge glacial lake near Fort Chipewyan, with the Pacific Ocean, Mackenzie made a series of ventures north and west into that mountainous arctic landscape.[17]

Mackenzie's guide, Aw-Gee-Nah, a respected Cree leader called "The English Chief" by North West Company men, told the explorer no water route existed, but Mackenzie insisted on seeing for himself. In 1789 "The English Chief" and his wife guided Mackenzie from Fort Chipewyan to the Arctic. As Aw-Gee-Nah had stated, Mackenzie found no route to the Pacific but instead found the Arctic Sea, clogged with ice and offering no advantage to fur traders.[18]

In 1793, after Mackenzie found no water route, the Nor'westers— senior partners of the growing North West Company—hired him to find a land route west. At the time Russia claimed the northern edge of the Pacific Coast, making any approach illegal and dangerous.

Even so, when Mackenzie asked that Alexander McKay be transferred to his command because "he would be of great Service to me should I undertake any expedition," the young man quickly agreed. Literate and ambitious, McKay joined Mackenzie's venture in the spring of 1793. With a party of six voyageurs, two Indian guides, and a dog, they made a seventy-four-day journey from Fort Fork on the Peace River to the Pacific Ocean. Just as their guides had warned, the grueling route took them through dangerous rapids and over mountain passes. After an even more difficult return that took three months, Mackenzie gave discouraging news to the North West Company: they could get to the Pacific, but there was no practical way to transport furs.[19]

After this adventure, Alexander McKay was rewarded with an appointment as clerk, the lowest tier of the fur trade officer ranks. Assigned to the Upper English River Department in 1795 in what is now Saskatchewan, he settled into the work of accounting, writing letters, and supervising food stores. His immediate superior was his older brother, William McKay, who had founded that post at English River (now the Churchill River) where the North West Company faced down the Hudson's Bay Company's York Factory.

Alexander McKay met Marguerite Waddens when pemmican became essential to the North West Company. Long a part of Native diets in the far north, pemmican—dried bison meat combined with extra fat and berries—now fed fur trade brigades. In more moderate terrain, teams of Native hunters traveled with brigades of hunters to shoot small game and birds to feed the group, often more than two hundred strong. But operating in this nearly Arctic region heightened the pressure to bring furs out and supplies back in during the brief window of time when rivers flowed. Pemmican became the fuel of choice for the fur trade in this region, and forts became pemmican factories and depots. In January 1795 a clerk at the English River post recorded that their storehouses held "112 Bales of beaver skins, bearskins, foxes, and 8,900 pounds of pounded meat" (pemmican), as well as 413 slaughtered bison to feed the inhabitants for the rest of the winter.[20]

We don't know much about the courtship of Marguerite Waddens and Alexander McKay, but we can surmise some details from others' accounts. Daniel Harmon, a wintering clerk for the North West Company, described the ceremony of taking a Cree woman as a "country wife." The European man would "make a present to the parents of the damsel, of such articles as he supposes will be most acceptable. . . . Should the parents accept the articles offered, the girl remains at the Fort with her suitor." Because Marguerite's Swiss father was dead, Alexander likely approached another Cree relative and offered proper gifts to the family.[21]

Alexander and Marguerite spent a decade moving between different posts as he worked his way up the North West Company ranks. As an officer, Alexander didn't have to paddle canoes or portage. Instead he accounted for and managed tons of fur and supplies. Promoted to brigade leader, he had the responsibility of five canoes, which meant twenty paddlers, two officers, and perhaps fifteen Indian guides and hunters. Each canoe carried thirty-five hundred pounds of gear, including birchbark and spruce gum to repair leaks in the delicate vessels. After several years of managing such complex human teams, McKay took on the responsibility of running an entire trading post.[22]

These large western posts allowed access to extensive hunting ranges and a network of Native villages. McKay, as chief trader, managed the entire operation. Big forts housed hundreds of people, mostly French-Canadian and mixed hunters and paddlers with their native families. They all spent five months together waiting for the rivers to melt. In bad winter weather, McKay gave workers moose or caribou skins to make moccasins, and Indian women taught them to sew with bison gut thread and British needles. To keep bored young men from creating trouble, he staged contests of strength and skill between European and Native men, with drams of liquor the prize. Everyone drank a lot. Rum kept North West Company men at wintering forts trading with Indians for furs. Rum, tobacco, cloth, and guns got Crees, Assiniboines, and Ojibwes to undertake the bloody work of processing furs for transport. In 1798 the North West Company shipped upward of 300,000 animal skins from the docks at Montreal.[23]

Marguerite's assistance was crucial to Alexander. She made clothing, tended to the sick, and supervised social events. Like most women in this era, she made clothing for her family. She and her children dressed mostly in European clothing, marking their elite status, but they wore warm Cree fur leggings and moccasins underneath for much of the year. She made and repaired woolen pants and coats for her husband, who as an officer also wore imported British suits. She also greeted Cree hunters and their bands when they arrived and encouraged them to trade. In 1795 Duncan McGillivray, who was stationed at a fort just up the river from McKay, described the traditions around trade: Cree traders were "disarmed, treated with a few drams and a bit of tobacco," then everyone smoked and shared news "with great deliberation and ceremony." Then they "named their prices" and began trading.[24]

Getting those valuable skins to Montreal required Alexander McKay, like most traders, to be absent from his family much of the time. The McKays had four children in those years: a son named Thomas in 1796, and then three daughters—Annie, born in 1798, Catherine in 1800, and Marie in 1804. The McKay family had their own house within the stockaded walls of Fort Chipewyan, while paddlers, hunters, and their families shared "shanties" in groups that included eight to ten adults and a dozen children. As he traveled and traded, Alexander expanded the North West Company's power and range. For his efforts, he earned £100 Halifax currency per year, a generous income. In 1800 he became a partner in the company. This rare status required him to go to Montreal (a distance of 3,500 miles) or attend the grand gathering of company partners, called a "rendezvous," at Grand Portage or Fort William in alternate years. His entire family occasionally accompanied him to the yearly rendezvous, but the arduous thousand-mile trip from Fort Chipewyan on the upper English River generally deterred them. Most summers the children stayed with Marguerite, learning to make clothing and collecting berries, medicinal herbs, wild plums, and nuts.[25]

By 1800, Marguerite Waddens McKay and her family linked Cree hunters and French paddlers with Scottish entrepreneurs, London businessmen, and Anglo-American sailors. After a hundred years, ledger books, canoes, and pemmican had changed life for everyone in the fur trade world. Five generations of Native women had married European men and spread mixed-descent children throughout the North American fur trade.

Braiding a Great Lakes Life

Fur trade marriage tangled many families in snarls of personal and business obligation. Thousands of miles south of Marguerite McKay's winter fort, Sault Ste. Marie lay on a spot that linked Lake Huron and Lake Superior, making it, like Grand Portage and Montreal, an essential site for the fur trade. The home of Ojibwes and Odawas, it had hosted French Jesuits and French and British traders for a century before the Johnston family arrived there in the 1790s. It sat on the border between the United States and British Canada. If you asked Ozhaguscodaywayquay (Susan) or John Johnston what country they lived in, like most people living there, they'd have no idea what you meant. They understood loyalty: Ozhaguscodaywayquay belonged to the powerful Crane clan of Ojibwes, and she had married a man who was both Irish and deeply indebted to French businessmen.

Marriage meant something different for Ojibwes than it did for their European neighbors. Even after marriage, which Ojibwes described as walking with another person, women remained in their own clans (or *doodems*). If a couple couldn't get along, both people could simply return to their bands and marry again. Building and testing new family ties, John and Susan Johnston stayed near her family for two winter seasons. After their first son, Lewis Saurin Johnston, was born at La Pointe in 1793, and after Susan Johnston's father, Waubojeeg's, death that same year, they moved to Sault Ste. Marie, several days' paddle from La Pointe.[26]

Sault Ste. Marie would be a fine place for the Johnstons' new business. Instead of trading furs himself, Johnston became a merchant who outfitted individual fur traders and traded with Indians in a spot called *Ba-wei-ting* by Ojibwes. Sault Ste. Marie lay on a river, the narrow place where a waterfall tumbles between Lake Superior and Lake Huron. As it was the only passage between two Great Lakes, geography forced travelers to pass there. John Johnston knew that scores of canoes came by each summer day on their way to Michilimackinac, eager to trade for Odawa-raised corn grown along Lake Michigan's shores and Ojibwe-caught whitefish from the St. Mary's River. Now everyone would see the enticing goods John Johnston imported from Montreal, New York, and London, and that Ozhaguscodaywayquay, now called Susan Johnston by her husband and their White neighbors, traded in their store.[27]

By the 1790s, when John and Susan Johnston moved there, Sault Ste. Marie comprised some twenty French and intermarried families, a North West Company post, and a British stockade. John, Susan, and baby Lewis lived in a house owned by Michel Cadot, a French and Ojibwe man married to Ozhaguscodaywayquay's sister, Equaysayway or Madeleine Michele. Jean-Baptiste Cadot, Michel's father, had been one of the earliest European settlers in the Lake Superior region. In the 1740s Jean-Baptiste married into a local Ojibwe band, also drawn to Sault Ste. Marie for its strategic location. Cadot developed such skill as an Ojibwe orator that, because of his crucial connection to the Crane clan, he served as chief of the Sault Ste. Marie band.[28]

After the 1763 Treaty of Paris ended the French and Indian War and New France turned into a piece of Great Britain, Cadot and his Ojibwe kin helped British traders understand that success in the region depended on having good relations with Native and mixed-descent families. With the connections of the Cadot family, the growing French, Ojibwe, and Odawa community at Sault Ste. Marie staffed the British fur trade. In 1771 the British superintendent William Johnson described Cadot as one of the "Two Most faithfull Men amongst the French," a backhanded compliment that recognized the web of loyalties in this place. Cadots made sure their children were French with baptism as Catholics and with Montreal educations. They ensured they were Ojibwe by marrying Ojibwe people and taking active roles in clan affairs. From that secure position, they did business with the large group of English traders who arrived after

1763, and with U.S. traders after 1783. In 1787 the Cadots joined the North West Company.[29]

The American Revolution and the political transitions that came after it made little difference in Sault Ste. Marie, especially since the border between British Canada and the United States remained undetermined. As a provisioning point for the North West Company, and surrounded by Ojibwe villages, Sault Ste. Marie had a future that seemed secure. However, in 1794 the Jay Treaty between the United States and Britain drew a border that put the southern shore of Lake Superior in U.S. territory, much to the fur trading community's surprise. Although the North West Company immediately began investing more heavily on the north side, its employees still chose to live in what would become U.S. territory. Their wives were Native women from the area, and their mixed-descent children had futures in the fur trade communities there. No American enterprises—banks, businesses, land offices, or courts—had yet arrived in the region, although they soon would.[30]

Susan Johnston continued to live an Ojibwe life. She and her sisters, married to White or mixed men, trapped birds and gathered maple syrup in the early spring. As the ground warmed, they waited for the annual whitefish run and planted corn. During berry season, they measured the short northern summer by gathering strawberries, then gooseberries, and finally blueberries with their female relatives and their children. They harvested corn and gathered wild rice in fall. These activities protected the essential Ojibwe qualities of their lives and made full use of their landscape.[31]

After a year or two of living with the Cadots, John Johnston bought a large building to house his business and family. He outfitted local fur traders for winter hunts and supplied military posts with a range of goods, but he did most of his business with local Indians. Susan ran the store. She traded with Indian and non-Indian customers and kept careful records of skins brought in, goods traded, and who bought what. She took beaver, otter, marten, mink, silver, gray and red fox, wolf, bear, and wildcat, muskrat, and smoked deerskin in trade, carefully noting what each pelt was worth. People also traded maple sugar, Indian corn, and *petit-blé*—parboiled and dried corn.

Another early resident recalled items that native women made and sold: "moccasins, hunting pouches, *mockocks* or little boxes of birch-bark embroidered with porcupine twills and filled with maple sugar, mats of neat and durable fabric, and toy-models of Indian cradles."[32]

Hardworking themselves and demanding of their employees, the Johnstons were successful. As their business and family grew, John furnished the house with mahogany furniture and Irish linens and crystal. He imported books for a large library. He and Susan had a ceremonial room for greeting Native visitors, with a separate entrance just outside John's office. White traders or visitors who arrived during the summer were always invited to dine with John at four p.m. On these occasions, Susan's place was just as important as it was in hosting Indians. Visitors commented on the food served: game prepared in Ojibwe fashion and puddings and pies adjusted to the English taste. Susan dressed to reflect her blended world with a black calico dress over beaded Ojibwe leggings and moccasins.[33]

Susan and John Johnston filled their house with children. Lewis was followed by George (Kahmentayha in Ojibwe), born in 1796, the same year Thomas McKay was born. The first daughter, Jane (Bamewawagezhikaquay, or "Sound of Stars Shooting in the Night") arrived in 1800, followed by two more girls, Eliza (Wahba-mungoquay or "Woman of the Morning Star") in 1802 and Char-lotte (Ogenobuoquay or Woman of the Wild Rose) in 1806. Their English names came from John's beloved Irish sisters. John and Susan would eventually have eight children, or nine if they counted young Nancy Campbell, the Ojibwe and White child who came to live with the Johnstons in 1808. Her father was John Campbell, a retired fur trader and U.S. Indian agent who was killed in a duel.[34]

Susan raised the children alone much of the time, relying on her extended family for help when John spent summers visiting traders and supplying military posts, and winters doing business in Mon-treal. Johnston's bankers and suppliers were in Montreal. Because it was impossible to travel back and forth between the Great Lakes and Montreal after November, when the snow fell and the rivers froze, John spent many winters entirely in town. By 1800, Montreal had grown beyond its crenelated walls into a colonial city. Great mansions, owned by Scottish and French fur trade grandees, circled downtown streets. John could entertain himself at dozens of taverns, coffee houses, and wine shops. He could buy clothing for himself and for Susan and the children at milliners, furriers, shoemakers, and hatters. His success in Canada enabled him to become a member of the prestigious Beaver Club, an elite men's group that celebrated those who had wintered in the interior but now could afford to spend winters telling stories in a smoky clubroom. John received his engraved medal signifying membership in the winter of 1807, right after Charlotte's birth gave Susan five young children to supervise.[35]

A different winter social scene, circumscribed by weather and isolation, unfolded in Sault Ste. Marie each year. Susan's sisters or cousins came to stay for long periods, small circles of people whom Susan trusted and confided in. She controlled a big piece of land on Sugar Island that she managed for her six brothers and sisters. This set of sugar maple stands and ceremonial villages kept her at the heart of family business, which maintained Sault Ste. Marie as a crucial place in Ojibwe life into the next century.[36]

When he wintered in Montreal, John worried about his family. He wrote long letters home, exhorting Susan to "attend to the children's health" and insisting that they "attend to their studies." During winters he stayed in Michigan, he taught his children to read and write in English, French, and Latin. When Lewis and George reached school age, John took them to Montreal and enrolled them in boarding school. He supervised them closely when he was in the city. He also monitored news about the fur trade but especially about growing tensions in the 1810s between the United States and Great Britain over Great Lakes and Atlantic shipping. A border war was brewing, and John Johnston would find himself right in the center of it.[37]

Family Heartache in the Fur Trade

Personal strife enveloped the Johnstons and other fur trade families. When Anglo- or French-Canadian men moved to different posts in those years, many left their Native and mixed wives and children in

Sault Ste. Marie, Michilimackinac, or smaller posts and communities that stretched up Canadian rivers. A friend and neighbor of the Johnstons, William McGillivray, was a Lake Superior winterer who would become chief factor—or company leader—of the North West Company. In 1800 he left his Native wife and three children for a Scottish bride he brought to Canada. McGillivray provided for his Cree and Scots children by educating them, finding jobs for them, and leaving them property in his will, but other men did not. John Johnston wrote to his family that he disapproved of McGillivray's "callous family management." He also knew that his decision to stay at Lake Superior with Susan and their children limited his career options.[38]

Abandoning Native wives and children was common for elite men as they moved up the company ranks. Alexander McKay and his two brothers Donald and William all left their Cree families in the north, rational career choices perhaps but emotionally painful as each decision unfolded. Some Native groups developed special clans for these fatherless children to provide them a clear place in tribal structures. Christian practices of establishing godparents and naming guardians blended with Native ideas about having a broad range of kin who could support orphaned or abandoned children.[39]

Enmeshed in that shifting context, Alexander McKay and his half-Cree wife Marguerite lived in North West Company forts one thousand miles north of Lake Superior. They tried to imagine their four children's futures and worried about how best to prepare them. Their daughters, Annie, Catherine, and Marie, might marry White traders or clerks in the fur trade world. Alexander taught them to read and write in English and to speak French, though they spoke Cree at home. Alexander wanted to give his son, Thomas, the tools to become a Canadian gentleman or an officer in the fur trade. Learning to read and write classical languages, developing excellent penmanship and accounting skills, feeling comfortable in the homes and lives of well-read and well-connected people, all required formal education. There were risks to sending a child away from home, and Marguerite and Alexander knew "how frail and perishing" their hopes in "such a promising son" might be. Childhood diseases, poor conditions at schools, inattentive guardians, and homesickness could and did kill children, and parents at isolated forts might not hear the news for months.[40]

Despite his parents' concerns, Thomas McKay left Fort Chipewyan in the late summer of 1803. He bade farewell to his mother and younger sisters not knowing when or if he'd see them again. At seven, it was exciting to travel with his father via canoe and portage to the unfamiliar city of Montreal, but it was hard to be left with his uncles' families to attend school in Glengarry, a Scots-Canadian community near Montreal.[41]

Thomas didn't see his father for nearly a year and a half. Alexander was now considering retiring from wintering and becoming a merchant or trader in Montreal. Retirement meant selling one's share of the company, a high-value item that allowed relatively young retirees to begin new careers or to form their own fur trade companies. Alexander spent one more season as chief trader at Lake Winnipeg with Marguerite and their daughters, then returned to Fort William for the last time in 1808. He received £1,000 for one share in the North West Company. Then he retired to Montreal.[42]

Retiring also required making specific family decisions. It meant leaving Native families behind but not exactly abandoning them. Men working in the upper echelons of the fur trade like Alexander McKay, most of whom had Native or mixed wives and children, understood that they could not enter Canada's elite without a White wife. So they made "arrangements" for their Native wives and continued to educate and find good positions for their children. When Alexander McKay retired, he "turned off" Marguerite, the phrase used to describe the process. He fully intended to support her when he married an Anglo-Canadian woman. He knew his old exploring partner, Alexander Mackenzie, had young, marriageable Scottish cousins.[43]

North West Company policy struggled to deal with the problem of families. The many Native wives and mixed-descent children who accompanied traders to winter forts and then required support and food had become "a heavy burden on the company." When twenty-eight of the wintering partners, including Alexander McKay, sat down to discuss this question at their annual company meeting in 1804, all had at least one "country wife." Many had more than one—

either sisters of their wives, or wives at different posts. The North West Company built extra housing for these families and kept them fed when the brigades were away. Clerks, shipping agents, paddlers, hunters, carpenters, and laborers had relationships with Native women "in similar proportion," meaning all of them did.[44]

Nor'westers knew that Native women provided essential services—feeding, clothing, processing fur, and bridging cultures; the problem was all those children. They agreed "to manage so great an Evil," though they knew that nothing "could be done to suppress it entirely." As a compromise, and because so many men had children they cared about deeply, they instituted a fine of 100 pounds for any officer who married an "Indian" and lived with her in "the Company's Houses or Forts." The 1805 edict continued that if an employee "consorted with," married, or "took" the "Daughter of a White man and an Indian," that would be "no violation of this resolve." Such words culled "half-breeds" out of the Native world by labeling them worthy of marriage to White men.[45]

Mixed-descent women, however, could not become part of White Canada. White men and women agreed that taking Indigenous wives and children to Montreal, Glasgow, or New York would be "inhumane." Abandonment was so common that Marguerite likely knew she would survive being "turned off." Some fur traders, and more rarely their wives, wrote about the heartache of abandonment, but we have no record from Marguerite. She and Alexander had lived together as partners and parents for more than twelve years. As he rose in the North West Company, she had enjoyed material comforts and the respect of other officers and their families. Without him, she had no status and four children to support. Thomas was just eleven when his father retired, and the girls were even younger. Alexander promised that he would provide for the family. Many traders found new husbands for their abandoned wives, but he did not.[46]

Marguerite could also rely on her Cree family—no one who was part of a Cree band would starve. She and her daughters returned to the cluster of forts near Rainy River, where she had spent her childhood. Her Cree family connections and an account set up by Alexander at the fort store provided them some safety. The human requirements of the fur trade made it likely she'd find another partner, either a mixed man or a European who wanted her experience and fur trade credentials. Marguerite's work as a mixed-descent mother was just beginning.

=3=

Fur Trade Migrants: Pacific McKays and Canadian Johnstons, 1800–1820

When Alexander McKay sold his share in the North West Company in 1808, he started a new life in Montreal as a rich Canadian. However, instead of discussing real estate investments during his winter evenings at the Beaver Club, McKay spun wild ideas about an international fur trade with a Dutch émigré and successful New York furrier, John Jacob Astor.[1]

Astor hoped to entice the North West Company into a venture linking Montreal, New York, the Pacific Coast, and Canton, China. He needed men like Alexander McKay with fur trade knowledge and connections to Native people. Alexander, often accompanied by his Cree-Scots son Thomas, now twelve, imagined the wealth and the new lands they'd see, all visible in Astor's words. In the Beaver Club's warm smoky rooms, reminiscent of Cree lodges and interior forts, anything seemed possible.[2]

U.S. Ambitions and Astor's Dreams

Three years after those conversations, Alexander McKay, not retired and not remarried, ended up on the coast of Oregon with his son. In

The Global Fur Trade, 1800–1820

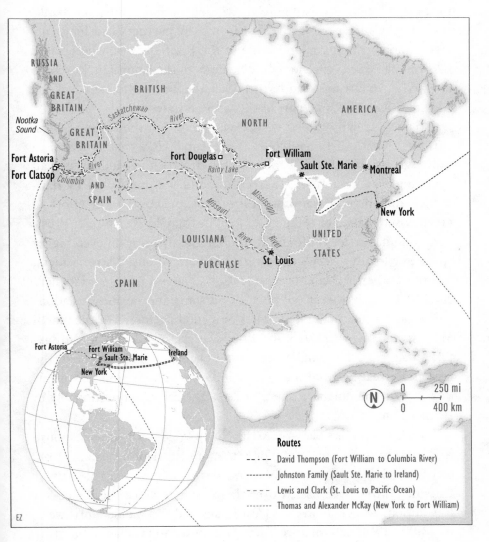

RUSSIA AND GREAT BRITAIN

BRITISH

Nootka Sound

GREAT BRITAIN

AMERICA

NORTH

Saskatchewan

River

Fort Astoria

Fort Clatsop

Columbia *River*

GREAT BRITAIN AND SPAIN

Fort Douglas

Rainy Lake

Fort William

Sault Ste. Marie

Montreal

New York

Missouri

Mississippi

LOUISIANA

PURCHASE

Missouri *River*

River

St. Louis

UNITED STATES

SPAIN

Fort Astoria

Fort William

Sault Ste. Marie

Ireland

New York

N

| 0 | | 250 mi |
| 0 | | 400 km |

Routes

- - - - - David Thompson (Fort William to Columbia River)

--------- Johnston Family (Sault Ste. Marie to Ireland)

- - - - Lewis and Clark (St. Louis to Pacific Ocean)

--------- Thomas and Alexander McKay (New York to Fort William)

EZ

April 1811, as they entered the mouth of the Columbia River, they surveyed the tumbledown huts of Fort Clatsop, where five years before, the U.S. exploring team led by Meriwether Lewis and William Clark had spent a miserable winter. Pacific sea otters and seals, as well as more prosaic beavers, all fantastically valuable in China, made the region irresistible to fur traders, sea captains, and bankers. McKay's former North West Company partners had long fantasized about finding a land route to the Pacific Coast, where those furs might make everyone rich. The news of the Louisiana Purchase stopped such dreamy chatter: in 1803 the entire watershed of the Missouri River became part of the United States.[3]

No one was happy about this development. For the United States, this huge swath of Indian country presented risks that appeared to outweigh any benefits. It had imposing deserts and mountains, had no boundaries that anyone agreed on, and was populated by dangerous Indians and traitorous Europeans. After years of effort to create a semblance of military control in the Old Northwest, President Thomas Jefferson found it troubling to imagine an even bigger space filled with even more powerful Indian nations. Native leaders, like most other backcountry residents, still envisioned a world where the Indian trade was at the heart of personal and business relationships. But would the United States be a good partner? For the North West Company, the Louisiana Purchase presented potential disaster: an aggressive United States could challenge its presence in the region. Retreating from the risk, in 1803 it rebuilt its company headquarters on the northern shore of Lake Superior, unquestionably in British Canada.[4]

John Jacob Astor's plan—and the North West Company's response to it—evolved at a messy diplomatic moment. Americans and Britons were close to war over borders, slave trading, and rules about shipping. They had tussled over these matters since the American Revolution, especially in the Great Lakes and the Pacific Northwest. In 1810 the Pacific Northwest was British territory, claimed first by British explorers such as Capt. James Cook. As trade with China made Pacific harbors more potentially lucrative, Russia, Spain, and the United States all sent ships to examine the region. With powerful Indian nations patrolling the coast, no Europeans had planted a successful settlement or trading post anywhere between San Francisco Bay and the Russian outposts in Alaska. Astor promised U.S. officials that his daring plan would finally open that lucrative space to American traders.[5]

Alexander McKay was frustrated with the North West Company's defensive actions, which left the Rocky Mountain and Pacific Coast trades to exploding numbers of American fur traders. To compete, Canadian traders needed to learn to transport trade goods and furs on a continental scale. In the spring of 1810, McKay, along with three other disgruntled Scots-Canadians—Donald McKenzie, David Stuart, and Duncan McDougall—traveled to New York to meet with Astor. He convinced them that his Pacific Fur Company could solve the large structural and geographic challenges crippling Canadian trade to the Pacific. Astor intended to develop Lewis and Clark's overland route and build a large fort on the Pacific Coast. That action would grab the fur trade right out from under the noses of the North West Company and put Astor's American ships at the center of the growing trade with China.[6]

The logistics were complex and the risks immense, but Astor's confidence was undimmed. As they heard rumors, the Nor'westers finally reacted. After the annual rendezvous in July 1810, North West Company partners sent their crack explorer and mapmaker, David Thompson, to investigate Astor's plan. Thompson's ability to travel the backcountry came from his wife Charlotte, a Cree raised in the far northern Athabasca lands. She and David Thompson had traveled, along with their growing family, through thousands of miles of Canadian forest, tundra, rivers, and ice. Now Thompson took Charlotte's brothers as guides and his oldest son as hunter, and they headed in six canoes for the Columbia River to find out what Astor and the Americans were doing.[7]

Alexander McKay would build a U.S. fort where the Columbia River enters the sea, the first piece in Astor's plan. To convince the U.S. government of the fully American nature of his enterprise, Astor needed American citizens to staff the overland trip to the site. He hired Wilson Price Hunt, a St. Louis merchant with no expedition experience but important political connections, to lead the overlanders. And he sent the Canadian fur trader Alexander McKay and his son Thomas aboard the *Tonquin* for a seven-month voyage around Cape Horn, then up nearly ten thousand miles of Pacific Coast to the Columbia River.[8]

Indian Policy and the Johnston Family's Michigan

Tensions over borders were also running high in what is now Kentucky, Ohio, Indiana, and Michigan, where the United States attempted to secure land for settlers and former soldiers through treaties with Indian nations. Congress failed at this central task. It couldn't enforce the new borders it drew with Indian nations; nor could it protect lands it opened for settlers. Unwilling to fund surveys that would establish which land belonged to whom, the United States was unable to keep White settlers out of Native lands. For their part, most settlers had no interest in the hard work of clearing land to farm it. When crops failed and soil wore out, they moved on, and with each move they invaded Indian lands. Government decrees and solemn promises were futile in the face of backcountry behavior.[9]

Indigenous nations weren't behaving as expected either. Thomas Jefferson believed that "Indians were in body and mind equal to the white man," and that once they gave up hunting for farming, they could "unite . . . with us and we shall all be Americans." Each carefully negotiated treaty called for Indians to accept missionaries and begin farming. In Jefferson's logic, the "arts and morals" of agriculture would be obvious and instantly beneficial. And agriculture was beneficial, especially for the non-Native squatters who invaded Indian farms and took their cleared land, livestock, and crops.[10]

Despite that emphasis on farming, federal and state Indian policies were inconsistent. Jefferson and his appointed officials wanted Native nations to continue one type of hunting—the kind that produced pelts for U.S. fur traders. In 1802 the United States passed a series of laws that designated most of Michigan and Wisconsin as Indian Country. Many new immigrants moving into these lands, stretching from the Great Lakes to the Mississippi River, sought to trade and intermarry with Native people. A different approach to Indian-White relations applied elsewhere. In the southern Appalachian backcountry, White citizens wanted to drive out the Indian people and seize their lands.[11]

The eight sons and daughters of John and Susan Johnston grew up in Sault Ste. Marie, a U.S.-Canadian border town at the heart of Great Lakes Indian country. New residents there faced an almost entirely Native world. In 1800 North West Company officials estimated that 8,000 Assiniboines, 6,000 Ojibwes, 4,000 Odawas, and perhaps 15,000 "Southern Indians" surrounded the Great Lakes. Fewer than one thousand White men worked in that same region, and most had intermarried with local Native people. White residents depended entirely on their Native and mixed-blood neighbors to make life safe and profitable. John Johnston and other traders outfitted wintering brigades who traded with Ojibwes, Assiniboines, Foxes, and Ho-Chunks. All successful traders had kin in those nations. Intermarriage still ran the business.[12]

By 1807, rumors of war between Great Britain and the United States and actual war between Great Lakes Indian people shifted the calculus around the fur trade. Ojibwe villages that had endured brutal attacks from Dakota raiders now spent several summers taking revenge. Ojibwe villages on both sides of the border were filled with Dakota scalps and captives, ensuring continuing violence. The Johnston children learned from their uncles about how Ojibwe warriors behaved in battle, how families cared for their kin, and how Ojibwe women died in the service of their nations. They heard the recent tale of an Ojibwe woman who killed herself when taken prisoner by Dakotas in 1804 because, as their uncle Waishkey explained, "The Great Spirit had made her a woman, but had given her the heart of a man."[13]

Beyond the crises of war, important family questions remained unanswered in this border region. Would John and Susan's children, Irish and Ojibwe, become Britons or Americans? Would they have lives in the fur trade, or should they be educated for other futures in other places? The oldest sons, Lewis and George, went to Mon-

treal to learn Greek and Latin and to make crucial personal connections with classmates of French, British, and Native descent. Big fur
companies, especially the Hudson's Bay Company, which controlled
so much wealth and social status in the region, discussed excluding
mixed-blood or "country-born" men from its officer ranks. One of
John Johnston's neighbors, Charles McKenzie, wrote to the North
West Company's chief officer. Worried about his own children, he
hoped that "unlike the Honorable HBC, who treat those born in this
country as if the Cain mark were stamped on their heads," the more
astute North West Company would employ "these native men with
fine education, families, and capacities."[14]

The Johnston daughters, Jane, Eliza, and Charlotte, educated at
home, became accomplished in both Irish and Ojibwe ways. The
eldest girl, Jane, or Bamewawagezhikaquay, was John's favorite. His
most studious and delicate child, she taught herself to read during
the long winters. She readily absorbed his lessons in scripture, handwriting, French, and arithmetic. To please her father, who had always
been a poet, she wrote poetry. Her Ojibwe grandfather, Waubojeeg,
or White Fisher, had also been a mighty poet, so her way with words
ran in her blood.[15]

Recognizing Jane's talents, John began a campaign with Susan to
take Jane to Ireland to be educated by his family. Michigan had no
educational opportunities for Jane, but sending her to an Irish school
five thousand miles away seemed to Susan an extreme solution. In
1809, when Jane was nine, Susan relented. She had already survived
sending her older sons to school, and her husband insisted that he
hadn't seen his Irish family in twenty years and wanted his children
to know them.[16]

By the time John and Jane arrived at the family home in Ireland,
Jane was sick and missed her mother. John left her to recover with
her unfamiliar aunts while he investigated Irish business and government opportunities. He was offered a couple of low-level government positions, but he couldn't imagine uprooting his family from
their North American lives. He traveled to London and met with
Thomas Douglas, Lord Selkirk, an old family friend who was just

beginning to consider a gigantic personal project: an agricultural colony in Canada's Red River Valley, a great treeless plain that runs from Lake Winnipeg into what is now northern Minnesota.[17]

In those years, European empires commonly transported poor people they considered unproductive to distant colonies: Britain sent debtors to America and prisoners to Australia. Selkirk's idea was to populate Canada with displaced Scottish Highlanders and to settle them among fur traders and voyageurs with their Native families. Selkirk pitched the idea to John Johnston and offered him the job of managing the first group of colonists scheduled to arrive in the summer of 1811.

Johnston saw fatal flaws in the plan. First, the North West Company wouldn't stand for settlements that cut off their access to the rich fur country in the far Northwest. Second, the brutal winters and short summers of that part of North America would doom any agricultural colony. Finally, the Red River ran over the contested border between the United States and Canada. Johnston turned the job down.[18]

When Johnston returned to Ireland, he found Jane unwell and unhappy. He decided to take her home. It took them almost until the ice settled in November to cross the Atlantic to New York, travel up the Hudson River, and finally manage steamer trips across three Great Lakes to reach their anxious family at Sault Ste. Marie. Susan Johnston knew that the St. Mary's River was about to freeze for the season and would block all large vessels. She later explained that one night a spirit called *Un watch e ga* had "fancied them near," so she sent her brother and some paddlers in a canoe to meet John and Jane's ship. The next day the river closed solid with ice.[19]

After that experience, John wrote to a friend that he would never "risk another child's health and happiness with such distance from home." That trip, with its two Atlantic crossings and the long separation from her family, broke Jane's health. She spent months each year confined to bed and recovering from winter respiratory illnesses and summer fevers. The trip also cemented John Johnston's decision to stay in North America.[20]

Thomas McKay's Big Adventure

In 1810, while John and Jane Johnston were sailing back from Ireland, Alexander and Thomas McKay left New York on another ship to advance John Jacob Astor's plan of a Pacific Coast trade. Aboard the *Tonquin*, the world of singing voyageurs, Cree hunters, and their spirits met an equally cosmopolitan culture of sailors. As they sailed, still another group of adventurers gathered in St. Louis. Led by St. Louis merchant Wilson Price Hunt, fifty-six men and "one squaw" prepared for an overland trip west. The guides, hunters, translators, and traders were all "half-breed French," according to Hunt, who worried about traveling with so many non-Americans on a venture sponsored by the U.S. government. After crossing the newly mapped Rocky Mountains, they would build boats to travel down the Columbia River to meet the *Tonquin* and its crew. If the whole plan appears sketchy, it was.[21]

Thomas McKay, then thirteen, enjoyed life aboard the *Tonquin*. The almost eternal daylight in the southern hemisphere's "winter," the flying fish that guided the ship at Cape Horn, and the warmth of the Hawaiian ocean all seemed miraculous to a boy from Canada. But the five ex–North West Company men whom Astor had hired to manage the trip clashed with the *Tonquin*'s captain, a bristly man appropriately named Thorn. He loathed the flamboyant French-Canadians and the free rein they gave their voyageurs and craftsmen. Captain Thorn complained about the Canadians' unseemly informality in reports to Astor, behavior that he believed endangered the ship.[22]

The ship landed in March 1811 in terrible spring weather. Chinook villagers watched as the ship negotiated the deadly sandbars and breakers that demarcated the Columbia River from the Pacific Ocean. As the new arrivals attempted to paddle to shore in Canadian river canoes, waves knocked them into the water. Four Chinooks watching onshore swam out, righted the canoes, and using some oceangoing paddles of Chinook design, got everyone safely to shore. They expected payment for their rescue effort and got it. With

Chinook assistance, Astor's men located a site fifteen miles up the river. Finally the *Tonquin* could anchor and they could build Astoria, on the northwest edge of present-day Oregon.[23]

Delegations of local people visited the new arrivals, wondering what advantage or danger they might bring. Any danger the Astorians presented seemed slight since they looked weak and hungry. Shipbound for months, they craved fresh meat and vegetables. The Chinooks could only offer the newcomers dried fish and root vegetables that they had stored for winter. When the Astorians turned up their noses at such items and had no gifts to exchange, the Chinooks stopped bringing food. Thomas McKay remembered the scanty rations of those first few months. It was a hard lesson, but later everyone "wished we had eaten more salmon with grace so that the Indians would have continued to provide."[24]

To survive, the Astorians needed to integrate themselves into this particular Native world. Access to ocean and land, combined with a temperate climate, made the Pacific Northwest a rich and comfortable place to live. More densely populated and more hierarchical than the Great Lakes world, Northwest Coast peoples lived in large villages that bumped up against each other. As the Iroquois had done in the seventeenth century, Chinookan-speaking people here had developed a powerful confederacy by the early nineteenth century. Chinooks, Clatsops, and Kathlamets protected their power aggressively from groups such as Wascopams and Wishrams living farther inland. They built status and wealth by capturing people in war and using those captives as slaves. Like those in the Great Lakes and Canada, the dozens of Columbia River nations controlled their region's resources by using watercraft. Huge oceangoing canoes carved out of northwest firs could carry seventy oarsmen to hunt whales hundreds of miles away. Flatboats for placid estuaries and nimble single boats for streams and smaller rivers enabled an ongoing trade between coastal peoples and those living inland. Native slaves chopped down enormous trees to build boats, ceremonial totem poles, and huge fish-drying platforms. Crowded villages along the Columbia resembled "the seaport villages on the east coast of the United States," according to one Astorian.[25]

By 1800, Pacific Northwest peoples had had plenty of contact with trading ships and European sailors. Russians trading with China hunted valuable sea otters along the coast north of Puget Sound. A few British and American ships had arrived in Puget Sound and made individual deals with village leaders. Some ship captains, bound by no rules and running no risk, had captured and enslaved Native people to force them to trade or hunt. By the time the Astorians arrived, local peoples were cautious, sometimes hostile, and capable of protecting themselves.[26]

As the Astorians waited for Wilson Price Hunt and the overland expedition to arrive, they had two tasks: to build a fort and to investigate the Indian trade. Building a fort required performing backbreaking work with axes too small for the Pacific Northwest trees.

Meanwhile the officers took on the task of learning about the local tribes. In June 1811 Alexander McKay sailed north with the *Tonquin*'s crew to explore the forbidding coast. Before leaving on that venture, he asked Alexander Ross to care for Thomas if something were to happen to him. He told Ross, "If you ever see us back, it will be a miracle." He was right.[27]

Near what is now Vancouver Island, at Clayoquot Sound, the *Tonquin* anchored to trade at a Nootka village. Alexander McKay went ashore to assess the possibilities. While he was gone, less experienced men invited some Indians onto the ship to trade. The Nootkas, knowing that ships sometimes sailed away before paying for their furs, demanded high prices and kept the furs just out of reach of the *Tonquin*'s sailors. Annoyed, the irascible Captain Thorn committed a serious breach of etiquette by throwing otter pelts at the village leader. When McKay returned to the ship he upbraided the crew for the dangerous encounter. But that insult, one of a series of bad encounters between traders on ships and these Nootka villagers, was the proverbial last straw.

The next day the Nootkas talked their way back onto the ship and killed most of the *Tonquin*'s crew. Alexander McKay, reportedly the first to be driven off the ship into the water, was beaten to death by women with paddles as he struggled to swim. A few survivors finally drove the attackers off the ship, but without sailors who knew how to get the ship moving, they were marooned. At dawn the next day five men escaped to shore, three of whom were killed when they reached the beach. In a climax to the violence, the last crew member on board lit the gunpowder magazine on fire. He blew up the *Tonquin*, himself, and local villagers who had returned to pillage the ship.

The only known survivor was a mixed Chinook-British man named Jack Ramsay, who had served as interpreter on the *Tonquin*. When Ramsay dragged himself ashore, he immediately offered himself up as a slave to a Nootka woman, the culturally appropriate way to deal with the situation. Only when he escaped from his enslaver several weeks later could Ramsay confirm the rumors that had been circulating since the *Tonquin* disappeared. That news took the heart out of the Astoria enterprise.[28]

What finally finished Astoria, however, was rescue by the North West Company. In July 1811, as the men struggled to put up buildings at Astoria, that prominent company man, David Thompson, "came dashing down the Columbia in a light canoe manned by eight Iroquois, chiefly from Montreal," according to an astonished Alexander Ross. From the beginning, Thompson had wanted to cooperate with Astor in Pacific trade. Now several years into his own adventure and without any intelligence from his superiors at the company, David Thompson told the shocked Astorians that Astor and the North West Company had surely done the rational thing and joined forces. He sent a sincere note to the Astorians to announce "with pleasure" that his "Wintering Partners" had accepted "Mr. Astor's offer for 1/3 of your business."

Astor had made no such offer and instead had wisely abandoned the Astoria venture once rumors of war with Britain made shipping risky. But no one in Oregon knew that.[29]

The loss of ship and employer left Thomas McKay orphaned and, like the other Astorians, broke and stranded. They didn't know if Wilson Price Hunt's overland expedition, now nine months into an expected six-month trip, would ever arrive. Life at Astoria was hard. The cold, damp fog of summer defeated the familiar crops they tried to grow. None of the Astorians were hunters, so once the last sheep was eaten and the pigs ran away into the forest, they depended on Indians to feed them. Everyone tired of the oily summer salmon and the dried meat they could purchase from the local Chinook leader Concomly and his large village.[30]

Facing this grim situation, the Astorians went to live with local Indian tribes in the winter of 1812. Chinook and Clatsop houses, built for rain and wind, kept them warmer than the leaky fort. Local Native women provided food and comfort, as they always had for Canadian fur traders. Thomas McKay, still too much of a boy to attract attention from these women, surely wished he had received more than food from women wearing "petticoats of cedar fibers" and "thick robes of weasel furs" who "bathed in the river and were no means shy."[31]

Wilson Price Hunt finally arrived with Astor's overlanders from St. Louis in the spring of 1812. They had suffered their own harrowing adventure: they had gotten lost in the Rocky Mountains, had been rescued by Crow Indians and then by Spokanes, and finally all their gear and boats had been smashed in the roaring Columbia. Nearly starving, the overlanders were pleased with the progress the Astorians had made on the fort. A large store, a dwelling house, a blacksmith shop, and several smaller buildings for storage and food preparation stood in a stout palisade, guarded by two cannons. Outside there were gardens, though they were ravaged by feral goats and pigs.[32]

Despite those steps forward, the fort's great fur press stood idle. After transporting the metal press around the world, the Astorians had made little progress in establishing that core business. That failure, and the arrival of only one U.S. ship in their first two years at Astoria, now concerned everyone at the fort. In January 1813 the news reached them that war had commenced between Great Britain and the United States. They knew that if British warships appeared on the Pacific Coast, they would hardly be welcoming to British citizens who had defected to an American company. They would no doubt claim Astoria for the British Empire. The remaining Astorians began packing up.[33]

Borderland Loyalties and the War of 1812

The War of 1812, mainly a rumor on the Pacific Coast, threatened life in Sault Ste. Marie. After the American Revolution, the Great Lakes region had remained a borderland mix of Americans, Canadians, and Indians. But the American invasion of Canada in the summer of 1812 forced the inhabitants to take sides. Like most people in the fur trade, Native and Canadian and British, the Johnstons supported the British after the American invasion.

The first volleys in the war hit the Johnston family. When the territorial governor of Indiana, William Henry Harrison, led an attack on Indian country just south of the Michigan border in November 1811, he lost to an Indian army led by the Shawnee warrior Tecumseh, who fought with British guns and bullets. The battle involved Native people the Johnston family knew, allies of their Ojibwe kin. American newspapers used Harrison's loss to warn their readers about the deadly combination of British ill will and Native perfidy that Canada encouraged: the perfect place, now, for an invasion. On July 12, 1812, Gen. William Hull led American troops across the Detroit River into Canada. The United States expected to achieve a quick victory but instead encountered a professional British military with powerful Native auxiliaries. U.S. officials misunderstood the depth of anti-American feeling in Canada. They had imagined Scots-, Irish-, and French-Canadians would become Americans the moment U.S. soldiers arrived. Instead, they faced people like John Johnston and his sons, resolute in defending their Canadian and Native lives.[34]

Outnumbered by the Americans, Canadian forces, both British and French, responded by gathering Native allies. They needed allies because Anglo-Canadians were outnumbered by Anglo-Americans, but Indigenous Americans outnumbered them all. Indian nations, still shocked by their defeats by American troops in the 1790s, vowed to reinforce their position in Canada and hoped to win back the Ohio Valley and the Great Lakes. The fur trade relied on Native and British control of the Great Lakes. Assessing this constellation of forces,

British military officials agreed on the strategic importance of Michilimackinac, now U.S. Fort Mackinac, and planned an attack there. To fight for Lake Superior, the sons of prominent traders—mixed-blood relations of the Johnstons—organized three hundred of their Ojibwe and Odawa kin. John Johnston, referred to in U.S. Captain Roberts's reports as the "Gentleman at the Sault of St. Mary's," brought a large flotilla of canoes manned by French-Canadians and Ojibwes. This quickly gathered force confronted the sixty-one American troops at Michilimackinac who, outnumbered and fearful of massacre by Indians, surrendered immediately.[35]

The easy victory at Michilimackinac made other Indian nations confident in a British victory. In the fall of 1812, Indian warriors attacked U.S. posts and settlements all over the Old Northwest. Fort Dearborn, now Chicago, fell in a violent attack that killed an entire garrison of soldiers but spared their mixed-race families. Next, the post at Fort Wayne fell, followed by Detroit. Not exactly an American stronghold, Detroit had one hundred U.S. soldiers to protect forty-seven hundred citizens, nearly all French-Canadians employed by British fur traders. The outpost was surrounded by tens of thousands of Indians.[36]

Such news, and the gory descriptions that came with it, were the material of nightmares for Americans. Atrocities from the French and Indian War and the American Revolution had occurred in living memory. A British naval officer commented that "the dread of the encounter with Indian foes was a striking feature among many of the Americans, even those who have never seen one." The British used that fear effectively and threatened to turn over U.S. captives to marauding Indians.[37]

The fall of the U.S. forts to British and Indian forces was good news to traders on the Great Lakes. The Johnston family felt secure in their decision to remain loyally Canadian while living in the United States. However, the war disrupted everyone's business. The naval war in the Great Lakes meant that few boats came from Montreal, leaving John Johnston with meager supplies to outfit Lake Superior trading posts. The canoes went out thinly outfitted that year. Concerned about his business, Johnston spent the winter of

1813 in Montreal buying goods. His seventeen-year-old son George was left to supervise the family business.

Johnston also worked at getting Lewis, his oldest son, a commission in the British Army. "Poor Lewis" had failed at running a store in Montreal and at several of the family trading posts because of a drinking problem. His father called in several favors to find a military position for him. When the war shifted to naval battle in September 1812, Lewis Johnston served on the HMS *Lady Prevost* on Lake Erie. The Battle of Lake Erie became a famous engagement because the American naval commander Oliver Hazard Perry bested the large British ships with his small but maneuverable force. Numerous men were killed and injured on both sides. Lewis Johnston was injured. The U.S. army surgeon who treated Lewis's injuries remembered him forty years later, amazed to learn that his patient had been an Indian. The surgeon noted, "I did not suspect at the time that he belonged to that race," but said he had wondered about Lewis's speech and assumed he was "French."[38]

The Johnstons were a perfect example of what the newly appointed territorial governor of Michigan, Lewis Cass, had feared when he asked for military assistance. Cass knew the Johnstons personally, but he never trusted them. They crossed borders so easily. The family spoke French and Ojibwe at home, and they had Native kin who were involved in military raids. John Johnston did business with the British North West Company, which so obviously supported the British Army. Crippling the North West Company by burning its facilities and stealing its furs became a U.S. military objective, and the Johnston family figured as a target. Cass vowed to destroy the posts of fur traders who fed Indians, armed them, and took them into their homes.[39]

In the summer of 1814, U.S. Army Maj. Andrew Holmes led American forces up the St. Mary's River to raid North West Company operations at Sault Ste. Marie and to capture John Johnston and confiscate his goods. Johnston wasn't there, but young George was, all alone. When Susan Johnston received news that American troops were coming, she took the five youngest children, including baby Anna Maria, six months old, to her brother Waishkey's village.

George tried to keep the troops from plundering his father's supplies and stores, but he ended up a prisoner himself. He watched as soldiers emptied the storerooms of furs, trade goods, and building supplies and burned all the buildings—except the Johnston house—to the ground.[40]

While U.S. troops were destroying his buildings, John Johnston was at Michilimackinac with fourteen-year-old Jane doing business. But the war came there too. When Major Holmes left Sault Ste. Marie, he moved toward Michilimackinac, where there was a garrison designed to withstand a naval siege. During the fruitless battle, the guns of Holmes's boats could not be raised high enough to hit the fortress. Afterward the American forces regrouped. They went around the back of the island to land and attack the fort from the rear. They had to cross a large open plain, and Native snipers cut down the U.S. soldiers at will, including Major Holmes, the very man who had pillaged the Johnstons. Fort Mackinac remained in British hands until after the war ended.[41]

John Johnston, inside Fort Mackinac with Jane, watched and wondered what had happened to his family at the Sault. With no word from George, his dread radiated across the page: "Oh why have you not sent Mr. Drew or Waishkey [Susan's brother] to deliver me from the torment of suspense." He and Jane waited anxiously for another few days until they got news that the family was safe, but their home and business were destroyed.[42]

That loss of goods and furs ruined Johnston's credit in Montreal and prevented him from outfitting for an entire season. Hoping he might be compensated by the U.S. or British government for his losses, he spent years applying to both. He went to Montreal to make his case to the British government and beg for supplies and extended credit from his bankers. Back in Sault Ste. Marie, Susan told anxious brigade leaders to head out early because provisions were so low at the Sault that hunters would do better living in the Ojibwe and Odawa villages. The Johnstons and their neighbors barely survived the following hungry winter of 1814.[43]

Farther south, the occupying U.S. army slaughtered livestock and burned farms to deprive the British army of supplies. Local

Michiganders watched bitterly as this happened, now dependent on British forts and their Indian friends to feed them. U.S. Gen. Duncan McArthur, fighting in Michigan, tried to form a militia from local volunteers, but they disappeared into the woods and refused to accompany him into Canada. Such behavior infuriated Territorial Governor Cass, who saw it as typical of the "old Michigan residents," code for mixed-blood trade families.[44]

The consequences of this dismal war surprised everyone. The United States had expected to take Canada and vanquish the Indians. Instead, after ten U.S. attempts to invade Canada, allied Indian and British forces still held it, the Indian war spread, and British troops burned Washington. From that position of strength, Canadian and British negotiators could have demanded much for their Native allies who had protected Canada so valiantly. They didn't. Canadian officials and military officers hoped to create a broad buffer zone along the U.S.-Canadian border inhabited by and patrolled by Native nations. They didn't. Instead, more concerned about Napoleon in Europe, British negotiators insisted only on a treaty article returning U.S. Indian nations to their "pre-war situation." Native people were supposed to put down arms, return captives, and surrender forts.[45]

When Native nations weren't invited to participate in the peace negotiations, they went to war. After their early success in the War of 1812, a series of influential prophets and military leaders convinced a significant coalition of Great Lakes and Ohio River nations to unite. The Shawnee leader Tecumseh had traveled up and down the Mississippi and through the Appalachians, explaining that Native nations needed to fight together to protect their remaining land and power. Huge armies gathered along the Ohio, threatening White settlements and river travel. But Tecumseh was killed at the Battle of Prophetstown, and their efforts failed. Still, the Native uprising disrupted the fur trade and challenged loyalties for a decade. Native armies retreated into Canada, escaping the U.S. Army in places like Sault Ste. Marie, where geography and family protected them. Military officials believed that the Johnstons supplied those warriors and their British allies. They were right. The Johnston children came of age during an era of powerful confederacies in the Old Northwest.

Their uncles and cousins fought with Tecumseh, and their father's friends were British agents. The Johnston family lived those mixed loyalties into the next generation.[46]

Meanwhile the McKays and other families made similar decisions about family and loyalty. During the winter of 1810, while Thomas was wandering among the seabirds at the Cape of Good Hope, his mother, Marguerite Waddens McKay, rebuilt her life in Canada. She would hear the grim news about the *Tonquin* and Alexander McKay's death a year after it happened, but she had no word of Thomas until she actually saw him several years later. Meantime she met John McLoughlin, a medical doctor and clerk for the North West Company, who wintered at Rainy River. In 1811 Marguerite and John married, according to the "custom of the country," blending a family from other marriages. Marguerite's three daughters were now seven, ten, and twelve, and McLoughlin's son, Joseph, whose Cree mother had died when he was a baby, was three. Marguerite and John had four more children together, and their partnership lasted until his death in 1857.

Thomas McKay, stranded and fatherless in Oregon, eventually made it home to Canada to meet this new family. In the winter of 1813, the event that the Astorians dreaded and prayed for since they'd heard the United States was at war with Great Britain finally occurred. A British warship, the *Raccoon*, arrived on the coast of Oregon. The Astorians surrendered as British officers claimed the Columbia River for Great Britain. Some former Astorians sailed off on the *Raccoon* when it left a month later, but Thomas had no desire to end up as a sailor.[47]

For Thomas, staying in the fur trade brought difficult choices. Though his father had employed him with an American company, Thomas wasn't an American. And despite his experience in the trade and his influential family, his mixed blood was a cultural fact that mattered more in some places than others. Thomas heard the derisive comments that U.S. ship captains made about fur trade marriages and the children who came from them. So with few other prospects, when a fur-trading brigade from the North West Company arrived in 1813, Thomas joined it. The Canadian paddlers, their French and Scottish bosses, and entourages of wives and mixed-blood children were familiar. And the Northwest men offered work, even though Thomas was demoted from clerk to servant. At last, in April 1814, Thomas left the Columbia. In a canoe built by Chinook craftsmen and paddled by Canadian voyageurs and a Hawaiian guide, he was bound for Fort William, the North West Company's headquarters on Lake Superior. He reunited with his mother, who was now married to John McLoughlin, late in 1814. Not even eighteen, he'd seen a lot.[48]

When the war ended in Canada, Thomas McKay was likely at Fort William for the grand summer gathering along Lake Superior's northern shore. For the North West Company, this was a heroic moment. The traders had lost the southern pieces of their territory to the United States, but with the acquisition of Astor's fort on the Columbia River, their dominion stretched from Montreal to the Pacific Northwest. Anchored by the Great Lakes world of Cree and Ojibwe hunters, and now by the Columbia, where Scottish traders did business with Chinooks, Spokanes, and Cayuses, the Canadian fur trade had, in tense accommodation with Native people, populated a new world with new peoples.[49]

The Pemmican Proclamation

Thomas McKay followed the Red River north, through the heart of bison country, now essential as a Pemmican Highway that supplied every fort, trade route, and wintering post. Pemmican made in Red River country powered winter travel in the fur trade. The northern Plains—treeless, windswept, and bitter cold in winter—looked bleak to the uninitiated. But abundant grass and winding, tree-lined rivers welcomed bison and the people who hunted them. Now, as part of a fully developed fur trade, retired hunters and traders and their mixed-descent families settled in new communities among Crees, Ojibwes, Dakotas, and Assiniboines who had hunted there for generations. They all made pemmican. A Canadian writer reminisced in 1909, "On the plain between the Assiniboine and the Saskatchewan, a half-breed community had sprung up." Because of "their dusky faces" they took the name Bois-Brulés, or "Charcoal Faces."[50]

Thomas McKay, like many young men around Lake Superior, used that Pemmican Highway to avoid ruin and seek work. Ruin could come from any direction: McKay's family worried he might make the wrong choices about a career or approach the wrong woman. His "ungovernable" temper and his frustration at not finding respect in the changing fur trade world led Thomas McKay to continue moving. He certainly found work—he paddled, he loaded heavy pemmican packs, and he obeyed his North West Company brigade leaders at Fort Ile-á-la-Crosse and Fort Gibraltar. His dark hair and dark eyes made him fit right in—at the center of a war over pemmican that threatened to ruin everyone.[51]

That war began because a Scottish lord, Thomas Douglas, the Fifth Earl of Selkirk, felt guilty. He had inherited fabulous wealth from his father, who had personally ousted thousands of Scottish crofters from their farms when he turned his land to raising sheep for Scotland's wool industry. The young Lord Selkirk watched this human crisis develop while reading reports about North America written by the Scots explorer Alexander Mackenzie. Selkirk saw a solution both to the crofters' misery and to his own guilt in the "vast emptiness" of Canada. In 1808 he traveled to Canada to meet Mackenzie, and together they planned a vast human experiment for western Canada.[52]

In 1808 Mackenzie, thinking of the challenge of supplying a fur trade that stretched from sea to sea, and Selkirk, hoping to solve the problem of the landless Scots, asked the British government for a huge land grant in the Red River Valley that extended from Lake Winnipeg into what is now South Dakota. British officials, hoping to avoid arguments with the United States, flatly refused. Unfazed, Selkirk and Mackenzie took another approach and bought shares in the Hudson's Bay Company. By 1809 the two men owned enough shares to demand access to some HBC land.

The Hudson's Bay Company, now losing money because of its

long corporate war with the North West Company, was willing to experiment. It might be good business to build an agricultural colony in the center of Canada that would cut off Nor'westers' trade routes. Lord Selkirk ended up with 116,000 square miles of land in Canada that spread into the United States, a chunk equivalent to New England and New York combined. That land, long settled, farmed, and hunted on by Native people, was now home to several generations of fur traders and their mixed-heritage kin. When Selkirk offered the position of governor to John Johnston, he turned down the job. Writing to his son George, John had predicted a "great effusion of blood" when Selkirk arrived in Canada.[53]

Ignorance and hope created a rolling disaster. Instead of Johnston, Selkirk hired a man named Miles Macdonell, a retired British Army officer beguiled by the Canada described in letters from his brother, a North West Company trader. They described fertile land, ideal for farming: "plains so extensive that a man may travel to the Rocky Mountains without passing a wood." This site, because of its strategic location for moving goods along Canadian rivers, would eventually become the city of Winnipeg, but it would never be an easy place to farm.

Selkirk had trouble recruiting settlers. The difficult Atlantic crossing and remote site attracted few Scottish crofters. Only seventy people arrived at the already frozen-in York Factory in Hudson's Bay in the fall of 1811. After a terrible winter, the Indians had to carry the colonists' remaining children south to the new colony at Red River, but at the price of "wedding rings" and "guns from the battle of Culloden."[54]

The new settlers arrived on the Red River late in 1812—too late to plant. By spring they had built a crude fort, named Fort Douglas for their benefactor, right next to the North West Company post Fort Gibraltar. A new crop of settlers arrived in the summer of 1813, and with another long Canadian winter setting in, feeding everyone became an immediate crisis. Watching their bison and rabbit-hunting neighbors, the colonists tried hunting but hardly ever filled their pots. Hungrily, they eyed the nearby North West Company storehouses filled with pemmican, ready to feed hunters and paddlers far to the north. Governor Macdonell believed he was in charge of his colonists and of North West Company workers. To demonstrate his power, he issued the Pemmican Proclamation in January 1814, declaring that no pemmican could be taken out of the colony and that it all had to be transferred to his fort. Since pemmican was essential for North West Company business, the pronouncement set off an armed conflict between settlers and Nor'westers, including Thomas McKay, who was now working as a clerk at Fort Gibraltar.[55]

When Macdonell's colonists began seizing pemmican and carting it off to their storehouses, the partners of the North West Company voted "to defend the Property at all Hazards." They sent Duncan Cameron, a Nor'wester with a reputation for both craftiness and violence, to head up Fort Gibraltar. Cameron threatened the settlers with starvation and attack by the local Indians. The settlers wisely left, scattering into the woods. Thomas McKay, along with his fellow Nor'westers—Anglo, Métis, Cree, and Ojibwe together—then destroyed Fort Douglas.[56]

Selkirk was still not ready to back down. The Hudson's Bay Company, always behind Selkirk, saw how much damage a settlement in Red River could do to the North West Company and came out in front. HBC officers appointed a new governor, Robert Semple, to rebuild Fort Douglas. He arrived with eighty new settlers in November 1815. Semple's first act was to destroy Fort Gibraltar, showing his power to snuff out the North West Company world. A mixed-blood man named Cuthbert Grant took the lead in responding to Semple's destructive act. In the end, he would get all the blame, part of a long tradition of accusing "hot-blooded" Métis men. Grant and a group of angry Red River men headed for Fort Douglas, stopping first at Rainy Lake, where North West Company partners and voyageurs joined his forces. The new recruits included John McLoughlin, now married to Marguerite Waddens McKay, and his stepson, Thomas McKay.[57]

When Grant's forces arrived at Fort Douglas on June 19, 1816, Semple and thirty of his colonists were outside at a spot called Seven Oaks. According to early reports, Cuthbert Grant's soldiers fired the first shot, though a royal commission eventually determined with "next to certainty" that Semple's men fired first. The Nor'westers were skilled sharpshooters and outnumbered Semple's forces; the "battle" or "massacre" of Seven Oaks lasted only fifteen minutes. Some of Semple's men were "finished off," shot in the head as they begged for mercy. Both sides acted out personal vendettas, desecrating the dead in Scottish, French, and Native fashion. The combined forces killed twenty-one men, including Governor Semple.[58]

Seven Oaks stands as a landmark in the American history of race. People with fur trade histories and whose families had mixed blood began to see themselves as Métis. The formal inquiries into the 1816 battle focused on the mixed-blood participants and how their race explained their actions. According to the testimony of John Pritchard, a clerk present at Fort Douglas, Thomas McKay was one of the ringleaders of the French-speaking and Indian-looking Bois-Brulés. Pritchard portrayed Semple's men as innocents requesting a surrender, rather than armed attackers shooting as they ran toward Grant's forces.[59]

Back at Fort William, the news of the Battle of Seven Oaks and the final "dispersal" of settlers seemed like a grand victory. Semple's rash act and Cuthbert Grant's response meant that the North West Company never took official action against Selkirk's colony or the Hudson's Bay Company. But the drama had not ended. Selkirk demanded that Canadian military forces round up the perpetrators. The governor-general of Canada refused, saying that "if the lives and property of the Earl of Selkirk's settlers are endangered," they had "brought it on themselves." Selkirk then came to Canada and hired a private force of British soldiers to take on the North West Company himself. Even as his flotilla of soldiers and cannons left the docks at Sault Ste. Marie, no one at Fort William took the threat very seriously. Within hours, Selkirk's forces had captured Fort William, the Lake Superior fortress of the North West Company.[60]

Selkirk arrested the partners of the Company, including Thomas's stepfather, John McLoughlin, and sent them to Montreal in a dangerously overloaded canoe. When a sudden storm struck Lake Superior, the canoe overturned and nine of the Nor'westers drowned, including two partners and a member of the Legislative

Council of Canada. When the remaining partners reached Montreal, they were not clapped in jail as Selkirk demanded, but treated as martyrs. Selkirk, who still imagined himself a hero to Canadians, announced that he would stay at Fort William for the winter to protect his new domain.

But Selkirk had become a pariah, and when a representative of the British Parliament arrived from London, he arrested Selkirk and took him to Montreal to be tried. Selkirk faced four separate offenses, all of which related to the unlawful occupation of Fort William. The case was so complicated that the *Montreal Courant* provided a handy checklist, updated weekly for its readers. The entire affair left Selkirk ruined.[61]

In the aftermath, as the North West Company and the Hudson's Bay Company got their businesses back in order, they faced hard questions. In the dangerous competition between the two companies, wintering men had acted like mercenaries, burning forts, stealing supplies, and inciting Indian war. Such activities destroyed profits and prevented both companies from developing new trade in Canada's interior Northwest or on the Pacific Coast. Both corporations now realized that if they didn't cooperate, the United States would soon have the upper hand in the fur trade.

After several years, the two companies merged in 1821. Neither company wanted to do this. They hated each other. Even with the facts plain, they couldn't sit down together until the British Parliament forced them to. The new company kept the name Hudson's Bay Company but used the operational structure created by the North West Company.[62]

The Red River country remained a question for the merged Company. The region had become a place where Anglo- or French-Canadian men with Native families made a living by hunting, farming, and producing pemmican and canoes, alongside their Native neighbors. Both the Hudson's Bay Company and the North West Company had found such communities essential and profitable but now also dangerous. No one in the fur trade world was sorry about Selkirk or his settlers, but someone had to be blamed. Red River's mixed-blood men offered a convenient solution.[63]

Worried about potential violence, even before the merger, Company leaders banished several "bad apples" west of the Rocky Mountains. Thomas McKay was among the crack brigade leaders with murderous reputations, mixed-blood sons of traders that the North West Company wanted under their control but at a distance. McKay's stepfather, John McLoughlin, was one of the North West Company men who brokered the deal with the Hudson's Bay Company. McLoughlin became a chief factor in the conjoined company, which now included 173 forts. He and Marguerite Waddens McKay McLoughlin, along with their blended family of nine children, entered the most elite level of the fur trade world. McLoughlin pulled some strings to send Thomas to the Columbia River, where McKay returned in the winter of 1820. Right where he had been abandoned eight years before by his father, Thomas McKay began a life in a different fur trade.[64]

Thomas was marked by his actions at the Battle of Seven Oaks. He was never formally promoted above the level of clerk, but his Seven Oaks reputation earned him enormous respect from Canadian and Native paddlers and hunters. Even in a mature fur trade, plagued with corporate trouble, the central feature of the business was building relationships with Native people. Now in his midtwenties, Thomas McKay married Timmee T'Ikul Tchinouk, the daughter of the local Chinook leader Concomly. This marriage gave Thomas access to fishers, hunters, canoe builders, and slave laborers, all essential to his work as a fur trader. Timmee gained trade goods and alliances for her family, which allowed her father, Concomly, to control who hunted and traveled in his Columbia River domain.

Marriage smoothed over some challenges in the fur trade business. Just underneath peaceful family life, however, roiled the violence that had killed Alexander McKay and turned fur traders like Thomas McKay into mercenaries. The stew of hatred leading to the Battle of Seven Oaks put men like Thomas McKay and their heritage under a new lens. Fur trade leaders, politicians, and settlers would soon see mixing race as a problem instead of the human core of trade and diplomacy. How would new American fur companies, struggling to break into an old business, regard an army of mixedblood men who didn't share the corporate goals of company leaders?[65]

=4=

"This Kind of Business Will Make Trouble": Remaking the Fur Trade, 1810–1830

A ndrew Drips stood on a newly built wharf in St. Louis in 1819. Surrounded by his meager belongings and a pile of goods he hoped to sell, he wasn't impressed by what he saw. St. Louis had no paved streets and few wagons or carriages to hire. Black and Indian slaves carried everything on their heads and backs.[1]

Andrew had left his Irish immigrant parents and joined an Ohio militia unit to fight Indians in the War of 1812. When that war ended in 1816, Andrew could have stayed in one of twelve new army posts the United States built along the Mississippi to police Native nations. Even though another war seemed likely, Andrew had options beyond the hard life of soldiering. Literate and hardworking, he worked his way west selling goods and keeping the books in river towns. He joined other young men, like the Louisianan Lucien Fontenelle, who poured into St. Louis from all directions.[2]

Lucien Fontenelle had arrived in St. Louis in 1816. Only sixteen, he had lost his parents in a hurricane that destroyed their New Orleans plantation. Lucien, a French speaker with only a little English, chose St. Louis because it remained part of a French world but offered new opportunities in the emerging West.

Any glimmer to St. Louis, however, was cheap paint hiding serious deficiencies. Andrew Drips, like too many others, learned that he was "unable to dispose of my stock for any price," leaving him with "the prospect of bankruptcy float[ing] before me." That prospect haunted all Americans in the first decades of the 1800s.[3]

Drips and Fontenelle hoped to escape such financial trouble. In an era when the population of the United States doubled every twenty years, that of St. Louis grew even faster. As opportunity and ambition moved west, however, so did their twisted twins, ruin and doubt. The city's commercial frenzy raced just ahead of economic calamity. Even as St. Louis businesses advertised land and goods for sale, newspapers like the *Missouri Gazette*, the first newspaper published in English west of the Mississippi, filled its back pages with long lists of creditors who threatened to jail people fleeing from debt. The *Gazette* was founded by the new territorial governor, William Clark, who stayed in St. Louis after his grand tour of the Louisiana Purchase.[4]

Debt and Hope in a New West

Everyone, including William Clark, expected the U.S. economy to boom after the War of 1812. Instead, Indian war and a perilous economic cycle culminated in the Panic of 1819, ruining a generation of young men and their commercial ambitions in the West. Those losses were reflected in the era's ubiquitous epistolary sign-off: "I'm indebted to you." It meant you recognized the power someone had over you. Being in debt was a crime. Many people, especially young men, found themselves in debtor's prison or in danger of being thrown there. They went west to escape prisons and poorhouses.[5]

St. Louis, however, offered no respite from economic failure. Between 1800 and 1820, the city added 150 stone buildings and 201 frame houses, but the accumulating burden of debt meant that no one could afford them. Banks closed, and land offices called in loans. Formerly comfortable St. Louisans found themselves suddenly "indebted to you." They sold Black slaves and Native servants to pay their debts. They certainly didn't hire young men like Andrew Drips or Lucien Fontenelle.[6]

Alongside the powerful economic downturn came a climate disaster. To be alive in the years 1816 to 1818 meant to be hungry. It began when the ash from a volcanic eruption in the Dutch East Indies blocked the sun. After the most powerful blast in recorded history, a "year without a summer" created a three-year worldwide crisis. Deep early frosts killed harvests, and droughts or flooding rains destroyed fields. Villagers in Vermont survived on hedgehogs and weeds, and peasants in Yunnan ate white clay. Summer tourists traveling in France mistook beggars crowding the roads for armies on the march. In New England, 1816 was nicknamed "eighteen-hundred-and-froze-to-death," while Germans called 1817 "the year of the beggar."[7]

When crops failed in 1816 and again in 1817, starving rural legions from China to Ireland to New York swarmed out of the countryside to towns to beg or sell themselves or their children for food. Across Europe and North America, devastated by a decade of war, tens of thousands of unemployed veterans found themselves unable to feed their families. Many families moved west, crossing the Atlantic Ocean and then traveling down the Ohio and Mississippi rivers, arriving in Missouri with few resources. Expecting the available land and healthful climate that government reports and speculators had promised them, new residents were instead attacked by local agues and fevers. They could hardly find the energy to farm places that flooded, froze, and occasionally shook from the aftershocks of the mighty New Madrid earthquake of 1812.[8]

In this unfamiliar place, the new migrants competed with a prospering mixed-descent world, not just in the fur trade but in the region's economy as a whole. New Missouri residents found themselves on land owned by Native nations and in communities where people married Indians and hunted with them to make a living. They didn't know how to fit into this world and resented people who did. When they couldn't get cash to start businesses or lost their farms, many found themselves on the streets of St. Louis looking for work. Their best hope was the fur trade, St. Louis's oldest and largest business.[9]

Andrew Drips and Lucien Fontenelle, among other discouraged young men, joined the St. Louis fur trade in 1819. In a new place, they found an old trade with old ways of doing things. New France might have dissolved as an empire, but French-speaking people still lived up and down the region's rivers in "creole" houses filled with families who married local Native people. And from upper management to lowly paddlers, French-speaking Americans ran the fur trade, much to the frustration of new Anglo-American residents. In this carefully regulated business, a young man couldn't just head up the Missouri and start trading. Only big players with capital and relationships with powerful Indian nations could participate. Big companies hired young men to paddle goods up the river to Indian villages and trading forts, paying them only after they had carried and paddled a season's worth of furs back down those rivers. A large conglomerate, the Missouri Fur Company, hired Drips and Fontenelle.[10]

As they paddled upriver in company boats, U.S. flags fluttered in front of army posts. However, French families—Chouteaus, LaClèdes, Papins—the original settlers of St. Louis who arrived in the region in the 1750s, controlled the fur trade. When the Mississippi Valley, coveted by many empires—European and Native— became Spanish in 1764, these French families endured and were enriched by that nation. Because the Chouteau men married Osages, the local powerhouse tribe, the Spanish gave them exclusive rights to build forts among the largest Native nations. Osages called St. Louis "Chouteau's Town." The traders who worked for the Chouteaus in these forts spoke French and a range of Native languages. Like their bosses, they married Native women. Intermarriage and diplomacy kept the peace.

After the American Revolution and the Louisiana Purchase made St. Louis part of the United States, these French survivors were confident they could manage Americans. French fur traders courted American officials and merchants, inviting them to balls and investing in their businesses. They also married Americans, a strategy ensuring that when English-speaking residents outnumbered French St. Louisans, they didn't control the economy or culture.[11]

In the 1790s, when Canadians like John Johnston and Alexander McKay entered the fur trade, Americans had not been significant to its operation. A Spanish spy who visited the Missouri River in 1798 reported to his bosses that everything about the trade was French and Indian, from the "birchbark canoes and the voyageurs' songs" to "the *engages* and *habitants*" who "refuse to grow food" and instead "live among Indian villages." Now, a generation later, U.S. fur traders wanted to end French influence and French ties to Native communities.[12]

As of 1820, they had failed. When U.S. interests entered the fur trade, they used a factory system largely inherited from the British. It required everyone to sell furs in the government-run trading posts (factories) that were now spreading up the Missouri River. Officials at those posts set prices and licensed traders, all to keep inexperienced and undercapitalized traders out of the trade. Since wars erupted when traders failed to deliver what they promised to their Indian partners, government rules preserved the delicate peace in Indian country by allowing French traders with capital and experience to monopolize trade in the region. New St. Louis residents, unable to buy land or to find work because of the terrible economy, didn't care about keeping peace with Indians. They raged against a U.S. government monopoly that was keeping them out of a lucrative business.[13]

The suspicion about these "foreigners" who operated the fur trade ran deep. The Louisiana Purchase had added long-settled French and Indian lands to the nation, and the lengthy arbitration over the U.S.-Canadian border that followed the Jay Treaty finally made Great Lakes residents into U.S. citizens in 1807. Despite this gloss of citizenship, wherever aspiring American fur traders went, they found French-speaking communities that were obviously in cahoots with British and Native peoples. Members of large French families intermarried with Indians all worked as interpreters, oarsmen, hunters, and traders in the fur trade. French town names like Carondelet, St. Charles, Des Moines, Florissant, Davenport, and Portage des Sioux reflected that history.[14]

In 1819 John Jacob Astor and his American Fur Company arrived in St. Louis. The same man who had created the Astoria venture that brought Alexander and Thomas McKay to Oregon now smelled profits in St. Louis. As Americans grew more suspicious of foreigners like John Johnston and Auguste Chouteau, who profited from the fur trade on U.S. borders, Astor, on his way to becoming the wealthiest man in the United States, opened an office in downtown St. Louis. He sent his right-hand man, Ramsay Crooks, to run his Missouri fur business. No one knew, in 1819, what would come of this effort.[15]

Andrew Drips set out to make a living as a fur trader at exactly that moment. Independent trapping required capital and a license. Andrew had neither. Selling furs on the black market was possible but risky. So he hired on with the Spaniard Manuel Lisa's Missouri Fur Company. Lucien Fontenelle, French-speaking and comfortable in St. Louis, made the same choice in 1819.[16]

Drips and Fontenelle signed contracts as *engagés*—engaged to work at the bottom tier of the fur trade. With those signatures, they began careers in an expanding Canadian-style trade, which was controlled by French-Creole families or by men like Manuel Lisa, who had married a wealthy French St. Louisan. Business depended on moving millions of tons of building supplies, trade goods, boats, people, and food upriver. Drips and Fontenelle agreed "to labor in rowing, towing, loading and unloading boats" as well as "trapping, hunting, and collecting Furs, meats, peltries," the broad duties a typical contract required. In return, they received a season's worth of provisions and the high-quality British and French trade goods (procured illegally from Canada) that Indians demanded. At the end of the trading season, they gave all furs taken in trade to their bosses to pay them back for the goods and supplies. Depending on the prices for furs, *engagés* might receive a little cash or they might be in debt. Many young men didn't last a season.[17]

In the late spring of 1819, Drips and Fontenelle started paddling and pushing upriver toward the large trading posts on the Missouri

River. These served as entrepôts for networks of smaller posts built for the convenience of their Indian partners, where men like Lucien and Andrew would winter. It was dangerous work that required leveraging the skills and goodwill of Indian people.

St. Louis fur traders wanted to build posts and harvest furs beyond the middle Missouri, an effort French traders had failed at for two decades. The first expedition to develop trade with upper Missouri River nations—the Blackfeet, Dakotas, and Crows—set out from St. Louis in 1795. After a year of effort, they concluded that "instead of happy and favorable beginning to the enterprise," they had "disenchantments" and "detriments." Boats sank, furs rotted, and Dakotas stole their guns and goods. Two decades later the failures continued. Upper Missouri nations, intent on protecting their territory, signaled their hostility by killing anyone who came near. The Missouri Fur Company, an early fur conglomerate, reported thirteen men killed in 1810 and another twelve in 1811.[18]

In 1819 a U.S. government expedition planned to renew the effort to explore the upper Missouri and extend the U.S. fur trade into that region. Led by Stephen Harriman Long, a major in the Army Corps of Engineers, the large party aimed to establish a fort at the mouth of the Yellowstone River, two thousand miles upriver. Long's team, the first western expedition of army engineers, imagined, as did the U.S. government, that the *Western Engineer,* a specially designed steamboat built in Pittsburgh, could revolutionize river travel. It would be the first steamboat to travel up the Missouri, and the first with a stern paddlewheel. It was also equipped with a mast and sail in case its innovations failed. Federal officials believed the expedition, a pet project of President James Monroe, would cement U.S. authority in the region. According to the optimistic *St. Louis Enquirer,* the expedition would enable American traders to "shut out the Northwest and Hudson's Bay Companies" so that a "commerce yielding a million per annum will descend the Missouri."[19]

Technology, geography, and human nature, however, conspired against the Yellowstone Expedition. But their diaries and records allow a view of every inch of the river the same year Lucien and Andrew began their fur trade lives.

THE MISSOURI RIVER TRADE WORLD, 1810–1840

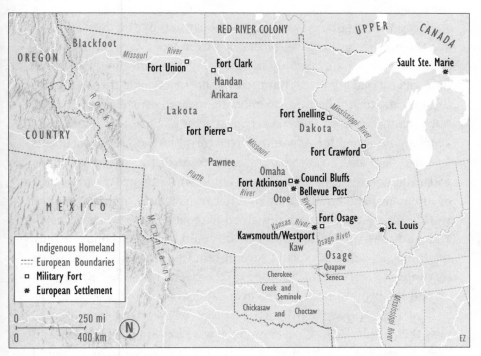

The Fickle Missouri and Its Native World

The river trip began between mountains of Indian graves. Great burial mounds suggested the magnitude of former Native populations, obvious even to the dimmest observer. The scientists and artists who accompanied Stephen Long noted twenty-seven mounds, each of which could cover several city blocks, towering hundreds of feet over the river. They grabbed bones and pottery as souvenirs, an activity that would raze the giant mounds as river travel increased.[20]

Andrew and Lucien, pushing upstream in flatboats, didn't have the energy to grab bones. Sandbars and piles of driftwood blocked their path upriver at every curve. Outside St. Louis, the river was wide, muddy, and not very deep. With depths that varied from three to nine feet, its snaking curves and wooded banks made the Missouri the snaggiest of rivers.

Every year it gobbled up boats and boatmen by the dozens. Indians traveled in bull boats—pieces of woven wood covered in watertight hides, with a draft only inches below the waterline. American flatboats carried big loads, but their flat bottoms made them slow and difficult to steer. The first steamboat appeared on the river in 1818, but it had foundered, expensively, just west of St. Louis. Keelboats, specially designed for Missouri River travel in the 1790s, used sails and paddlers and a very shallow draft to meet the challenge of the 850-mile upstream trip. Keelboats could travel upstream at a speed of fifteen miles a day, but they couldn't transport much cargo. So the workhorses of the industry remained flatboats like those that Lucien and Andrew manned, and those boats could sometimes manage only two miles in a day. In spring several hundred flatboats, each rowed by twenty to forty people, headed up the river. Everyone helped push or pull the heavily loaded boats over sandbars and rocks.[21]

The trip upriver highlighted a piece of complicated old business that troubled St. Louis and its new vision of itself: Indians and their mixed kin. As Lucien, Andrew, and their companions could see, thousands of Indian people lived along the Missouri River. Like everyone else who lived there, they had adapted to decades of change. In the early 1800s, at least 300,000 Indians lived in the broad region where the Missouri and Mississippi rivers come together. Warfare and epidemic disease threatened some groups, but overall the region's Native population had increased. The growth of the fur trade attracted Indians from the upper Mississippi, while warfare and White settlement pushed Ohio River and Illinois Indians west across the Missouri. Because of earlier land exchanges and forced removal, Missouri's native Osages now contended with Sacs and Foxes, Shawnees, Delawares, Miamis, Potawatomis, and Wyandots and their intermarried relatives. These nations moved their villages into the heart of Osage country—prairies and woodlands stretching south from the Missouri River to the Ozark Mountains in what is now southern Missouri and Arkansas.[22]

Osages fought hard to protect their country, and no governor or army could make those places safe for White immigrants, repeating eighteenth-century patterns from the New York, Pennsylvania, Ohio, and Kentucky backcountry. St. Louis newspapers reported on Osage raids, with details about terrifying night attackers who used tomahawks to destroy "goods that they could not carry away" but who took children and horses. Through treaties made in 1808, 1811, and 1815, negotiated by the Chouteaus and their Osage relations, many Missouri Osages exchanged their land for large sections of what would become Kansas and Arkansas, now designated Indian country. Despite those treaties, St. Louisans felt threatened by Indians as daily reports continued of "depredations," "sinister plots," and "threatened attacks."[23]

As all this unfolded, Fontenelle and Drips continued up the river. Just outside St. Charles, the first town past St. Louis, the travelers passed Shawnee and Delaware villages where Ohio-immigrant Indians had settled. These villages included Euro-American traders who had married Shawnee or Delaware women and raised Indian families. Joseph Jackson, a former salt maker, Charles "Indian" Phillips, and Jimmy Rogers, now the village chief, sold fresh fish and plums to passing boatmen. They sent their French- and English-speaking children to help with boats, for a price.[24]

Farther on, they passed old Osage villages and the Chouteaus' Fort Carondolet, where the Osage River heads south from the Missouri. French–Osage and French–Iowa communities had been part of the region for fifty years as Indian traders and farmers. Major Long noted that no "settlers" lived above Fort Osage, only people who craved an "adventurous, unsettled life of hunting." Hardly unsettled, many second-generation French families such as the Papins, Roys, and Sarpys had left Americanizing St. Louis for lives in Indian country.[25]

When they finally arrived at Chouteau's Landing, which would become Kansas City, travelers stayed in large Kaw villages. The Kaws, eager for traders and trade goods, prepared cool arbors to shade their guests from downriver. Women, dressed in colorful blue and red dresses that showed off their tattooed legs, offered corn soup, watermelons, and bison meat. Kaw men, bedecked in eagle feathers and furs, took the opportunity to demand their own post with its own trader. The closest post, some sixty miles north, near what is now St. Joseph, Missouri, served only Otoe and Iowa villages. Joseph Robidoux, head trader for the Chouteaus' French Company, wintered there with his three wives (one Otoe, one Kaw, and one Iowa) and their families.

The flotilla of boats carrying scientists and fur traders kept going. North of what is now the Nebraska-Kansas line, a war party of Pawnees interrupted Major Long's evening camp. Some Kaw Indians, led by a Frenchman married into a Kaw chief's family, rescued them. The Pawnees got their horses but not the valuable trade goods. Minus horses, the boats reached the next large river, the Platte, famously wide but only inches deep, where Otoe and Ponca villagers gathered for much of the year.[26]

In early September 1819, the flatboats reached Manuel Lisa's trading post, Fort Lisa. Surrounded by Omaha villages, it stood across the river from the new government post of Council Bluffs, established in 1818. Lucien and Andrew stopped here, having reached their boss's objective. Council Bluffs divided the middle Missouri world of river gardening from the upper Missouri world of bison hunting. Long a place where peoples from those two worlds—often at war—gathered to trade and solve problems, its name indicated its prominence. The *Western Engineer* and its crew stopped at Council Bluffs too, still only halfway to their objective. Out of supplies and replacement parts, the government steamship, its engines clogged with silty mud, could travel no further. The engineers would have to wait until spring for parts to replace everything the river had worn down. At their winter camp, they had time to visit Indian villages, dine with traders, and rethink their ambition of bringing steam power to the Yellowstone.[27]

A few traders went farther north to winter in Dakota villages, but the whole upper river enterprise failed because novice traders had failed to develop relationships with local people. Instead of bringing down boatloads of furs, those upper river pioneers had their goods stolen and their boats destroyed by Arikaras and Omahas who guarded access to the upper Missouri. Those same Indians made clear that traders who did business with Dakotas or other enemies would be murdered. The traders stood down.[28]

Lucien and Andrew's boss, Manuel Lisa, understood that diplomacy and kin-making had to come before business. The wealth of furs on the upper Missouri, in Lisa's view, required strong trading relationships with the middle Missouri nations: Omaha, Otoe, Arikara, and Iowa. Those nations needed guns and allies to protect themselves from the warrior nations on the upper Missouri. Only traders made loyal to them by intimate family connections could meet their needs. Once Missouri River Indians had White traders living in their villages, Lisa believed, the traders could convince Indian villagers to become middlemen instead of enemies. It was tricky diplomacy, but Plains nations like the Dakota, Lakota, Crow, and Blackfoot needed the corn, horses, and trade goods that middle Missouri nations had. Could furs, guns, and ammunition become part of that exchange? In the fall of 1819, Lisa sent Andrew Drips and Lucien Fontenelle to Otoe and Omaha villages to live and to explore those possibilities.[29]

Omahas and Otoes

That same year Omaha leaders negotiated a land cession with the U.S. Army. In return for protection from the Dakotas, Lakotas, and Pawnees, they would allow the army to build a fort. Omahas, like other middle Missouri nations, were confident they could manage change. The tribe or *uki'te* had always appreciated new ideas and useful objects. Omahas moved regularly and absorbed new peoples without losing a clear sense of themselves.[30]

There were costs. A French post commander reported that "our young Canadians and Creoles" arrived in native villages and ran "at full speed, like escaped horses, into Venus country." Soldiers and boatmen often left a "foul distemper," venereal disease, to mark their visit. Missouri River women often convinced White men to stay. In 1819 the Omaha leader Big Elk warned a military officer that too many traders could harm his people. "Your traders come among my nation, give medals, and make chiefs out of every man," he noted, a situation that challenged his leadership. Big Elk was right. As hunting became a way to purchase goods from traders, its role in tribal life increased. New possessions—guns, whiskey, kettles, axes, and cloth—created distinctions and strife among Omahas. They hoped that with French or American men married into their communities, everyone would keep their bargains.[31]

One who did was Andrew and Lucien's superior, Manuel Lisa. In 1815 he had married an Omaha woman named Mitahne, daughter of Big Elk, as part of his effort to build trade. In return, Lisa agreed to erect a post at the Omaha villages and to live among the Omaha with his new wife during the winter. Lisa had a White family in St. Louis and two children with Mitahne, but he viewed all these families as part of doing business—he recognized all his children in his will. To satisfy his Omaha partners, he staffed a permanent post at Bellevue, a site across the river and just south of Council Bluffs. In 1820 Lucien Fontenelle began trading there as part of a new Missouri Fur Company operation.[32]

Andrew Drips went south to a cluster of Otoe villages that spread west from the Missouri River along the Platte. A much smaller nation than the Omahas, the Otoes shared their neighbors' attitudes toward trade and toward Dakota and Lakota warriors who had expanded south into middle Missouri lands. These peoples, speakers of Siouan languages, were labeled *Sioux*—an abbreviation of the Ojibwe word for adders—by French traders. Middle Missouri nations lived reasonably peacefully along the Missouri River as European contact and Sioux expansion shifted their lives. They shared diplomatic practices and ideas about kinship and reciprocity, even if they spoke different languages. Using pipes carved from sacred red stone, they developed ceremonies that clarified behavior and belonging to manage an increasingly troublesome outside world.[33]

You were a person of the pipe before you were part of a family or a nation. Over some two thousand years, sacred pipes had served as tools to manage problems among neighboring villages. Lewis and Clark, like other travelers before them, had learned this crucial lesson as they traveled up the river: never dismiss a pipe, never turn down a chance to smoke one. These pipes, and the ability to create allies in war, enabled Omahas, Otoes, and Arikaras to broker trade between a broad range of people: western bison hunters, northern fur-hunting peoples, and corn cultivators living near the river along with European traders. Drawing outsiders in had saved river nations when disease and war rolled into their communities in the 1780s and again in the 1810s.[34]

By 1820, the Otoes controlled commerce and agriculture in what is now eastern Kansas and Nebraska. To protect their bounty, they reminded the larger Pawnee and Dakota nations of their power by occasionally raiding and burning their villages. An Otoe village was home to Andrew Drips during his first winter as a Missouri Fur Company employee.[35]

Macompemay and Mehubane

Macompemay and Andrew met in the winter of 1821. Her Otoe village, home to three to four hundred people in what is now eastern Nebraska, lay deep in the trees and well back from the river. Friendly or unfriendly Native or European traders could find the village by the smoke floating through it and by the sounds of horses, dogs, and people. The winter settlement was a half-circle of winter lodges, each home to forty people, their belongings, and a few visitors. Winter lodges were made of clay, mixed like cement or adobe, and dried over a huge wooden frame. Windproof and roomy, thirty to forty feet in diameter, these earth lodges had raised beds along each wall, storage pits, and several fireplaces.[36]

Macompemay probably sat across from the entrance and against a wall so she could observe people entering. Who was worth further inspection? Andrew might have seen her from the doorway. We have a description of Macompemay from a decade later, still vibrant and strong, riding a horse bedecked in white sheepskin and long fringe. She wore a scarlet blanket that underscored her confidence and panache. When Andrew met her that first winter, she was not quite twenty, with vitality and strength that surely attracted him. If she was part of a prominent family, she would have had distinguishing tattoos on her forehead, and if she came from a less significant family, the tattoos might be hidden discreetly on her wrists. Andrew, at thirty-three, showed a few miles on his face. His literacy and business acumen distinguished him from the usual men who wintered in Indian villages. The two observed each other carefully through the smoke and heat of the evening fires, knowing that more immediate pleasure would have both benefits and risks.[37]

White traders hoped for more than a winter with a warm young person in their arms. They needed to be ceremonially linked to an Otoe family. Older men, leaders who wanted American traders to be obligated to them, adopted them in ceremonies that reminded everyone of their roles and celebrated the animals they would hunt together. They encouraged those same traders to take wives, ensuring that they would consider Otoe interests. Life in Otoe villages centered around producing food, linking families and clans, and instructing children and men like Andrew Drips who needed to learn the basics of Otoe life.[38]

Macompemay had reasons to consider a relationship with someone like Andrew Drips. In the early 1820s, when she met Drips, her village and family were under stress. Her people had lived along that piece of the Missouri River for many generations. It had never been an easy life, but now raiders from the north threatened the riverbank gardens that yielded corn, squash, pumpkins, and tobacco, and they took the horses that made hunting possible. And now as the Otoes made the fur trade their business—not entirely by choice—they sought to create kin with British and American traders to get the guns, ammunition, and allies they needed for protection. Macompemay's family would have encouraged a liaison with Andrew Drips. Other Otoe women had made connections to the American world. Only a year earlier, an Otoe woman named Hayne Hudjihini (Eagle of Delight) was painted by Charles Bird King when she traveled to Washington, D.C., as part of a diplomatic mission.[39]

Young women didn't make these decisions alone, and marriage outside the tribe wasn't an easy choice. Macompemay's place in the world was determined by her membership in a clan. Nine clans organized the Otoe world, all living in separate lodges with different tribal functions and status. Otoe people could marry and adopt between clans, but that didn't change their status. A beaver clan person could never become a bear clan person, the group that created tribal leaders.[40]

We don't know the status of Macompemay's family, but her decision makes sense for someone from a family with modest resources. Macompemay knew that the assets she gained from marrying a trader could improve her family's situation. She wouldn't lose her Indian self, but aspects of her life would change. She could live near her family at least part of the year, but she would spend much time with her husband at forts where the business of the fur trade was conducted. She surely didn't know how much time she would spend without her husband, or how much childrearing and family business she would conduct alone, without her Otoe relations.

Such future concerns likely evaporated in the warmth of the winter lodge. Macompemay put aside the otter skin bag she was beading to look at Andrew Drips more carefully. After their first glances and conversations, they spent time getting to know each other amid the winter rhythms of the fur trade. Since Andrew spoke only a little Otoe and even less French, they resorted to the basic sign language developed for business and exactly such intimate moments. Through Macompemay's efforts to teach him some Otoe and through his efforts to give her some English, they arrived at some common words. In that winter season, they had nothing but time.[41]

Life seemed to go on as usual. The only excitement that winter of 1821 occurred when the Kaws stole fourteen Otoe horses, requiring a group of young men to retaliate. They didn't get the horses back, but they did get two French-Kaw boys. A demographic deluge of American settlers was coming, but no one could see it yet. As Macompemay and Andrew began their family life, the Otoe world tilted.[42]

Thirty miles to the north, Lucien Fontenelle wintered in one of the Omaha villages. Luck or wisdom had brought him into Big Elk's large household that season. Lucien knew of the big drama that had unfolded around Manuel Lisa and his Omaha wife Mitahne. In

1819 Lisa had shown up in Omaha territory with his St. Louis wife. Mitahne didn't like it and left him, taking their two children, Christopher and Rosalie, to a distant village. Later that winter Lisa stole the children and took them to St. Louis. The entire village was in an uproar over this breach of trust, and Mitahne was inconsolable.[43]

Lucien Fontenelle wanted to make sure he stood out as loyal to Big Elk. He began a relationship with Mitahne's younger sister, Mehubane (Rising Sun). He promised Big Elk that he wouldn't live at Council Bluffs but would stay in the Omaha villages with Mehubane and trade out of the new post at Bellevue. In a winter that saw the Omaha eating wild oats rather than meat and stealing Pawnee corn, Lucien impressed everyone by traveling into dangerous Dakota territory to hunt for elk.[44]

That spring, when snowmelt in the Rockies raised river levels so boats could travel, information in the form of newspapers, letters, and gossip came up the river. In the early 1820s, little of that news was good. The biggest shock was the report that Manuel Lisa had died while visiting St. Louis. Neither Lucien nor Andrew knew who their next boss would be or who would buy their furs. In that moment of flux, they discussed forming a partnership. They hardly knew each other, but they shared family circumstances and ambitions. They decided to run a trading post themselves. They would, in the end, be lifelong partners, an island of stability in the fur trade world. However, no trader or trapper could operate without the front money, suppliers, and transportation systems of a large enterprise.[45]

In 1823, Andrew and his Otoe wife Macompemay, and Lucien with his Omaha family, moved to Bellevue to operate the trading post. Living there meant that their wives wouldn't spend their summers as most Otoe and Omaha women did, raising corn, turnips, squash, and sweet melons. Traders' wives helped run the trading operation and translated for their husbands. They stood in as storekeepers and managers when their husbands made trading trips.[46]

That first summer the "fort," only partially built, barely sheltered Macompemay and Mehubane. Bellevue was just north of the Otoe villages and surrounded by Omaha villages. The rich land in the deep bend of the river was ideal for crops, and Omaha women planted here each summer. Macompemay set up her summer lodge in the trees above the fort, hoping that spot would be airier and less buggy than the muddy fort. In 1832 the artist George Catlin commented on the beauties of Bellevue but attributed them to European "improvements" rather than the work of Native women who had farmed here for generations. He described his "pleasure" at seeing "in this great wilderness, a civilized habitation" surrounded with cornfields and potatoes, with "numerous fruit-trees bending under the weight of their fruit."[47]

Trade made this long stretch of the Missouri River, from Fort Osage in Missouri to the Arikara villages in what is now the Dakotas, a fertile site for mixed-descent communities. Like Sault Ste. Marie and the Columbia River, it attracted trade families from everywhere. At least thirty families of French-Indian ancestry settled around Council Bluffs. One St. Louis fur trader, Thomas Forsyth, reporting on the western fur trade to U.S. officials, explained that Missouri River trade was operated by "many half-breeds brought up to hunting in Canada . . . but now part of the American concern." French and Indian and Anglo-American and Indian, these mixed-descent communities were comfortable places for the Dripses and Fontenelles to raise children. For Macompemay or Mehubane, however, unknown risks could always come up the river.[48]

Policing the Western Fur Trade

Six hundred miles down the river in St. Louis, the former explorer and governor William Clark limped out of his front door, his rheumatism aggravated by the damp spring weather. At fifty-four, although his lush hair contained more white than red, he remained a man of enormous influence. After his trip with Meriwether Lewis to the Pacific Coast, Clark had settled in St. Louis and, like nearly everyone else there, invested in fur. Employment in the Missouri Fur Company proved less stable than military service, so Clark kept his government job. He served first as Indian agent, then as territorial governor, and now in 1824 he was superintendent of Indian affairs for all of the Louisiana Territory.

Clark's personal life reflected St. Louis's shifting milieu. His was a combined family of nine children that he and Harriet Radford had created when they married in 1820. The family included two adopted wards, Pompey and Lisette Charbonneau, the children of Tous-saint Charbonneau and his Shoshone wife Sacajawea, who had died after accompanying Clark on his journey west. Clark's staff included twenty-two slaves, both Native and Black, who worked alongside three French and Indian "serving girls." Clark owned a family pew amid the Chouteaus, Prattes, and Labadies in the great new Catholic cathedral, but he also founded the city's first Episcopal church. Twenty years after Clark's first visit in 1804, St. Louis retained its French heart and its Native feet and hands, even if its head was now American.[49]

The American part, however, now troubled William Clark. He knew that the system of government trading houses staffed by U.S. officials had kept Indians at peace in the backcountry. His own life-time of work had made St. Louis the Montreal of the Missouri River, a powerful fur trade center that Indian nations respected. Americans had finally made inroads into the fur trade, even though the British continued to control it from Hudson's Bay Company forts in Canada, the Great Lakes, and the Pacific Northwest.[50]

Clark's efforts had combined trade and diplomacy. In 1818, with mixed-blood translators at his side, he had negotiated a peace between the Osage and the Cherokee, who had been at war since 1806, when the U.S. government had put Osage reservations in the middle of Cherokee lands. Clark had also created détente between the Lakota and the Dakota through traders who supplied the guns and fine-quality trade goods they demanded. The Shawnee and Del-aware, removed from communities surrounding St. Louis, now lived over the Kansas border with their French and mixed-blood relatives and their American agent. It was a delicate balance. Indian agencies staffed by government officials now licensed traders and occupied trading posts.[51]

Clark knew that the bureaucracy he had created gave advantage to old St. Louisans like Pierre Chouteau and Manuel Lisa. They had the respect of Native nations that more recent American settlers did not. But Clark miscalculated the populist politics that had come with Missouri statehood in 1820 and its thousands of new residents. Frustrated at being jobless in St. Louis and shut out of a business that looked so easy, as boatloads of furs just floated down the river, Missouri residents demanded change. In 1822, urged on by John Jacob Astor, the fur tycoon who was still seeking to monopolize the fur trade, and by Missouri senators, the U.S. Congress deregulated the fur trade and dismantled the factories and stores. Beginning in 1823, it became William Clark's job to issue a trading license to anyone who could afford one.[52]

Such legislation reflected long-held American suspicions of regulation from afar, whether from Britain in the 1770s or Washington in the 1820s. American men thought they could and should manage their own affairs; but state and federal officials, who had to keep peace with Native nations, were not so sure. In that deregulated moment, the first large group of independent American fur trappers traveled up the Missouri River. Trappers still needed infrastructure and front money, but these White men would trap furs themselves. They would keep half the skins they trapped and give the other half to a larger company—in this case, William Ashley's new Rocky Mountain Fur Company—as compensation for feeding, housing and transporting them. The simple system would circumvent forts, winter camps, British traders, and Native people.

The trappers imagined, as did their bosses, that they would make a quick killing. As boatloads of Euro-Americans headed up the river, they passed Bellevue and Fort Atkinson. One of Andrew Drips's friends watched them get stuck on the river and then pass Big Elk's Omaha villages without issuing proper greetings. He reported that the new trappers "were from all nations, but all, gen'lly speaking, untried." He warned, accurately, that "this kind of business will make trouble." John Jacob Astor, eager to buy up failed trading enterprises, waited for just such trouble to develop.[53]

In June 1823 the boatloads of trappers got as far as the Arikara villages, a few days' journey past Council Bluffs. The Arikaras understood the threat that the new trappers presented to their lives as river

traders. When the men demanded horses and women without offering presents, Arikara warriors attacked. They killed fifteen traders,
burned their boats, and took their supplies. When word of the attack
got back to Fort Atkinson, Col. Henry Leavenworth combined his
230 U.S. soldiers with 750 Dakota and Lakota fighters, intending to
drive the Arikaras away permanently.[54]

Colonel Leavenworth's forces attacked the Arikara village in
August. The Arikaras, outnumbered but with better positions along
the river, held them off. Leavenworth ordered an artillery bombard-
ment that also proved ineffective when the shots missed the village.
A day later he attempted an infantry attack, but the troops failed
to break into the village. After those failures, Leavenworth negotiated a peace treaty, which infuriated his Dakota allies. They left the
scene, disgusted. That night the Arikaras, seeing the Dakotas leave
and fearing an attack from that enemy, sneaked out of their village.
Leavenworth, with no victory, no treaty, and no chance of finding
the Arikaras, burned their villages to the ground and returned to
Fort Atkinson. It was a complete disaster.[55]

The bad news spread quickly. Superintendent Clark took to his
bed after he read the dispatches. Sioux war parties now attacked Arikara villages and brought back horses and captives. When Arikaras
and their Sioux enemies exacted revenge on each other, the violence
worsened the situation between river nations and traders.

Now, in 1824, Clark limped to his office to manage the dangerous situation created by the ignorance of American men. Congress
had made the task even harder when it created the Bureau of Indian
Affairs as a separate office of the War Department. The new bureau's
function was to manage the Indian land business. Signing treaties
would replace the fur trade as the engine of diplomacy. Peace commissions, made up of federal and state officials, local land speculators, and mixed-descent translators, would travel to Indian country
and convince tribes to sign away land. Clark now had to plan such a
trip up the Missouri River, making treaties with peoples who were
still at war. When Thomas Jefferson first appointed Clark to manage
Indian affairs, the president had reminded him that "Commerce is
the great engine by which we are to coerce them, not War." Now war

had replaced commerce, and Superintendent Clark had to clean up the mess. Only families, peace pipes, and new marriages could mend such wounds.[56]

Families in the Rocky Mountain Fur Trade

In the aftermath of the Arikara War, Andrew Drips and Lucien Fontenelle considered several risky options. They had to decide which company would survive the corporate reorganizations and financial implosions of the early 1820s. John Jacob Astor, who had failed spectacularly with his first fur trade venture, Astoria, had now partnered with British and Canadian investors to create the American Fur Company. American politicians and investors found his involvement in British fur companies distasteful or even treasonous. However, he emerged as the sole person with the capital and business acumen to challenge the Canadians. In 1823 he used the chaos created by the Arikara War to get into the business in St. Louis.[57]

Despite the recent congressional action deregulating the fur trade, Astor knew that success would depend on involving Indians in the trade. A trade in which Native people purchased goods with furs they hunted and trapped was the path to peace and profit. Manuel Lisa had understood this, and so had the Chouteaus. Astor made exclusive arrangements with the suppliers of Indian goods in St. Louis, Detroit, and New York, including the Chouteaus' operation, run by a cousin, Bernard Pratte. As they always did in the fur trade, business dealings required a marriage. In 1825 Ramsay Crooks, Astor's partner, married Pierre Chouteau's niece, Emilie Pratte. The couple settled in St. Louis, and in December 1826 the head of the Chouteau family, Pierre Jr., signed an agreement with Astor, naming B. Pratte & Co. the sole western merchant of the American Fur Company.[58]

But not even Astor could figure out how to succeed on the upper Missouri after the Arikara War. Hostile Arikara warriors were now stopping travel up the river by stealing horses and killing men. Those who managed to venture farther met the "Blackfoot Wall." In a single season, Blackfeet killed eighteen White and mixed men and took $14,000 worth of furs and robes. The experiment of taking non-Native trappers into that region failed utterly.

Between 1820 and 1840, the fur trade in the United States was remade. Regions, business models, agreements with Native nations, the furs and hides traded—all changed and recombined as the trade spread south from Canada and west from the Great Lakes and upper Mississippi, that old Native, French, and British core. With trade on the upper Missouri River too dangerous, frustrated traders and their investors looked west to the Rocky Mountains. An unknown wealth in furs might be tapped with a different business model, inaugurated in 1822 by William Ashley's Rocky Mountain Fur Company. Four years later Andrew Drips and Lucien Fontenelle found themselves in this new enterprise when their old bosses in the Missouri Fur Company recombined once again to compete with Ashley. John Jacob Astor sat back and waited to see what would happen.[59]

As Andrew and Lucien cast their eyes westward to the Rocky Mountains, their personal lives at Bellevue went on. In the early spring of 1824, the month of the little frog, Charles Drips was born in an earth lodge at his mother's Otoe village. Logan Fontenelle arrived in May 1825 in his mother, Mehubane's, summer lodge. Mehubane named her son White Horse, and his father, a Frenchman born in Louisiana, named him Logan after the famous Mingo Indian leader. Charles's mother, Macompemay, and his uncles surely gave him an Otoe name, but we don't know it. Andrew named his first son to honor his own Irish-American roots. These babies, though they had White fathers, were born in Native places. Their mothers' clan networks and their uncles' and grandfathers' lodge societies would link them forever to Otoe and Omaha ways of being. They would also be shaped by the rapidly changing fur trade.[60]

The Rocky Mountains presented new challenges to all parties in the trade. The British and Russian empires claimed the region in the Northwest, the United States in the central part of the great mountain chain, and New Spain and then Mexico in the south. Despite those claims, the region was really a vast hunting ground shared by dozens of powerful Plains and mountain tribes: Crows, Flatheads, and Utes, Cheyennes, Arapahos, and Shoshones. Although they wanted guns and horses to patrol their lands, so far they had refused to allow American trading posts. Drips, Fontenelle, and their new partners would have to compete with the Hudson's Bay Company, which sent hunting brigades south from the Canadian Rockies and east from the Columbia River, still British territory. No company had yet built a permanent fort in the fur-rich central Rocky Mountains.[61]

In this unstable situation, fur traders and Indian nations worked out a new organization. Modeled on the Native trading fairs long held in the southern Rockies, hunters and traders agreed to meet each summer in a particular spot high in the mountains, like Pierre's Hole, Sweet Lake, or the headwaters of the Green River. These Indian trade fairs became, in the 1820s, the great "rendezvous" of fur trade lore. Using the French term for "where you gather," White and Indian hunters, rival trading companies, and Indian nations met to trade furs for the next year's supplies. Traders brought food, kettles, clothing, and especially spirits from St. Louis, Mexico, and the Pacific Coast. They made fortunes trading these with hunters who brought in a season's worth of furs. At the end, after everyone agreed where next year's gathering would be held, traders packed up their furs, and the hunters and Native families packed up their children and supplies.[62]

Andrew and Lucien wanted their trading post at Bellevue to become a cog in this developing system. They needed cash to buy enough supplies to participate. In 1826 and 1827, they joined a large partnership that intended to challenge the Hudson's Bay Company's effort to grab the Rocky Mountain trade. In the fall of 1826, they led forty-five men and a hundred horses laden with thousands of dollars of trade goods into the mountains. They left their young families at home and were gone for nearly a year. It didn't go particularly well. When Crow Indians stole most of their horses on the trip out, they were forced to bury (cache) their supplies. But they didn't seal the packages properly, and water destroyed everything. Still, they had enough trade items for the Bear Lake Rendezvous and came home with sufficient furs to pay back their investors. Andrew and Lucien decided to stay in the Rocky Mountain fur trade.[63]

That decision would define their lives. The two families would run different ends of the business. Andrew and Macompemay would spend winters in hunting camps in the Rocky Mountains, organizing winter hunts and keeping an eye on pelts, traps, and guns. They would stay through spring and summer to do business at the annual rendezvous, held at an isolated spot deep in the mountains. When the rendezvous ended, Andrew and Macompemay would return to Bellevue, leading a retinue of horses and mules carrying packs of fur. Meanwhile, Lucien, Mehubane, and their extended family would make sure Andrew had trade items to exchange for all that fur. Lucien would spend winter and fall purchasing goods in St. Louis and New York. Spring and summer meant packing boats and horses and transporting the tons of items into the mountains to meet Andrew and the hunting brigades.[64]

For the next decade, Andrew and Macompemay led large hunting and trading groups into the mountains. From Bellevue, they traveled six hundred miles to the Rockies to staff winter hunts. Accounts depict such mountain camps of fur hunters as lustily and solely male, but women and children participated in every piece of the enterprise. For example, Andrew's 1831 brigade included "115 souls" with "41 armed, 38 men, besides a slave and two youths, 29 women, 22 boys and 23 girls." With 272 horses and mules, it was a cavalcade of humans and animals. The men were Indians, mixed-blood Canadians, and Anglo-Americans. Longtime participants in the trade remembered that White trappers "generally had an Indian wife and half-breed children." Charles and his younger sister, Mary Jane, born in 1827, now also traveled with Macompemay and Andrew.[65]

This innovation, which linked great trading fairs in the heart of the Rocky Mountains with steamboats on the Missouri and fur trade markets in New York and London, is now viewed as the classic expression of the fur trade. In fact, it was a short-lived and unsuccessful business model. The cost of mounting an expedition into the mountains each year was immense. In their first years, Drips and Fontenelle partnered with different investors who fronted the money to buy and transport tons of expensive trade goods into the Rockies. In 1828 their corporate partner, the Missouri Fur Company, fell to pieces.[66]

John Jacob Astor seized this grim moment to take over. With the

Chouteaus as his St. Louis partners, he had the experience and connections to compete with anyone. By 1830 the American Fur Company, which economic historians label the first American monopoly, had swallowed up the Rocky Mountain and Missouri River trades. Astor ran the company from his headquarters in New York. Mackinac Island and St. Louis served as production centers, where most furs were gathered, packed onto boats, and sent east. Astor's agents staffed posts throughout fur country and supplied the company's vast network of traders, who lived with Indians and convinced them to hunt and process animal furs for trade.[67]

Andrew and Lucien, having gained expertise and connections through their marriages, joined Astor's new firm. They now ran what Astor called the "mountain business" for the Upper Missouri Outfit of the American Fur Company. The other crucial partners were Macompemay's Otoe band along the Platte River, and Mehubane's father, Big Elk, and his family, who lived just north of Bellevue. As fathers, sons-in-law, husbands, traders, and businessmen, Andrew and Lucien made lives in this phase of the fur trade.[68]

Other American traders looked southwest, where growing trade with Mexico and its Native nations beckoned. Like other fur trade locales, the region offered traditional pelts, but this one also offered bison hides, horses, slaves, and silver. And here too the trade required Native partners. This time Cheyennes and Arapahos from the north and Comanches and Kiowas from the south converged in the great open landscape around the Arkansas River. Together they built another trade system. Brothers and cousins, mothers and sisters, parents and children made a human chain that now stretched from the Great Lakes to Santa Fe and from New York to the Columbia River. Capital—and debt—followed these families. St. Louis, Detroit, and Chicago, up-and-coming cities with fortunes built in the fur trade, had bankers and investors who loaned money to people headed to the Pacific Coast, the Rocky Mountains, and Mexico.

In the 1820s babies who would grow up to be "half-breeds" appeared all over the American West. Charles and Mary Jane Drips, and Logan, Albert, and Tecumseh Fontenelle, would grow tall at Bellevue and in the Rocky Mountain fur trade. In Michigan, heart of the old fur trade country, Johnston children anchored a new generation on the shores of the Great Lakes. Far to the west, still outside the United States, Thomas McKay, having reached Oregon along with the Hudson's Bay Company, would marry the Chinook Timmee and bring their first two children, Joseph and William, into a blended Cree, Canadian, and Chinook world.[69]

=5=

From the Sault to
Oregon Country: Mingling
Blood and Land, 1818–1838

John Johnston read a letter while sitting at his large desk. Imported from Brussels and made with wood from tropical islands, the desk had endured many Michigan winters. In 1818, despite that material testament to his success, Johnston, after twenty-five years of trading furs around the Great Lakes, was denied a business license. The letter explained that he could no longer do business as an Indian trader because "none but bona fide American citizens properly shall be admitted to the Indian Country." Johnston pounded his desk and penned a letter to the governor of Michigan. "What have I done that I should draw upon my head the anathema and the persecution of the United States?" he asked.[1]

The answer was simple. In 1818, to end competition in the Great Lakes fur trade, John Jacob Astor intended to drive John Johnston and other Canadian traders out of business. Astor's plan was to build a monopoly while taking advantage of shifting politics about capital investment and government support. Three entwined developments on American frontiers formed a powerful knot that served Astor and choked off the ambitions of John Johnston and Ozhaguscodayway- quay's eight children. A brutal consolidation of the western economy put resources and jobs in the hands of distant owners. Forced removals and military encounters turned Indian country into American states, a process that required establishing governments that could enforce their will. And a westward wave of evangelical religion brought missionaries who hitched citizenship to Christianity.[2]

Corporate battles didn't occur in a distant stratosphere of politics and business. They were personal. John Jacob Astor, the German immigrant who had begun in New York selling furs, was now the wealthiest man in the United States. After Astor's Astoria venture failed in 1813, he made sure his Great Lakes and upper Mississippi operations would have government support. He lobbied hard to get Congress to pass new fur trade regulations. Now Canadian and British traders had to purchase every trade item from U.S. merchants, and only U.S. citizens could trade with Indians. Taking advantage of those new restrictions, Astor "destroyed" Canadian traders, including John Johnston. To manage the disaster, John had his son George take an "oath of fidelity" to the United States, affirming George's citizenship. Since his brother Lewis served in the British Army and his other brothers weren't yet old enough, George had to be the citizen in the family. Then George applied to Astor's American Fur Company for a license to trade. He received it, and the family business survived but as an American Fur Company franchise.[3]

Testing Opportunity in Territorial Michigan

George Johnston's, or Kahmentayha's, experience shows how confusing citizenship and race had become for individuals and communities. As Ozhaguscodaywayquay's son, George attended Ojibwe council meetings as a Crane clan member, but without credentials as a warrior, he had little sway. However, as an educated man with important parents, George met the legal requirement of White citizenship. In 1818 in Michigan, "White" still included French-Canadians, "half-breeds," and some Native residents. As an adult free man, George could vote and work with customs officials at Mackinac Island and Sault Ste. Marie.[4]

George spent the winter of 1819 in Montreal, away from his family, learning the back end of the business. With American Fur Company credit, he bought supplies for the upcoming season. Even wearing the fine shoes and suits expected for gentlemen doing business in the city, George was miserable. His family troubles in fur trade politics and his "Canadian lineage," as his father delicately called it, made it hard for George to find friends. He complained about "the wealth and ostentation, the boasted civilization of Canada," but mostly he felt ostracized. He would visit Montreal again but never spent another season there.[5]

The Johnston family had more to worry about than being snubbed. John and Ozhaguscodaywayquay's eldest son, Lewis, had joined the British Army and was now stationed close to home at Fort Drummond, Michigan. He had gotten himself into trouble by drinking, gambling, and running up debts. Lewis disgraced the family, at least in his father's eyes, by consorting with "abandoned women." George and his sister Jane tried to make up for their brother's bad behavior. Jane's delicate health limited her social activities, but her father hoped she might marry the son of a fur company trader or a local merchant.[6]

In 1822 George married a Sault Ste. Marie neighbor, Louisa Raimond. Louisa and her family, French and Cree, had migrated south from Canada to Massachusetts during the War of 1812 and moved to the Sault in 1819. George's parents and sisters thought Louisa was a step down for George because she wasn't literate and was Catholic. Given such family coolness, George and Louisa began their married lives at some distance from the Johnstons. George became a fur trader.[7]

He and Louisa moved three hundred miles west of Sault Ste. Marie, where George ran a trading post for his uncle, Michel Cadot, in the old Ojibwe stronghold at La Pointe. Cadot, who had married Susan Johnston's sister, had generations of family in Ojibwe bands. Connected and comfortable in La Pointe, George designed a coat of arms for his new life and family. It intertwined a Johnston family crest with an Ojibwe Crane clan symbol. An elegant mink sable lay on top, linking the Ojibwe man Kahmentayha and the Michigan trader George Johnston through a sacred animal.[8]

While George managed the family business during changing

times, another young man who would soon enter the Johnstons' lives struggled into adulthood. Henry Schoolcraft, born in 1793, was the same age as George Johnston, Andrew Drips, and Lucien Fontenelle. Like those other young men, Henry was literate and ambitious, but he was ruined by failure at age twenty-five. He moved west seeking opportunity as a writer but became a federal bureaucrat.

Henry Schoolcraft wanted to become a famous scientist and explorer. His family couldn't afford to send him to college, so he read about travel and mineral wealth in distant places. He and his father opened glass factories in upstate New York, then lost them, leaving the family penniless. In 1818, to escape this financial embarrassment, Henry went west to Missouri's lead rush. Instead of joining the fur trade, he tried to make a living publishing descriptions of the mining region just south of St. Louis. Few Missourians bought his self-published *A View of the Lead Mines of Missouri*, but he remained confident about his prospects for future success. He prepared a collection of western mineral samples, traveled to Washington, D.C., and presented himself and his rocks to scientists and congressmen.[9]

Henry networked. He gathered introductions, letters, and invitations and used them like a stepladder to meet, finally, John C. Calhoun, the powerful southern secretary of war who managed western exploration. As Henry remembered it, on the day of their meeting in November 1819, Calhoun received a letter from Michigan's territorial governor asking for an exploration of the Great Lakes and a scientist to accompany the expedition. Calhoun wrote Henry a letter of introduction, the early nineteenth-century equivalent of a job contract, and Henry magically became a government scientist. The post was temporary and poorly paid, but he gladly abandoned $747.20 of unsold books and left for Michigan to meet his new boss.[10]

Lewis Cass, a rising star in the Democratic Party and territorial governor of Michigan, would be essential to Henry's career. Cass had the life and family Henry craved. Born to an old New England family, Cass had been educated at Exeter and read for the law. With those credentials, when Cass moved west to Ohio, he married the daughter of an important local politician and joined the local militia. That enabled him to serve as a colonel in the War of 1812, where he was heroic. These were all things Henry Schoolcraft was not, which made him obsequious in person to Cass and bitter behind his back.[11]

In 1813, as reward for his heroism and his loyalty to the Democratic Party, Lewis Cass became Michigan's territorial governor. Having now added the huge and mostly unknown Upper Peninsula to Michigan Territory, Cass hoped the region would offer more than ice and fish. In the spring of 1820, he and his new geological expert, Henry Schoolcraft, headed north from Detroit to search for mineral wealth. They traveled in canoes paddled by Ojibwes, Odawas, and French-Canadians, Henry's dreams come true.[12]

Power and Love in Sault Ste. Marie

Lewis Cass's job was to encourage enough new settlement in Michigan Territory that it could reach the population threshold to graduate to a state. He had to build a bureaucracy to bring law and property rights to a place that didn't want them. When Cass and Schoolcraft arrived in Sault Ste. Marie in June 1820, four canoe loads of that bureaucracy came along. Cass brought twenty-two soldiers, one officer, twelve paddlers, two interpreters, a doctor, and three clerks to protect the governor and his geologist, Henry Schoolcraft. Cass's first task was to convince powerful Indian nations who had taken U.S. forts during the War of 1812 to give up their Michigan land. However, as Schoolcraft reported, local Ojibwes "entertained a spirit of hostility toward the United States" and threatened to stop the expedition's passage onto Lake Superior.[13]

This challenge was carefully managed by John and Susan Johnston. Cass and his officers, including Henry, stayed in the Johnston household, where they enjoyed hospitality that made "us forget our isolated situation." Everyone knew Cass and his entourage had traveled to Sault Ste. Marie to establish a U.S. fort, but no fort could be built until the Ojibwe agreed to cede land. The Johnstons knew that only a properly run treaty session could achieve any such agreement. Lake Superior Ojibwes who could negotiate and sign a treaty were mostly members of the Crane clan, including Susan Johnston and her sons George and William, who translated for their relatives who didn't speak English.[14]

The Johnstons organized such a treaty session, but the initial meeting went poorly. Cass had not brought the proper gifts to begin the session, and he continued to deny that he planned to build a fort. Knowing that he was lying and angry at the impolite way the session had begun, two "war chiefs drew their lances and stuck them furiously in the ground." They kicked away the measly gifts and the U.S. flag that Cass had presented. Henry had no idea what this meant, but Ozhaguscodayway-quay did: the war chiefs were threatening to kill Cass.

Then the chiefs hoisted a British flag over the council ground, indicating their disgust with the proceedings. Using her son William, then fourteen, to interpret, Susan explained to Cass that he had to present himself, immediately, at the chiefs' lodge. He must do three things: apologize for his poor behavior, demand that a U.S. flag be hoisted, and issue a few threats of his own. William would interpret, since the angry leaders were his uncles. Cass paid attention and did exactly what Susan laid out. According to William, after apologizing, Cass told the chiefs that if they flew a British flag again, "the United States would set a strong foot upon their necks and crush them to the earth." Message received on both sides. A few minutes later a treaty was signed.[15]

That exchange set several precedents. First, the land was Ojibwe territory, and the United States would have to pay to use it. Second, local Indians demanded that the diplomacy be conducted on their terms with presents, proper ceremonial language, and recognition of traditional use rights. And mixed-descent people, like the Johnston family, had to intercede and translate.[16]

After completing that trip with Lewis Cass, Henry Schoolcraft sought a permanent government appointment. In grim economic times, stable employment on a government salary appealed to many men. Henry decided that his economic future lay in the Office of Indian Affairs. Next to the army, the Indian Office employed more people than any other government sector. Indian agents fell into two categories. Many had long experience with Native people as fur traders and often had Native or mixed-blood families. Others had no experience with the region and received government appointments as a political bonus. Schoolcraft would begin his career in the latter category but end it in the former.[17]

At the moment when Schoolcraft eyeing a possible appointment, the Indian Office had seventeen agencies and twenty-three subagencies. This bureaucracy increased exponentially in the next few years as its aims shifted to getting Indian land out of the hands of Indians and managing the fur trade. As the only representative of the United States in many communities, Indian agents also served as postmasters, judges, and jailers. They worked closely with local military commanders. For this work, they received $1,500 per year, an upper-middle-class salary. These positions were family sinecures: wives, children, and in-laws all benefited from these appointments and from the other jobs and pay that came with them.[18]

It took a year and several expensive visits to Washington, but in December 1821 Secretary Calhoun appointed Henry a U.S. Indian agent. He had little idea what he was in for, either as a bureaucrat or as an Indian country resident.

Schoolcraft came to his position holding a common set of beliefs about Indians, beliefs that would make it easier for him to justify expelling them from their homelands. First, Indian people were in their twilight on the American continent. Their history and legends needed to be captured and preserved as relics of a savage past. As Indians were positioned lower on the evolutionary scale from advanced people like Henry, contact with White frontiersmen, Catholic priests, and the fur trade had already ruined them. Humane policy makers saw their task as protecting these corrupted savage "children" while White America rolled over them. Nothing, neither policy nor science, could save Indians from their own inevitable decline. However, no matter what Henry Schoolcraft believed about imaginary Indians, his position existed because real Great Lakes nations held military and economic power.[19]

Schoolcraft's was the largest Indian agency in the United States, having jurisdiction over sixty thousand square miles of what is now upper Michigan, northern Wisconsin, northern Minnesota, and Lakes Huron, Michigan, and Superior. Many people in this juris-

diction called themselves Ojibwe, but at least twenty-five different bands lived here, with distinct names and leaders, in territories
spread over twelve hundred miles. Tens of thousands more Native
people traveled through the area to hunt, fish, and trade. The core
of Henry's job was to enforce the morass of conflicting state, federal,
and international laws governing that trade. The giant monopolies of
the American Fur Company and the Hudson's Bay Company, however, did whatever they pleased in the isolation of the Great Lakes.
Henry, in reality, worked for them.[20]

Henry's eastern friends and relatives worried that he'd vanish, his
career snuffed out in that distant place. His sister Maria teased him
that he might "disappear with the savages and never more be seen."
The new agent did in fact disappear, but into the bosom of the Johnston
family. Because his Indian agency had no building, Henry boarded at
John and Susan Johnston's home in Sault Ste. Marie. He reported to a
friend with relief that "the polished circle" of the Johnston household
could protect him from other Michiganders who were "ignorant of the
conjugation of a verb." Henry would use the Johnston family and their
Ojibwe connections over his entire life as bureaucrat and scholar.[21]

Henry took the job because he wanted a government position that
would support his career as a scientist, but he stayed for personal
reasons. As he wintered in isolated Great Lakes communities, he fell
in love with his hosts' daughter, at least the part of her that seemed
well mannered and White.

Jane Johnston's Ojibwe qualities may not have been visible to
Henry during their brief courtship, but they were there. She had
grown up in a world entirely without White women, so she wasn't
conscious of what Henry expected. Aside from her trip to Ireland in
1810, she'd never left Michigan. However, in that community at that
time, if Henry wanted to marry, the Shakespeare-quoting, maple-
sugar-offering Jane Johnston seemed wondrous.

What Jane saw in Henry is harder to know. Henry, ever anxious
about his status, was self-centered and cripplingly dependent on the
opinion of others. By October 1822, the two were writing love letters,
but Jane still had to apologize one morning for having corrected his
conjugation of a Latin verb. She hoped, in her third placating letter

of the morning, that Mr. Schoolcraft "would forgive my correction" and understand "how much I value your excellence in everything." He was, however, deeply literary, and he loved her for her mind. He published some of her poetry in upstate New York newspapers, advertising her as "an unknown savage poet." Henry's sister complimented him on the "wild writers" he had uncovered in Michigan who "write such pretty poetry."[22]

In 1823, after a winter of poems and a summer of picnics, Jane and Henry married. Their marriage was hardly remarkable in the Great Lakes world. They entered it discussing the children they would create. Henry, a metallurgist and glassmaker, believed in the power of amalgamation, a metallurgical analogy for racial blending that many argued could create a vibrant new race. Like metals blended into alloys, their offspring would be stronger and more flexible than unmixed people. As he listened to his new family's stories, he wondered "who could have imagined these wandering foresters should have possessed such a fund of fictitious legendary?" His look into "the Indian mind" focused his intellectual and literary efforts. Ozhaguscodaywayquay and her brother Waishkey told the stories, Jane Schoolcraft and her brothers and sisters translated, but Henry published them and took the credit.[23]

Henry and Jane married in a cultural moment when American thinkers hoped amalgamation between Indigenous and European Americans could push the republic forward. "Your blood shall run in our veins," President Jefferson promised visiting Delawares, so that "we shall all be Americans." Many early republic thinkers, including Jefferson, James Madison, and Benjamin Rush, embraced the idea of White men marrying Native women to keep American blood vigorous. There were, however, clear limits to racial mixing. The same year Jane and Henry married, two White women, Sarah Bird Northrup and Harriet Gold, wed Cherokee men, John Ridge and Elias Boudinot. They met at a school for young missionaries that mixed Native and non-Native scholars. White women choosing Indian men stepped over lines of power and gender. As the story became news all over New England, missionaries locked up their daughters, and the school shut down.[24]

Missionary families, a new arm of the American state, arrived in Michigan just as Henry Schoolcraft was planting the flag in front of his agency. Among those who arrived in Sault Ste. Marie in the 1820s were William and Amanda Ferry, Michigan's first Protestant missionaries. Sent by the American Board of Christian Foreign Missions, founded in 1810, the Ferrys were part of a powerful surge of evangelical Protestantism sweeping the United States and western Europe. Its American version, confident and competitive, became embedded in U.S. Indian policy. Converting Native Americans to Protestant Christianity would be seen as essential to American expansion.[25]

Missionaries were hardly new in frontier Michigan. French and Spanish Jesuits accompanied early traders and moved deep into the interior of North America in the 1600s. Few such "Black Robes" actually lived around the Great Lakes, but itinerant priests from Montreal, St. Louis, and France showed up every summer to baptize children and marry couples, linking Indian and French Catholic worlds.

Henry Schoolcraft and the missionaries changed Sault Ste. Marie. In that mostly Catholic world, the Johnstons were one of few Protestant families. When Protestant missionaries arrived, they wanted to preach to Native people in their own languages. The deeply Presbyterian Johnstons became translators and then teachers of the Ojibwe and Odawa languages. Right before her marriage to Henry, Jane wrote a poem called "The Contrast." In her youth, "Friends on every side appeared, from whose minds no ill I feared," but in her life now, "how changed is every scene," now that the Sault "half in joy, half in fear / Welcome the proud new Republic here." When Henry arrived in the early 1820s, he described Sault Ste. Marie as "scraggy-looking and antique." The town had eighty or so French-style long lots interspersed with groups of Indian lodges, but it now had added twenty-five Anglo-American square lots.[26]

Henry and Jane settled into their marriage in this Native, French, and now American place. At first, they lived with Jane's parents, a common arrangement for Ojibwe and Anglo-American couples. Since they didn't have much privacy, they wrote intimate letters that laid open details about their relationship. He had married her for her wealth, status, and knowledge of Indian languages and traditions, but he resented her wit and intelligence. Her ability to speak several Native languages became a critique of his failures. In his efforts to learn the Ojibwe and Odawa languages, with the help of his Ojibwe relatives, he developed extensive vocabularies and elaborate grammars. Even so, he never got past memorizing words.[27]

Later in life, Schoolcraft would take pride in his lifelong labor to preserve Indian languages and to civilize Indian people. Early in his career, however, he loathed the fur trade community that seemed to smother his personal and scholarly ambitions. He worried that he might become savage himself. He wrote regularly to a young Detroit lawyer, James Doty, who shared his interests in geology but who had married a White New Yorker. Henry wondered if his "red and exotic bride" could ever befriend Doty's wife. He disliked the "odious caribou" that appeared for dinner. Later, he would use every aspect of that life as writerly material.[28]

The newlyweds bound over some of their differences with shared religiosity. The Second Great Awakening, a vast revival of popular Protestant religiosity begun in the small towns of interior New England and upstate New York, spread across the early republic and deeply affected young people like Henry and Jane. They both had fierce conversion experiences before their marriage and took heart in a powerful Protestant God who could lift them from earthly worries. They wrote to each other and to a set of close advisers about their spiritual development. They read the scripture aloud in the evenings, and they both wrote poetry about the spiritual world, Jane's mixing Christian and Ojibwe beliefs.[29]

As soon as the rivers unfroze enough for trading and hunting, most of the Johnston men and now Henry Schoolcraft left Sault Ste. Marie. Jane hated it when Henry left. She hadn't liked winters when her brothers and father left for Montreal, and she complained in the summer and fall when they traveled around the Great Lakes. Now she wrote poems like "Absence," in which she laments that "while Henry strays far from sight, Stranger I am to all delight." Her father and her husband both had wide circles of friends to whom they wrote, but Jane had no literary acquaintances beyond her family. She depended on them for intellectual stimulation and emotional connection that no one else could provide.[30]

This intensely private circle was interrupted by the birth of William Henry Schoolcraft in June 1824. Both parents worried about the challenges a mixed-race child would face, even though their family represented the most elite level of this mingled world. Jane hoped the wealth and skills of her Ojibwe family would sustain her own children. However, Henry Schoolcraft himself represented the leading edge of a powerful settler society that saw even the Johnstons as shiftless and barbaric. He remained optimistic that his children would have a different reception. They would, he hoped, be seen as exotic and capable, a strong alloy of "an American type," as he wrote to a friend.[31]

The flexible racial categories of Michigan's fur trade world were, however, being challenged. In 1824 Sault Ste. Marie experienced a brouhaha over an election when new residents claimed that mixed people weren't citizens. The debate centered on Jean-Baptiste Piquette, a mixed-blood Sault resident, and on whether he looked and acted more like a White man or an Indian. Some claimed he had "the habits and mode of life assimilated entirely to Indians of full blood," meaning he hunted in the winter and didn't have a farm. Others pointed out that he "didn't wander, lived in a house, dressed like a white man," and in general "benefitted the community." The community ultimately decided that mixed-descent residents could vote, because "they were numerous in the community" and "could be future Americans," a phrase threatening in its conditional form.[32]

By now, Henry had spent three winters at Sault Ste. Marie. He equated the long dark winter and its bitter cold with being "trapped in a tomb for eight months." He mourned the loss of his connections to the literary and scientific world. So in the fall of 1824, Henry, Jane, and baby Willy traveled to New York City. Jane's youngest sister, Anna Maria, then ten, accompanied them. Jane, never hardy, fell ill on the steamer between Michilimackinac and Lake Erie. By the time they arrived in Manhattan in early December, she had developed a serious bronchial infection.

This would be a pattern. Jane never did well away from home, but especially away from Henry. This time he left her in rented rooms near the New-York Historical Society, sick and with a baby to mind. He hired a nurse when he traveled to Washington, D.C., to lobby for increased funding for his agency. Lonely and ill, Jane wrote pitiful letters back to her family, including pleas to her sisters to write along with encouragement to her youngest brother, now seven, who had fallen in a vat of boiling lye and nearly died. John Johnston wrote with alarm once he understood Jane's "dangerous condition." John instructed Henry about taking proper care of Jane and making sure that she wore flannel undergarments. However, flannel wouldn't cure Jane's loneliness. Her ten-year-old sister and seven-month-old son didn't replace a lively circle of familiar adults.[33]

When Henry returned in February, Jane recovered a bit. He would remember these months in New York as providing "gratifying intercourse with a high moral and refined portion of society" and that Mrs. Schoolcraft had excited much attention for being "a person of Indian descent with refined manners and education." Jane was embarrassed by this attention. She hated it when Henry called her a "northern Pocahontas" and asked her to speak Ojibwe in front of guests. She couldn't leave New York fast enough.[34]

They got home to Sault Ste. Marie in early May 1825, accompanied by Henry's younger brother James. Not nearly as ambitious or judgmental as Henry, James Schoolcraft was a welcome addition to the family. They all moved into the house and agency building that Henry built, called, rather pretentiously, Elmwood. Indian customers streamed in daily, asking Henry for the tobacco, guns, traps, knives, and food supplies guaranteed to them in treaties. Some visits were purely social and gave Henry time to work on his Ojibwe. He relied on hired translators or Jane's brothers to conduct his daily business.[35]

A big part of Henry's job was ending the wars between Great Lakes nations and their enemies that endangered White settlement and disrupted the fur trade. Accompanied by George Johnston, he spent the entire summer of 1825 negotiating a peace treaty between the Ojibwe and the Dakota. Now someone needed to make sure that all parties kept their bargain, including the United States, which had promised to build new posts and to pay annuities if Native people stayed peaceful. To manage that peace and to control unlicensed traders, Henry wanted to add an agency at La Pointe, the Ojibwe community where John Johnston had met Ozhaguscodaywayquay.[36]

In 1826 Henry dispatched Jane's brother George to serve as La Pointe's subagent. George Johnston, of course, knew the community well. He had worked there as a trader until 1824, using his Ojibwe language, personal connections, and writing skills. The new post served villages of Ojibwe, Odawa, and Potawatomi who did business with traders from everywhere. George issued trading licenses and made sure American Fur Company traders paid the prices they had guaranteed to Native hunters. With his wife Louisa and their two young children, Louisa and John George, George began a rocky stint as a Henry Schoolcraft's Indian Office employee.[37]

Rendezvous in the Rockies

As the federal bureaucracy expanded in the Great Lakes and George Johnston became an Indian agent, a fur trade experiment was taking place in the Rocky Mountains. There Andrew Drips and Lucien Fontenelle, with their Native wives, Macompemay and Mehubane, were building their business and families through the fur trade rendezvous. The summer peak of the trade's seasonal cycle, the rendezvous was a huge monthlong gathering where traders, hunters, and Native communities met, in a different place each year, to trade furs, buy supplies, and carouse. For large fur trade companies, the evolving rendezvous was enticingly cheap. As a trading system, it required no permanent structures, and all of the risk fell to individual employees who trapped and traded for furs and got them to the rendezvous site.

The business looked familiar in many ways. Andrew Drips took brigades of hunters—White, Indian, and mixed—into the mountains each winter. Some years he and Macompemay didn't return to their home in Bellevue at all. Meantime Lucien Fontenelle worked in Bellevue and St. Louis, buying and packaging an entire season's worth of trading goods and then transporting it, by boat, wagon, and horse, to the rendezvous. The site moved each year to provide fresh grass for horses and clean camping sites for humans. Because inter-marriage still bound the fur trade, mountain camps were mixed-blood family affairs. Macompemay raised her children in the field, at winter hunting camps and at the summer rendezvous.[38]

Charles Drips and his sister Mary Jane, now six and three, fit right into this mélange of custom and innovation. The children rode horses, explored mountain meadows, and crossed rivers on top of huge bison-skin balls. These carefully stitched teepee coverings were filled with household goods and secured at the top with a rope. Children rode while their mothers swam the floating houses across rivers. The noisy cavalcade of children, horses, mules, dogs, and wagons wasn't just fun. The presence of women and children with a traveling party signaled its peaceful intent.[39]

Managing family life in a Rocky Mountain camp took effort. Even experienced hunters and boatmen with generations of Canadian and Missouri River life behind them underestimated the difficulty of mountain winters. They ran out of supplies or bartered them away for alcohol or sex. Macompemay and other women with the hunting party had to feed and clothe the ill-prepared and the irresponsible. They sewed moccasins and leggings out of worn-out skins from last year's lodges and made clothing out of deer skins. In addition to car-ing for their own children, women handled the ailments common in winter camp: fevers, frostbite, vermin infestations, broken bones, animal bites, gunshot wounds, and venereal diseases.[40]

After a long winter, the July rendezvous was a celebration. As win-tering groups gathered for the trading sessions, Macompemay and the children washed grimy winter clothing and bedding in the river. One writer recalled that the gathering men, clean for the first time in months, argued over using the few available hand mirrors to shave and trim to look their best. Sir William Drummond Stewart, a Scot-tish hunting enthusiast who accompanied the caravan with Drips and Fontenelle for several years, outdid them all. To remember the grand rendezvous of 1837, he commissioned a portrait of himself dressed in his finest white leather hunting jacket and specially made tight trousers of Stewart tartan plaid.[41]

Such occasions allowed White men to test boundaries of race and sexuality, affirming their growing power over other people on those frontiers. Drinking, gambling, and having exotic sex with women of other races and with other men was romantic adventure that made White men hardier. Sex tested and reaffirmed the racial order but could upend it if non-Indian men stayed in the Indian world. Sex endangered Native women and men, who were supposed to be available and acquiescent in that risky economy.

The rendezvous also had more prosaic purposes: buying and selling furs and resupplying for the next year's winter hunt. How that cycle played out in 1832 demonstrates why the business was so risky. Because Andrew and Macompemay spent the fall arranging for Charles to attend school in St. Louis, the whole brigade got to their winter site late. Macompemay was pregnant. In May, when they all reached the rendezvous site at Pierre's Hole on what is now the border of Idaho and Wyoming, Andrew was anxious about her condition and the whereabouts of Lucien Fontenelle.[42]

As more than one thousand people gathered in the isolated mountain valley in 1832, Drips waited for Fontenelle to appear with the company's trade goods. The timing of his arrival was critical, but it was dependent on things they couldn't control—weather, the mood of tribes, and the workings of steam engines. Fontenelle had left Bellevue in April with men and horses, planning to meet a steamship loaded with a season's supplies at Fort Union. That spot on the upper Missouri in Montana was the farthest point goods could be transported by boat. From there he, forty men, and 110 horses would pack and carry tons of supplies to Pierre's Hole, at least five hundred miles distant and around the Grand Teton range. Fontenelle was supposed to arrive in June, but Drips wrote to another trader in July that he was "looking with much anctciaty for news from Missouri."[43]

His anxiety was about more than losing profits. Their biggest competitors, the Rocky Mountain Fur Company, had arrived on time but had encountered Blackfoot raiders who stole their horses.

The Rocky Mountain men warned everyone to stay in large groups because of that danger. Drips and Macompemay stayed at Pierre's Hole, still waiting for news from Fontenelle and, now, for the new baby. Catherine Drips arrived July 12, born at the foot of the Tetons in the green midsummer along the Snake River.

Meanwhile a group of hunters and traders, led by Milton Sublette and his Snake wife, Mountain Lamb, headed south from Pierre's Hole toward the Great Salt Lake. On July 17 they ran into a band of traveling Gros Ventre Indians who appeared to be peaceful. But some Native hunters from Sublette's party recognized this particular band as the murderers of their own relatives the summer before. Exacting revenge, they shot the Gros Ventre leader, and his murder provoked an intense battle. White and mixed-blood trappers, and their Flathead and Nez Percé allies, engaged 250 Gros Ventre warriors who took cover in a thicket of willows. An inconclusive battle raged for hours. As night fell, the Gros Ventre, still hidden in the willows, warned that many more warriors were coming. Worried about the rendezvous site with its valuable furs, newborn Catherine, and many other children, the trappers returned to Pierre's Hole. The Gros Ventres then disappeared, leaving twenty-six Gros Ventre bodies and twelve dead trappers.[44]

That episode ended the 1832 rendezvous. Andrew Drips, frantic about Lucien Fontenelle's location and everyone's safety, packed up and headed east. They met Fontenelle in the Green River Valley, but they had missed their chance to sell food, clothing, guns, ammunition, and alcohol at the usual 2,000 percent markup. Fontenelle simply turned around, and they were all home in Bellevue by fall. The poor timing didn't ruin them, but Drips never again trusted Fontenelle to manage the supply caravan.[45]

Both families had more children. The Dripses added William, born in 1834, and Glorvina, who arrived in 1836. Lucien's family now included four sons and a daughter: Logan, Albert, Tecumseh, Henry, and Susan. They stayed in Bellevue and went on summer hunts with Mehubane's Omaha family in the years when Lucien led the company caravan west or took furs to St. Louis for sale. In 1833, when Prince Maximilian of Wied, a Prussian explorer and naturalist, headed up the Missouri on a grand tour, he was hosted by Lucien Fontenelle. He raved over Bellevue's beautiful scenery, the children who spoke "innumerable" languages, and the "delightful native wife."[46]

That idyllic description hid alterations in the relationship of Native people to the American government. To meet the terms of treaty agreements, the U.S. Indian Service created agencies up and down the Missouri River, including one that Lucien Fontenelle and his Omaha family lobbied for at Bellevue. In 1834, when soldiers and federal officials turned out to be challenging tenants, Lucien sold the Bellevue post to the U.S. government. With the $1,000 he got for the "entire establishment, all the houses and the fort," Fontenelle built a new post a few hundred yards down the river. He assumed that a brisk Indian trade would continue as traders and hunters came to the new agency.[47]

Too many people came. Indian removal from east of the Mississippi sent tens of thousands of Indians to Nebraska, Iowa, and Kansas. In exchange for cash annuities and trading posts, local Indians ceded thousands of acres of their land to refugee Indians. As the fur trade shifted westward, money paid out to Indian nations floated the economy in older frontier areas, a situation that encouraged White men to continue to marry Native women. And the mixing of people and livelihoods created tension. Trouble simmered between Omahas and Iowas who had been pushed into each other's territory.[48]

Henry Fontenelle, the youngest son of Mehubane and Lucien, would remember "an incident" from 1834. One day a party of Iowas ambushed Henry's Omaha aunts and cousins. They tortured an aunt and "pinioned her with lances to the ground along with her son and left them to die." Mehubane didn't forget such a "cruel assault." When some Iowas drank too much during a visit to Lucien and Mehubane's store, they boasted about their attack on the Omaha family. Henry's mother "picked up a small handaxe and buried it in the head of one of the Iowa." For safety, Mehubane and her children hid in her father's village. In 1836, to avoid further such trouble, Omahas and Otoes ceded their lands east of the Missouri. Macompemay and Mehubane's people would no longer live or sow crops east of the river. They shifted their focus west to the growing fur trade.[49]

The Chinook McKays and the Oregon Fur Trade

The successful Rocky Mountain fur trade heralded new competition for British traders in Oregon Country, a place formally shared by Britain and the United States. However, whatever "joint occupancy" might have meant on the ground, after the corporate consolidation of 1821, the new Hudson's Bay Company controlled the Columbia River. And in that competitive place, Thomas McKay worked for the company and for his stepfather, John McLoughlin, who had arrived with Thomas's mother in 1825 to lead Fort Vancouver.[50]

Fort Vancouver, like other Hudson's Bay Company forts, became a fur trade factory. Local Native communities provided labor. Local hunting patterns and demands from London headquarters created a yearly cycle. Late each spring, a supply ship from London sailed into the Columbia's mouth, carrying new company recruits and goods that everyone wanted, especially guns, tobacco, and alcohol. Letters from mothers and sisters and instructions from company headquarters all fell into eager hands. News of the ship's arrival brought canoes laden with furs down the river from Native villages. Inside the fort, Indian workers processed those furs. Using huge fur presses, they flattened and packaged the soft pelts into dense waterproof bundles. These fur pallets were loaded onto the London ship, which left in midsummer. Then new recruits, old traders, and their families headed up the river to interior forts for fall and winter hunting.[51]

The Hudson's Bay Company operated a dozen large interior forts west and north of the Columbia River where traders and hunters lived permanently with their families. These forts, built where Native communities wanted them and designed to build trade relationships with those communities, were the biggest difference from the Rocky Mountain rendezvous system that Drips and Fontenelle managed. Forts and families were expensive. And because Hudson's Bay was a big British company, with a chain of command, company officers kept daily journals recording their expenses. Details on their families and what they wore, ate, and bought fill those journals.

Company officers in the Columbia district all married Native women. Thomas McKay was married to Timmee, a Chinook woman and daughter of the local leader Concomly. McKay worked for chief trader Peter Skene Ogden, who had children with two Native women, a Cree from Canada who raised their son at Red River, and a Nez Percé–Shoshone woman. John Work, a young man recruited from Scotland's Orkney Islands, came to the Columbia District as his first posting. Work married the Spokane Josette Legacé and they had eleven children.[52]

The expanding webs of the trade could also carry threats. When Thomas McKay took a large expedition into southern Oregon and northern California to develop trading relationships with the Umpqua, Klamath, and Umatilla nations, they returned with a new danger: malaria carried in their blood and in mosquito larvae hidden in furs. Traders and boats spread the disease up and down the Columbia River in the early 1830s. Chinook people, with no resistance, suffered terribly. Timmee's father, Concomly, died in 1830 from malaria, and so did Timmee and Thomas's eldest son, Joseph McKay.[53]

Waves of malaria were followed by smallpox. A worldwide pandemic, it reached the Northwest Coast in 1833 and killed people by the thousands. When Timmee died during that 1833 epidemic, Thomas was still managing fur brigades. He left his remaining children, William, nine, Alexander, eight, and John, six, with their grandmother, Marguerite McKay McLoughlin, at Fort Vancouver.[54]

In 1835, McKay and his hunters ran into the first party of Americans who came to stay. They were the advance team of an ambitious Boston entrepreneur, Nathaniel Wyeth, who planned an outpost in American Oregon. He promised investors he'd trade furs, grow potatoes and tobacco, and develop a salmon industry to rival New England cod. After meeting the new Americans, McKay hurried to Fort Vancouver. He and John McLoughlin decided to drive Wyeth out not by force but by the Hudson's Bay way: a price war. So McKay built a post directly across the Snake River from Wyeth's new fort.

This became Fort Hall, three hundred miles east of Fort Vancouver and thirty miles north of present-day Pocatello, Idaho.[55]

Wyeth's American Trading Company, the first U.S. effort to challenge the Hudson's Bay Company in the Pacific Northwest, withered away when McKay offered higher prices for furs and lower prices for goods. John Townsend, a member of Wyeth's expedition, described McKay as an exotic cultural combination of "forester" and "Frenchman" who managed to "discipline his men, most of whom were Canadians, half-breed and Indians and ruled them completely." After a few months of taking Wyeth's business, McKay and the Hudson's Bay Company magnanimously stepped in and offered to buy Wyeth's entire operation. This purchase ended Wyeth's magnificent dream but only delayed the American presence in Oregon.[56]

The real threat to the Hudson's Bay Company, the wedge that would destroy its world, opened in a more innocuous form. In 1831 four Flathead Indians from Oregon arrived in St. Louis and allegedly requested that William Clark, the Indian superintendent, send them a missionary. The story had a kernel of truth that expanded like popcorn into something else indeed. The Flatheads had heard about the Black Robes, Catholics willing to live among the Indians, at the 1831 fur rendezvous. Some Flathead men had been curious enough to accompany Lucien Fontenelle back to Bellevue with the American Fur Company's wagons. Fontenelle, who was Catholic himself, saw no reason not to take them.[57]

The plea for Christian succor from the "poor Flatheads" reverberated through a United States bursting with evangelical energy. The report appeared in evangelical newspapers like the *Missionary Herald*, which was read aloud in homes and from pulpits every Sunday. Wherever American merchants arrived in the West, American evangelical missions now followed with the hope of converting Native "heathens." The Flathead request to William Clark had expressed curiosity about languages and agricultural techniques, not about changing where they lived, how they married, or which gods answered their prayers.[58]

In the Pacific Northwest, Methodists arrived first, raising funds for an "Aboriginal Mission west of the Rocky Mountains." Reverend

Jason Lee and two young missionaries-in-training received $3,000 and instructions to build a string of Great Plains "mission stations." The earnest travelers arrived on the Missouri River in 1834 and from there hitched a ride with an American Fur Company supply train that was led, of course, by Andrew Drips and Lucien Fontenelle. They left the Missouri River in April, reached the Green River rendezvous in July, and got to Fort Hall in August, where they met Thomas McKay. The missionaries were now escorted by "Mr. M'Kay and his Canadians," who traveled with "wives mounted in the fashionable native style, astride, and bearing muskets." Frightened a little by women carrying guns and riding astride, the Methodists were relieved to arrive at the Hudson's Bay Company's stronghold. To help them, but also because he wanted to warn John McLoughlin, Thomas McKay took the Methodists to Fort Vancouver in August 1834.[59]

John McLoughlin, gracious to people he didn't perceive as threats, welcomed the Methodists. He gave Reverend Lee supplies, workers from the fort, and advice about where to locate a mission. He suggested the Willamette Valley rather than eastern Oregon, where powerful tribes had been stirred up by smallpox epidemics and the resulting waves of captive taking. He offered Cyrus Shepherd a job teaching school at Fort Vancouver, where the young missionary reported that "all the laborers here are Canadian French, with Indian wives," and even "the gentlemen of the company have native wives." Shepherd's school taught not the "poor Flathead Indians" that Methodists had fundraised for but "trappers children, half-breeds all, as well Japanese children rescued from a ship, and Hawaiian boys."[60]

The mission, built by Jason Lee's French-speaking neighbors in 1835, had a barn and crops in the ground, but Native Oregonians showed no interest in agriculture. Some left their children with Lee at his Manual Labor School that first winter, but after all the children died or ran away, few other families did the same. Lee remembered that in the spring, even the most "docile" boys, "when some work was called for, and a little submission required," left, "running onto the plains, free as a bird escaped from its cage."[61]

While the missionaries settled in, wishing for neighbors who spoke English and Indians who would farm, Thomas McKay worked out of Fort Hall. He had his three sons with him, but he had also begun a relationship with a Cayuse woman with crucial connections to eastern Oregon's Native hunters. Convinced by his mother, Marguerite McKay McLoughlin, that his Chinook sons needed formal education, McKay considered sending them to schools in St. Louis or Canada. In June 1838, however, when missionary Jason Lee arrived at Fort Hall heading east to raise funds for the Oregon missions, Thomas considered another solution. Lee agreed to escort McKay's three sons—William, now fourteen, Alexander, twelve, and John, ten—to New England where he would enroll them at his own Methodist alma mater in Massachusetts.[62]

Lee had five "Indian lads" with him, including the McKay sons. For seven months they served as the central attraction for Lee's fundraising show, which began in Shawnee Mission, Kansas. After a swing through the Midwest, they ended up in New York City. Lee's talks, along with the "thrilling descriptions of Oregon's land and salmon" by the "Indian boys," were reported in scores of newspapers. New Yorkers were so eager to meet the McKay boys that the mayor invited them to City Hall in January 1839. A writer described their comportment, amazed that "sons of the forest could adopt our customs to such an extent and learn to behave with such perfect propriety at table."[63]

Their grandmother, Marguerite McLoughlin, who had presided over grand tables at Fort Vancouver and instilled manners in her grandsons, would have laughed at this. How William, Alexander, and John felt about being paraded around as ignorant Indians, we can only guess. When they arrived at Wilbraham Academy a few weeks later, they were described as "not pious, though seriously disposed and of good morals." The school's pastor prayed that the Indian McKays would "return to their own country devoutly pious and extremely useful both as men and Christians." The McKay brothers would indeed become useful men, but only after their racial status had been clarified.[64]

George Johnston and a New Racial Landscape

Race was proving a problem for George Johnston in Michigan. When Henry Schoolcraft appointed George, Jane's older brother, as subagent in the U.S. Indian Office that choice angered local people. It was not because of the obvious family favoritism, which no one objected to, but because appointing George raised racial alarms. Even though George's heritage and experience made him a logical choice, people complained to Henry that only a "white man" should receive a government job. George, with his black hair and dark skin, looked like an Indian. When he drank too much, spent money with abandon, or handled personal affronts poorly, people attributed it to his race.[65]

Henry Schoolcraft didn't trust George Johnston. He warned George that "many eyes are upon you" and that people watched "to espy any thing that may be seized upon to form an accusation." Because the subagency at La Pointe was so far from the Sault, George operated on his own. Over the three years that he and Louisa lived there, George did reasonably well in keeping Henry informed. However, George gave in to pressure from traders to ignore illegal activities, and he kept his Ojibwe relatives happy with lavish gifts.[66]

Those three years were hard ones for the Johnstons in Sault Ste. Marie. In 1825 the oldest brother, Lewis Saurin Johnston, did what his father John had feared most: he died after drinking, fighting, and falling down in the bitter winter cold. He left two little girls and a son from relationships with an Ojibwe woman and with a local mixed-blood woman. Then only eighteen months after Lewis's death, little William Henry Schoolcraft, not even three, died of a childhood fever. Six months later Jane miscarried. And barely a year after that, John Johnston died, leaving his family bereft.[67]

Jane almost didn't recover from these losses. She wrote these lines ten days after Willy's death:

> *Who was it nestled in my breast*
> *And on my cheek sweet kisses prest*

And in whose smile I felt so blest?
Sweet Willy
Who was it wiped my tearful eye
And kissed away the coming sigh
And smiling bid me say Good bye?
Sweet Willy

Henry corrected her words, copied the poem, and sent it to his friends in Detroit. He described it as writing "fit to be preserved as a specimen of native composition." Henry suffered, deeply, from little Willy's death, but his ability to turn Jane's agony into an ethnographic project seems a little heartless. And Henry's constant traveling that summer, surely to assuage his own grief, hurt Jane to the quick.[68]

New baby Jane Susan Schoolcraft, named after her grandmother and mother, born in February 1828, provided a glimmer of cheer. George wrote from La Pointe to congratulate Jane and Henry on producing a "little yellow-haired angel," telling us something about what she looked like. Jane loved the little girl but continued to grieve by writing poetry about dead babies and God's mysterious will. Henry never took the same pleasure in baby Jane, soon nicknamed Janee, as he had in Willy. He chided himself for his "idolatry of a child" and believed that God had rebuked him for "placing his affections too deeply." What a burden for that new child to bear.[69]

Isolated in La Pointe, George Johnston fought to keep his own family together. In 1829 the Indian Office in Washington decided that supporting two operations on Lake Superior was too expensive. To get George reappointed and save the subagency, Henry probably would have had to travel to Washington and lobby personally. After the death of his son and his father-in-law, and with Jane's precarious health, he just didn't have the heart. He also needed to protect his job. If the Indian Office insisted on only one agency, Henry wanted to make sure it was his. So George and Louisa and their three children came home to Sault Ste. Marie, where George worked as Henry's assistant. Henry tried to put a positive face on it, saying that "your residence here during the season will be pleasant." However, he warned George that "great reductions have been introduced in the expenses of the whole department," so that he might lose even that pittance of a job.[70]

This situation imploded immediately. George resented his demotion to clerk. In 1830, when Henry departed for his usual summer treaty negotiations, he left a set of orders for George, who refused to follow them. Instead, to take on anything he thought menial, George hired his brother William Johnston, now eighteen, and several other Ojibwe relatives, all at government expense. Henry fired George when he returned to the Sault office.[71]

Insulted, George moved to Mackinac Island, a bigger town with a busier port, and tried to find work. He schemed about running a store or shipping enterprises, but they required money he didn't have and that no one was willing to lend him. In the middle of the drama, George's wife died, leaving him with three young children. His mother, Susan Johnston, took in the two younger children temporarily, but Louisa, now seven, stayed with George. He tried to get his life back on track in Mackinac. A proud man, he didn't want to rely on his mother or on Henry.[72]

George had hoped, like everyone else in the family, that his money troubles would be solved by the settlement of John Johnston's long-standing claim against the United States for losses in the War of 1812. In 1828, the last year of his life, Johnston gathered more affidavits to prove that he had not been a British agent. In 1830, two years after his death, Susan received the final news that all their claims had been denied. The claims commission decided that confiscating Johnston's goods and burning warehouses was an "expected part of war against foreign nations." Therefore, the letter said, "the petitioner is not entitled to relief."[73]

That crushing disappointment added to George's difficulty in finding what he considered his due. Mixed-race men had trouble getting work more typical of Anglo-American settlers, as farmers, merchants, bankers, or ship operators. These jobs required family with land they could use as collateral, tax records, and connections to eastern banks, all benefits of White citizenship that fur trade families found harder to obtain. More troubling for the old mixed-descent fur trade world, the Indian Office became the Indian Service and no longer focused on the fur trade. When Andrew Jackson became president in 1829, Henry's Sault Ste. Marie Indian agency became a cog in a great bureaucracy to move Indians off their land. Henry continued to issue trade licenses, but his job was removal: negotiating treaties and moving Indians to smaller pieces of land in the West.

By 1830, a fine mesh of new bureaucracy and ideology spread through the fur trade West, following rivers the same way the trade itself had. Mixed-descent communities could see that land was the new coin of the realm. At first, when Native people ceded land, they continued to hunt and tap sugar maples in places where they always had. Property lines were invisible. However, before new White residents even arrived, a growing state would plat towns, build roads on Indian trails, and convince Native people to sign treaties giving up their land.[74]

At their simplest, treaties between the United States and Indian nations involved exchanges of land. However, what was really being exchanged was a community and a way of life for a piece of land in a random place that was anything but home. In the pressure of treaty negotiations and with few other options, mixed-blood translators from intermarried families convinced their people that their communities could begin anew. In hindsight, however, we can see that to protect their livelihoods, trader families colluded in creating land deals that destroyed much of Native life and the trader world alongside it.

More than fifty of the treaties written between 1800 and 1871 included "half-breed tracts" that were part and parcel of removal and dispossession of Indian land. Also called "mixed-blood reserves," these tracts were created to solve a problem facing White men with Native families. Because federal officials, and most White Americans, could only imagine property being owned by men, Indian mothers or wives often lost their property and access to future tribal lands in treaty negotiations. When non-Native men with Native wives and children realized such treaty language was robbing them of land, they found a solution. Intended to solve the problem of fur trade marriage and the children it produced, half-breed tracts promised special land arrangements on future Native reservations.[75]

These treaties looked like a boon for mixed-heritage people. Negotiated by fur trade fathers and translated by their mixed-descent sons, they created land arrangements that gave mixed people a stake in the new settler societies arriving on their doorsteps. But that stake could also be driven straight through their hearts.

Andrew Drips and Lucien Fontenelle, who had married into Otoe and Omaha families, benefited from a treaty made in 1818. An agreement between Indian nations and the United States to exchange land east of the Missouri River, the treaty promised extensive reservations for "half-breed" Osage, Otoe, Shawnee, and Kansas people in what is now Kansas and Nebraska. The promise got more specific in 1833 when treaties with the Omaha and Otoes laid out land near Bellevue for "half-breeds of the tribe," including Mehubane and Macompemay's children. Henry Schoolcraft negotiated treaties in 1826 that provided land for "Mixed Blood" Dakotas and Sioux in Wisconsin, and in 1836 for Potawatomis, Odawas, and Ojibwes in Michigan. This special notice for mixed families, however, created seeds of future trouble. Mixed families who had influence because of their fur trade connections got deals that other Native families did not. More portentous, the treaties introduced the category "half-breed" into Indian policy, though no one had yet defined what it meant.[76]

Native nations signed treaties with addendums for families of French, English, or American men who were residents of Native communities because of the long history of intermarriage. Since Indigenous groups had always recognized the children of Native women who married White or Black men as fully Native, they agreed to treaties protecting them. But for U.S. officials, "half-breed" children had blood that enabled them to be trusted with land ownership that the government was not willing to give to "full-blooded" Indians.[77]

Whatever trouble those words—*mixed, half,* and *full*—might cause in the future, Andrew Drips, Lucien Fontenelle, George Johnston, and Henry Schoolcraft, like thousands of other fur trade fathers, hoped that their families would find places in the new economies. The Johnstons had a specific treaty clause granting "Oshauguscodaywayquay and her descendants, including her 7 living children and her grandchildren" land on Sugar Island, where Susan hoped her grandchildren could visit each spring. John Johnston died believing his family would make their way in the world that was developing around them. "Half-breed tracts," granted in treaties from Michigan to Nebraska to Colorado to Oregon, extended those promises as the frontier moved west.[78]

=6=

Forging Peace on the Southern Plains, 1821–1840

Mistanta could ride a horse almost as soon as she could breathe. A Cheyenne child born about 1817, she could hear their nickering at night. She lured horses close with handfuls of corn, smelling their clean sweat as she leaned against the animals she loved. Her father, the Cheyenne leader White Thunder, had convinced some of his people to move a thousand miles from their northern Plains homeland to a new place where they could increase their horse herds. Like the Shawnees who had traveled far and settled the Mississippi Valley, and the Hurons who had left Lower Canada to regather with other Algonquian nations after war had ground them down, Cheyennes decided to move south.[1]

Horses made Mistanta and her people, *Tsétsêhéstâhese* or Southern Cheyennes, but it was bison that kept them alive. Mislabeled buffaloes because they resemble Asian water buffaloes, bison are unique to North America. Designed for Great Plains weather, they use the enormous muscles in their humps to drive their heads through snow, powerful natural plows that clear paths for other animals. A bison's double-coated skin, called *pelage*, has ten times the density of hair per square inch as cattle, enabling it to withstand subzero wind and driving snow. That trait made bison-skin lodges windproof and winter robes luxuriantly warm. Worn-out lodge skins clothed people and diapered babies. Bison horns made cups and stored powder; bison muscles made bowstrings and thread. Dried bison excrement, "buffalo chips," made clean-burning fires on a treeless Plains landscape. Fresh bison hearts and tongues, eaten at the moment of a kill, were a special delicacy, but dried meat fed people all year. Bison hides also bought horses, and guns to protect those horses.[2]

A growing trade in bison hides, horses, and guns developed on the southern Plains in the 1820s. In a place that was not yet Mexico or the United States, traders and distant markets made new lives possible. Like earlier fur trades in the Great Lakes or the Rocky Mountains, this business required family making between cultures. Undertaking such a life demanded bravery and imagination.

The Bent Family and the Southern Plains

Like the Cheyenne, the St. Louis trader Charles Bent moved south because of bison. Born in Virginia, he had moved with his family to St. Louis in 1806. Bent's father, Silas Bent, was part of that city's first Anglo elite. He served on the Missouri Supreme Court while he and his wife Martha raised eleven children in the first decades of the nineteenth century. Their daughters married well and created generations of St. Louisans. Even with connections and capital, their sons became mountain men. Heroic adventure and potential profit drew many St. Louisans into the trade. After years of business and personal risk, Charles Bent decided that the fur trade had lost its allure. His partnership with the Missouri Fur Company had been undercut by John Jacob Astor's American Fur Company. Dragging boatloads of goods up the Missouri River was brutally hard work. Trapping in icy water and facing attacks by Native raiders made winters deadly. In 1827 and 1828 Bent lost dozens of his men and most of his furs in altercations with Arikara, Sioux, and especially Blackfoot.[3]

Now nearly thirty, a ripe old age in the fur trade, and having lost fortunes and friends, Charles wanted something new. He had four younger brothers who needed livelihoods. As the fur trade evolved into the Rocky Mountain–style rendezvous and the upper Missouri and upper Mississippi fort-based systems, two new elements entered the fray. Newly legal commerce brought silver, enslaved Native people, and horses from Santa Fe and Mexico. Simultaneously the forced expulsion of Native peoples from east of the Mississippi brought hundreds of thousands of refugees into western Indian country. Trade with Mexico, federal contracts and forts, and a huge potential labor supply ignited a trade with Indian peoples from Arkansas to California.[4]

Bison, the "monarch of the Plains," became a capitalist's dream, just as beaver had generations earlier. Bison meat fed soldiers in U.S. and European armies, but the hides were most important. The dense leather that came in long single pieces attracted international demand as material for industrial pulleys. Bison leather ran British cotton mills and German looms before the era of rubber. Smaller pieces made army boots and shoes for slaves. And bison seemed limitless in number. Zebulon Pike, the first U.S. explorer in the region, described the prairies in 1806 as entirely covered with bison, a sight that "exceeded imagination." Travelers and businessmen on the Santa Fe Trail found themselves similarly speechless at their first sight of bison. They were here "innumerable," reported William Becknell, an early Santa Fe Trail traveler.[5]

That endless supply of animal wealth lured many people to the southern Plains. Cheyennes (and their close relatives the Arapahos) had successful lives on the northern Plains, hunting in the Black Hills and sowing corn and tobacco on the Missouri River. They lived well there because of trade in global markets. Mexican silver, British guns, Comanche horses, and American alcohol appeared on the Plains because of the fur trade and now the business of bison. The wealth to be found in Cheyenne homelands drew expanding Sioux and Blackfoot nations, who pushed Cheyenne bands closer to their most hated enemies, the Pawnees. Both Pawnees and Sioux stole Cheyenne horses when they visited the Missouri River. Without horses, Cheyennes couldn't hunt for the furs and bison that they traded for corn and guns. Without those essential items, the Cheyenne might starve.[6]

Traveling south on long fall hunts and summer trading expeditions, the Cheyennes met southern Plains peoples—Utes, Comanches, and Kiowas—who had everything they needed. Native and Anglo raiders brought horses and slaves from Mexico. New Mexican villages had corn, tobacco, and cloth. French and Spanish traders exchanged guns in return for bison robes. If Cheyennes partnered with southern Plains peoples and helped them to protect their world from Apaches and Navajos, everyone could hunt bison.[7]

A new nation with old local roots enticed both Cheyennes and white St. Louisans. In 1821, after years of revolution, Mexico became independent of Spain as the Estados Unidos de México. The Arkansas River marked its border with the United States. Mexican officials knew that trading with the expanding United States was dangerous, but two centuries of Spain's efforts to keep Americans out had only increased smuggling and reduced tax revenues. Powerful Indian nations, however, had completely stopped cross-border trade and were a far greater threat to Mexico's interests than were White Americans. After the revolution wound down, the desire of Mexicans for guns, money, and population as a bulwark against Comanche and Apache raiders outweighed their fears of Anglo-Americans.

In 1822 the Mexican government officially opened the Santa Fe trade, making a long-tolerated illegal trade legal. American demand for Mexican silver, mules, and captive slaves, traded for U.S. manufactured goods, especially textiles and ammunition, increased exponentially. In response, the United States opened a route called the Santa Fe Trail that covered one thousand miles between the Missouri frontier and Mexico's northernmost state. It began at Chouteau's Landing, now called Westport, where the Missouri River turns north toward Andrew Drips and Lucien Fontenelle's post at Bellevue. It ended at Santa Fe, the old capital of northern Mexico, founded in 1612. Because the trail crossed international borders in Indian country, in 1825 a team of U.S. negotiators requested permission from the Kaw, Osage, Pawnee, Wichita, and Comanche nations to allow passage through their lands. Guided by not-yet-famous William Sherley Williams, the negotiators carried $20,000 in gifts appropriated by Congress. Williams had raised a family among the Osage,

INDIAN COUNTRY AND EMPIRE: THE GREAT PLAINS

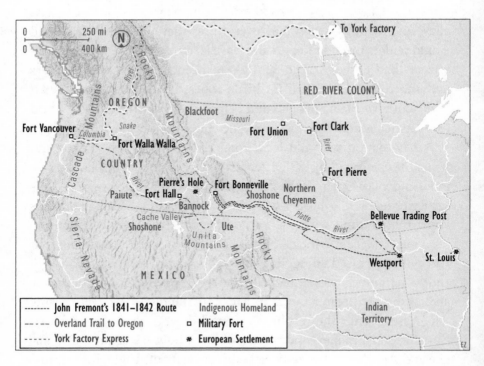

so he knew to hire mixed-blood translators with the language and diplomatic skills to get permission to enter Indian nations. Through planning and presents, U.S. officials and Indian diplomats traveled safely to Santa Fe and back.[8]

In 1826, with permissions granted and a road marked, large wagon caravans began trundling east and west. Taxes and profits flowed into government coffers and built fortunes in both St. Louis and Santa Fe. Native communities, both those who had been removed from east of the Mississippi and those who were indigenous to the region, welcomed traders. This part of Indian country remade itself once again as teamsters, mule drivers, and guides who came from places built by the fur trade in Kansas and Arkansas.[9]

For the Bent brothers, such opportunities were irresistible but also risky. Charles Bent and his younger brother William, then nineteen, set out in their first wagons to Santa Fe in 1828. They joined a caravan of thirty-eight carts heading southwest from Missouri, knowing they would meet Plains nations who demanded gifts as the price of travel. If travelers were stingy and didn't tolerate a little theft, they would run into trouble. The 1827 caravan had been attacked, disastrously, by Indians. So in 1828 President Andrew Jackson provided a military escort. In June, three companies of infantry accompanied the creaky wooden carts driven by Native and mixed-blood teamsters. The troops took them to the Mexico–U.S. border at the Arkansas River, about four hundred miles into the trip.[10]

As soon as the soldiers left Bent's caravan at the border, Kiowa and Comanche raiders ran off its horses and mules. The humans were never threatened, but without animal power to pull the loaded wagons, the caravan was trapped. Ninety-five men from Taos, alerted to the danger by a brave rider, came to the rescue. The addition of mules and manpower convinced the Comanches to leave, and the wagons rolled into Santa Fe in late July. Another young Missourian, Kit Carson, just beginning his career as mountain man and soldier, was part of the rescue team. After that shared drama, Kit and William Bent became lifelong friends. They would eventually share businesses and households, building families as *compadres* (coparents) in Indian country on the southern Plains.[11]

The Bents considered business possibilities in Santa Fe and in Taos, an old trading town two days north of New Mexico's capital. They consulted Taos residents and old St. Louis friends, Ceran St. Vrain and Sylvestre Pratte, whose success came from marriages into important local Mexican families and from the financial (and familial) support of old French fur-trading companies. The Bents' business decisions took a new twist when young William Bent didn't follow instructions. Bored with unloading carts and selling goods, William wandered off to hunt and trap along the Gila and Rio Grande.[12]

William's actions were illegal. U.S. citizens had limited trading options in Mexico. They could bring in manufactured goods that New Mexicans wanted, and they could take Mexican manufactured goods back to St. Louis, as long as they paid hefty customs fees on both sides. They could not, however, trade directly with Indians; nor could they trap beaver, hunt bison, or take any "products of the landscape," according to an 1824 Mexican law. Along with other scofflaws, in 1829 Bent and a party of French and Anglo-American trappers wintered on the upper Arkansas River, talking and trading with Cheyenne hunting parties.[13]

In 1830 William trapped farther south along rivers in what is now Arizona. He weathered an Indian raid, lost most of his furs and his loyal dog Lolo, and reconsidered life as an independent trapper. Barely twenty, he saw that men who succeeded had Indian families to protect and feed them. Such relationships didn't eliminate danger entirely in the world of southern Plains raiding and trading, where honor and status turned on violence, but kinship connections and the rituals that wove them reduced the risk. William's entrée into the Cheyenne world came when his quick thinking diverted a group of Comanche warriors searching for Cheyennes who had stolen their horses. He hid the guilty men and sent the Comanches in the wrong direction. Bent's decision began his life with the Cheyenne.[14]

William Bent convinced his brother Charles, as well as the Bents' future partners, the St. Vrains, that trade between Santa Fe and St. Louis could be more lucrative with fur and bison hides in the mix. Marriage into Indian nations and into local Mexican families would make that trade legal and possible. The families went into business together, forming a partnership that lasted longer than many marriages. These Bents and St. Vrains never again lived in St. Louis, though their banks and business managers remained there. In 1832 Charles Bent carried more than thirteen thousand pounds of fur and 355 buffalo robes in his caravan to St. Louis, garnering a huge profit and attention in Missouri newspapers.[15]

The Bents knew they had been lucky. They had seen U.S. traders dragged off to Mexican prisons. They also knew how vicious the competition in the fur business could be. The Bents and St. Vrains specialized in a mostly legal niche. Rather than hiring White trappers, they convinced Indians to hunt and trade bison hides. They chose to trade along the Arkansas River, right on the new U.S.-Mexico border. Native people could trade and hunt across borders that stopped Anglos and Mexicans. Whether their business came from the United

States or from Mexico, the Bents were in the heart of Indian country. Huge encampments, with thousands of lodges each, outnumbered all Anglo and Mexican settlements.[16]

The Bent brothers' timing was perfect. The fur trade was entering its last golden age along the long spine of the Rocky Mountains. For Plains nations, the bison trade provided a vehicle for successful expansion and new wealth. Along with their U.S. neighbors, the Cheyenne, Sioux, and Comanche were rapidly changing and expanding. All these ambitious peoples saw opportunity along the Arkansas, a place where they could build new lives and where Indians and Anglos required each other to succeed.

As the southern and central Plains spread around the Bents' new trading post on the Arkansas River, the visual feast of grassland, cool river bottoms, and millions of animals captured everyone's gaze. Pronghorns, horses, prairie dogs, roadrunners, beavers, otters—and the wolves, coyotes, bears, and bobcats that feasted on them—ranged over the entire region. The bison, the largest land mammal in North America, dominated that landscape and the hopes of humans who ventured there.[17]

Cheyennes Along the Arkansas

When White Thunder decided to move south, his decision mattered because he was an arrow keeper for his people. His life's purpose was to protect the *mahouts*—four sacred arrows given to the Cheyenne by Sweet Medicine, their prophet. Sweet Medicine gave the Cheyenne horses, the Sun Dance, military societies, and *mahouts*—everything important to them. An arrow keeper first earned his status because of military prowess, but he stopped fighting to care for the arrows and become a voice of wisdom for the tribe. Cheyennes governed themselves and wove clans and villages together with military societies that recruited members from many clans. The head men of the Fox, Elk, Shield, and Bowstring societies organized hunts and raids. A fifth military society, the Dog Men or Dog Soldiers, evolved in the 1830s as raiding and pressure from U.S. troops intensified.

The Dog Soldiers prided themselves on their military discipline and courage. To make decisions for the entire Cheyenne nation, a Council of Forty-four comprised clan and village leaders, all respected elders who had retired from raiding.[18]

White Thunder and his wife, Tail Woman, also a clan leader, convinced many Cheyenne people to follow them, including many Dog Soldier bands. Most of the Council of Forty-four questioned White Thunder's judgment in splitting the people, but the appeal of a richer life drew many people south. In 1820 U.S. explorer Stephen Long visited a large Indian trading camp along the South Platte River, where hundreds of Cheyenne families traded British guns, ammunition, and beads for horses from the Kiowa. A year later they were reported as "greatly settled" in villages along the Arkansas River, where they hunted bison and pastured huge horse herds. These Cheyenne villages now housed most of the Hairy Rope Clan, led by White Thunder and Yellow Wolf, both renowned horse raiders.[19]

Mistanta, whose name meant "Owl Woman" in Cheyenne, grew up in this new *Tsétséhéstâhese* place. Because the Cheyennes had moved so much and avoided some waves of epidemic disease, their population grew in the early nineteenth century. Unlike Ojibwes in Michigan and Chinooks in Washington, Cheyennes had always been a small nation of about 3,000, more like Otoes. But as Mistanta and her sisters grew up near the Arkansas, their population nearly doubled. Arapaho and Kiowa villages grew as well, dramatically increasing the number of people in the region. As populations and horse herds grew, Mistanta and other Cheyennes felt new pressures to find bison robes and to prepare them for market.[20]

Skinning a bison and preserving its robe in a single piece required immense effort. First, women removed the skin of a thousand-pound animal, requiring skillful use of a sharp knife to keep it in one piece. The next steps required pinning the large bloody hide to the ground, hair side down. Using rocks and bones or metal scrapers, women and boys removed every bit of sinew and fat. Next, they flipped it and removed the outer hair with an elkhorn tool. Finally, girls and boys tanned the now smooth hide by rubbing it with a mixture of bison brains, pulverized soapweed, and grease, making the robe soft and durable.

Bison robes bought Cheyennes guns, ammunition, food, and silver, but most significantly they bought horses. Horses gave young men the ability to fight and raid. As the price of a wife, horses were the only means for young people to become fully adult. Gifts of horses began diplomacy, ended wars, and created kin. But these glorious animals rarely reproduced themselves in the harsh landscapes of the northern Plains. They thrived on the southern Plains, where the grass grew thick and winters were less brutal. The final ingredient in this southern Plains economy, then, was a constant supply of captive herders and guns to protect the horses. The focus of Cheyenne life thus shifted to managing the trade in bison, captives, guns, and horses, and competing with the Comanches and Apaches who fiercely patrolled the same landscape.[21]

The Plains economy shifted the position of women in Cheyenne life, since they were the key labor source in producing bison robes for trade. Girls like Mistanta felt this change most deeply. Brothers and boy cousins were still trained as hunters and raiders, lords of the Plains. But women wielded significant spiritual power. While men protected the *mahouts* or sacred arrows, women guarded the *Issiwum*, the Sacred Buffalo hat. Formed from a female buffalo's scalp, it carried the power to renew bison herds, so caring for it with proper ceremonies was essential. As the daughter of White Thunder and Tail Woman, Mistanta understood her role in protecting and feeding the people, even if it required doing the dirty work of preparing bison robes for traders.[22]

William Bent knew that bison would be the center of his life in the Indian trade. In 1831 he set up a temporary post where Fountain Creek flows into the Arkansas River, at present-day Pueblo, Colorado. A group of Cheyennes arrived to trade, accompanied by Yellow Wolf, their leader. Bent politely offered tobacco, and they began a translated conversation—Bent had English, Spanish, and some Lakota, and the Cheyennes had several languages and a little Lakota, so they could discuss business.

Yellow Wolf wanted a personal relationship with a trader who wasn't already indebted to the Comanche or Kiowa. He also sought a trading post where Cheyennes could repair their guns. For his part,

Bent wanted a trading house along the Arkansas that could serve those Cheyenne needs, and where Taos and Santa Fe trail traffic would bring steady business. With those shared goals, the Cheyenne welcomed him into their trading circles, and Bent began a new life. Yellow Wolf suggested a place called Big Timbers as the site of the new post. The shady wooded thickets attracted summer encampments but allowed bands to winter there as well.[23]

Bent convinced his brother and other investors to build several temporary posts in 1833 and 1834, but the final site, a compromise, was thirty-five miles west of Big Timbers, close to the Purgatoire River. Yellow Wolf convinced three large bands of Cheyenne to migrate south from the Platte River. At this place, these Southern Cheyenne—and the Bents—would create something new along the Arkansas.

From some perspectives, this place was the middle of nowhere. However, in the early 1830s, Bent's Fort, on the north side of the Arkansas River, stood at the center of a trade system linking St. Louis and Mexico. More significantly, Bent's Fort stood on the northwestern edge of Comanchería, that vast territory controlled by Comanche warriors and their skilled diplomats. Situated between southern Plains peoples like the Kiowa and Comanche and desert war experts like the Apache and Navajo, Bent's Fort survived by offering the western Comanche secure access to American markets. It wasn't just bison robes. Comanche and Cheyenne also traded stolen people— Mexican and Indian captives—for guns and horses. Those people, used as herders and laborers at Bent's Fort, were also sent east to the Missouri border and south into Texas.[24]

William Bent's first year at this crossroads did not go well. To attract traders and warn intruders, Bent planned a building that could be seen for miles and offer protection from attacking raiders. With few available trees, the best building material was Spanish adobe brick, made from mud and fired in ovens. It offered protection from the wind, and it stayed cool in summer and warm in winter, but it required expertise to produce and use. Bent hired groups of Mexican workers and *genizaros* (mixed Indian and Mexican slaves) to make bricks, but they brought smallpox. Bent caught the pox, which left his face badly pitted for the rest of his life. As he took to his sickbed, he sent a messenger north to the large Cheyenne villages to warn them against coming near.[25]

Though Mistanta and her family avoided smallpox, White Thunder's years as arrow keeper brought the Cheyenne other challenges. In 1832 Pawnees attacked a Cheyenne raiding party along the Platte River. It was an embarrassing defeat for the Cheyenne, who retreated to their new home along the Arkansas and planned a retaliation. This time, led by White Thunder and carrying the *mahouts,* they couldn't fail. But their attack in 1833 did fail, and the loss was devastating. Early in the battle, the Pawnees struck down the man chosen to carry the sacred arrows. Cheyenne warriors fled in fear, and women and children followed, furious at their leaders.[26]

This was a cultural and military disaster. The Cheyenne knew that until they recovered the *mahouts,* life would be grim. In November 1833, after a year of bad luck and weather, poor raids and harvests, the stars fell in a great meteor shower. Elders remembered that "all the Indians thought the world was coming to an end and the camps were full of mourning." White Thunder and a group of medicine men and leaders created new *mahouts,* but they were a poor substitute. Desperate, White Thunder and Tail Woman made a secret visit to a Pawnee village in 1834. Unarmed and entirely vulnerable, the Cheyennes promised great peace and numerous horses if the Pawnees would return the sacred arrows. That village had only one arrow, having sent the rest to other Pawnee villages to protect them. The Pawnees returned the *mahout,* in hopes of concluding a peace that would allow everyone to hunt safely on the western Plains. With peace, perhaps the other *mahouts* would reappear.[27]

Owl Woman Takes a Husband

In the summer of 1835, William Bent and Mistanta married. Mistanta, or Owl Woman, the seventeen-year-old daughter of the arrow keeper of the Cheyenne, and William Bent, the twenty-six-year old son of a St. Louis judge, joined lives in a great public ceremony. They bound two networks of relations—siblings, parents, aunts, uncles, and in-laws—into extended family obligations. The marriage promised Mistanta's father, White Thunder, increased prestige and wealth, which he could use to regain the remaining Cheyenne *mahouts*. Finding safety amid Pawnee, Kiowa, and Comanche required guns and sacred power. A good life for the Cheyenne meant having more horses, more food, and more luck. Marriage and new kin could create the first threads of a web that made possible a peaceful trade world along the Arkansas.[28]

Trading wasn't just transactional—it took place within the circles of kinship and obligation that ran through the world of Bent's Fort. Relationships required loyalty. In 1834, to show his loyalty to the Cheyenne, William Bent led an attack on a group of Shoshones camped outside a small stockade just up the river from the fort. He killed and scalped three and encouraged the Cheyennes with him to steal all the Shoshone horses. The Cheyenne, surprised at Bent's ferocity, were delighted that he had demonstrated that their bitter enemies were now his enemies too.[29]

His marriage the following year to Mistanta ensured that William Bent would care for his Cheyenne relatives, and that Yellow Wolf and White Thunder's families would protect Bent's family. Bent gave presents lavishly, demonstrating his understanding of Cheyenne expectations. He gave silver beads, swords, and knives from Mexico, blankets and clothing from England, tobacco and alcohol from Missouri, and most significantly, hundreds of horses and guns. He killed dozens of cattle and prepared bison hearts, tongues, and livers. Black slaves and Mexican servants baked cakes and pies and prepared tortillas to serve at a feast that lasted days.[30]

When she appeared at the marriage ceremony, probably carried in by her uncles, Mistanta wore Cheyenne clothing befitting her lofty status. She wore a soft, nearly white buckskin dress, belted with a leather and brass sash, ornamented with silver beads and elk teeth. Yellow-and-black-striped tights covered her legs. Iridescent shells sparkled in her ears, and silver and brass bracelets adorned her arms. She wore a symbolic chastity belt under her clothing, a knotted rope that hung between a young woman's legs until she chose to take it off.

Some brides wore the belt for several months until the couple were accustomed to marriage and sex and felt ready for intercourse.[31]

Mistanta and William lived much of the time in a bison-skin lodge located next to Tail Woman and White Thunder's lodge at the center of the Cheyenne village. The couple also spent time inside the fort, and Mistanta redecorated William's ground-floor quarters to suit her tastes. She covered the hard dirt floor with bison robes and set up seating rests next to the adobe walls, but nothing could make the dark rooms as airy as her lodge. She soon shared both spaces with her two sisters, Island and Yellow Woman. They were co-wives to William, as suited his elite status in the Cheyenne tribe. This shocked some Anglos, but few dared to comment in William's presence.[32]

Mistanta and her sisters continued to live in a world of women. Their work shifted between supporting men as warriors, cleaning bison skins, and feeding families. Because these responsibilities involved unending work, most important families included co-wives and daughters whose men hunted for the household. Dozens of non-Native men lived in the households of each Cheyenne village. In the account of William Boggs, one of Bent's traders, the Indian wife of "Gary a Canadian Frenchman" took Boggs to the "teepee of old Cinemo, the old Cheyenne chief" whose wives ran a bison robe production facility. He explained that White and Native hunters supplied bison to "the squaws of the village" to dress and prepare, all for the "benefit of the Bents Company."[33]

While women produced robes, men raided for horses. In 1836 the Cheyennes conducted a successful raid against Buffalo Hump's Comanches. They got hundreds of horses, and gave William Bent the great Comanche leader's personal horse, a great honor. A day later Comanche warriors came to avenge this insult. Hearing that Comanches were approaching, Bent acted to protect the sacred arrows that were in White Thunder's lodge. He sent a team of men out to dismantle the huge lodge and carry it into the fort. When the Comanches arrived in the village, they demanded to know who had stolen horses and where the Cheyenne leaders were. Bent claimed he had no idea about either, and the Comanches left to continue their search.[34]

William Bent and Mistanta's first child arrived on a January morning in 1838. Mary, or Ho-Ka (Little Woman), started life in a Cheyenne winter lodge along the Arkansas River. She was the granddaughter of White Thunder, the arrow keeper of the Southern Cheyenne, the most powerful man in the tribe. Her birth took place auspiciously, just after the Cheyenne recovered the last sacred arrow after it had spent six years in enemy hands.[35]

The Cheyenne felt safe in the great cultural hinge that was Bent's Fort. Mary's birth, followed by her siblings Robert, George, Julia, and Charles Bent, offered hope that the hinge would stay open for years. The peoples and villages who traded bison skins with the Bent and St. Vrain Company became "wealthy" with guns, horses, and the magical fetishes required for success in warfare. But wealth, once created, had to be protected. White merchants in New York, New Orleans, and St. Louis sent smoothbore shotguns by the hundreds of thousands into the hands of Native people on the southern Plains. White Thunder thought he had saved the Cheyenne by moving south, but he had only shifted the risks.[36]

In the summer of 1838, the year of his granddaughter's birth, White Thunder was killed. He was the only arrow keeper ever to be killed in battle, surely a bad sign for the Cheyenne. His widow, Tail Woman, carried the arrows back to camp, where William, Owl Woman, and her sisters Yellow Woman and Island tried to comfort her. The forty-four Cheyenne chiefs chose a new arrow keeper, a Tsistsista named Lame Medicine, related directly to the great prophet Sweet Medicine. They hoped their luck would return.[37]

Many other people tried their luck in this emerging mixed-blood world. Alexander Barclay, an English immigrant to Canada in 1833, moved to Bent's Fort after a few bitter Canadian winters. Hired to supervise the fort store and keep the books, Barclay assured his family that his new post wouldn't be dangerous, but he hoped for "a little Indian fighting that would add a great deal of interest to my adventure."[38]

Barclay arrived at Bent's Fort in October 1838, right after Mary Bent's birth, and settled right in. Styling himself a mountain man, he sent bearskins and Indian arrows to his admiring family, even as he added columns of numbers and inventoried items as a good storekeeper should. He joked about "bartering for an Indian squaw" in a letter to his brother, claiming she cost too much. His family laughed at such a preposterous claim. Barclay, however, like most Euro-American men at the fort, began a relationship with a Cheyenne woman.[39]

Much like Michilimackinac, Fort Vancouver, or Bellevue on the upper Missouri River, Bent's Fort was a cosmopolitan place built by the mixed-blood families of the fur trade. Fragile sites of contested power in an expanding nation, their success and stability depended not only on delicate human relationships but on distant matters like the price of bison leather in New York and the administrative rules of the Indian Service. Trade on the Arkansas River could be damaged by too many bison hunted in drought years, or too many young men killed in warfare between the Apache and the Comanche. It turned out that neither prices nor warfare nor drought brought ruin to Cheyenne villages. It was Christian missionaries, bellwethers of the ambitious nation, who carried ideas that unraveled lives on the southern Plains. They challenged the blood mixing and kin making that characterized the edges of Indian country from Minnesota to Mexico.

Missionaries in Indian Country

For three decades between 1820 and 1850, the violent removal of Native nations from the entire region east of the Mississippi forced Indigenous families and peoples west. William Clark, superintendent of Indian affairs for the western region, described people who arrived there as "starving, with no clothes, amidst Indians who would not welcome them." In those desperate conditions, missionaries found opportunities to make Christianity and agriculture part of Native lives in new places. All the major Protestant denominations established missions along the Missouri River in the 1830s and 1840s. Churches, firmly part of military and civilian efforts first to remove and then to replant Native nations, devoted enormous financial and human resources to the missionary project. Indian agents, many of them converts themselves in this evangelical age, rarely questioned the effort to make Indians into farming Christians. Removed Indians, who started over with no resources on enemy land, used missionaries, who sometimes migrated and settled with them, as intermediaries between tribes and the federal government.[40]

Missionaries traveled along the same paths through fur trade communities that traders and officials followed. In 1831 Henry Schoolcraft made a treaty with the Ojibwe to exchange land in Michigan and begin removing west. That treaty included providing money for missionaries to teach Ojibwe children to read. Moses and Eliza Merrill, devout Baptists from Maine, were appointed to a mission in Sault Ste. Marie and became Jane Schoolcraft's first teachers. The school operated for only one winter because the Baptist board sent the Merrills west to convert Indians in Kansas and Nebraska.[41]

In a coincidence that shows the tight network of missions and trading communities, the Merrills were also teachers for the Drips and Fontenelle children. In 1836 the Merrills moved to Indian country to preach to Otoes. They found space in Lucien Fontenelle's old trading post buildings, now the Bellevue Indian Agency. Merrill wrote, after his first winter, that he had received no supplies from the government or from the Baptist board. Even so, he reported some progress: "The S. School, Bible Class, and religious exercises in Otoe and English are continued as usual." He listed some challenges: "ardent spirits and the French," whose Catholic children filled school seats more readily than "reluctant Otoes."[42]

The old mixed-blood world continued on. Many missionaries reported that the only real success they had in conversion came among "half-breeds." Missionary tracts proclaimed them to be "industrious and intelligent, well-versed in the English, French, and Kaw languages." One missionary admitted that among Kansas Indians, "the Canadian French in my opinion have done more to civilize the Kansas and Otoes than all the missions that have ever been established" because they are "willing to marry."[43]

By the 1830s, the problem of too many competing missions forced dueling Protestant churches to cooperate. They formed the American Board of Commissioners of Foreign Missions (ABCFM), a Christian umbrella group, to consolidate missionary activity. The ABCFM directed Isaac McCoy and his wife, Christiana Polke McCoy, to organize all Protestant missionary activity among western Indians. Isaac and Christiana had genuine frontier credentials. Christiana's family had been taken by Shawnees during a raid in Kentucky in 1780. Christiana was born during her mother's yearlong sojourn with the Shawnee. At sixteen, Christiana Polke married Isaac McCoy, and they immediately set off to convert Indian country. In 1819 McCoy performed the first Baptist marriage in western Illinois, between two mixed-blood people—Noel Dagenet, a Miami-French trader, and Mary Ann Isaacs, a Mohegan from upstate New York.[44]

Decades of experience in marrying and preaching to Weas and Miamis in Indiana and Potawatomis and Odawas in Michigan prepared the McCoys to supervise the ABCFM's vast missionary project on Indian country's new frontier. Those experiences also convinced them that Native people surely needed saving, but more from White settlers than from hellfire. The Shawnee, for example, who lived on 1.6 million acres along the Kansas-Missouri border, faced squatters who "removed them from their neat cabins" every time they had "fields broken and tilled." The removed Indians then became easy targets for Pawnees and Dakotas who swept in for raids.[45]

After witnessing such setbacks, Isaac McCoy made creating an Indian state his life's work. Native people needed a place, away from evil traders and settlers, where they could learn how to govern themselves. He insisted that tribes who had created written laws, like Creeks, Choctaws, and Cherokees, could be models for the "less civilized tribes, viz.: the Pawnees, Omahas, Otoes, Kickapoos, Kauxaus, Putawatomies, Delawares, Shawanoes, Weas, and Peorias and Kaskaskias, Ottawas, and Osages." He hoped those tribes could emulate the "Five Civilized Tribes" and "form the confederacy and adopt laws."[46]

McCoy wanted to convince Washington officials that Indians were not, as most White Americans hoped and assumed, disappearing. In 1837 he estimated that "Mexican Indians make about 5,400,000 and the Indians in this country about 1,800,000." These inflated, entirely invented numbers were supposed to prove McCoy's claim that Native populations had expanded because of intermarriage. (According to current estimates, Indigenous populations in the United States were in fact increasing in these years, but the total population was perhaps 800,000.) McCoy also claimed that his "estimate" didn't include "2,500,000 mixed offspring of whites and Indians and about 1,000,000 of descendants of Indians and Negroes," groups that he insisted had "increased in numbers." Many White Americans and policy makers shared McCoy's concern but didn't like his solution of an independent Indian state. No matter how many Indians there were, they didn't want "flourishing Indian populations," "Indian confederacies," or "half-breed led states" in the center of the continent.[47]

McCoy got several bills before Congress. In 1836 "an act to provide for the exchange of lands with the Indians residing in any of the states or territories for their removal west of the River Mississippi" reached the House floor. The commissioner of Indian affairs, missionary groups, and friendly congressmen mapped the "Western Territory." It began at the eastern boundary of Arkansas and Missouri and included everything west to the Rocky Mountains, where the United States ended in 1836. In the vast plains between the Arkansas and Missouri rivers, Indians would govern themselves in a "Confederacy with a General Council of delegates." With the help of agents, missionaries, and teachers, the bill promised that Indians would become citizens.[48]

McCoy wasn't alone in such efforts. A few years later Abelard Guthrie, a Baptist preacher and Nebraska territorial representative, tried to have "all the Indian Territory between Kansas and Texas" made into the territory of "Lanniwa" and provided with "a Territorial Government." Guthrie and a like-minded congressman from Kansas introduced legislation into Congress. They wanted Indians to be safe from "Kansas whites" and claimed that a "half-breed led state could protect them." The U.S. House passed a bill, but after some debate it died in the Senate.[49]

A Great Peace on the Southern Plains

As Congress debated these proposals in the early 1840s, in the heart of Indian country the Bent children lived during a peaceful interlude. A Cheyenne universe of bison, tall grasses, and horses, and a White world of oxen, wagons, and Christianity gave them a glorious childhood. But that peace had been hard won the decade before. Removal of eastern Indians had brought war to the nations living farther east along the Arkansas River. Indian commissioners looking for suitable lands for southern and midwestern Indians found resolute "hostiles" already in place who fought for their land.

These troubles led to the first U.S. military expedition into the region. Its goal was to "scour the landscape between the Arkansas and Canadian Rivers of Indians." While scouring, military officers hoped to convince Kiowa, Comanche, and Wichita leaders to come to a peace meeting at Fort Gibson in the fall of 1833. The expedition was a disaster. Instead of being scoured out, Comanches and Kiowas ran off the soldiers' horses and captured and tortured their Indian scouts. Such "constant harassment" forced the troops "to abandon the object of the expedition and return to Fort Gibson."[50]

The next year Col. Henry Dodge, an Army man who had battled Indians successfully in the Midwest, made another try. Dodge and his superiors, including the secretary of war, believed that properly outfitted and trained horse-mounted troops could best any Native warriors. But Colonel Dodge ended up with untrained troops who had to endure a grueling winter's encampment along the Arkansas without proper supplies. So many of their horses died and were eaten that the crack dragoons that he imagined he would have in the spring turned into sick infantry with no horses. Fortunately he had hired Cherokee, Seneca, Osage, and Delaware warriors, and he had some captive Kiowa and Wichita children he hoped to use to negotiate peace. This army had an embedded artist, George Catlin, to capture the scene. Catlin described five hundred regular troops and a retinue that included "Frenchmen who had long lived among the Indians" and "half breeds of the various nations who could hunt and translate." They doubled Dodge's force to nearly one thousand.[50]

William Bent and the Cheyennes knew who and what was coming. The news had traveled south to Comanches and Kiowas who intended to hunt that summer between the Arkansas and Canadian rivers, just where the troops were heading. Bent knew that the Plains tribes viewed the U.S. military as buffoonish at best. Rumors of the grand peace expedition concerned Bent because he knew a poorly managed effort would further destabilize a region that was already dangerous.

And so far Dodge's troops, ordered to catch Indians of any sort, had just aggravated everyone. Smaller groups of soldiers found Comanche camps and Wichita villages and tried to convince them to attend a council hosted by the president, "the Great American Captain," so that "red brothers could stop fighting." The result of that patronizing invitation was a sparse meeting in 1834 between "the half-naked and wild-looking representatives of the western tribes," as one soldier described them. When the "wild-looking representatives" saw the shameful offering from Dodge—thirteen guns and $250 worth of merchandise—the western Indians just left, unimpressed with U.S. power.[52]

Bent and the Cheyennes knew the U.S. Army couldn't broker a peace. Between 1835 and 1837, a series of violent, unprofitable years, which the Kiowa called the "winter that they dragged the head" or the "summer that the Cheyenne were massacred," roiled the Plains. The U.S. Army took over several trading posts on the central Plains and in Texas, but when soldiers and sutlers didn't seem to know how to trade, Bent's Fort became the only game in town. The fort was crucial as the arms depot for the Cheyenne and Arapaho expansion into Comanchería. It was profitable, but supplying competing enemies from martial cultures had risks.[53]

A truly shocking event, far to the south in the old Mexican trading town of San Antonio, drove the Comanche into the Bents' arms. In 1839, facing pressures from the Cheyenne and Arapaho to the north and the Osage to the east, along with the ravages of smallpox and cholera, the Comanche decided to consider peace with the new Texas Republic. The Comanche had long enjoyed good relationships and ongoing trade with many Mexican towns. To protect those relationships, Comanches agreed to meet with Texas officials in San Antonio and discuss the return of White captives. It went all wrong.

In March 1840 sixty-six Comanche peace diplomats arrived in San Antonio to begin discussions. They brought only a few White and Mexican captives, instead of the scores, among them children, whom the Texans wanted returned. Sure that the Comanches would never return their children, Texas officials sent soldiers into the council house where the unarmed diplomats were meeting. The soldiers were supposed to take Comanches hostage and hold them until all the captives appeared. Instead, the soldiers killed the unarmed Comanches who were standing outside the council house. In the melee that followed, most of the Comanches who were inside escaped. Comanches would never make peace with Texans again. By breaking basic rules of Indian diplomacy, Texans had proved themselves uncivilized and, more than that, inhuman.[54]

The result was mayhem. The Comanches killed their captives and went on a series of revenge raids, remembered forever in Texas history as the Great Raid. Hundreds of warriors attacked outlying communities, murdering men and women and capturing children. Comanches killed twenty-five White Texans in the Great Raid and took many more as prisoners. They burned many towns to the ground and took tons of goods. The Texas militia responded in August 1840 with a battle at Plum Creek, where neither side claimed victory. These battles made the Comanche more interested in allying with the Cheyenne, who could get them guns and ammunition and help them protect their southern Plains empire against the perfidious Texans.[55]

War grew so costly for everyone that it became predatory. Comanches and Cheyennes raided each other, leaving villages destroyed and thousands of horses and children stolen. The Cheyennes offered peace first, sending messengers among the Comanches and Kiowas. White Thunder's successor, Lame Medicine, and the Comanche leader Buffalo Hump decided that they had to seek peace. William Bent served as broker. Five nations sent leaders to meet at Two Butte

Creek on the Arkansas. After exchanging gifts and prisoners, they planned a great peace conference for the following summer at Bent's Fort. Because trade was the center of their discussion, and Bent's Fort was run by a man who understood trade and had good manners, the location made sense.[56]

They all met southeast of Bent's Fort in the summer of 1840, a year the Cheyenne called "Giving Presents to One Another Across the Water." Weeks of gift giving, feasting, and trading led to a long-lasting general peace on the central Plains, in what is now Colorado, New Mexico, and Texas east of the Rockies. Rather than the thirteen guns and measly pile of blankets that the U.S. government had offered in 1833, William Bent brought hundreds of guns and thousands of blankets, hats, and dresses. He slaughtered dozens of cattle and cooked chicken and lamb for thousands. He understood that generosity now would create powerful obligations into the future. It meant his children could grow up safely with the love of their White and Indian families.[57]

George Bent, born in 1843, didn't experience the summer of 1840, but he later understood that the "Great Peace" had made his childhood glorious. A gorgeous piece of ledger art, done by the Southern Cheyenne Howling Wolf in the 1870s, depicts the joy and peace created when Comanches, Kiowas, Arapahos, and Cheyennes hugged each other and danced under the stars. They exchanged horses, and George Bent's father offered beautiful Mexican saddles and bridles to celebrate this hopeful moment, a peace that would keep bison hunting a profitable enterprise for the entire Plains region. A hundred traders, nearly all of them married or kin to native people, worked at Bent's Fort in those years. Thousands more worked in other trading posts along the Arkansas and Red rivers, or in Santa Fe and Taos. Cheyenne, Arapaho, Wichita, and now Kiowa and Comanche people gathered in huge summer villages to trade and marry.[58]

When the 1840s began, the bison and hide trade boomed, the Cheyenne and Arapaho expanded their human and horse populations, and the Bent family had wealth and influence. Whether in Michigan or Oregon, along the Missouri River or the Arkansas, mixed-descent lives seemed possible. William Bent, who married three Cheyenne women and a mixed-blood Blackfoot woman, hoped it would last forever. But the good times proved fragile. Peace meant many more bison could be killed, too soon destroying the resource that provided safety and plenty.

=7=

Rivers of Trouble in
Indian Country, 1831–1843

Everyone in Indian country looked forward to the arrival of the spring boats carrying trade goods upriver. In busy Otoe villages, clustered just south of the Drips and Fontenelle post at Bellevue, happy children greeted boatmen and helped unload boxes of goods. But in the spring of 1831, nestled amid hair ribbons, combs, and sugar, there were invisible smallpox germs. Days later people broke out in pustules. The bales of pressed furs they loaded on boats heading downriver to St. Louis carried even more smallpox virus. People fired guns to warn others to stay away from boats carrying smallpox victims.[1]

In 1832 the river brought another deadly load. Boats carried New York City and St. Louis newspapers with headlines that reported, "There is no business except that by Cholera: Doctors, Undertakers, and Coffinmakers." Cholera had arrived from Europe, then traveled up the St. Lawrence and Hudson rivers and west through the Great Lakes and down the Mississippi. Spread by fecal matter in water, no river town escaped cholera. At Bellevue, ten White men died, and the disease spread to nearby Otoe villages. Violent cramps, vomiting, and diarrhea caused such rapid dehydration that victims' blood thickened and couldn't circulate. Without sufficient oxygen, cholera sufferers' lips and skin turned blue. Victims could die in just hours. With brutal efficiency, by the end of 1832, cholera killed one-fourth of the Otoes.[2]

The disease was cruelly unpredictable. Pawnees, Dakotas, Crows, and Kaws, who took their entire families on summer hunts, were away from the Missouri River when the infection arrived. Macompemay protected her children by spending long seasons in the Rocky Mountains. Her kin, however—Otoes living near Missouri River forts and growing crops along riverbanks in summer—suffered disproportionately when a second wave of smallpox arrived in 1837. Indian agents and Native leaders reported bodies in every Indian lodge and stacked up in shallow graves. The loss could have been as many as fifty thousand among nations living along the Missouri River.[3]

Across the St. Mary's River from the Johnston and Schoolcraft family compound in Sault Ste. Marie, cholera struck with special force in French villages that staffed the fur trade. Many French-Canadians blamed poor Irish and English immigrants for carrying the disease. They accused their English rulers of sending poor and sick English people to Canada to take French jobs and, now, French lives. In 1819 Britain's Parliament had passed a law encouraging poor workers to emigrate to Canada instead of crowding poorhouses. Thousands had come, and now cholera spread in those poor communities. How the contagion spread and why some populations seemed so vulnerable remained a bitter question. Like blood, disease was hard to police.[4]

The mixed-descent families of Indian country had to be nimble as they faced the wholesale change brought by disease, alcohol, new trade practices, and new laws. Along with germs, every boat traveling up the river carried kegs of "spirits," the illegal whiskey and moonshine that now flooded Indian country. Different animal skins were now driving the fur trade, shifting how and where people made a living. When people moved, changed their work, and created new communities, citizenship and its associated rights and obligations—voting, taxes, and schools—became a concern. In some places, citizenship became an instrument used by state governments to keep new immigrants, free Black people, and Indigenous Americans from obtaining those rights and duties. That power to keep the United States a "White" nation was challenged by the West, where frontier conditions reshaped ideas that White immigrants carried about citizenship and property rights.[5]

Mixed-descent families managed this shifting ground with different tactics. At Bent's Fort and at Fort Vancouver in the Pacific Northwest, the 1830s still held out a future that needed and welcomed blended families. Along the Missouri River, however, people either had to change, move, or die as waves of smallpox and cholera, alcohol, and Sioux and Pawnee raiders came down the river. Facing that load of trouble, the Dripses remade themselves, while the Fontenelles simply couldn't.

Rivers of Alcohol

Alcohol was as destructive as smallpox. No one seemed immune to it—man, woman, or unborn child, White or Native, Catholic or Baptist, Otoe or Omaha. Alcohol, debt, and bad luck ruined the Fontenelle family. Lucien, Mehubane, and their five children lived at Bellevue and up the river with the Omaha, both places soaked in alcohol. That family's hopes did not survive the 1830s.

Every set of Indian trade regulations enacted by Congress from 1790 to 1840 made it illegal to produce or sell alcohol in Indian country, but no one enforced the law. Liquor, cheap to produce and easy to transport, brought heartache and murder. In 1838 illegal alcohol resulted in forty-three deaths at the Otoe and Iowa agency at Bellevue. Peter Sarpy, the agent, requested help from the military to stop whiskey smugglers. The army sent two hundred dragoons who policed the agency and the docks around the river, but they had little effect given the scale of the problem. Another Kansas agent wrote to his boss, Supt. William Clark, that he could see five distilleries just over the river in a Missouri county where alcohol was legal. He estimated that three-quarters of the local fur traders smuggled whiskey. Liquor trafficking boomed in the 1830s, when fur trade monopolies drove small operators out of business. Alcohol filled an economic gap for former fur trade workers and their Native families. Former traders distilled alcohol, and their French and Native employees transported it and drank it. Everyone became addicted.[6]

Lucien Fontenelle's White skin didn't protect him. Like so many men who endured the hard lessons of nineteenth-century boom and bust, he had a drinking problem. In 1835 another trader complained that "Fontenelle they say leads near about the same life as usual, merry-making instead of paying my debt." Because of Lucien's unreliability and his debts, the American Fur Company banished him to a distant fort along the North Platte River. Built in 1834 to test the growing bison robe trade, the little wooden post, initially called Fort William or Fort John, would become Fort Laramie. At first the trading post didn't do well, especially after Lucien arrived. Unable to afford school tuition, Lucien brought his entire family to Fort Laramie in 1837. The older boys, Logan and Albert, in their early teens now, became their father's assistants, learning the blacksmithing trade. They also worked in the post store when Lucien was "indisposed."[7]

Mehubane hated the isolation of Fort Laramie. Throughout Lucien's career, she had remained close to her Omaha family. Because Lucien rarely took his family into the field during his Rocky Mountain trading days, their children spent their lives with Omaha, French, and American blended families around Bellevue. Dusty Fort Laramie, only eighty by one hundred feet of roughhewn cottonwood palisade, seemed like a punishment to the whole family even though Lucien tried to create a semblance of his former life. In 1837 a Scottish hunting enthusiast, Sir William Drummond Stewart, made his fifth trip west to hunt and enjoy the revelry of the rendezvous. Stewart's party visited Lucien Fontenelle at Fort Laramie and noted approvingly that he had decorated the rough fort with fine engravings and that he served his visitors a meal with imported brandy. Despite Lucien's effort at grandeur, the Fort Laramie post lost money. In part, the failure was beyond his control: by 1838, smallpox had killed so many Indians that the few remaining hunters brought in only a paltry few furs.[8]

Because his salary depended on how much profit the fort made,

Lucien now owed enormous sums to the American Fur Company. Broke, the family moved back to Bellevue. The town had many mixed families, including the Dripses and their longtime friend Peter Sarpy, who ran the trading post along with his Iowa wife Nico-mi. The Sarpys and the Dripses, both surviving the challenges of the moment, paid for the older Fontenelle boys to return to school. As Lucien's fur trade fortunes disappeared, he tried everything. He begged for money from his sister in New Orleans and got a small loan to keep afloat. As his health failed, he asked a traveling Jesuit to baptize his children and to recognize his marriage with Mehubane in the Catholic Church. Lucien Fontenelle died at home in Bellevue in early 1840. He was only forty and he left five children.[9]

From Kawsmouth to Westport

That spring of 1840, saddened but not surprised by Lucien's death, Andrew Drips left Bellevue to lead the American Fur Company wagons west, for what would be the last big fur trade rendezvous in the Rocky Mountains. Macompemay no longer accompanied him even when he wintered with his hunting brigades in the field. She stayed behind to care for their growing family, the children now attending school in St. Louis and Kansas City.[10]

To enter the evolving fur trade, the Drips children needed formal education and connections to a range of ambitious frontier families. Education offered a path to the middle-class security that Andrew sought for his children. Several times when he felt his life was in danger, he wrote letters to friends requesting that if anything happened to him, they should educate his children. The Drips boys, Charles and William, would both enroll at the preparatory school for Jesuit St. Louis University. Mary Jane and her younger sister Catherine attended the Convent of the Sisters of St. Joseph in an old St. Louis neighborhood. The girls learned French, English, mathematics, and drawing. Along with the daughters of other elite St. Louisans, French-Osage girls, Omaha and Sac-Fox daughters of prosperous traders, and Kaw and Shawnee "half-breeds" all became "well-educated, well-read, and accomplished young ladies."[11]

Unsure of his future after that "last" rendezvous, Andrew Drips returned to Bellevue, where he received more sad news. Their youngest child, three-year-old Glorvina, had succumbed to a fever, endemic on the river that summer. By 1840 the Missouri River fur trade world had become dangerous. The rules for coexistence between Indians and Whites, settlers and fur traders, had changed precipitously. Andrew's Native family gave him options as he considered leaving the fur trade. Because of Macompemay's Otoe heritage, the family could live on the Otoe reservation. But instead they decided to explore the settler world of merchants, real estate, and slaves. Late in 1840, after two decades of living at Bellevue near Macompemay's Otoe village, the Dripses moved to Westport, Kansas.[12]

Westport began as a trading community called Kawsmouth because it stood where the Kansas or Kaw River flows into the Missouri. It would become Kansas City in the 1850s. Whatever people called it, for decades the town was the border between the United States and Indian country. Federal legislation in 1834 laid it out: "All that part of the United States west of the Mississippi, and not within the states of Missouri and Louisiana, or the Territory of Arkansas . . . shall be deemed Indian Country." Indian country started at Kawsmouth on the Kansas–Missouri border and extended west to the Rocky Mountains. Its southern borders were the Red River and the Arkansas, where William Bent and Mistanta had built a life.[13]

What had once been a Native place, then a tensely shared trading world of Europeans and Native people, was shifting into an American settler world that saw little use for Indians. In the 1840s those changes transformed Kawsmouth into Westport. There local Indigenous people and refugee nations, driven from their homelands by U.S. policy and warfare, all remade their lives. Old French families like the Chouteaus settled in Kawsmouth and made families among Osage, Kaw, and Shawnee people. The first baptism by a Catholic priest took place at Ligueste Chouteau's house. It celebrated little

Henri Mongrain, son of Noel Mongrain and his Osage wife Ton-papi, indicating how that community built itself.[14]

The Drips family fit right in. People like Andrew Drips—traders and hunters and boatmen—set up new businesses in Kawsmouth. Some trader families farmed, while others opened lumber mills, ran freighting companies, or brewed alcohol. Real estate speculation and town site planning fed the new economy. Trader families also came because the U.S. government had promised Native wives and mixed-descent children land on nearby Indian reservations in what is now eastern Kansas and Nebraska. Macompemay and her children were entitled to land designated the "Otoe Half-Breed Reserve," but that land had been in legal limbo for a decade already, so Westport seemed like a better bet.[15]

There is a myth that the fur trade ended in the 1840s. In fact, aside from a brief dip in numbers of pelts shipped to London in 1840, and again in 1848 and 1849 when the California Gold Rush filled wagons and ships with prospectors rather than goods, the fur trade expanded throughout the nineteenth century. The business matured, in the way that all western extractive industries did, so that a few large companies controlled almost everything. The Hudson's Bay Company and the American Fur Company drove most of their competitors out of business. Prices for beaver in New York, London, and Canton steadily increased. Half a continent had been trapped out, but a vast supply of beaver, mink, marten, muskrat, otter, and bison remained. The individual trapper and hunter became anachronisms in a corporate enterprise. Many aging fur traders like Andrew Drips, worn down by the physically demanding work, considered moving on to other trades in the early 1840s. Thousands of people still depended on the trade, but fur was no longer the sole business in western communities.[16]

As its core economies shifted in the 1840s, the Missouri River borderland became an Anglo-American settlers' frontier. To succeed in this new setting, the Drips family adapted. They bought town lots and used Black slaves, always part of western settlement, to do the hard work of building in this new setting. To make it easier for Andrew to manage business and property records, Macompemay changed her name. Now Margaret Jackson Drips, she and Andrew "married" in 1841, so Andrew could have her operate his affairs in his absence. In 1844, Charles, the eldest son, bought an interest in the riverboat *Omega*.[17]

Andrew Drips struggled to find work that supported his family. Some Kawsmouth residents opened trading posts that specialized first in the Indian trade, then in groceries, clothing, or lumber when the community evolved into Westport and then into Kansas City. The fur trade still created a lot of business for merchants. Barges or flotillas of canoes coming downriver from the upper Missouri delivered hundreds of men with a season's pay in their pockets. They jumped off the boats eager to buy booze, tobacco, new guns, and clothes. Andrew tried selling goods but found that too many other men operated such businesses. His decades of fur trade experience didn't translate into profits.[18]

So in 1842 Andrew Drips went back to work for the American Fur Company. He made long trips west along the Platte River and headed north into what is now South Dakota trading for bison hides with Pawnee and Dakota villages. However, his income was sporadic and the work dangerous as Plains nations protected their interests. When the chance came to take on a government position for the Indian Service—regular and well-paid work—Drips jumped at it.[19]

The Indian Service was becoming increasingly significant to Indian country economies and politics in the 1840s. Fur trade families, once central to the economy, were now policed by federal bureaucracies aiming to keep Indians away from land they had ceded to the United States and to keep White people out of reserved Native land. But who was White or Native? Andrew Drips made his choice as a White man, but his Otoe-White children faced their own choices amid shifting global intellectual currents on race and bitter debates over federal policy, increasingly mired in Christian theology.

Race and Family Tension on the Great Lakes

The challenges facing intermarried people on the Missouri River were honed in the Great Lakes. In his years as an Indian agent and

husband to Jane Johnston, Henry Schoolcraft adjusted to changing responsibilities. Instead of regulating the fur trade, Henry's job
became pushing Indians out of Michigan. The aim of Indian policy
now was to turn Ojibwe hunting lands into profit-making forests and
farmlands. The new policy put Henry and Jane's marriage, their relationship with her Ojibwe relations, and Henry's position in the Great
Lakes community into conflict. Native resistance to the U.S. policy
of removal brought American troops to Michigan and trouble into
the Johnston household. In December 1830 Jane Johnston Schoolcraft faced another Great Lakes winter and another family disaster.[20]

Jane's terrible Christmas began when James Schoolcraft, Henry's
younger brother, got into a brawl with a local soldier and "stabed him
in the sid with nif or Dager." The fight took place in Mackinac, a full
day's paddle in summer and a four-day winter snowshoe trip from
Sault Ste. Marie. James was arrested and tossed in jail. Jane heard
the news when the Mackinac jailer sent a letter notifying them of
James's crime. Henry wasn't there. He'd decided to spend the winter
of 1830 in Detroit, pursuing his political and literary interests. Stuck
in the Sault with three-year-old Janee and one-year-old Johnston
Schoolcraft, Jane and her brother George Johnston managed Henry's Indian agency and now James's mess.[21]

So it was Jane who received James's suicide threat, his "only
recourse" if he were to be jailed for his actions. His letter included an
expression of his wish to run away "like an Indian" and "be killed in
the woods," indicating how law enforcement often worked in frontier
Michigan. Jane sent family friends, a minister and a lawyer, to coun-
sel him. To add to the family morass, James had recently announced
that he intended to court Jane's younger sister, Anna Maria, now
eighteen. Susan Johnston, Jane and Anna Maria's Ojibwe mother,
didn't trust James and made a great effort to keep the relationship
from developing. Keeping them apart, however, proved challenging
in Michigan winters when they all lived so close together. To demonstrate her love for James, Anna Maria threatened to run away and
help him escape from jail.[22]

When the young man that James stabbed did not die, James
avoided a murder charge and now faced trial on a lesser crime.

Despite that good news, in February 1831 James escaped from jail in Mackinac and returned to Sault Ste. Marie. Henry Schoolcraft and his mother-in-law, Susan Johnston, lost patience. Lacking judgment or a job, James was hardly the husband Susan wanted for her youngest daughter. Henry forced James to return to Mackinac for trial and to pay his fines. Jane demanded that he become a good confessing Christian and "avert wrath of that Holy Being he had hitherto so despised." Henry and Susan arranged to have James work as a purchasing agent for the family business, so that he would spend most of his time in Albany, Detroit, and Mackinac, away from Anna Maria.[23]

The episode reveals telling racial patterns. James's actions had few consequences. He continued to enjoy himself in ways that infuriated Henry and that were permissible only for White men in the region. James wrote to a friend in January 1832 that "we had a Grand ball here last night and I danced till I was Blue." He added that the "Gala broke up" when soldiers ejected some "Indian lads who didn't like our dancing." White men could be forgiven a stabbing or two, and they could "take" Native women who didn't want to dance. Native men were killed in the woods.[24]

What we can't fully see in family letters, Indian agency records, and account books is how Susan Johnston's Ojibwe family experienced such changes. Her uncles and brothers had much say over who did what in the Johnston family. These men were Ojibwe leaders descended from the first settlers at Sault Ste. Marie in the eighteenth century. Now they were dealing with the United States. Ojibwe villages encircled Sault Ste. Marie. Two of Susan's sisters, Charlotte and Madeleine, Ojibwe women married to successful French-Canadian traders, lived in town and spent a great deal of time in the Johnston household. Susan never traveled alone: her brothers and sisters accompanied her on fishing, trading, and rice-gathering trips. They cared for, advised, nagged, and now grew to depend on their Johnston nieces and nephews as translators of news carried in by Henry Schoolcraft. Jane described the change in a poem: "to gain one sordid bit of gold," her forested world had been replaced with "lawsuits, meetings, courts, and toil."[25]

That news now concerned Indian removal, official policy of the

United States. Several developments made targets of Native communities: Indian war in the Old Northwest, the discovery of gold on Cherokee lands in Georgia, and demands from settler families for access to the fertile, already broken and fenced land that Indigenous families had long worked. The federal government, working with full support from states, unfurled an arsenal of weapons. Supreme Court decisions in the 1820s made "removing" Indian people legal. In 1830 President Andrew Jackson announced a program to move Indian communities west across the Mississippi, bringing intense pressure to exchange their homes for land elsewhere. That year, in a rehearsal for what would happen to southern Indians, Senecas and Delawares were evicted from their land along Ohio's Sandusky River, despite treaties promising them that land, signed by presidents Jefferson, Madison, and Adams. As refugees, they marched to Kansas. When some Native communities refused to leave, as happened in Sauk and Fox towns on Illinois's Bad Axe River in 1832, White men burned their villages and fields and drove them out of their houses at gunpoint. The U.S. military completed the task.[26]

Removal, carried out by the military and paid for out of sales of Indian land, put Henry Schoolcraft, and all Indian agents, in an impossible position. Since furs were still bringing in huge profits, powerful fur companies wanted Native people to hunt, but now government policy required Indians to sign treaties and move to small reservations. Henry's job required making and enforcing peace treaties between Indian nations, so that they could hunt and share territory. Because of removal, bands of Fox, Ho-Chunk, and Dakota hunted and built villages on land that had been promised to relocated Ojibwes. It was a formula for conflict.[27]

The change in policy caused Henry to worry justifiably about losing his appointment. To impress his superiors and to demonstrate how essential fur trading remained in Michigan, Henry prepared a chart of his Lake Superior agency. He emphasized its scale, with forty Ojibwe trading posts serving "6252 Indians, 50 traders, and 268 Boatmen and Clerks," who brought in "peltries worth $72,716.23." Such big business reflected the work of generations of traders who had built trading posts where Native people wanted them and entered kin relationships that cemented trust and loyalty. Removal, pressure to give up land, and war threatened such efforts. Henry described the tense treaty negotiations that he managed around the entire Great Lakes. Many Ojibwes, angry that the U.S. Army had not punished Sioux and Fox raiding parties for crossing the line they had all agreed on in 1826, snubbed Henry and refused to participate in talks. A warrior named Flatmouth warned that he was no longer willing to "see our young men, our wives, and our children murdered." He dramatically threw his peace medals, wampum belts, and treaty papers at Henry Schoolcraft's feet, claiming they were stained with blood.[28]

Henry's lobbying was fruitless: he soon learned that all the Great Lakes agencies would be consolidated into a single office in Mackinac. In the summer of 1832, he rehired George Johnston to repair the new agency in Mackinac while Henry traveled. George was still angry at Henry for firing him two years earlier. He had attempted to find work outside the fur trade as a merchant and importer but had failed miserably. George didn't want to rely on Henry, but after his wife's death in 1831, he had few choices and three young children to support. Swallowing his pride, George agreed to assist Henry in Mackinac. He brought his daughter Louisa but left his two boys with their grandmother, Susan Johnston, who took them with her to the annual summer Ojibwe gathering to fish and hunt northwest of Sault Ste. Marie.[29]

Henry traveled all summer and came home only for a brief visit before he headed to Detroit, New York, and Washington, D.C., to spend the fall of 1832 lobbying to keep more Indian agencies open. Maybe he felt guilty—the next boat after he left carried back a black silk dress for Jane made by a Detroit dressmaker, a load of pears and quinces, and six new pairs of shoes for the children. Henry came home six weeks later, taking the last boat to cut through the already icy lake waters. Because his efforts in Washington failed, the entire family would move to Mackinac. He knew that move would be hard for Jane, who never flourished away from her Johnston and Ojibwe kin.[30]

Jane agreed to the move because she wanted more educational opportunities for her children. She knew her own poor health made her an impatient "first teacher" for her children, in either Ojibwe or English. But Jane also wanted them to have Ojibwe values and strengths. She dreamed about the children, including dead little Willy, and told Henry that they "were sometimes delightful animals." Henry certainly knew Ojibwe dreams mattered. If Jane dreamed of hawks or moose, it was a good sign, but deer or hares meant threats were near. She ensured that her children spent a lot of time "with their dear Grandy and Aunty's."[31]

Jane put a good face on the 1833 move to Mackinac, but their first winter away proved to be a disaster. James Schoolcraft was back in Sault Ste. Marie, using Henry's Indian Service connections to get appointed as a sutler to Fort Brady, a lucrative position that involved purchasing goods for the entire fort. He also renewed his relationship with Anna Maria Johnston. Anna Maria wrote to Jane and Henry in Mackinac that she expected a proposal and that her family had become "reconciled to it." Hardly reconciled, Jane's younger sister Eliza began a smear campaign, accusing James of "whoring (excuse the term) drunkenness and all manner of lewdness and the like," as James wrote indignantly to Henry.[32]

James defended himself vigorously, but Susan Johnston fought even harder. She found an ally in her new son-in-law, William McMurray, a Scottish Anglican minister who had recently married Charlotte Johnston. Susan and William forbade James from entering the Johnston house, but James and Anna Maria simply ignored the order. McMurray reported that "Maria has acted in every way contrary to her Mamma's wishes." James wrote that he had to protect "poor Anna Maria" from her mother, who in anger had hit Anna Maria with a fire poker. Jane, stuck in Mackinac, could only remind her family that "we all cannot plead ignorance of their attachment for it has existed for years." Six months later James and Anna Maria would wed, though the Johnston family never liked the match.[33]

The excitement over James and Anna Maria dimmed, but only in contrast to that which George Johnston now provided. Because of his drinking or because he was easily swayed by power and money, George had failed in several positions of trust. After Henry appointed him Indian agent at La Pointe in 1828 and 1829, George had allowed unlicensed traders to operate in his region, and he had bought their furs on the side, entirely illegal and entirely commonplace. Henry had fired George in 1830 from the post of subagent in Sault Ste. Marie for insubordination. When the Indian Service reshuffled agency appointments, George was dealt out. In 1830s Michigan, government jobs and other political favors went only to White men. Lewis Cass, now secretary of war under President Jackson and an old friend of the Johnston family, explained to Henry that George's "Indian nature" made it impossible for him to avoid being "unduly influenced."[34]

White men were hardly less "influenced," since the point of having a government job on the frontier was personal profit. Many Indian agents operated stores right next to their agencies, sold government goods as their own, and bought land from tribes they served. Graft was as common along the Great Lakes as water and was limited only by lack of imagination. Like his neighbors, George invested in some businesses that failed and in others that were in direct conflict with his government positions. For most agents, the cost of bad behavior was a reprimand, but because George was an Indian, he lost his position.

In 1834 George and Henry had another falling-out that followed what was now a continuing pattern of conflict. When Henry traveled to Detroit or New York, George stepped in, looked after the agency in Mackinac, and reported on the Schoolcraft children, visitors to the office, and the funeral of his Ojibwe cousin, "Waish-kees son Caw-kot, attended by almost every person at this place." Trouble came when Henry returned after five months and began ordering George around. According to George's version of the final "battle" with Henry, which he sent to Lewis Cass, George arrived at the agency in Mackinac one morning and perceived "in Mr. S's manner that a storm was brooding in his heart." Rather than endure the storm, George went to the blacksmith shop to make a doll bed for Janee. Henry called George into the office and "accosted" him in "angry severe language," saying he had left the office unattended while building toys. Schoolcraft listed the duties that George had ignored, including sweeping, going to the post office, and opening the agency on time. George retorted that he wasn't paid to undertake such lowly tasks and quit in a huff.[35]

Henry and George barely spoke for a year. George moved his family back to Sault Ste. Marie, where his extended family could support him. George tried hard. He offered up his services as an Ojibwe linguist, he wrote to his father's relatives in England hoping they might have some business opportunities for this poor "American relation and son of the forest." He wrote to Jane, regularly, and to James Schoolcraft, who teased him about being in the "selective club" of people who had not lived up to Henry's standards. James tried to make George feel better by listing the nasty things Henry had said to him over the years.[36]

James enjoyed every benefit as a White man in frontier Michigan. After assaulting a man, being arrested for drunkenness, and being fired for stealing from the government, he was elected to several county offices. He supervised elections and licensed people to marry. Meanwhile George, an Indian, was shut out from banking networks and barred from serving on juries. The line between Indian and White, formerly quite flexible, was growing sharp and distinct, dividing even members of the same fur trade family.

Thomas McKay's Columbia River

Similar changes were afoot in 1830s Oregon Country. Shared by the United States and Great Britain since 1818, it included most of British Columbia, Washington, Oregon, and Idaho. Alaska was still claimed by a Russian fur trading company. Joint British-American occupation of Oregon Country meant that both nations could trade across the entire Pacific Northwest and colonize the region. Both sought sole occupation of the Columbia River and the potential ports around Puget Sound, although only the Hudson's Bay Company had any real presence there. Fort Vancouver, built by the Company on the north shore of the Columbia, served its vast trading area from San Francisco Bay in Mexican California to Russian Alaska. Throughout the 1830s, Company brigades had roamed inland to the Rocky Mountains of Montana and Utah, unchallenged by U.S. fur traders even when they ran into American Fur Company outfits.[37]

Thomas McKay, a mixed-blood Canadian with Chinook-British children, made a life in the Oregon of the Hudson's Bay Company. While McKay's three Chinook sons attended boarding school, he began a relationship with a Cayuse woman. They had two children, Donald and Wenix. When McKay left the fur trade and eastern Oregon, just as his own father Alexander had three decades earlier, Thomas left that family behind. In 1838, Thomas married a young French-Cree woman, Isabelle Montour, the daughter of Nicholas Montour, Jr., and Susanne Umfreville. Migrating from French Canada, Isabelle's family had worked in Oregon since the 1820s. Her uncles and father, former servants of the Hudson's Bay Company who had moved west with the fur trade, now lived as hunters and farmers in the Willamette Valley. They had all married Cree or French-Cree women from the interior of Canada and brought those family traditions to the Columbia River. Because so few priests came to the Columbia region, local fort leaders conducted most marriages. Representing the authority of Hudson's Bay Company, chief factor John McLoughlin,Thomas's stepfather, signed civil marriage contracts between HBC employees and Native or mixed-blood women.[38]

Despite such common civil contracts and informal family weddings, the first Catholic priests at Vancouver found themselves in great demand because people wanted their marriages and children recognized by the church. Many people remarried when a priest became available. Thomas and Isabelle were married by the first Catholic priest to appear at Fort Vancouver, Father François Blanchet, on December 31, 1838. Isabelle's parents, informally married at Fort Dauphine around 1815, joined their daughter and her new husband in a mass marriage ceremony for dozens of couples that welcomed the New Year of 1839.[39]

Thomas, well past forty and now with three families of children to provide for, managed several Hudson's Bay Company farms along the Willamette River. Thomas and Isabelle soon had five children, beginning with Maria, born in 1839, and followed by Thomas, Catherine, George, and William. McKay never settled much into farming and began to lead expeditions to southern Oregon and California. In 1840 he bought 3,600 sheep and 661 cattle from Mexican ranchers in California and drove them to the Willamette Valley, hoping to introduce sheep and cattle ranching to the HBC suite of enterprises. In the early 1840s, as American migration to the region slowly increased, the McKay family's world was still Native, French, and controlled by the Hudson's Bay Company.[40]

Concerned over the HBC's power in Oregon, expansionists in the U.S. Senate began bringing the Pacific Northwest and its potential into public view. Between 1838 and 1842, Congress funded an ambitious and expensive expedition to circumnavigate and explore the Pacific, repeating what British Capt. James Cook had done fifty years earlier. Led by Capt. Charles Wilkes, the grandly named U.S. Exploring Expedition comprised a navy of six ships carrying sailors, artists, and scientists. U.S. politicians and investors watched reports from the expedition carefully to determine opportunities in the Pacific. The ships visited the Columbia River and Native nations up and down the Pacific Coast. In 1841 members of the expedition's overland party met and breakfasted with Thomas McKay at his Willamette farm. U.S. Navy officers described him as "one of the most noted individuals in this part of the country . . . and the hero of many a tale."[41]

Even as U.S. and British diplomats argued over borders and legal arrangements, few Americans actually lived in Oregon Country. Rhetoric in U.S. newspapers about the need to colonize the region to protect settlers' "rights" bubbled up over only a few dozen residents. They included the founders of two Methodist missions in the Willamette Valley where Thomas and Isabelle lived in 1839, plus a few Americans who drifted up from Mexican California. Those new arrivals saw that the Hudson's Bay Company built and owned everything: docks, sawmills, fields, boats, and houses. It even owned the cows. To develop the Company's agricultural interests, John McLoughlin gave both Canadian and American settlers access to livestock, loaning them out in pairs to farmers but never selling them. All calves born were Company property. One American, Ewing Young, built a saw mill and a flour mill in the Willamette Valley, but without access to British and Russian ships that controlled Pacific Coast trade, such businesses remained small.[42]

The first effort in 1838 to form a government, a "mass meeting" in the old French and Indian village of Champoeg, included thirty-six people, many of whom were French speakers. One longtime settler recalled a peaceable kingdom, a happy combination of French-Canadian former HBC employees, whose "gentle dispositions caused them to take kindly to retirement," and ex–mountain men who had "settled in the Willamette Valley after years of hardship, privations, and daring." These settlers, Canadian and American, he wrote, had "Indian consorts who were patient, obedient, and . . . constant workers." The Oregon residents "lived in an easy and careless fashion with their Indian wives and their half-breed children, without cares." "What more could they ask?" he mused. But the idyll would soon end in conflicts over race, citizenship, and who deserved this place.[43]

Andrew Drips, Special Agent

Mixed-blood families struggled to protect themselves in other places. Andrew Drips tried a career as a merchant in Kansas City but found that work unstable and boring. He'd gone back to trading with Dakotas and Pawnees, but his business remained uneven. When in 1842 he was offered a longer-term government appointment as special agent to the upper Missouri, he took it. The promise of a stable government salary convinced him to become an alcohol policeman for the U.S. government. It was, simply, an impossible job in that alcohol-soaked world. Paternalistic laws meant to keep alcohol away from Indians did not deter soldiers, priests, traders, and Indian agents from drinking and selling it. Immeasurable in both quantity and value, liquor flowed up and down rivers and along trails throughout Indian country.[44]

The success of the alcohol industry was reflected in the mounting efforts to stop it. Hefty new fines appeared in the 1830s: $500 and trade licenses revoked for selling alcohol to Indians, and $300 just for bringing alcohol into Indian country. With average yearly incomes of about $800 per household, those fines were steep. In addition, anyone who sold or transported alcohol had their furs, hides, or trade goods confiscated.[45]

The enforcers were Indian Service officials and the U.S. Army. "Informants" were rewarded with half the "goods, boats, packages, and peltries" of anyone they turned in. People turned on their competitors. As the biggest operator on the Missouri River, the American Fur Company received the most accusations of selling liquor to Indians from the federal government and other traders. And if the American Fur Company couldn't sell whiskey, it didn't want anyone else to sell it either. So it decided to support the U.S. government's move to hire Andrew Drips, who had just retired from their company, as special agent.[46]

In the spring of 1842, Drips became a government agent charged with "preventing the introduction of ardent spirits into the Indian Country." According to his instructions, he was to "traverse the whole country within your limits," a vast space that included all forts and posts north from St. Louis to the Canadian border and west to the Rocky Mountains. His instructions breezily told him to leave the Sioux country "well scoured" of alcohol, and to see that all stills in Arikara, Gros Ventre, and Mandan villages were "emptied and destroyed" by spring. Then he could head farther up the Missouri, which the superintendent in St. Louis, ensconced in his comfortable office, promised "would be a pleasant journey through picturesque country." The trip would take Drips to Fort Union and the Blackfoot posts, where dozens of traders had recently been killed.[47]

Earnest but soon frustrated, Drips found that alcohol mysteriously disappeared whenever he arrived at a fort. He got reports of "rascals in their drunken frolicks" and of boats heading up the Missouri with kegs of alcohol and new stills, but news of his arrival beat him up the river. Even when he did find barrels of whiskey and brandy to pour into rivers, or managed to break down a few stills, he had to contend with loopholes in the law itself. The federal laws passed in 1834 held that the only people who could legally trade alcohol in Indian country were Native people, and traders who had married Native or mixed-blood women. A trader with Native kin could accept furs or hides from Native hunters in exchange for alcohol that he had produced or bought just outside the borders of Indian country in places like New Mexico, Missouri, and Iowa. William Bent had used this loophole for years to sell Mexican and U.S. alcohol from his fort and in all the Cheyenne villages around it.[48]

Government attempts to enforce laws about drinking and trading, however, highlighted a new agenda to reshape the fur trade world. When Andrew Drips left his family in Westport for the dangerous work of stopping illegal alcohol, he knew that no matter what happened to him or to the fur trade, his family would have land. Andrew had bought land in Kansas City to supplement what the government had promised to the Drips children as "half-breeds" of the Otoe nation. That promise, created and upheld in treaty after treaty, now, in the 1840s, became a place: the Great Nemaha Half-Breed Tract. There, in small villages that had belonged to Otoes for generations, south of the Platte along the Great Nemaha River, blended families and their Native kin settled. Native peoples, having steadfastly refused to give up lives that mixed hunting, farming, and gathering—and to continue just as their White neighbors lived—had also steadfastly refused to give up their land or their understandings of family. They just added cattle and pig production and lumbering to hunting and gardening. The Nemaha tract seemed reasonably safe—even as more American farmers, merchants, and missionaries arrived in Kansas and the value of Great Nemaha land increased.[49]

The Drips family plan fell apart when Macompemay died on June 1, 1846, in her mid-forties. She had borne five children and had watched too many of her relatives die from the sicknesses that plagued river towns. We don't know what she died of or how long she suffered, but Andrew resigned from his position as special Indian agent and was quickly back home in Westport. Approaching sixty, with complicated responsibilities, he had to figure out what to do next about his family and fortunes.

The "Half-Breed Army"

Like Andrew Drips in Kansas, George Johnston in Michigan had children to launch into a world that was developing new rules about livelihoods and land ownership. But Johnston, unlike Drips, faced those challenges as Indian or Irish-Ojibwe. As the expanding American state and its settlers pressured Native nations to give up land, new treaties required Indians to move to ever smaller reservations. Mixed-descent people explained the new rules and helped their Indian families develop new ways of making a living. Shut out of the world of elite fur traders, George and his brother William instead worked as translators for the Indian Service. As bearers of bad news about unwelcome change to Indian communities, these translators did uncomfortable duty.

George and William held these positions in an era when the United States was expanding its borders faster than it could police them. As war, land theft, and removal increased the size of the nation, the question of who had the right to the benefits and responsibilities of U.S. citizenship became a dangerous issue. Could non-White people be citizens? Former slaves and Indian leaders petitioned for citizenship. White reformers, especially Christian activists engaged in the abolition movement, began a fierce debate over Indian removal. New Englanders worked with Cherokee, Creek, and Shawnee leaders to demand that the U.S. Congress grant Native people citizenship, now that so many were farmers and Christians. To slave owners, who wanted to expand their own operations into Indian land, any discussion of broadening citizenship was a mortal threat. They shut down national debate, and federal officials refused to engage the citizenship question.[50]

The era of expansion, roughly from 1830 to 1860, also included filibustering, an extreme version of expansion carried out by private expeditions. One of its advocates defined the activity as "wars of conquest waged by the strong against the weak" that allowed "provident and skillful whites to gloriously civilize." Groups of Anglo-Americans, Frenchmen, and Mexicans sailed or marched over borders intending to form their personal fiefdoms or build slave plantations, regardless of what people actually living in those places thought or did. Certain of their superiority and the rightness of their vision, filibusters never apologized for attacking foreign nations or killing local citizens, and much of the American public cheered them on. The same disdain for any rule or limit encouraged Americans to defy weak federal and state authorities in their own nation during the era of "try and make me."[51]

Amid such disturbances, George Johnston and a group of Canadian fur trade sons considered embarking on their own nation-building adventure. In 1831 a new CEO of the Hudson's Bay Company, George Simpson, had announced that "country-born Canadians" could never be HBC leaders. Using a polite term for young men with Native mothers married to HBC fathers in the "custom of the country," Simpson told a generation of talented, well-educated, but mixed-descent traders' sons that they weren't part of Canada's White world. Those young men also understood that their Native kin needed protection from expanding White America. Bitterly, they proposed a solution: what if such men, shut out of advancement in the fur trade, created a separate North American nation as a haven for Indian families?[52]

In the summer of 1836, George Johnston ran a trading post on isolated St. Joseph's Island, partway between Sault Ste. Marie and Mackinac. Proud and poor, without anyone to lend him money or employ him, George had gone into the Indian trade again. He'd left his children with his mother and sisters in Sault Ste. Marie. Because of his confrontation with Henry and his subsequent firing, only the efforts of his Cadot uncles, married to his Ojibwe aunts, had gotten him this post. After a lonely winter and a summer with little trade, George received an invitation that promised to change his life.[53]

Earlier that year a mysterious man named James Dickson, calling himself General Montezuma II of the Indian Liberating Army, appeared in East Coast cities. Claiming variously to be a Scottish fur trader, a Mexican Army officer, and a Native chief, Dickson was most notable for a dashing uniform of his own design. With those credentials, he raised money and gathered followers to invade either Mexico or California. In that 1830s moment, so overheated by news of rebellions everywhere—Texas, France, Mexico, California, Canada—Dickson's vision of invasion was hardly noteworthy. His plan to establish an "Indian kingdom in the far west," ruled by "half-breed gentlemen," however, got attention.[54]

That vague and alluring description enabled Dickson to recruit troops. In 1836 his recruits, disgruntled men from fur trade families, rendezvoused in Buffalo, New York. They chartered a schooner to travel around the Great Lakes gathering more officers for the Liberating Army. William Nourse, a Sault Ste. Marie fur trader, warned Canadian officials about Dickson's activities. His army's plan, Nourse wrote, was to head to New Mexico to "plunder Santa Fe." Next, with Cherokee help, its members would march to California where "they mean to endeavor obtaining possession of that Country." Once they had their "kingdom in California," they would locate "all Indian tribes there, ruling them under a Military Government, preventing all except those of Indian blood from possessing an acre of land." This time blood would keep White men out.[55]

The fur trade world looked on with some alarm. Dickson's first sixty commissioned officers were the sons of elite fur traders, including Hudson's Bay and American Fur Company men who lived all around the Great Lakes and in Montreal. As captains, majors, and colonels in a "half-breed Army," as one concerned letter writer put it, "God only knows and where and when it may end."[56]

In September 1836, George Johnston received an appointment as colonel in the Indian Liberating Army. Dickson offered to give him a fantastic salary and benefits package if he could raise a "Chippewa Cavalry" of four hundred men to join the "band of brave hearts." A detailed contract from Dickson promised George a uniform that came with "swords and holster pistols . . . also a rifle," along with a salary appropriate for his title: "Colonel $2000." The commission George was being offered paid more than Henry Schoolcraft would earn as Michigan's Indian agent. Dickson's letter explained that such positions were to be held by mixed-blood men alone, for no "white officers [would] be appointed to the Regiment."[57]

George probably knew it was too good to be true. The contract explained that actual pay, and uniforms, would only come after the Liberating Army plundered Santa Fe, a year hence. But thereafter money "to purchase necessary arms and saddles and military accoutrements"—and "provisions necessary for the journey to the Rocky mountains"—would flow to the marching army. Still stinging from Henry's dismissal and surrounded by Americans who wouldn't hire him, George began recruiting. He sent letters to Ojibwe relatives telling them that Dickson was "the red man's friend" and that they should "listen to what he will say to you." George laid out the plan of "the emancipation of the suffering tribe of Indians" in a "country beyond the Rocky Mountains" that could be "a place of refuge for your women and children forever." No Ojibwes joined the "Chippewa Cavalry," but many of George's mixed-descent acquaintances did.[58]

Dickson's poor grasp of geography meant that the operation started too late in the season, and he hadn't planned for the difficulty of transporting his troops from the Red River of the North to Santa Fe. Since he hadn't been quiet about the plan, the troops were arrested for stealing cattle near Detroit and for lacking proper papers on Lake Huron, where authorities confiscated their schooner.[59]

When the much-diminished army reached Sault Ste. Marie in October 1836, George decided not to take up his commission after all. He did give Dickson's men letters of introduction, which got them boats and supplies from friendly traders. In late October they crossed Lake Superior guided by Ojibwe men and began the long trek to the Red River. One of the participants wrote that "Gauthier our boatman who is a metiff (*métis* or mixed)" warned them about the risks of traveling on Lake Superior. He told the inexperienced men that they faced "dangers & difficulties attendant upon the navigation of it at this late season."[60]

The nearly frozen Indian Liberating Army arrived at the Red River to find George Simpson, governor-general of the Hudson's Bay Company, waiting for them. Newspapers had reported every move made by "Pirates on the Lakes," so Company officials knew they were coming. Simpson used Company power and pressure from the young men's own families to get them to quit the enterprise. He offered them the golden ticket to middle-class success in Canada: appointment as officers in the Hudson's Bay Company. He knew that their families desperately desired such status for them, but the racial limitations now laid out in HBC policy had barred them. Given that reality, few mixed-descent men turned down Simpson's offer, ending the saga of James Dickson and the Indian Liberating Army.[61]

George's family teased him about his flirtation with Dickson and his Half-Breed Army. William addressed him as "the Colonel," and James Schoolcraft, now married to George's sister Anna Maria, wrote that he was having "dickson war" with Henry about management of "the Estate's affairs" and was "determined to make a vigorous siege of it." After some ribbing, George got back to work. Henry, who in January 1837 had been appointed superintendent of all of Michigan's Indians, hired George to work as an Indian Service translator.

Few people now know this story, and most accounts dismiss Dickson as a fool or a madman. But if we put Dickson's alternative vision of Indian country alongside other similar demands for equal opportunity, representative government, and shared authority bubbling up from the frontier, it looks more serious.

In 1837 the Indian agent at Bellevue, Nebraska, reported to his St. Louis superintendent on an "uprising" among Otoes and Omahas. Recent news about the victorious Seminole Indian leader "Osceola and his string of victories in Florida," the alarmed agent explained, had created some trouble. Indian victories had inspired the men of mixed descent living at the Bellevue agency, including the Fontenelle brothers, Logan and Albert, to consider mounting "a supportive uprising."[62]

The same summer Michigan Indian superintendent Henry Schoolcraft faced down "Half-Breed Chippewas" furious over an unpunished murder of one of their own. The case went to local courts, but the jury decided that because the victim was not a White man, his murder had not been a crime. Outraged, the "mixed bloods took things into their own hands," according to Lyman Warren, the trader and agent at La Pointe, where the murder had occurred. The "Half-Breed Chippewas" wrote to President William Harrison, warning that if they "were not protected by U.S. Law as citizens, they would enforce Indian Law in Indian Country." They also refused to work without contracts, creating a sudden drop in the number of furs sold in New York. Seeing a serious threat to his authority, Henry Schoolcraft summoned the "mixed bloods" to a "Chippewa council for Lake Superior and the Upper Mississippi" in the summer of 1837. A new agreement granted them more rights, and big fur companies increased the number of mixed men who were licensed to hunt and trade with Indians.[63]

Even larger rebellions brewed all over Canada. In 1837 French-Canadians mounted a series of uprisings known as the Patriots War against British authorities and the Hudson's Bay Company. Those well-planned and well-armed revolts seemed "a dangerous and evil precedent" to Henry Schoolcraft, who worried that local Native people would join. However, the French-Canadian rebellions brought an instant response from British troops stationed in Canada. They crushed the rebellions and killed or exiled the participants. French-Canadians and their allies, however, went underground to form secret organizations, called Hunter's Lodges, just over the border in the United States. There French, British, and mixed-blood refugees from Canada plotted and organized.[64]

Disgruntled mixed-descent people caused a world of personal and professional trouble for Henry Schoolcraft as he tried to improve his own situation. Aiming to be appointed governor of the new Wisconsin Territory, he wrote to the new president, Martin Van Buren, but his two pompous letters failed to win him that office. As Indian superintendent of Michigan, he decided to move Jane and the children to Detroit where, he hoped, they could escape the Johnston family turmoil. Jane insisted that Henry leave the family in Sault Ste. Marie with government jobs and monetary support. So Henry appointed William Johnston, Jane's younger brother, keeper of the "Indian dormitory," which meant he supervised workers and visitors who needed a place to sleep. George worked as a translator and interpreter at treaty negotiations between the Ojibwe and the Sioux in 1837 and again in 1839, and between the U.S. government and the Ojibwe in the 1840s.[65]

Those treaties, all of them, included a clause guaranteeing land to the tribe's "half-breed" or "mixed blood" members, which included the Johnston family. Henry Schoolcraft had previously exchanged some of those Johnston family claims—with Susan, William, and George's knowledge—for land in Detroit and speculative railroad stocks. By 1838, George's children—ages sixteen, fourteen, and thirteen—needed school fees and clothing, so he tried selling those stocks, but no one was buying what he was selling. To make Jane happy, George joined a local church. To make his mother happy, he worked with his uncle Waishkey in Ojibwe clan business. At church, he met Mary Rice, a New Englander and Baptist missionary, aged thirty-seven and never married. George, a widower since Louisa's death, needed help managing his life, and Mary wanted to learn Ojibwe. They set up housekeeping in 1839 and began a family.[66]

Watching the Johnstons struggle to find middle-class respectability increased Schoolcraft's anxiety about his own children. He made a will in 1835 stipulating that Janee attend a female seminary "in the east" and that Johnston, no longer Johnny, receive a college education to study divinity. Janee and Johnston's uncles, George, William, and John Johnston, well educated and with powerful families, continued to hope that just a little more cash or connection could make them succeed. Jane, Charlotte, and Anna Maria did better than their brothers because their White husbands provided them with protection in this increasingly unfriendly world. They prayed about "how Indian" their children would look and how they would proceed through their lives in Michigan as it became a U.S. state. Facing such new realities, at the same moment that the Drips family moved to Kansas City, the Schoolcraft family took their children east to find "suitable" schools.[67]

In December 1838, Henry reported that the family stopped in Princeton, New Jersey, and "left Johnston at the Roundhill school." The next day Jane, Henry, and Janee went to Philadelphia to visit the "Academy of Natural Sciences," where "Dr. Samuel George Morton's extensive collection of Indian crania" was displayed. They left Janee at "the private school of the Misses Guild, South Fourth Street," in Philadelphia. While Henry switched easily from measuring Indian crania to considering his children's minds, Jane felt the loss more deeply. That day she composed an elegy titled "On Leaving My Children John and Jane at School in the Atlantic States." It began in Ojibwe *May kow e yaun in*, or "my heart fills with pleasure and throbs with a fear."[68]

=8=

"Marked for Slaughter":
Borderland Violence in the 1840s

While Jane Schoolcraft wrote elegies to her past, Mistanta and her Anglo-Cheyenne family made a blended life in the present. In the early 1840s, they spent each summer in a Cheyenne village of bison-hide tepees. Along with their Cheyenne cousins, the children—Mary, Robert, and George Bent—learned how to ride horses and shoot bison and antelope with guns and arrows. In winter the family moved into the fort, where an enslaved Black cook prepared meals and old men told stories. The children learned to write in English and Spanish, and how to make deals with St. Louis and Santa Fe traders.

But that same decade brought the Mexican War, followed by gold rushes in Colorado and California. The same hunger that justified seizing Indian land in Michigan, Ohio, and Georgia, and the same White nationalism that challenged the Johnstons' mixed-blood world, also animated the Mexican War. In the 1840s, slaveholders' visions of cotton empires in the West and in Latin America drove expansion policies that led to war. But it took the powerful idea of manifest destiny to justify the blood and treasure that conquest required to the nonslaveholding majority of White Americans.

That idea recast outright land theft as God's will. People who didn't own slaves could still believe that they were doing God's work by tak-ing land from lesser peoples like Mexicans and Indians. The racial dimension was key. *New York Herald* editor James Gordon Bennett demonstrated this on his front page, announcing: "When the white races multiply . . . all the colored races will disappear." With such racist clarity illuminating their path, U.S. soldiers invaded Mexico in 1846. Undisciplined volunteer soldiers indulged in plunder, rape, and murder as they marched through Mexican and Native communities. By 1848 the outcome of that brutal war and the surprising annexation of Oregon suddenly doubled the size of the country. However, the U.S. flags that now flew over forts in the Southwest and in Oregon Country did not convey American control of these places. White set-tlement would not be easy. Conquest would run up against families like the McKays and Bents, who had not disappeared.[1]

By 1840, these families reflected the long heritage of mixed-blood life in the West. Many could trace their families back ten genera-tions. Some families stayed in the communities where they had made a success of themselves and bought property. Others built roads, drove wagons, and became mule tenders and cooks as new business came to old communities. Some mixed families incubated leaders for Native nations as they moved west, adjusting to land cessions and suing to uphold treaty rights. Others, first or second generation, still did the work of *hivernants*—wintering in Indian villages and moving animal skins along rivers.[2]

How mixed-descent families managed the changing western econ-omy and the growing legal framework around race depended on cir-cumstance. Some were educated in the non-Native world and owned land. Others hunted for a living and moved with Native villages. Some lived in households with many mothers, which were still com-mon in many communities. Many lived with a single parent or were hired help in other people's households. As race and blood became central to defining U.S. culture, mixed people imbibed prevailing ideas about racial hierarchy that elevated those who adopted White culture above those who spoke Indigenous languages and wore Native clothing. But blended families took measures to protect themselves in a White world that opposed mixing blood and recommended racial separation. We can see these strategies working in four of our families that carried on after the deaths of Native mothers.

When Mehubane, the Omaha widow of Lucien Fontenelle, died in 1840—almost immediately after Lucien's death—she left five orphaned children. Their Native families stepped in. The older boys, Logan, Albert, and Tecumseh, stayed with their Omaha grandfather, Big Elk, and his wives, but were educated to join the shifting border world of Indian country. The younger children, Susan and Henry, attended mission schools on the reservation but often lived with family friends in Kansas City.

When Jane Johnston Schoolcraft died in 1842 while visiting her sister in Ontario, she was buried in Sault Ste. Marie, next to her baby son, Willy. Her surviving children, Janee and Johnston, never returned to Michigan. Their father, Henry Schoolcraft, did his best to erase their Native heritage by marrying a White woman who hated his and Jane's children for their racial makeup.

When Macompemay, Andrew Drips's Otoe wife, died in 1846, her children were well ensconced in Missouri border life built by the fur trade. They didn't return to their Otoe families. The oldest daughter took care of her younger siblings until their father married a French-Dakota mixed-blood woman, whom he brought into the family home in Kansas City. Comfortable in their skins, the Drips children created new versions of mixed-descent lives.

And, in 1847, when Mistanta, William Bent's Cheyenne wife, died, her sisters, also William Bent's wives, simply took over. The Bent children, Mary, Robert, George, Julia, and Charles, surely missed their mother, but their Cheyenne relatives stepped in. William Bent never considered moving outside the world he had created along the Arkansas, even as expansion brought the United States ever closer.

The Fontenelle Children as Omahas

Lucien Fontenelle and Mehubane's five children, left adrift by their parents' deaths, remained members of the Omaha nation. As Big Elk's grandchildren, they had status and responsibilities. Big Elk remained a powerful leader by building kin relationships with trad-ers and military officials. He kept the Omaha together through waves of epidemic disease and moves to new reservations. An Omaha artist remembered many years later that Big Elk's bison-skin lodge was adorned with traditional symbols but also had a steamboat painted on it, now important in Omaha life. Big Elk negotiated treaties that included large tribal payments, trading posts near Omaha villages, and a training school for Indian children.[3]

Along with other Omaha children, the Fontenelle boys attended the Indian Manual Training School when it opened in 1843. Located near Fort Leavenworth, the school's curriculum included English, blacksmithing, and carpentry, skills for an evolving Missouri River world. Susan Fontenelle, the youngest and only girl, lived in Andrew Drips and Macompemay's home while she attended school in Kansas City.[4]

Logan Fontenelle, the eldest, also known as Shon-ga-ska or White Horse, was in line to lead the Omaha tribe. Logan's skills and his personal connections got him a job as a translator for the Omaha at the Council Bluffs agency and then at Fort Leavenworth starting in 1841. At only seventeen, he was paid $300 a year. A favorite of his grandfather and increasingly useful as he interpreted paper and peo-ple from the non-Native world, he also learned ceremonies and led hunts. Big Elk had no living sons, so he sought a successor among his grandsons, both adopted and natural.[5]

Because Mehubane's children had a White father, they could become hereditary leaders only if their grandfather adopted them. Big Elk did not adopt the Fontenelle boys but instead selected another mixed-descent adoptee, Joseph La Flesche. Joseph, or Iron Eye, was the son of Waoowinchtcha, a Ponca-Omaha woman, and a French-Canadian fur trader. Big Elk realized how important his choice would be as he had previously watched the Otoes devolve into a destructive fight over leadership after losing chiefs to war and illness. In 1843, to avoid a recurrence of such chaos, he designated young La Flesche as his successor, which surely caused resentment among his other grandsons. Fluent in French, Ponca, Pawnee, and

Iowa, in addition to Omaha, Joseph also studied tribal history to prepare for the chieftainship that would come with Big Elk's death.[6]

Their location in eastern Nebraska, however, placed the Omahas in harm's way. They were now under daily pressure to abandon
their villages in the path of White migration and the raids of Plains
warriors. Overland immigrants burned Omaha fields and stole their
livestock. Pawnees and Lakotas attacked Omaha villages and hunting camps, killing and taking captives, in their efforts to expand into
Omaha territory. Lakotas, with seven clans including Dakotas and
Yankton Sioux, meted out harsh violence to anyone who hunted or
camped in territory that they now considered their own. Logan Fontenelle saw the costs of this warfare when the Omaha agent sent him
to investigate a brutal attack made by Yankton Sioux in 1846. He
found seventy-three dead Omaha women and children. The Omaha
men had gone on a winter hunt and left them sleeping. Sioux raiders
found them, killed them, and cut off their noses, a grisly fact Fontenelle included in his terse report about the incident.[7]

Logan Fontenelle moved closer to his Omaha family by marrying an Omaha woman named Gixpeaha or New Moon. Using his
education and family background, he handled many Omaha land
negotiations. But when deals went sour, or when Omaha people discovered how little land and money they actually received, many of
them blamed Logan. In August 1846 he acted as interpreter for Big
Elk to negotiate a treaty with the Mormon leader Brigham Young.
Young wanted to house Mormons exiled from Missouri and Illinois
on Omaha land, as a temporary respite to prepare for their trek west.
Big Elk hoped that Mormon camps and villages could serve as a barrier from Lakota raiders and American overland travelers. Instead,
the Mormons brought disease, immigrants who required Omaha
charity, and increased attention from the U.S. military. Logan, as
translator and negotiator, was accused of bringing both hungry Mormons and White soldiers into Omaha lands.[8]

Logan's younger sister, Susan, only five when her parents died,
lived with the Drips family in Westport, Kansas. Susan attended
mission schools and found friendships and a husband from other

mixed-blood families. The Fontenelle children, as "half-breeds of the Omaha nation," had been promised land on the Great Nemaha Half-Breed Tract. However, without a White trader father to demand their status as "Half-Breeds of the Nation," only Susan, protected by the Drips family, got her land. Hoping to make a life on that land, she married Louis Neals, French-Canadian and Omaha, who also grew up on the Missouri River. Whether land and marriage could protect the Omaha amid the settlers building towns around them remained a puzzle.[9]

Cheated and Chiseled on the Great Lakes

Like other fur trade parents, Henry Schoolcraft and Jane Johnston Schoolcraft provided their family a safety net of mixed-descent people. The 1836 treaty with the Chippewa and Ottawa, signed on Henry's forty-third birthday, included a census of the "mixed bloods of the tribes" and reserved land on Sugar Island for Susan Johnston and her children. Henry wrote to Jane to "rejoice with me" because their "half-breed relations were provided for, every man, woman and child of them." He also wanted to celebrate that Michigan Ojibwes would get schools, missions, agricultural implements, and blacksmith shops, as part of a "20-year Christianization program." He was genuinely happy about what he had achieved, certain that his Johnston family relatives would benefit.[10]

Instead, they sued him. The Johnstons were angry about annuity payments—a combination of goods and cash, paid annually, that Native peoples received for the land they ceded in treaties. Henry's new job involved buying and distributing annuity goods. But the blankets, coffee, flour, agricultural tools, fish baskets, clothing, dried peas, seeds, and bacon were of such poor quality that the Ojibwe sent them back, preferring to wait an entire year in protest. For traders and storekeepers like George and William Johnston and James Schoolcraft, Ojibwe hunters with no cash and no goods meant financial disaster. They would have to go into debt themselves to pay their Indian customers who brought in furs, corn, and maple sugar. The

This pictograph appears on an 1847 treaty between the U.S. government and the Okanagon band of Lake Superior Ojibwes. It is a formal signature depicting the crane *doodem,* or clan, who negotiated the treaty. Their plaid dress signifies their marriages with Scottish traders. That clan included Susan Johnston, her brother Waishkey, and the Johnston children.

(Pictograph redrawn by Seth Eastman for Henry Rowe Schoolcraft, ed., Historical and Statistical Information Respecting the History, Condition, and Prospects of the Indian Tribes of the United States [Lippincott, 1851], 1:418.)

Jane Johnston Schoolcraft, Bame-wawagesihkaquay in Ojibwe, or Sound of Stars Shooting in the Night, was born in 1800 to Ozhagusco-daywayquay (Susan Johnston) and the Scottish-Irish fur trader John Johnston. This photograph of a small locket painting that has since disappeared shows a very young Jane, likely before she met Henry Schoolcraft in 1820. *(Johnston Family Papers, Bentley Historical Library. Courtesy University of Michigan Digital Collections.)*

Henry Rowe Schoolcraft married Jane Johnston in 1822 and moved up the Indian Service bureaucratic ladder. With Jane's continuous assistance, he established himself as an ethnologist and expert on Native languages. This 1854 woodcut engraving, by Wellstood and Peters, was made to accompany his six-volume study, *The Indian Tribes of the United States. (Getty Images.)*

Charlotte Johnston, daughter of John and Susan Johnston, married the Anglican minister assigned to Sault Ste. Marie, William McMurray, in 1832. Both photographs were taken in the 1850s in Dundas, Ontario, where William served as minister. They are wearing formal clothing, suitable for elite Anglo-Canadians.. *(Diocesan Heritage Collection, P2005.79.13.1. Courtesy Algona University Archives.)*

A marriage at a fur trade rendezvous in Wyoming, as painted in 1845 by Alfred Jacob Miller. Miller accompanied the Scottish lord William Drummond Stewart on two fur trade expeditions as Stewart's personal painter. He painted many versions of this romantic scene, which he called *The Trapper's Bride*. *(MPI/Getty Images.)*

Margaret Campbell McKay was born to a fur trade family in 1833 along the Peace River in northern Canada. Herself Cree and Scots-Canadian, she married William Cameron McKay—Chinook, Scots-Canadian, and Cree—in 1856. The couple raised five children in the eastern Oregon reservations at Warm Springs and Umatilla. This photo of Margaret was taken in Portland in 1883. *(Courtesy Oregon Historical Society.)*

Donald McKay, seated, was the son of Thomas McKay and a Cayuse woman. Donald's older half-brother, Dr. William McKay, born in 1824 to Thomas McKay and Timmee, a Chinook woman, stands with his son, William McKay, who did not survive to adulthood. This 1870 image was produced by a commercial photographer offering reproductions of "Oregon Indians" to interested buyers. *(Courtesy Oregon Historical Society.)*

Donald McKay, leaning on a rock, poses in 1873 with his fellow Warm Springs scouts at an army camp in northeastern California. These Cayuse men rounded up Modoc warriors after they held out for months against the U.S. Army. *(Eadweard Muybridge, The Modoc War [stereograph], 1873. Courtesy George Eastman Museum/Getty Images.)*

In 1833 Prince Maximilian of Wied, on a tour of fur trading country, visited Bellevue, the trading post on the Missouri River established by Andrew Drips and Lucien Fontenelle. Three family groups likely Omahas or Otoes, appear in the scene, along with two structures: Lucien's home on top of the hill, and the trading post closer to the water. This watercolor was painted by Swiss artist Karl Bodmer who accompanied the prince on his tour. *(Gift of the Enron Art Foundation, 1986.49.371, Joslyn Art Museum, Omaha.)*

Hayne Hudjihini, or Eagle of Delight, an Otoe, visited Washington in 1822. At about the same time, Andrew Drips moved to the Otoe villages as a trader and married Macompemay. Hayne Hudjihini, who was married to Sumonyeacathee, an Otoe leader, is shown with a blue tattoo on her forehead denoting her royal status. *(Charles Bird King, Hayne Hudjihini [Eagle of Delight], Oto, c. 1822, White House, Washington, D.C. Corbis via Getty Images.)*

Breakfast at Sunrise, painted in 1837 by Alfred Jacob Miller, depicts a Rocky Mountain fur brigade beginning their day. Native and French men eat breakfast, surrounded by Native women and children typical of the personnel involved. (*Walters Art Museum, Baltimore. Photo by Mondadori Portfolio via Getty Images.*)

Louise Geroux Drips, of French and Dakota heritage, was Andrew Drips's second wife. This photograph was taken in Kansas City about 1862, two years after her husband died, when she was in her midthirties. *(Courtesy of Bancroft Library, University of California, Berkeley.)*

Andrew Drips and two of his sons, Andrew Jackson and Thomas Nelson, aged seven and four. Taken in 1858, these small photographs were designed to be carried in a pocket. After nearly fifty years in the fur trade, Andrew looks careworn at age sixty-nine. *(Courtesy of Bancroft Library, University of California, Berkeley.)*

LIST OF

Half Breeds and Mixed blood Indians

OMAHAS, IOWAYS, OTTOES, YANCTON & SANTIE *bands of* SIOUX

entitled to participate in benefits of

HALF BREED RESERVATION

between the

Great and Little Nemaha Rivers

NEBRASKA

Under Act of Congress
approved

July 31. 1854.

The federal government had promised land to mixed-heritage peoples in treaties with Otoes, Omahas, Iowas, and Dakotas. This ledger book, kept by Indian Service officials in 1854, contains the list of people entitled to land on the Great Nemaha Half-Breed Tract in Nebraska. The list eventually grew to thousands of names, including members of the Drips and Fontenelle families. *(Records Relating to the Nemaha Half-Breed Reserve, Lists of Allotted and Unallotted Mixed-Bloods, 1854–1857, Office of Indian Affairs, RG 75, NARA. Photo by the author.)*

Three generations of Drips and Barnes women, photographed in 1899 in Kansas City. Catherine Drips Mulkey (center left) was born at the 1832 rendezvous. Her older sister, Mary Jane Drips Barnes (center right), is seventy-two. Above them is Catherine Barnes Dickey, Mary Jane's only daughter. Below them is Catherine Mulkey Drips, Mary Jane's and Catherine's great-niece, born in 1880. *(Courtesy of Bancroft Library, University of California, Berkeley.)*

Lucien Fontenelle, as sketched in 1837 by Alfred Jacob Miller. Miller, along with Sir William Drummond Stewart, accompanied Lucien's American Fur Company supply train from the Missouri River to the Wind River Mountains. *(Alfred Jacob Miller, Fontenelle Chased by a Grizzly Bear, 1837. Joslyn Art Museum, Omaha. Museum purchase, 1988.10.87.)*

A young Omaha boy with a freshly shaved head, earrings, and an elegant white feather attached to his hair, indicating his band and clan status. He was painted by Karl Bodmer in the summer of 1833, when the Swiss artist visited the Omaha villages and Lucien Fontenelle's trading post at Bellevue. *(Joslyn Art Museum, Omaha. MPI/ Getty Images.)*

Emily Papin Fontenelle, photographed in 1915, near the end of her life. Of Omaha, Pawnee, and French heritage, she attended the Omaha boarding school in the 1850s and then married Lucien's youngest son, Henry Fontenelle. *(Courtesy of Nebraska Historical Society.)*

What was important to Cheyenne people was bison and human families. Below, men and women court outside their tepees at a summer hunting encampment. Above, hunters on horseback hunt bison that float through the air. All were part of the world that Mistanta (Owl Woman) and William Bent helped create on the southern Plains in the 1830s. Bear's Heart (Nock-ko-kist) drew this memory of his Southern Cheyenne life while imprisoned at Fort Marion in St. Augustine, Florida, in the 1870s. *(Fort Marion Ledger, c. 1878. Courtesy of National Museum of American History, Smithsonian Institution.)*

William Bent, photographed at age forty-nine, likely in Kansas City. The proprietor of Bent's Fort, William married three Southern Cheyenne women: Mistanta, and her two sisters Island and Yellow Woman. Taken just before the 1858 gold rush to Colorado would destroy his southern Plains world, the photograph shows Bent at the height of his influence. *(Courtesy of History Colorado.)*

George Bent, William and Mistanta's son, and Magpie Woman, Black Kettle's niece, shortly after their marriage. In this 1867 photograph, George and Magpie are wearing formal garb, including his beautifully beaded moccasins. It was taken at the Medicine Lodge Council, likely by a U.S. Army photographer who traveled with treaty commissions. *(Courtesy of History Colorado.)*

n 1868 William Bent met with Arapaho fathers at Fort Dodge, Kansas, to try to negotiate a solution
the continuous violence on the Plains. From left to right: Little Raven, Little Raven's granddaughter
Grass Woman, William Bent, and Little Raven's sons Little Bear and Shield. The photograph was
taken a year before Bent's death. *(Courtesy of National Archives and Records Administration.)*

Julia Bent (George Bent and Kiowa Woman's daughter) and her older half-sister Ada were among the first Cheyenne children to attend the Carlisle Indian Industrial School in Pennsylvania. In this 1887 photograph, fourteen-year-old Julia poses with another Southern Cheyenne student and rests her hand on her uncle Edmund Guerrier's shoulder. *(John N. Choat, photographer. Courtesy of National Anthropological Archives, Smithsonian Institution.)*

In 1905 George Bent, Julia's father, was at a low point. None of his four wives would live with him after he tricked Cheyenne leaders into signing a corrupt deal that gave away almost all of their land reserves. Toward the end of his life he would regain some trust in the eyes of Cheyenne elders and his family. This photo was taken at the Seger Indian Agency in Indian Territory. *(Unknown photographer, 1905. Courtesy of Oklahoma Historical Society.)*

family was angry also because in 1836 Henry fired William Johnston. Now twenty-six and recently married, William had been appointed keeper of the Indian dormitory, a place to house Indians when they came to do agency business. However, William continued his trading business from the Indian dormitory, which was strictly illegal. Henry had to fire him.[11]

To support their suit, William Johnston lined up Henry's enemies: Catholics resentful that Henry had refused to fund their missions, Whigs bitter over his appointment of Democrats, traders who had their licenses and liquor taken away, and most damaging of all, affidavits that William and George gathered from their Ojibwe relatives about poor-quality goods. But Henry had ardent supporters, and despite the extensive evidence against him, he kept his job. T. Hartley Crawford, the superintendent of Indian affairs in Washington, wrote grudgingly to his own superior, the secretary of war, that "Mr. Schoolcraft has experience and connections we need." In 1840, aware that his government career was likely coming to an end, Henry resigned. In his memoir, he wrote that he had been "triumphantly acquitted" but had "become tired of politics."[12]

Before he left office, Henry mollified the Johnstons by giving everyone jobs at the new Grand Traverse Bay agency. He made George a "carpenter" and George's wife Mary an "interpreter," even though the new Mrs. Johnston spoke no Ojibwe. John McDougall Johnston, the baby of the Johnston family who had been fired at Sault Ste. Marie for negligence, became a farmer and his wife, French and Ojibwe, the assistant farmer. Some 150 miles south of Sault Ste. Marie and now the largest Ojibwe reservation in Michigan, Grand Traverse had a short growing season and poor soil. It made a terrible model farm, but it was the best Henry could do. Having spent a decade watching his efforts to introduce "Civilization" be destroyed by a tightfisted Indian Service and by ungrateful Indians who saw little attraction or profit in farming, he was bitter. Long an advocate of assimilation, he now wrote a long treatise recommending the rapid removal of all Indians from Michigan. Then he and Jane, having literally sold the family down the river, fled to New York.[13]

By 1840, the Johnston family, who had brought their children into the world with such great expectations, was foundering on the seismic changes in Michigan. Mixed-descent men could no longer find jobs except as laborers in the fur trade, mines, or lumber mills. Henry and Jane left Michigan because of these troubles and because Henry wanted to enroll their children in elite East Coast schools. When Jane expressed concerns about sending the children away, Henry reminded her that they had special responsibilities as parents because their children were "not simply of unmixed blood."[14]

While remaking his children into White citizens, Henry intended to remake himself as a scholar and a gentleman. His years in Michigan had left him with Detroit real estate, a collection of Indian tales, alphabets, and linguistic treatises, and knowledge about the mineral resources of the Great Lakes. His interests in geology and metallurgy had long fueled an imagined career as a scientist, but he had no scientific training at a time when science was moving from a gentleman's activity to work by trained professionals. His ethnographic work, representing years of effort by Jane's now–estranged family, seemed easier to develop. Henry got publication contracts for his Indian stories, which he recast as original linguistic research to build his stature in that growing field. His contribution to linguistics was to insist that Native people across the world spoke simple languages and were incapable of complex thought, an idea that was both dangerous and convenient for policy makers who wanted to expel Indians.[15]

Henry's ambitions, however, were much bigger. He envisioned a great, all-inclusive history of Native America, a grand edifice of salvage history, ethnography, and linguistics. Henry didn't need scientific training for the work: his authority came from his experience in Michigan, his exploitation of his Ojibwe family, and his connections. Now he just needed the right sponsor: a great university, a wealthy patron, or the U.S. government. His poor science and racist ideas about "simple" Native people would have immense consequences for public policy and his own family.[16]

Through the winter of 1841, Jane pined away in her lonely house on Nineteenth Street in Manhattan. It was filled with carpets and cutlery, but she missed her children, now students in upstate New

York boarding schools, and her Michigan family. Her siblings Charlotte and George wrote, but no one came to visit. Henry's driving ambition kept him on the road almost constantly. He gave talks at the New-York Historical Society, consulted with authorities on Indians, and kept up his connections in Washington, D.C. Much to Jane's dismay, he planned an extensive trip to England and Europe to meet with publishers there. As he gathered letters of introduction from literary luminaries, Jane's health, always precarious, took a turn for the worse. Refusing to stay alone in New York as she had done with little Willy in 1826, she planned a long visit to her sister Charlotte, who lived with her Anglican minister husband and their children in Dundas, Ontario.[17]

In the spring of 1842, Henry boarded a ship for London. Jane took a steamer up the Hudson to Albany and continued north to Ontario. By the time Henry arrived in London, Jane was dead. She died at Charlotte's house on May 22, at the age of forty-two. Her mother insisted that her body be brought back to Sault Ste. Marie and buried next to her baby son, William. Henry didn't find out about her death for some weeks, though William McMurray, Charlotte's husband, wrote him immediately. Henry wrote a devastatingly cold letter informing his children, then fourteen and twelve, of their mother's death.[18]

Even if we allow for nineteenth-century formality, we cannot forgive Henry for that letter. It spewed his deep pessimism about Native people and his anger at Jane for not being White. In assuring his children that they could survive without a mother, Henry wrote: "Reflect that your mother herself, had not the advantages of a mother (in the refined sense of the term) to bring her up . . . that she had many and peculiar trials to encounter in coming into the broad and mixed circle of society." After insulting their beloved grandmother, he wrote that the children could take comfort that their mother's "taste in literature was chaste" and "she wrote many pretty pieces." Cold comfort indeed.[19]

Henry decided to stay in Europe for another six months attending to business, but he was unmoored by Jane's death. The trip did not go well. He couldn't find a publisher, and his writing career seemed endangered. He briefly changed his name to Colcraft, which he thought was the original version of his family name, but he gave it up when others found it puzzling. The children spent time with their Schoolcraft relations, and Jane's sister Charlotte offered to take them in, but Henry insisted they stay at Mr. Porter's school in Albany.[20]

Henry didn't want them to associate with any Johnston family cousins. He worried that the racial taint his children carried would show. Perhaps young Johnston's inability to excel in school came from his "Indian lineaments and dark hair." Because he didn't think he could afford to send his son to an expensive preparatory academy for college, Schoolcraft attempted (and failed) to enroll him at West Point or Annapolis, military academies that required an appointment but were tuition free. Janee, "bonny and blonde," excelled in deportment and academics, but Henry remained concerned that her family heritage might affect her "marriage prospects."[21]

Dangerous Business on the Southern Plains

While the Schoolcraft children grieved in Albany, Owl Woman and her Cheyenne sisters did their best to manage the changing world of the southern Plains. The Great Peace of 1840, the fragile agreement that had halted hostilities between the Comanche and the Cheyenne, could not stop the lucrative raiding for horses and human captives that had been ongoing for decades. When the new Mexican nation, desperate for cash to infuse into its war-depleted economy, demanded workers to reopen silver mines in central Mexico, the raiding increased. Native raiders stole other Native people, along with White and Mexican residents, and sold them to Mexican traders who marched them all south in long human chains. By the early 1840s, these profitable endeavors became large-scale military campaigns involving thousands of Comanche warriors in carefully coordinated attacks. The region stretching from the Arkansas River south through Texas into northern Mexico's deserts became nearly impassable for traders and caravans bringing goods from Mexico or Missouri. Such instability became intolerable in Mexico and the Republic of Texas.

U.S. policy around ransoming captives evolved in these years. Indian agents, instructed to pay cash to redeem White Americans, also assisted Anglo and Mexican families in brokering ransom deals. The agent assigned to Fort Gibson in what is now western Arkansas reported to the secretary of war that "the Comanches and some of their allied bands" held between thirty and forty "white prisoners" but perhaps one thousand "Mexican children . . . still in captivity," suggesting the scale of the human trafficking.[22]

Many people profited from this volatile situation, including the Bent brothers and their Cheyenne and Comanche partners. As frontier economies expanded on the United States' western border and on Mexico's northern border, demand for horses and mules, guns, and humans increased exponentially. But it was a dangerous business. A Comanche raid in 1841 took the life of Robert Bent, William Bent's older brother, just outside the fort.[23]

In the midst of this dangerous success, the Bent family grew. Mary, the eldest child of William Bent and Mistanta, now had two brothers, Robert or Octavi-wee-his, born in 1840, and George or Ho-my-ike, born in 1843. They were named after their Bent uncles but raised as good Cheyennes. Mistanta had many responsibilities as the daughter of a chief and the wife of the fort's leader. Her decisions about when and where to hunt, camp, and trade remained invisible to most White visitors, who commented only on her "striking appearance" and her elaborately beaded buckskin dresses. A very young and very interested visitor described her dress as "reaching obliquely to the knee." He noted her "bracelets of brass, which glittered and reflected in the radiant, morning sun" all, as he put it, "a profusion . . . of allure."[24]

The business conducted at Bent's Fort depended on women like Mistanta and on intermarriage. The men Bent hired as traders needed families in Cheyenne villages. Alexander Barclay, the storekeeper and accounts manager at the fort, wrote to his brother that all the men who worked at the fort full time "have squaws of various tribes." The chief traders for the Bents, Marcellin St. Vrain, John Simpson Smith, and Lancaster Lupton, and their fiercest competitors, the Janisse brothers, who ran forts for the American Fur Company on the Platte River, all had Native families. Lupton, a West Point graduate and army officer, married a Cheyenne woman named Thomassa. They had eight children, but Lupton initially kept that secret from his family. After the birth of his fourth child, however, he wrote to his parents about his marriage and children. His father merely wondered, "Why have you kept this truth from us all through those years?" and was grateful that he had "acted like a man." Lupton and his Cheyenne family moved to California in 1849 during the Gold Rush.[25]

The Bent children, as young Cheyennes, had few responsibilities in a place that they all would later recall as wondrous. Stables with donkeys, blacksmith shops, kitchens, and storerooms enticed children to visit. The fort even had what some visitors called a "petting zoo with bald eagles, baby antelopes, and otters," but these were kept to provide feathers and special furs for ceremonies rather than to entertain children. Outside the fort, every summer a cacophony of Cheyenne, Arapaho, and Wichita voices filled the air from villages spread along the shady river banks. Herds of horses and mules, taken far from the fort to graze, marked the outer edge of the Bent's Fort world. In wintertime, only a few hundred lodges stayed near the fort, as hunting parties moved out over the Plains. Life is never as idyllic as children remember it. George Bent's first memories, like his mother's, were of horses and their smells and sounds, but those memories could have been of war, continuously brewing and then boiling into fierce battles throughout his early years.[26]

Charles Bent, William Bent's brother, lived in Taos and managed Bent and St. Vrain's trade with Mexico and the United States. Aware that raiding sometimes benefited the company and sometimes didn't, he warned Mexican officials about trouble when it suited his needs. In 1841, for example, he warned Manuel Alvarez, a former Indian trader and now U.S. consul to Mexico, that Cheyenne and Arapaho Indians planned a great raid on New Mexico. They intended to recover horses stolen from them and "will play the divil with the frontear settlements." A year later Bent described a Comanche war party heading to New Mexico. He warned Alvarez that local volunteers should not try to fight the Comanches, that "they are too numerias and too well armed, they will be found a verry different enime from the Apachies and Nabijos."[27]

After giving such advice, in 1843 Charles and William made lucrative deals with the Mexican and U.S. armies to supply troops marching against Native raiders. Another significant business opportunity came along with the permanent presence of the U.S. Army, which now needed to manage the disruption and war created when eastern Indians were removed to the West. Policing the Plains required provisioning soldiers on the move. Feeding, arming, and entertaining the U.S. Army profited the Bents for a time, but in the end it would destroy their lives.[28]

The Whitman Massacre

Like people living around the Great Lakes or along the Arkansas River, people in the Pacific Northwest were surprised by the trouble that arrived in the 1840s. In Oregon Country, or Owyhee as local people called it, Chinook, Spokane, and Cayuse, as well as mixed-blood McKays, used the fur trade to create wealth. Blending Indigenous trade networks and fur trade systems was profitable but also unstable. Just as in Kansas and New Mexico, the 1840s brought business opportunities, foreign settlers, and violence.

When ships and diplomats from the United States, Mexico, and Russia pushed into the Pacific Northwest in the 1840s, Hudson's Bay Company leaders could no longer monopolize the region, so they accepted tense shared ownership. The Company had a strategy: strip the region's furs, develop a broader business base in agriculture and shipping to supply food and manufactured items along the Pacific Coast, and settle the region with retired employees. Thomas McKay and his family, part of that Company plan, lived and farmed at Fort Nisqually at the southern end of Puget Sound.[29]

After ten years of effort, the Company farm produced some potatoes and peas but failed at wheat, oats, and cattle. The fort traders did business with local Indians, a range of coastal villagers including Cowlitz, Snoqualmie, and Klallam. Local hunters brought in a wealth of furs and fishes: "large beaver, small beaver, otter, musk-rats, wood rats, raccoons, lynx, minks, fishers, badgers, martens, foxes, bears, elk, wolf, tiger, fresh salmon, fish, ducks, and grouse." In return, they wanted high-quality trade goods like cloth, hats, but-tons, needles, and axes, as well as guns, powder, and alcohol. When French-Canadian and American immigrants arrived, HBC officials lent them tools and milk cows, helped them fell huge trees to build houses, and provided potatoes as seed.[30]

But Fort Nisqually officials also recorded trouble. Cows ate the potatoes and local Salish villagers ate the cows. Bored during the long winter, rainy and cold, Frenchmen and Iroquois hunters started a brawl over a horse race, causing the fort leader "to give them all a good drubbing." On May 1, 1849, chief trader William Tolmie wrote about a more serious incident involving Americans. He explained to his bosses that "a large party of Snoquamish and Skegwahmish . . . had an assay with our people," and unfortunately "the American Wallace was killed." Tolmie laid out the fuller story. A group of armed Indian men came to the fort, upset that one of their women was being beaten by her new husband, a young man from a neigh-boring village. Tolmie invited the leaders to come inside, but one of Tolmie's traders fired his gun. A shooting match began before Tol-mie's men could close the gates. Two recent American arrivals, Wal-lace and Lewis, were outside the fort "when the affray commenced" and did not respond to the call of "all hands come in and shut the gates." Wallace lay dead and Lewis grievously wounded. Because they were Americans, Tolmie concluded that "trouble would come from this affair."[31]

Everyone expected a U.S. war with Great Britain over control of the region. Instead, late in 1846, news reached Oregon that the United States and Great Britain had signed a treaty setting a bound-ary between the United States and Canada at the forty-ninth parallel. With that agreement, the Hudson's Bay Company began withdraw-ing from the Columbia River, leaving no source of authority about property, life, or labor. Everything felt unstable, to Native villagers, to new Anglo-American arrivals, and to Thomas McKay, who had lived there for nearly forty years.

Rumors flew. Fort Nisqually chief trader William Tolmie heard Klallam warriors blaming recent immigrants for measles epidemics. A newer settler, A. B. Rabbeson, even more skittish, claimed he had overheard chiefs inciting "a gathering of thousands" to drive Whites out of the country. American newcomers and missionaries began building forts. Anglo-American settlers raged about Indians who had guns, cattle, and horses and complained about British despots and their Indian-coddling ways. The HBC's Columbia district leader, chief factor Peter Ogden, reported gloomily to his London superiors that he expected disaster any moment as "we are looked upon with a suspicious eye by one and all."[32]

Like all old Oregonians, Thomas McKay had to figure out how to operate in this unfriendly situation. He and his third wife, Isabelle, had a growing family. McKay's sons, William, Alexander, and John from his marriage to Timmee, had returned in 1843 from boarding school, college, and medical school in the East and now expected to make lives in Oregon. Instead of a powerful trader family, American settlers considered those McKays suspicious mixed bloods who seemed a little too British.[33]

To be essential in the new American present, Thomas came up with a road-building scheme. The fur trade had relied on river and ocean travel to operate its business. The steep, densely wooded Cascade range blocked the huge wagons of American immigrants, as well as the mail, the army, and anything else that needed to come overland. In 1846 McKay petitioned the new Oregon government to survey and build a road across the Cascades. Recognizing the disadvantages of his "alien" status, he declared himself a U.S. citizen as part of his request. He was granted the work but found the task of building a mountain road "through the great breadth" of the mountains, "in combination with snow," too challenging. He completed the survey but not the road. The Oregon government labeled him an "unreliable half-breed" and abandoned the project.[34]

Success in attracting new settlers was stymied in part by missionaries, who had been at the heart of American efforts in Oregon. An evangelizing duo from New York, Marcus and Narcissa Whitman, had arrived in Oregon in 1836. They ignored John McLoughlin's advice about where to settle and set up a Congregationalist mission in what is now central Washington. In this isolated spot—Waiilatpu (now known as Walla Walla), two hundred miles from Fort Vancouver—they preached to Cayuse, Spokane, and Walla Walla people but never learned their languages. The Whitmans' bulletins about the savages who surrounded them—and who needed saving—made good copy when read aloud in churches every Sunday but also frightened away potential settlers.[35]

Over ten years, the Whitmans themselves created their own fairly savage situation. The only "Indians" Marcus and Narcissa permitted into their household were mixed children of trader families, such as Helen Mar Meeks (Joseph Meeks's daughter) and Mary Ann (Jim Bridger's daughter), both servants. Narcissa described their dispositions in a letter to her sister as "easily governed" and making "but little trouble." She also sent the terrible news that "the Lord has taken our own dear child away," but justified her loss as "fruitful," giving her time to "care for poor Nez Perce and Cayuse children." She described that care: "we confine them altogether to the house and do not allow them to speak a word of Nez Perces." The Whitmans' habit of confining children and refusing to share food during long winters made them enemies to the powerful Columbia Plateau tribes.[36]

Those Indians, irritated by continuous wagon traffic through their lands, required only a tiny instigation to turn violent. During the dreary fall of 1847, measles arrived—it made young children among the settlers mildly ill, but it killed Native people. From the Cayuse perspective, Marcus Whitman seemed able to cure new settlers but failed to cure any Cayuse. After thirty Cayuse died, leaders agreed that they had tolerated the dangerous Whitmans long enough. As a failed shaman, Marcus and his entire family had to be killed.[37]

So on November 29, 1847, a morning when Marcus Whitman buried Chief Tiloukaikt's third child, that same chief led a band of Cayuse to attack the mission. They killed Marcus and Narcissa Whitman and their children. Everyone in the household died in the vicious attack, including eleven-year-old Mary Ann Bridger. The Cayuses captured forty-seven other White and mixed-descent women and children and fled into the mountains.[38]

Oregon dissolved into panic. U.S. Army troops might take months to arrive. Peter Skene Ogden of the Hudson's Bay Company, with long local experience, left Fort Vancouver and rushed into the mountains on December 7, the morning after he heard the news. He took sixteen of his best hunters to ransom the hostages. His action infuriated newly arrived Anglo-Americans who didn't trust Ogden's group of "all half-breeds and Indians." The head of the American provisional government at Oregon City, Gov. George Abernethy, took two different approaches. First, he called up companies of volunteers to "chastize" the Cayuse nation as a whole. The five hundred volunteers, however, lacked the guns, ammunition, and supplies to make a winter campaign and turned back. Second, Abernethy formed a peace commission of three White missionaries—Joel Palmer, Henry Lee, and Robert Newell—to work with friendly bands of Indians who might convince the Cayuse to turn over the hostages. That approach also failed.[39]

The HBC party led by Peter Ogden and Indian scouts found the hostages and by December 24 had negotiated their release. Cayuse leaders responded to Ogden's plea that he and his traders "have mixed our blood with yours." This was a triumph for Ogden and for the Hudson's Bay Company. Ogden pointed out to his bosses in London that "without [the Company's] powerful aid and influence nothing could have been effected." However, it wasn't enough for the frightened new settlers, who now realized how vulnerable they really were. Demanding vengeance, a large contingent of volunteers rushed into the mountains early in 1848 and began killing Indians.[40]

Thomas McKay understood that to prevent a general Indian war, the Cayuse band that had instigated the Whitman massacre would have to be punished. Like Peter Ogden, he knew that only experienced local men with Native kin could bring them in, so he created a troop from the French-Native community. They successfully tracked Cayuse bands through the winter landscape, but new White settlers reacted with fear and anger, suspicious of the networks of trade and knowledge shared by powerful Indians and their mixed-descent kin. When McKay brought the Cayuse in, he was not labeled a hero but was remembered instead as a "hot-blooded" French-Indian "centaur," foreign and maybe not even human.[41]

The End of Bent's Fort

Far from Oregon, another international hot spot was moving from rumor to war. Throughout 1845, stories reached Bent's Fort about troops shooting near the Rio Grande, Texans attacking New Mexico, and Britain taking Oregon. Caravans from St. Louis arrived with newspapers that elevated some rumors to fact and demoted others to forgotten worries, although the news was always outdated. In early 1846, rumors of attack worried everyone in northern New Mexico, but old friend and Mexican governor Manuel Armijo assured the Bents that he had heard nothing from Mexico City. With war seeming distant, Charles Bent arranged to lead the spring caravan trip to St. Louis to resupply the fort and sell last season's hides.[42]

But at the same time frontier stories floated back east that fed the furor for war. Accounts of the long war between Native nations and two struggling republics—Mexico and Texas—filled American newspapers. Politicians described the battles Mexicans had waged unsuccessfully against "*los bárbaros*," and they explained Mexico's failures with racial logic. Texas and New Mexico had been reduced to a land of deserts and burned villages not because Indians were strong but because Mexicans were weak. Mexico had to be saved from barbarism and from itself, and the United States would have to do the saving. The lands of Texas were perfect, opined Robert Walker, a senator from Mississippi who had never set foot there, except for the Indians. It "just needed a hardy people, willing for the sake of a small portion of soil, to go in and subdue them."[43]

The next piece of logic involved making the Comanche, Kiowa, Wichita, and Apache into foes that Americans could easily beat. Matt Field, a *New Orleans Picayune* writer, claimed that "Comanches dread the Americans" and that fifty armed Americans could take on all of Comanchería. There were press reports of Apache raiders "fading silently" into the desert on encountering Anglo-Americans.

Continuous boasting about Anglo-American might, Indian savagery, and Mexican laziness spread through the press like poison. It
infused a national culture that already believed in the natural superiority of something called the Anglo-Saxon race, and it drove the
nation toward war.[44]

President James K. Polk had been elected to expand the nation
from sea to sea, whether that meant the Arctic, the Caribbean, the
Gulf of Mexico, or the Pacific. He and his advisers initially hoped
that they could just buy New Mexico and California and annex Texas,
but Mexican officials had refused to entertain such ideas. Ignoring
those signals, Polk, willing to go to war, told his negotiators to treat
Texas annexation as a "settled fact" and to present Mexico with $2
million. Mexican politicians, newspaper editors, and military officers vowed to die before giving up an inch of Mexican soil. When the
United States offered to pay for what it called Texas's "annexation,"
Mexico took the illegal land grab as a grave insult to its national
honor, requiring a response.[45]

In that heated setting, a war was easy to start. In January 1846
Gen. Zachary Taylor moved his troops from near Corpus Christi to
the Rio Grande to ensure U.S. control of the Mexican land annexed
as the new state of Texas. They reached the Rio Grande in March
and set themselves up within gunning range of Matamoros, where
the Mexican Army was stationed. In May 1846 "shots were fired."
Americans lay dead, and Polk immediately declared war.[46]

In June 1846 Charles Bent, while leading Bent and St. Vrain Company wagons toward St. Louis, ran into a special emissary from the
secretary of war who was rushing to Santa Fe. American citizens
living there needed to know that war had been declared and that
they now lived in an enemy nation. Charles made an important personal decision. Instead of continuing to St. Louis with his traders, he
offered up his services to Gen. Stephen Watts Kearny, who had just
been ordered to lead U.S. troops to secure California. Bent had long
reported to Manuel Alvarez, an old friend and the Mexican consul
to the United States, about rumors and business dealings in Taos,
in Santa Fe, and on the Arkansas. Because of such connections to
Mexican officials and his deep knowledge of the region, Charles Bent

became one of Kearny's most useful advisers. Bent also continued to report to the Mexican consul.[47]

At first, war continued to be good business for the Bent family. The early campaigns took place by land: expeditions from Missouri to California, via New Mexico, and from Texas to Mexico City. The small regular army swelled with eager volunteers from 6,000 soldiers to 115,000, most of whom went to Texas and Mexico. Another 2,000 soldiers took to the Santa Fe Trail. General Kearny and the Army of the West arrived at Bent's Fort in July, the height of the summer trading season, to stage an invasion of New Mexico. U.S. troops needed horses, mules, guides, guns, and supplies. Anglo-American, Mexican, and Native traders converged on Bent's Fort, lured by the irresistible presence of an army with money. Comanche and Kiowa raiders saw rolling supply trains and army camps as a bonanza. They took considerable numbers of horses, mules, and cattle, and the raw troops could do little to stop them.[48]

The extended Bent family gathered at Bent's Fort as soon as they heard the news about the war. The situation in New Mexico had become dangerously unstable. Ignacia Jaramillo, Charles's wife, left alone in Taos with her three children, sought the safety of Bent's Fort, which now lay across an increasingly real border. She and her sister, Josefa, married to trader and mountain guide Kit Carson, packed up for an indefinite stay. They were escorted by George Bent, Charles's younger brother, who had just been attacked by a mob of Taos citizens, now angry at "Americanos." Even though George was married to María de la Cruz Padilla, born and bred in Taos, he no longer felt secure. The whole family sought the safer side of the border when war began.[49]

Situated at the fort he had built, William Bent considered his options as he took in the news from Taos and Santa Fe about preparations for war and the anger of Mexican citizens. His livelihood as an American citizen who traded and made families with Mexicans and with Cheyennes depended on personal and political flexibility. But Mexico's northern states had become unstable with uprisings and a long, tiring war with Indians. Bent's wives, Mistanta and her two sisters, Yellow Woman and Island, took refuge in the Cheyenne village. Like other Cheyenne and Arapaho women, they wanted to protect their children from U.S. troops and their own warriors, all of whom had too many guns to be trustworthy. William Bent's children, Mary, eight, Robert, who was five, and George, who turned three the day the troops arrived, spent the summer with their grandmothers and uncles across the river. They later remembered that William Bent greeted the army with a cannon salute. The cannon had been sitting idle for years, and when the inexperienced crew loaded it with too much powder, it exploded, sending out a stream of sparks that lit fires everywhere.[50]

Nothing could protect the Bent children from streams of vitriol about lazy Mexicans and subhuman Indians that filled soldiers' conversations around campfires at Bent's Fort. By early August, nearly twenty thousand horses, mules, and oxen had decimated the grass near the fort. William tried to meet the army's needs but found his stores depleted, his repair shops destroyed, and his Native allies spread far from the fort. When Kearny asked Bent to form a company of Indian scouts to figure out where Manuel Armijo's Mexican troops had gathered, William initially refused. He worried what such an assignment would do for his business, but he gave in to the pressure after several days and agreed to serve the United States.[51]

On August 3, 1846, guided by William Bent and his Native and mixed-blood scouts, U.S. troops left Bent's Fort and made their way over the difficult mountain passes into the heart of New Mexico. No one knew exactly what to expect. The Mexican Army had not yet arrived, but whether local citizens would fight an occupying army remained a question. U.S. soldiers marched into the town of Las Vegas, New Mexico, unchallenged, but heard rumors that New Mexico's governor, Manuel Armijo, had gathered five thousand men in Apache Canyon, whose steep walls would make a direct attack nearly impossible. Armijo, however, was a wealthy local landowner and a smart politician. He had no desire to lead a group of volunteers against the U.S. Army. He sent out spies to meet with William Bent and Kearny's advance team. After that meeting, Armijo sent his men home and fled south to safety in El Paso. U.S. soldiers marched into a silent Santa Fe.[52]

The conquest of New Mexico is often described as bloodless, but that description only fits the experience of U.S. politicians. For people living in the region, facing urgent choices about how to protect their families, conquest could be bloody indeed, as the experiences of William and Charles Bent show. William Bent, married to three Cheyenne women and operator of a trading enterprise spread across lands bordering three empires—the United States, Mexico, and Comanchería—remained at his fort. Respected by Cheyennes and Comanches, he had a partnership that required careful balance. Like Cheyennes and Comanches, he saw his biggest risk as being corralled by any single nation.

William's brother, Charles, considered himself both New Mexican and American, an identity he assumed he could maintain. When the war began, he and his family returned to Taos, where they had built a home and a business. He had achieved that good life by exploiting New Mexicans over whom he had power. Like other wealthy New Mexicans and their colonial predecessors, Bent claimed Indians as mistresses or menial laborers. He had Black slaves who shared household duties with Native servants in both Taos and Santa Fe. Though he lived among them, he had also been outspoken about his "disgust" with "ignorant and aviritious" New Mexican leaders, and he disparaged his Mexican neighbors.[53]

In September 1846 General Kearny appointed Charles Bent to govern occupied New Mexico. Bent should have known that the appointment would brand him a traitor. The Taos region boiled with anger over American occupation. Bent assumed that his marriage, his long residence in Taos, and his friendships with businessmen, government officials, and priests would protect him. Instead, he became a man with whom nearly every Taoseño could find fault, now that he served the occupying Americans.[54]

Early on January 19, 1847, a group of angry Taos residents, led by a Pueblo Indian man named Tomás Romero, ignited a revolt. The rampage began when men from the Taos Pueblo stormed the local jail demanding the release of their friends. A mob gathered outside the jail to enjoy the excitement, and when the officer in charge scolded them, they hacked him to bits. Emboldened by this bloody moment, the group of local men, both Mexican and Native, decided to march to Charles Bent's house, a person they agreed needed chastising.

Charles and Ignacia met the approaching mob on the porch while the other family members hid. Before Charles could even speak, arrows flew through the air, striking his head and Ignacia's shoulder. Ignacia handed Bent his pistols and then hid in a back room, where she and the other women devised a desperate plan. While Bent held off the mob, the rest of the family would break through the adobe wall that adjoined another house and drag everyone to safety. While the shouting mob fired bullets and arrows into the house and began to tear the roof off, the family dug desperately with fire pokers and spoons. Somehow they succeeded; Bent and his entire family escaped to the house next door, but not to safety.[55]

The mob, in its rage to get to Bent, followed them. As his children Teresina, Alfredo, Estafina, and Rumalda watched, the angry men scalped Bent, shot him with arrows and bullets, and completed the task by stripping the body and mutilating it. They tacked Bent's bloody scalp to a board and paraded it through the streets. The Bent family huddled on the floor next to what remained of their father's body. In an occupied New Mexico, Bent's children, the fruit of racial mixing, now reminded people of who had power and who didn't, a dangerous status. A Taos trader, Dick Wootton, later claimed that "the half-breed children were . . . marked for slaughter." Since "Mexicans and Indians all had dark complexions," hair and eyes were made "the test of blood." In this setting, blood could tell: "children who had light hair and blue eyes" had to be hidden from a mob.[56]

Ignacia Bent and her sister, Josefa Carson, understood the grave danger their once-powerful status now created for them. They dressed like Indian women and took their blue-eyed children to the homes of trusted Mexican friends to wait out the growing war. A thousand men—Mexican, Native, and Anglo—marched from Taos toward Santa Fe, intent on expelling Americans. The news spread quickly, north and east to Bent's Fort and south to Santa Fe. Col. Sterling Price, a Missouri volunteer charged with the task of protecting the capital, decided to meet "the rebels" head on. He was accompanied by Ceran St. Vrain, Charles Bent's partner, and a company of volunteers, Bent family friends with personal scores to settle. They slogged through deep snow along the Rio Grande and met the Taoseños in two nasty battles. Their New Mexican opponents, without much ammunition or military experience, retreated to Taos after two days of fighting. By February 1847, thousands of people, Hispano and Native, had barricaded themselves inside the Taos Pueblo, willing to make a final stand.[57]

The battle for Taos raged for three days. In the end, three hundred Taoseños lay dead alongside thirty Americans. The pueblo itself was a smoking ruin. Although the uprising had broad support across northern New Mexico, the Taos Pueblo Indians bore the brunt of U.S. blame. President Polk wrote in his diary that the victory was "one of the most signal" because it showed occupied communities the costs of resistance. Dozens of Taoseños were hanged as traitors several weeks later. Ignacia Bent watched as the men who had killed her husband swung from the gallows, but the sight provided little comfort. Her world, the mixed-race melding of family and business in the border region, would never be the same.[58]

William Bent, who had stayed at the fort on the Arkansas, fearful that violence would sweep away his family and fortune as well, received the news of his brother's death, the battle, and the hangings in silence. Now personal tragedies overwhelmed the family. His loyal younger brother George had recently died at Bent's Fort of consumption, leaving George's widow and children to endure the Taos rebellion alone. Mistanta died after giving birth to their fourth child, Julia, in early 1847, just after the news reached the fort that the Taos rebels had been hanged. William's wives, Island and Yellow Woman, would care for Julia and for baby Charles, born to Yellow Woman in 1846 and named for his dead uncle.[59]

While the family adjusted to its new situation, the U.S. war with Mexico ended first in California and then in Mexico. Through the Treaty of Guadalupe Hidalgo, signed in early 1848, Mexico ceded California and its ports to the United States. What is now Utah,

Nevada, Arizona, New Mexico, and an expanded Texas became U.S. territory. The Bent family no longer lived on a border. The discovery of gold in California in February 1848, only days after U.S. and Mexican officials signed the treaty, made Bent's Fort into a way station to a gold rush. Bent watched as wagons crowded trails, many of their passengers carrying cholera. Hundreds of Cheyennes died. Reeling from personal losses, Bent saw that the life and business he had built at Bent's Fort would likely not survive American conquest. So in 1849, according to his son George, William Bent blew up his fort.[60]

In Oregon, Thomas McKay, like the thousands of men who rode past Bent's Fort, was lured by the stories of gold that replaced stories of war in Oregon newspapers. Eager for an adventure, in the summer of 1849 McKay led a pack train to California along with his sons William and Alexander. The former brigade leader agreed to test a new route through northern California recommended by an enterprising road builder. The trip was a disaster. The supposedly smooth, easy trail went over giant granite walls and through impenetrable forests. The well-built and carefully packed wagons had to be broken down into handcarts that the frustrated miners dragged and pushed.[61]

Shocked by the chaos he found in the California diggings, where "no man could trust another," Thomas and his sons returned to Oregon without any gold. McKay's half-brother, David McLoughlin, who accompanied him on the trip, recalled that the brutal winter expedition broke McKay's health. Thomas died attended by his mother, Marguerite Waddens McKay McLoughlin, in December 1849. The New Year opened with a group hanging just outside his mother's door on the main street of Oregon City. It had taken more than a year and the U.S. Army to do it, but they found five Cayuse men to blame for the Whitman Massacre. Troops brought them to Oregon City where the men—Teloquoit, Tomahas, Clokomas, Isiaasheluckas, and Kiamasumkin—appeared in an Oregon courtroom. Days later they were hanged in a public show of justice, even though the guilt of those particular Cayuse men was never clear.[62]

The hanging only made new Anglo-American settlers angrier. How Oregon would create and maintain new settlements would now be decided by people with eyes blindered by the racism and distrust created by Indian war. Mixing blood, long regarded as a solution, now seemed a dangerous problem. Thomas McKay was lucky enough to die before these ideas bore bitter fruit. His children faced the consequences.

=9=

Surviving War and
Peace in the 1850s

I n the summer of 1855, five thousand warriors of the Cayuse,
Yakima, Spokane, and Walla Walla nations gathered with their
families on the plateau above the Columbia River. A newly
appointed American governor had threatened to take their weapons,
horses, and land. Now these nations demonstrated their power to
resist. Isaac Stevens, governor and Indian superintendent of Washington Territory, was an ambitious railroad man who knew nothing
about Native nations. As he traveled west in 1855, he made treaties
with Nez Percés, Blackfeet, and Coeur d'Alenes so he could start
building railroads. In making those treaties, he had enlisted "local
half-breeds" as his interpreters.[1]

William Cameron McKay, the oldest son of Thomas and Timmee, served as Stevens's interpreter in Washington Territory. Born
in a Chinook village and educated in Connecticut, McKay had the
languages and personal connections Stevens needed. McKay took
his life in his hands to interpret at this moment. No matter who
translated it, the message to Stevens was that Pacific Northwest
nations had decided on war.[2]

Everything Isaac Stevens did, from offering poor-quality tobacco
to trying to get one chief to represent the gathered nations, made

matters worse. His proposal to the assembled crowd was for them to cede land and live on reservations. William McKay duly translated. When Stevens demanded a quick answer, McKay warned, "I am afraid we shall all be killed before we leave these grounds."[3]

Stevens and McKay survived, but starting in 1855 war spread over what is now Washington, Oregon, Idaho, and northern California. For three years, Pacific Northwest Indians protected their lands and lives by killing hundreds of White immigrants and U.S. soldiers. They also threatened William McKay, now considered a traitor for standing next to Isaac Stevens.

In the 1850s mixed-descent people negotiated four different frontier conditions: war, peace, removal into a new Indian country, and U.S. efforts to restrict their movement. They had managed such situations before, but now they faced them in an era of failed federal authority. Following dramatic expansion into the West, the U.S. government and the army could not keep their promises about opening land, upholding treaties, or keeping peace. Instead, Native nations, no longer willing to be pushed west and no longer imagined as part of an American state, went to war.

Indian war covered the western two-thirds of North America for thirty years, briefly interrupted by the Civil War. In the early 1850s, the violence spun out from two centers: the Pacific Northwest and California, and the northern Plains. Later in the decade it spread to the southern Plains and the Southwest. In those wars, people with Indigenous heritage who spoke European languages had the job of communicating with both friends and enemies. What they heard and saw was often inconceivable. When war erupted in the Pacific Northwest and in Colorado, the McKay and Bent families served as army scouts and interpreted at treaty sessions. In both positions, they struggled to find words to describe the violence of gold rushers and squatters who invaded Indian villages, or the vicious response of Native and U.S. soldiers.[4]

These wars, and the peace agreements that followed them, evolved in an era of strengthening racial distinctions. After the Mexican War, amid building tensions over slavery and abolition, the possibility that Native Americans would have full and unquestioned citizenship in the developing United States narrowed. Each state and territory developed its own rules about who could vote, sue, and serve on juries. These racial distinctions all had an effect on mixed-descent families. While the Drips family managed and even profited in the Missouri River trade world, the Fontenelles struggled on their Nebraska reservation. The Johnstons, meanwhile, protected the lives they created with new White neighbors along the Great Lakes.[5]

White Citizenship on the Great Lakes

When Janee and Johnston Schoolcraft left Michigan in 1840, they left behind a dense set of relations extending back to the 1700s. Their Johnston aunts and uncles, all "half-breeds," as that term came to be used in treaties beginning in the 1820s, had extended that world. They continued to make kin with White immigrants and with local Ojibwe and Odawa families. Janee and Johnston faced challenges in remaining part of Native families and convincing a White world they belonged.[6]

Their task got harder because their father, Henry Schoolcraft, was building the intellectual architecture to make mixing blood illegal. Along with other race scientists and policy makers, Schoolcraft intended to protect White blood, narrowly defined as flowing from Anglo-Saxons, against pollution by Indians, Africans, and Mexicans. Human progress would continue, he believed, only if the fittest and purest members of the White race became citizens. Despite evidence from his own Johnston family and their successes in Michigan, Henry believed that Indians, even the Johnstons, were trapped by a tragic inability to move along the evolutionary scale. They simply could not become part of a world of "Saxon northmen and Huguenots." Henry praised removal because it protected Indians, an "idle, pastoral, unphilosophic, and non-inductive race" who were "playing the very last bit of their dramatic history." He anticipated that they would soon disappear from the edges of the civilized United States, while more deserving White settlers took their land.[7]

Even as Indians faded away, however, Henry wanted to create a grand accounting of their history and present circumstances. And with the Southwest and the Pacific Northwest now added to the United States, Congress worried about what sorts of people lived in the new territories. In that context, Henry's ambitious promise to count and to "assess the level of civility" of every Indian nation became easier to sell. As a Christian who understood that Indians could never be incorporated into "our system," Henry promised to discover "the mode of rightly governing and managing them as wards under a governmental guardianship." In early 1847 Congress approved a huge Indian census with Henry Schoolcraft as its director.[8]

Even while he was traveling, writing, petitioning Congress, and keeping tabs on his children, Henry somehow found time to court a new wife. Mary Howard was a wealthy, unmarried South Carolinian approaching thirty. After several failed courtships, she wanted a husband, and Henry's financial needs made her plantation wealth appealing to him. They met, of course, at church. As an introduction, Henry sent Mary a long lecture about God's plan for the universe. After receiving that sermon of a first letter, Mary rejected him as "cold hearted," making her prickliness evident from the beginning. Henry and Mary were kindred spirits: they knew that the world rarely appreciated them because so few people measured up to their standards.[9]

Henry and Mary may have been a match, but Janee and Johnston deserved better. Once Mary accepted Henry's attentions, she grilled him about his children and their blood. Henry assured her that few "signs" presented themselves. Janee had "a lily complexion, set off with blue eyes and auburn hair." She had a "fierce intellect" and played the piano, sang, and had joined the church. Johnston had "dark hair, full, large, hazel eyes, and a proud hasty temper." Henry did not mention Johnston's "dark complexion," which he and his family worried about. After a brief courtship, almost entirely in letters, Henry and Mary married in January 1847 and settled in Washington, D.C.[10]

Their new domestic life required some family reshuffling. The relationship between Mary Howard and her new stepchildren began with suspicion over their racial makeup and got worse. When Johnston, age seventeen, failed at several jobs in New York City, Mary saw it as "proof" that "the issue of a mixed marriage" inevitably turned out badly. Johnston reluctantly returned to Washington, where his father hired him as copyist on the Indian statistics project. Living at home had to have been a misery.[11]

Janee tried to escape that misery. While the family lived in New York, Henry had befriended the poet Charles Fenno Hoffman, a famous eccentric. Hoffman took an interest in Janee, nearly thirty years younger. An amputee and avid traveler, he had published several books about his western travels in search of good health and sanity. Hoffman had settled in New York to edit the *New York Mirror* but missed his western adventures. He loved the idea of Janee's "savage blood" and asked her to put his poems into Ojibwe.[12]

When Janee moved to Washington with her father and new step-mother, she and Hoffman began corresponding. After a year of writing, they planned to marry in 1849. Henry and Mary agreed, since even if Hoffman was old, unstable, and legless, he was White and willing to marry Janee. However, a week before the wedding, the groom had what Henry labeled a violent attack of dementia. Hoffman never recovered and spent the rest of his life, thirty-five years, in an institution. Janee, shocked by this turn of events, went to Canada to recover with her aunt Charlotte and her White and Ojibwe cousins.[13]

Henry Schoolcraft meanwhile soldiered on with his great work, the six-volume *Historical and Statistical Information Respecting the History, Condition and Prospects of the Indians of the United States.* He had two co-authors: the artist and military officer Seth Eastman, and trader and politician Henry Sibley. Both men had begun their careers in Michigan's fur trade and had mixed-race children of their own. After Henry suffered strokes that paralyzed his writing hand, Janee and Johnston returned to Washington to help Henry manage the data he received from hundreds of Indian agents, subagents, military officers, missionaries, and fur traders. Overwhelmed with information, it took Henry seven years and almost $127,000 to collate and publish the tomes.[14]

As Henry's project went on and on, Janee found the best possible way to spite her stepmother: in 1855 she married Mary's beloved younger brother, Benjamin Howard. Henry was delighted; Mary was horrified. She wrote to a friend about her "anguish" that her "morally elevated and idolized brother was to be connected to that hateful Indian race." In her "hopeless grief" over this turn of events, Mary Howard Schoolcraft developed her own great project.[15]

She began a novel titled *The Black Gauntlet*, intended to defend the South against Harriet Beecher Stowe's 1852 *Uncle Tom's Cabin*. Outraged by Stowe's unflattering view of slavery and slave owners—and by Janee's marriage—Mary wrote furiously. She produced not exactly a novel but a collage of characters who discussed God's approval of the plantation South. The book concluded with a lecture on the dangers of racial mixing. Borrowing autobiographical details from her husband and stepchildren, Mary invented a Mr. Roland Walsingham who married a half-Indian with defective blood, a poet who went insane. Poor Mr. W is left with two children from this "abominable amalgamation." She used Henry's connections to get her book published and dedicated it to him.[16]

Interpreters and Scouts in the Pacific Northwest

While Mary Howard Schoolcraft wrote fiction about racial amalgamation and Henry Schoolcraft built science around it, mixed-descent men and women who worked for the Indian Service or the army as interpreters or scouts had to translate the consequences of that race science to their Indian kin. Misunderstanding and resentment were baked into the position. Interpreting what other people didn't understand or couldn't see made interpreters untrustworthy. Their ability to speak several languages made them double-tongued and gave them power, even though the position stood on the bottom tier of Indian Service employment. But being paid by the government made their role even more suspect. It wasn't clear whose interests they served.[17]

As Ozhaguscodaywayquay's sons, George, William, and John Johnston had always been interpreters. In the 1840s, federal officials—invoking treaties negotiated by Henry Schoolcraft—pressured them to move their Ojibwe families, long residents of Michigan, Wisconsin, and Canada, west to Minnesota, home to the fiercest enemies of the Ojibwe, the Dakota Sioux. Sioux raiders, protecting their land, attacked the new Ojibwe villages, stealing Ojibwe children and burning fields. Watching this, the Johnstons' kin refused to leave their lands east of Lake Superior. They stalled by getting George and William Johnston to write treaties demanding millions in payment, which they knew Congress would never accept. They held out for decades. In 1854 the Sault Ste. Marie, L'Anse, and La Pointe Ojibwe bands traveled to Washington to negotiate a treaty to allow them to stay home. They chose a delegation of "12 Indians and four half-breeds" including George Johnston, a "half-breed of the Sault Sainte Marie band," who served as interpreter. The La Pointe Ojibwe elder, Bizhiki, made a powerful statement to George Manypenny, a commissioner of Indian affairs who believed in local reservations. With George Johnston translating everyone's words, they signed a treaty protecting Michigan Ojibwes from removal.[18]

After that small victory, many Michigan Ojibwe did exactly what George Johnston and his brothers and sisters did: they disappeared into logging, fishing, and mining jobs that required local knowledge. New settlers recognized the essential role the Ojibwe played in the regional economy. Mining towns along Lake Superior depended entirely on Ojibwe farmers, hunters, and fishermen for food. Ojibwe women produced the clothing, snowshoes, fur coats, and hats that made life in Michigan possible. White newcomers came to see that mixing blood still made for good neighbors.[19]

Such particular, and delicate, relationships, however, could never be knitted in the violent Pacific Northwest. When Washington, Oregon, and Idaho became part of the United States in 1846, the paramount aim of settlers was to get land away from its Native and old trader residents. Faced with White squatters who stole crops and burned villages, and who were still angry over the fallout from the Whitman massacre and the "Cayuse War" that followed it, many Native communities stepped up cycles of raiding and killing. White newcomers responded in kind. No one was safe.[20]

In 1850, amid this conflict, the Oregon Land Donation Act sorted out how local land would be handed out. The governing assumptions were that Indian nations would sign away their rights and that U.S. citizens—in this case, residents from old trader families and new immigrants—would control the reallocation of land. Oregonians, new and old, wrote and voted on the donation act. White married couples could get 640 acres, with each person owning 320 acres in their own names. Single White male settlers, eighteen years of age, could claim 320 acres. "American half-breed Indians" were eligible for land claims under the law, but not Blacks, Hawaiians, single women, or all other "Indians." To get actual title to land, claimants had to fulfill three other requirements: take up residency on the land, cultivate it for four years, and become territorial citizens before December 1, 1851.[21]

But who could actually become a citizen? New immigrants saw old French fur trade communities as foreign: Catholic, loyal to the British Hudson's Bay Company, and suspiciously related to Indians. Should such "foreigners" be allowed voting rights or citizenship? As scientists like Henry Schoolcraft encased racial and gender hierarchies into law, the path to citizenship proved a rocky one. In Oregon, legislators from the Willamette Valley introduced a bill to allow some "half-breed Indians" to qualify for "citizenship in this Territory." They had to meet numerous requirements: have a "white father and Indian mother," speak and write English, have "in all respects the education habits and associations of a white person," and be a person of "good moral character." However, legislators from southern Oregon, where a brutal war raged between White miners and Rogue River Indians, made sure even that limited bill failed.[22]

When Washington Territory was carved from Oregon in 1853, the McKays and their Native kin ended up in Washington, where no treaties had been made and no land could be claimed by new settlers. The recently appointed governor, Isaac Stevens, the Massachusetts-born railroad promoter, wanted all land to be in American settlers' hands, and all Indians ensconced on small reservations. But on the plateaus of eastern Washington, he found independent Nez Percé, Spokane, Coeur d'Alene, Walla Walla, and Cayuse warriors who had no intention of giving up their land.[23]

FORTS, GOLD RUSHES, AND RESERVATIONS, 1848–1868

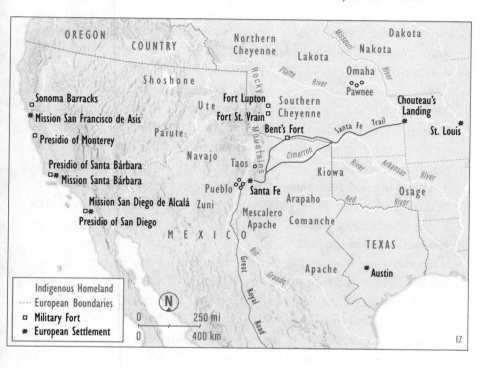

The danger increased as the nations of the Pacific Northwest gathered in the summer of 1855, when William McKay interpreted the discontent and danger to Stevens himself. McKay noticed a Cayuse chief who walked up to mark his X on the treaty, while biting his lip to contain his rage and leaving his mouth covered with blood. McKay knew that the gathered leaders intended war, no matter what they signed. Stevens ignored it all, convinced that a few Xs on a piece of paper meant that he had won. The peoples of the Columbia now knew that Governor Stevens could be educated only by war. Two months later, as William McKay had warned, three separate Indian wars spread over the region.[24]

The government had promised Indigenous Washingtonians food, sawmills, blacksmith shops, and cash in return for allowing immigrant traffic to pass through their lands. When none of that came, they stole cattle and horses from immigrant trains. Angry immigrants shot Indians. Cayuses and Walla Wallas killed their agents. Yakimas attacked white miners. Rogue River Indians burned saw-mills and gristmills in new towns. Native resistance stopped immi-grant wagons, miners headed to goldfields, and town building for nearly three years.[25]

In 1855, with this deadly situation unfolding around him, William McKay opened a store along the immigrant trail where it crossed the Umatilla River in northeastern Oregon. He hoped to sell supplies to immigrants as they approached the mountains and start a cattle ranching operation. The war interrupted those plans. Cayuses and Yakimas burned the houses and stole the cattle, pigs, and horses of White residents in the region. McKay, who had credibility with the Cayuse because he had not lied to them at the recent treaty meeting, received a warning.

In the late winter of 1855, as frightened residents abandoned their homes and poured into tiny army forts, the U.S. Army tried to orga-nize and respond. In February 1856 it sent two companies of regular troops from Fort Dalles—with some civilian horse packers, Indian scouts, and a mountain howitzer—into Yakima lands. But the out-numbered Yakimas held their familiar ground, and U.S. troops retreated, leaving their howitzer behind.[26]

The news that the army had failed, routed by Native warriors, shocked everyone. The governor quickly issued a call for volunteers, and nearly five hundred men gathered at Fort Dalles. As his father had in 1847 during the Whitman crisis and the Cayuse War, William McKay rushed to the defense of his community: Anglo-American, French, and Native. Like other Oregonians, he and his neighbors responded to the crisis by forming a militia company. They called theirs the French Company as it consisted mostly of ex-traders and local French settlers. This made them especially suspect to White newcomers; local newspapers called speaking French a "code" and "treasonable." One of its members recalled later that the company's name wasn't accurate as "there was only one Frenchman, the balance all being mixed bloods, like Dr. W. G. McKay, Antoine Rivet, Joseph Depart and Augustin Delard, Narciss Vivet, Es. Groggier." McKay would later remember proudly that "in battle with the Indians they were heedlessly brave." Oregon and Washington both tried to make it illegal for mixed men to serve in militias, to vote, and to own land that winter.[27]

William McKay, like many other mixed-descent men, now took up arms as a scout for the U.S. Army. The decision to lead enemy troops into the heart of Indian country broke hearts and minds. Was it a choice, or did people make these decisions under such duress that *choice* isn't the right word? The Pawnees looked at the situation on the Plains in the 1850s and decided that allying with the United States and using their talents as warriors would be a safer choice than any other. William McKay and others made similar choices under terrible pressure.[28]

The U.S. Army, like scouts and interpreters, struggled to understand its role in western conquest. After the war with Mexico ended and the cession of Oregon was completed, the army had a vast new territory to police. The number of regular troops almost doubled in those years to more than eighteen thousand, but the army's size never caught up to local needs. As a peacetime army with "constabulary" duties, it was supposed to keep order and enforce the law. This benign charge, however, hid what it actually did. It waged war on Native nations but rarely enforced the law on White civilians who trespassed on Native lands. Such contradictions disgusted professional army men. Officers stationed across the West had nothing but contempt for impatient immigrants who "had no respect for law and order."[29]

We don't know how William McKay felt about his service in that confusing war. It expanded in scope as more powerful nations— Walla Walla, Palouse, Snake, and Umatilla—joined the war. Accusing the U.S. Army of incompetence, Gov. Isaac Stevens demanded that the remaining regulars leave so that his volunteers could take over. In 1856 the war spread west, and fighting flared on both sides of the Cascades. When gold mining immigrants sparked vicious encounters while crossing Indian lands, President James Buchanan intervened and sent in Gen. John E. Wool, commander of the Department of the Pacific.

Wool reviled U.S. citizens who invaded Indian lands and then demanded federal support when Native peoples resisted. He responded to Buchanan's command by closing every immigrant road into Oregon and Washington while his troops prepared for a campaign. Governor Stevens and local newspaper editors grew apoplectic as federal soldiers methodically built forts and gathered supplies, while travel to Oregon stopped and Indian attacks went unchallenged.[30]

In the midst of the crisis, in October 1856, William Cameron McKay and Margaret Campbell got married. Both were from Hudson's Bay Company families. Margaret, of Canadian-Cree descent, had spent her childhood in HBC forts in Canada. She attended schools in Red River, where trader families sent their children for an education and to find suitable marriage partners. She had arrived in Oregon, still single, with her newly married sister, Mary Campbell Sinclair. Mary's husband, James Sinclair, was Cree-Scots Canadian, and educated at Edinburgh University. He took an officer's position at the HBC's Fort Walla Walla. Sinclair arrived with his new wife Mary, and four of her brothers and sisters, in 1854.[31]

They all ended up as refugees at Fort Dalles in the fall of 1855. James Sinclair was killed by Yakima warriors during a bitter fight to protect army supplies and ammunition in March 1856. After his death and as another winter of war brewed, a decision to marry may have seemed hopeful. In any case, William Cameron and Margaret Campbell McKay moved to a community around Pendleton, Oregon, one hundred miles east of Fort Dalles, hoping to escape war and build a business.[32]

Instead, William got pressed back into service as a scout for a brutal, and effective, campaign through Yakima and Cayuse country in 1857 and 1858. Led by Col. George Wright, the troops were directed to find and defeat individual bands so thoroughly that they would sign treaties agreeing to move to reserve lands in northeastern Washington, far away from the Walla Walla Valley and the Columbia River. Scouts moved ahead of the troops, finding bands of Indians and deciding whether to take hostages or burn their villages. William McKay worked at this dangerous job through one long winter and spring. He "mustered out" in the fall of 1857, when General Wright planned a campaign through eastern Washington. Wright's troops

and howitzers killed hundreds of Cayuse and their allies, slaughtered thousands of Indian horses, and burned their camps. A Cayuse leader, Howlish Wampoo, summed up the terrible situation: "We
had thousands of horses and cattle; the hills and valleys were covered with them. Now . . . not an animal is to be seen." After General
Wright hanged sixteen warriors who had refused to sign a treaty, the
Cayuse agreed to stop fighting.[33]

William and Margaret McKay fled the violence on the Columbia
Plateau. They moved to Champoeg, the old French settlement in the
Willamette Valley, near Fort Vancouver where William had grown
up. In the 1860 census, they had two children, Flora and Thomas,
and a farm worth $2,000. Their next-door neighbors were Peter and
Mary Waggoner, a White man and an Indian woman. The census
taker didn't note the McKays' race.[34]

This moment in Pacific Northwest history usually plays as prelude: with the Indians vanquished, real settlers could get to work.
But after so many towns had been burned and farms and trading
posts devastated, violence still simmered on both sides. Indians
still attacked isolated settlements, stole animals, and robbed immigrants on the Oregon Trail. White settlers, army men, and miners
still set up camp on Indian lands, kidnapped women and children,
and burned villages. Men like William McKay were caught between
emerging racial categories. It wasn't clear if they could vote, own a
gun, pay taxes, or run a business, or whom they could marry.

In 1859 three large reservations in Oregon (Umpqua, Grande
Ronde, and Warm Springs) and three in Washington (Yakima,
Colville, and Quinault) officially became home to the region's
"defeated" Native nations. The big reservations offered some respite
for mixed-descent families, increasingly under pressure to become
Indians. Many French and Native families left the Willamette Valley
and joined their Native kin on Indian reservations in eastern Oregon
and Washington. Still others migrated to less settled areas throughout the Pacific Northwest, places like Frenchtown in eastern Washington and the French settlement near Roseburg, Oregon, or the
traders' town in Pendleton, Oregon.[35]

In 1862 William McKay moved to the Warm Springs Reservation

with Margaret and their three children. A trained medical doctor, he became reservation physician in mountainous central Oregon. His reports to his superiors about tuberculosis, scrofula, and cirrhosis suggest something about the dire conditions in which people found themselves there. The McKays and their Native neighbors at Warm Springs were also in constant danger from raiding Snakes, Bannocks, and Paiutes. In 1860 the Indian agent reported to his superior that the reservation had failed as an "asylum" for Indians, because of "the loss of life and property by the frequent forays of the predatory and treacherous Snake Indians." Because of the raids, the only building on the reservation was a "commodious blockhouse, built for the defense of the resident employees." During Indian raids, William, an employee of the agency, could take his family into the blockhouse, but his neighbors and patients could not.[36]

The continuing trouble convinced the army and the Indian Service to arm a group of Native men from Warm Springs. According to the local superintendent, the Indians enlisted with the understanding that they could have "booty won from the Snake Indians but were armed and rationed by the government." William Cameron McKay and his half-brother Donald McKay became captains of this guard. They and the Warm Springs guards joined other local troops to drive Snake Indians out of southern Oregon. Between the rock of being an Indian in frontier Oregon and the hard place of serving as a "half-breed scout" for the U.S. Army, the McKays soldiered on.[37]

Bleeding Kansas

Life was for a time more peaceful along the Missouri, where the Drips family continued to place their bets on the fur trade. After Macompemay's death in 1847, Andrew Drips couldn't bear to stay in Westport, so he re-upped with the American Fur Company. He became chief trader or *bourgeois* at Fort Pierre along the upper Missouri. Named for the St. Louis fur trade mogul Pierre Chouteau, this busy post was eight hundred miles upriver from St. Louis in what is now South Dakota. Hundreds of people—traders, boatmen, herders, tailors, carpenters, blacksmiths, and tinsmiths—supported the work that hundreds of Native women did to process 100,000 hides coming down the Missouri each year.[38]

The Gold Rush changed everything. With more than 100,000 miners rushing to California in 1849, the federal government bought Fort Laramie from the American Fur Company as a site to support and rescue ill-prepared travelers. Drips's bosses sent him to manage a store at the fort. It was an exotic world to the migrants. In 1849 J. Goldsborough Bruff described Fort Laramie as a place where "you can buy whisky for $5 per gallon; and look at the *beautiful* squaws of the traders." But Drips hated his demotion to storekeeper and soon returned home to Kansas City.[39]

He didn't come home alone. Sometime in 1849 he married a young woman named Louise Geroux, whom he likely met at Fort Pierre. Louise was "French and Yankton Sioux" and twenty when she married Andrew.

Drips, respected in the fur trade and with property in Kansas City, could have done what many fur traders did—marry a White woman with good prospects in the new settler world of Missouri, Kansas, and Nebraska. In marrying a Dakota and White woman, he made a different gamble about his family's future. His oldest daughter, Mary Jane, now nineteen, had just married Leonard Benoist, a trader descended from two generations of French-Canadian men who had married Dakota women. Mary Jane and Leonard comfortably joined a new iteration of the mixed-blood world in eastern Kansas.[40]

Louise stepped right into Andrew's household there. Literate, with beautiful handwriting, she spoke English, French, and Dakota. Andrew and Macompemay's Kansas City home revived under her care. William and Catherine, still at home, attended St. Louis schools much of the year. Mary Jane, with a new baby, found herself a widow in 1849 just a year after her marriage to Leonard Benoist. She and Louise, about the same age, became friends and lived near each other for most of their lives. Andrew and Louise added five more children to the family between 1849 and 1857. Andrew, still working in the fur trade, was often absent, but other fur trade wives, like the Omaha Therese Picotte and James Kipps's two Mandan wives, Mary and Earth Woman, lived nearby. Another retired trader, William Laidlaw, and his Dakota wife, Mary Ann, bought property next to the Dripses. Nested in these familiar relationships, Andrew Drips's older children helped Louise manage a growing household.[41]

Everyone's plans, however, depended on land. Decades of treaty making and land swaps that had removed Indians from the Midwest and South left every bit of what would become today's Kansas and Nebraska assigned to immigrant tribes or Native nations who had been there for generations. Surprised visitors described Kansas towns "full of Indians," with "Sacs and Foxes, Shawnees and Delaware, Wyandottes" among the twenty thousand who had been "removed" from the old Northwest. They lived amid Kaws, Omahas, Otoes, Iowas, Osages, and Pawnees—the original inhabitants who still numbered in the tens of thousands.[42]

This crowded landscape was where the Drips family envisioned their futures. Using the legal entity called a half-breed reserve that traders had first deployed in the 1830s to protect their mixed-blood families, the Dripses waited as the Great Nemaha Half-Breed Tract, first described in an 1830 treaty, now appeared on Nebraska and Kansas maps. Turning an old promise into an actual place meant that the category of "half-breed" would be defined, measured, and made into law. U.S. treaty commissioners, eager to open up Nebraska and Kansas for White settlement, conducted a census in 1857 that counted 1,125 "half-breeds." Mary Jane Drips Benoist, a widow with a seven-year-old son, would be allocated land on the Great Nemaha in 1860, along with her three siblings, her stepmother, and her five half-brothers and sisters.[43]

Andrew Drips meanwhile applied for trading licenses along the Platte and upper Missouri that included his sons and sons-in-law. He served as bondholder for his son William's license in 1856. Trading with Plains Indians was dangerous work in the 1850s. Gold Rush migrants were pushing Indian peoples away from roads and rivers and into each other's paths. Droughts and overhunting eroded bison populations, ensuring that Plains nations fought over hunting areas. Drips continued on trading trips until he turned seventy, a long career in a hard business. He suffered a last personal blow in

1859 when his younger son William died from a summer fever along the Green River in what is now northern Utah. Andrew buried him there since they were many weeks from home when he died.[44]

Andrew came home from that last trip in poor health, and he died at his Kansas City home on September 1, 1860. His death, noted in the St. Louis and Kansas City newspapers as the loss of a rare old pioneer, left nine Otoe, Dakota, and White children and a widow. After forty years in the fur trade, the family had Kansas City property and promised allocations on the Great Nemaha Half-Breed Tract.[45]

Andrew's still-living children with Macompemay—Charles, Mary Jane, and Catherine—settled into adult lives. Charles, the eldest, tested several careers, not unusual for young men trying to establish themselves in the mid-nineteenth century. After working for his father as a trader and hunter, he owned part interest in a riverboat that went bust almost immediately. Mary Jane, the widowed eldest daughter, lived close to Louise and often took in her children. In 1857 Mary Jane married a St. Louis man named Francis Marion Barnes. Barnes had no property when they married, but he brought a crucial asset to the marriage: as a White man he could buy or sell any land he wanted, including his wife and stepson's claims on the Nemaha tract.[46]

Catherine Drips married William Mulkey, a White man from North Carolina, in 1853. They lived in Kansas City near Louise and Mary Jane. They had one baby, Mary Celestine, who died at only three months in 1857. Catherine housed and educated a number of local mixed-race children, including her own half-siblings. In 1860, right after Andrew Drips's death, Catherine's household was full. Mountain man Jim Bridger's half-Spokane daughter Jane, aged eleven, boarded with her, as did Louise Drips's children, all labeled as "Indian" in the 1860 census. She and William Mulkey lived on property that Catherine brought to the marriage, including two Black slaves, part of Andrew Drips's Westport household.[47]

With White migration into the Kansas-Nebraska region increasing and debates over slavery and landownership growing more heated, deadly warfare with the powerful Plains nations erupted.

To protect overland trails and end expensive wars, state and federal officials decided that Indians needed to be "concentrated" in zones where settlers who followed rules and settled legally could be protected from them, but settlers who squatted, sold alcohol, and stole cattle could be kept away. It remained unclear who would police such borders and how.[48]

Mixed-descent families lived in places where those hard questions got tested: the earliest western reservations. In 1853, just as these decisions on land and race were being made, a new commissioner of Indian affairs, George Manypenny, took over. Like most political appointees, Manypenny had few credentials as an Indian expert, but he was enthusiastic about reservations. He envisioned them as places where Indians would develop Anglo-American-style agriculture and learn about private property and individual wealth. Manypenny planned to cluster Indian colonies around the Overland Trail, where Indians would farm and sell produce to White migrants heading west. Needing a powerful bureaucracy that could force Indians to relocate and keep new immigrants off reservation land, he doubled the number of agencies in the region and quadrupled their employees.[49]

Lucien Fontenelle's sons, who grew up at Bellevue and now as adults lived in Omaha villages, worked for these new agencies. Logan Fontenelle helped to create Manypenny's model reservation in the northeastern corner of Nebraska. He persuaded his relatives to cede 4 million acres of land in Iowa and Nebraska to the United States. In return, the Omaha were promised annuities of $40,000 for thirty years, and the protection of U.S. troops from Plains raiders. On the northern edge of familiar territory, the reservation was removed from the heaviest overland traffic. It offered good deer hunting but poor farming, and more worrisome, the reservation bordered Dakota hunting territory. To demonstrate its safety, Logan Fontenelle, Joseph La Flesche, and their families moved to the Omaha reservation in 1855. Many Omahas refused to move to such a dangerous spot, but together La Flesche and Fontenelle ran a ferry business that capitalized on Gold Rush traffic.[50]

The Kansas-Nebraska Act of 1854 introduced another sort of

violence to the Omaha as Indian country jarringly became part of the United States. The act, which organized a vast territory west of the Missouri River, was premised on the concept of popular sovereignty: residents could decide for themselves whether their territories allowed slavery. Violent abolitionists and militant slave owners poured into Kansas and Nebraska, both intending to steal the popular vote. They moved onto Indian land, built competing towns and governments, and then engaged in open warfare. Under the spotlight of national attention because of the intensifying sectional controversy, tens of thousands of Native people disappeared. Through military conquest, land theft, and simple murder, the Kansas–Nebraska Act delivered land to White migrants when not one acre was actually available. Only violence and a complete disregard for law made Kansas and Nebraska into White settler states.[51]

Manypenny hired Daniel Vanderslice, a White man with an Iowa son, to run the Indian agency that included the Otoe reservation and the Nemaha tract. Together they managed perhaps the most violent patch of ground in the United States. George Manypenny's vision of Native farmers settled amid White farmers did not survive territorial Kansas with its fur trade past. White men fought over politics, sold liquor and guns, and shot each other. An agent working for the Otoe and Omaha complained that "there are no fine settlers to be models, only many unprincipled persons who locate themselves along the river for the purpose of trading whiskey to the Indians." Sioux and Pawnee raiders increased the violence.[52]

The old trade world, in which Native people protected their interests by intermarriage and local alliances, provided some cover. Vanderslice's account books show Anglo or French men whose Native wives made claims for annuity payments and land. Families with French names dominated payrolls and school enrollments. Native customers with a little cash made stores and trading posts lucrative businesses.

Many people profited from these arrangements, but ready cash also attracted criminals. One July day in 1852, Pvt. Joseph Dodge and three of his soldier friends deserted from Fort Leavenworth. To get transportation and cash, they attacked a Delaware Indian and his sister who were driving thirteen horses and carrying their families' annuity money. Leaving the two Delawares for dead, the thieves took the money and horses to Independence and boasted about their success. The Delaware woman survived and told her story to Agent Vanderslice. Because the deserters had bragged about their crimes so brazenly, they were hanged after a public trial. Most thieves on the reservation, however, were bigger: railroads, banks, and large land firms that took Native annuities, stock, and land without any threat of hanging.[53]

The Omahas, living on reservations north of Kansas's chaos, had their own enemies. In 1855, while picking gooseberries, Logan Fontenelle ran into Sioux raiders. After a brief skirmish, the warriors killed and scalped Fontenelle and five of his party. Joseph La Flesche later described long lines of horses that accompanied Fontenelle's body as "the Indian chiefs and braves, mounted on ponies, with the squaws and relatives of the deceased, expressed their grief in mournful outcries." Different accounts of his burial, at Bellevue and at the new Omaha reservation, reflect Logan Fontenelle's complex life. According to one version, a trader and an "Otoe half-breed" (probably Charles or William Drips), stood over the grave. The trader read the Episcopal funeral service while a female Baptist missionary sang hymns. Another account describes a Catholic wake, while another makes it an entirely Omaha occasion in which "the Indians had their own oratory and chanted funeral songs into the night." While none of these accounts is completely credible, their variety suggests Logan Fontenelle's importance in the community.[54]

Logan's death saved him from suffering Omaha life in the 1850s. The reservation in the Blackbird Hills where Fontenelle had been killed continued to be dangerous. In 1856 Sioux raiding parties took fifty-nine horses. In 1859 Sioux raiders attacked a party of seventy elderly Omahas and children out gathering food. In 1860, when agents and missionaries wanted to build a school on the northern edge of the reservation near the Dakota border, the Omahas warned, "Do not go there. The Sioux will kill the children." They were right. The next year Brulé Sioux attacked Omahas in a schoolyard. Finally, the Omahas convinced their agent that they needed military protection. They created a cavalry unit led by mixed-race men, Whites, and English-speaking Omahas, all "suitable to arm," according to their agent.[55]

After Logan died, his wife Gixpeaha stayed on the reservation. Their daughters went to the mission school, married Omaha men, and raised families. Logan's brothers barely outlived him as Omaha and Otoe lands became settler Nebraska. Tecumseh Fontenelle, the middle brother, stayed near Bellevue but was murdered in a fight with his brother-in-law, Louis Neals. Albert became the blacksmith at the Pawnee agency but was killed in an accident in 1859. Removal and reservations nearly destroyed that generation of Fontenelles.[56]

The Fort Laramie Treaty, 1851

The Bent family, adjusting to life without Mistanta or Charles Bent, still believed they could find a solution to Great Plains violence. As Indian raiders poured north from Texas and Mexico, and as cholera epidemics swept the Platte and Arkansas river overland routes, the Bents and their Cheyenne kin spent the summer away from the river. In 1851 they joined an unprecedented gathering of Native people to discuss safety on the Plains at Fort Laramie.

President Millard Fillmore and the superintendent of western Indian affairs, D. D. Mitchell, had convinced Congress to allocate $100,000 for a grand assembly of Plains nations. Through diplomacy, bribery, and threats, U.S. officials urged attendance by tribes "residing south of the Missouri River, east of the Rocky Mountains, and north of the lines of Texas and New Mexico, viz, the Sioux or Dahcotahs, Cheyennes, Arrapahoes, Crows, Assinaboines, Gros-Ventre, Mandans, and Arrickaras." Mitchell's team of commissioners— federal officials and Native interpreters—spent several weeks camped with fifty thousand Indigenous warriors and their families from both sides of the Platte River. A surprised observer noted that "hereditary enemies smoked and feasted together, exchanged presents, adopted each other's children according to their own customs," all indicating "their peaceful and friendly intentions." Their efforts to create new alliances and rebuild old ones reflected the grim demographic facts of peoples decimated by smallpox, cholera, and Plains warfare.[57]

The Bent family, like many others, arrived in early August. William Bent allowed a Catholic priest to baptize his children, an act that Island and Yellow Woman protested. Baptism would not protect children from the new worldly dangers of Plains life. Native peoples wanted two things from any treaty: access to annuities and trade goods as a safety net in years when bison failed them, and protection from the Lakota. U.S. officials, however, had different goals: to move Plains nations away from the overland trails and to stop Indian war and raiding.[58]

The treaty agreed to at Fort Laramie in 1851 drew clear boundaries for the purpose of creating separate Indian nations within Indian country. In return for land exchanges and the promise of peaceful passage through Indian lands, the U.S. government promised to protect Indian borders from Native and White intruders. While Native nations learned to live in their new independent states, the U.S. government would pay them annuities—yearly cash payments and agreed upon lists of goods—for ten years. These items would be delivered to each nation's agency, which would distribute the agreed-upon cash and goods to Indians whom the agents decided had lived up to their end of the agreement. From the perspective of Washington, it seemed viable: Indian people could be sequestered in a vast reservation at the center of the Plains, supervised inexpensively by a few federal officials.[59]

William Bent, skeptical of a plan in which Indians promised to stop fighting and Whites agreed to stop trespassing, had already hedged his bets. After destroying his fort, he became a rancher and invested in Kansas and Colorado real estate but kept his hand in Arkansas River Indian trade. The evolving world the Bents inhabited along the Arkansas remained mired in the chaos of the disputed U.S.-Mexico border. A panicked commissioner of Indian affairs reported that New Mexico Indians were "plundering and murdering the inhabitants without fear or restraint." He added that the "entire population is reckless, mixed, and heterogenous." In other words, he couldn't tell who was Indian, Mexican, or White. That heterogeneity made New Mexico "so discreditable and deplorable as to render its acquisition a misfortune." War came from every direction, continuously ignited by Comanche, Apache, Ute, and Lakota raiders.[60]

In 1852 the Bents sent their older children away from that war. Mary, the eldest, was fourteen; Robert and George were eleven and nine. They would attend school in Kansas City, preparing for lives in the new agricultural and mercantile economies that might offer safety and success. Island and William accompanied the three children along the Santa Fe Trail leading from their southern Plains home. The road was now rutted and treeless. Council Grove, the center of the Kaw reservation, had been stripped of trees and filled with liquor traders. When they reached the outskirts of Westport, they crossed Shawnee lands where saloons, gambling dens, and wine shops clustered along the road. Island, who had surely seen her relatives drink, and William Bent, who had made a fortune selling liquor in Colorado and New Mexico, were shocked at what they saw.[61]

Like so many other fathers in the fur trade, including Andrew Drips, William Bent bought property in Kansas City. Albert Boone, son of Daniel Boone and father to his own Native progeny, agreed to supervise the Bent children. Island stayed several weeks to get them settled, erecting her lodge outside Boone's house. The newspapers commented on William Bent's "tipi-wife" and admired her equestrian skills. Mary and Robert attended Mr. Scarritt's "Western Academy" located at the Shawnee mission, three miles west of town. Founded by Methodist missionary Nathan Scarritt in 1848, the school was radical in welcoming both girls and boys, and Native, White, and Black students who were put "in close competition for the race for knowledge."[62]

The school closed in 1857, when life in Kansas became dangerous. Mary remained in the Boone household until she was old enough to marry, and Robert and George continued their educations in St. Louis. Another old fur trader, Robert Campbell, who steered the boys of numerous trader families through elite education, supervised Robert, George, and a few years later, Charles, at the Christian Brothers' College. Underprepared in Greek, Latin, and Catholicism, they didn't enjoy the long years away from home. They saw their father once a year when he came to St. Louis to buy trade goods.[63]

William Bent got himself a new job. As in Michigan and Oregon, the first Indian agencies on the Plains were trading posts where traders became part-time agents. To support the promises to distribute annuities to many nations made in the Fort Laramie treaty, William Bent became an Indian agent and Bent's Fort the site of the new agency. The U.S. government paid Bent $400 per wagon to pick up promised goods in St. Louis and Westport, load them onto his wagons, and carry them eight hundred miles west. In late summer, as the train trundled along the Santa Fe Trail, Bent sent runners to villages announcing the wagons' arrival. Annuities were paid and goods were given out, but never as much as the government had promised, or as much as people needed in drought years when bison were hard to find. Even in difficult times, Cheyenne families erected tepees around the fort, and everyone celebrated the temporary plenty with feasts, dancing, and gift giving.[64]

When the 1850s began, the fur trade and the buffalo hide trade anchored a vibrant regional economy centered on the Platte and Arkansas. Highlighting a bright spot beyond Kansas's dangerous political turmoil, the Kansas City board of trade boasted that nearly ten thousand wagons trundled west to Santa Fe each year filled with 60 million pounds of merchandise. Wagons returning from Santa Fe carried $500,000 in bison and deer skins, beaver and otter pelts, and sacks of silver coins. Dead animals, the raw material of shoes, coats, hats, and leather straps, remained a crucial sector of the West's economy. The Cheyenne, Arapaho, Pawnee, and Kiowa controlled that trade and provided the legs and arms of its workforce.[65]

As the 1850s ground on, though, and as drought and war depleted bison populations, the Southern Cheyenne and Arapaho could not maintain their traditional lives in the southern Plains and Rocky Mountain region. Bent tried to position his extended Cheyenne family—the relatives of his two wives and his own five children—so that they might survive whatever happened. He spent a decade working to create a Cheyenne and Arapaho reservation in Colorado with a half-breed tract at its heart. His ranch, nestled along the Pur-gatoire River, lay on the southern border of the reservation. The land was treeless and windblown; only irrigation made anything green. But it was Cheyenne country, and Bent's relatives had been prom-ised significant land there. Bent and other fur trade fathers, present at every negotiation, carved out a possible future for the region.[66]

Colorado seemed like a good bet. Many New Mexican families—Indian, Anglo, and Mexican—moved there. People like the Bents and their neighbors started cattle and sheep businesses. William Bent began a cattle operation on the Purgatoire River but continued to trade with hundreds of Cheyenne families who had once gathered near Bent's Fort each summer. Moving to the cattle ranch, however, upset Bent's domestic life. Yellow Woman refused to live in the new place and had moved back to the Cheyenne camps several years ear-lier. When Bent came home from a trip east with gonorrhea, Island left him as well.[67]

In a pattern we have seen in Kansas, Michigan, and Oregon, trad-ers on the central Plains moved with their Native families to trading posts and ranches along the Platte and Arkansas rivers. Colorado communities like Pueblo and Boggsville evolved into towns with eth-nically complex populations. Boggsville, for example, included ex–Bent's Fort employees and Bent family members Thomas Boggs and his wife Rumalda Bent (one of Charles Bent and Ignacia Jaramillo's daughters), Kit Carson and his wife Josefa Jaramillo, and John Prow-ers and his wife Amache (daughter of the Southern Cheyenne leader Ochinee). Similar populations gathered in Julesberg and La Bonte, located north on the Platte River. Native and mixed men repaired carts and wagons, sold wine and whiskey, raised horses, sheep, and cattle, and developed the first irrigation projects in Colorado.[68]

These towns offered a glimmer of a future for mixed-descent fam-ilies. William Bent begged the federal government to "give them a start" toward a future of Native trading and ranching by developing Indian reservations near these mixed-blood communities. However, before anyone could move into that potential future, an especially vicious war ruined the present.[69]

War in Colorado

The Fort Laramie treaty had promised Plains nations that if they kept away from the Overland Trail, then the U.S. Army would protect them. That promise failed when the 1858 Pikes Peak gold rush flooded Cheyenne lands with travelers and their mules, horses, and cattle. Native groups lost the ability to hunt and move freely without running into White gold seekers. As wagon roads crisscrossed Cheyenne lands, the U.S. Army didn't protect anyone.

It was a desperate moment for the Southern Cheyenne, who were going hungry as the bison disappeared and White people overran their land. They were divided over how to live, whether to choose war and bison hunting or peace and farming. William Bent had to convey this impossible situation to Native kin and federal officials. He warned federal officials to limit contact between Whites and Plains raiders. He wrote that "a smoldering passion agitates these Indians, perpetually fomented by the failure of food." The Cheyenne, Bent knew, had nothing to lose.[70]

Native people saw gold miners as invaders but also as convenient food caches. White miners viewed the Indians as "hostiles." A popular guidebook to the Colorado gold country warned readers that for Indians "it is as natural for them to steal as to breathe." Indians did shoot, but mostly when attacked by White men. In April 1860 the Arapaho leader Left Hand left his village near Denver with a hunting party. The women and children who remained in the village were dragged from their lodges by drunken White men, then raped and tortured. The Arapaho, who couldn't identify the attackers, retaliated by stealing cattle and horses. White residents then demanded government protection from such "depredations," a nineteenth-century word describing enemy pillaging during war. If people suffered "depredations" rather than just theft, the U.S. government would reimburse them, making depredation claims a lucrative business.[71]

Depredations and violence spiraled up along the Platte River and around Denver. To avoid mayhem, many Cheyenne villages moved south to the Arkansas River in the summer of 1860. There drought and overhunting had depleted the bison, and travelers' cattle had eaten the grass of Cheyenne ponies. Kiowa and Ute raiders took advantage of the chaos and raided sleeping Cheyenne villages. Many young Cheyenne and Arapaho men joined war parties. Watching these developments with dread, William Bent went with his eldest son to talk to the people camped along the Arkansas. Bent didn't need a translator, but by bringing his son he highlighted his connection to the *Tsistsista* or Southern Cheyenne. They still numbered at least four thousand, and few wanted to move to a reservation. Much had changed about Cheyenne and Arapaho life, but summer villages still offered relaxed sociability: children played with dogs, women sewed moccasins or repaired lodges, and men talked, cleaned guns, and made arrows. Robert and William Bent knew how to approach such villages and how to help people listen. The Bents understood exactly what was at stake—Indians had to join the settler world, and quickly, or be wiped from the earth. Many Cheyennes, however, were inclined to fight.[72]

Late in 1860, recognizing the dangerous situation, the new commissioner of Indian affairs, A. B. Greenwood, traveled to Bent's Fort to negotiate a treaty. Greenwood, a political appointee who had never met an Indian, sought a quick agreement. He made the same mistake that Isaac Stevens had made in Washington: he demanded a treaty ceding all Native title to Colorado so that White miners, storekeepers, and farmers could claim land. Robert Bent and John Smith, both from Southern Cheyenne families, translated for the few Indians present that the treaty would put Colorado Indians on small reservations and open the territory for White business. They explained to Commissioner Greenwood how unhappy the chiefs were and how few were even willing to come to the meeting.[73]

Disgusted by this episode and prescient about the danger coming, William Bent resigned as Indian agent. He turned the post over to his old friend Albert Boone, the father of six White and Native children and the Bent children's guardian in Kansas City. In the winter of 1861, while Boone went to Washington, D.C., to work out the final details of the Treaty of Fort Wise, Robert Bent and John Smith agreed to travel among the tribes to persuade them to sign it. The young interpreters, under enormous pressure from the territorial governor, the commissioner of Indian affairs, and their own families, had to sell a document that no Cheyenne chief would sign. Most chiefs refused because the new reservation was too far from where they actually lived and hunted. Others refused because the annuities would go to government agents, farmers, teachers, and blacksmiths, leaving nothing for Cheyennes and Arapahos. With threats and alcohol, Bent and Smith coerced a few men who were not leaders to sign the treaty.[74]

The Fort Wise treaty, rushed through Congress, may be the most duplicitous of all Indian treaties. Its provision of land for Robert Bent and John Smith, the two "half-breed interpreters," further corroded an already bad deal. However duplicitous, some Cheyennes and Arapahos, truly starving, would sign anything to get food and supplies. But Northern Cheyenne and their Arapaho allies, who lived and hunted along the Platte and Republican rivers, refused to settle on the Arkansas Reservation, long the home of Southern Cheyennes. Such divisions brought on war.[75]

Dog Soldiers, once a respected division of elite Cheyenne warriors, now became outlaw bands that split from the nation, an option that appealed to many angry Cheyennes. Disdaining any move toward accommodation with Whites as anathema to Cheyenne culture, Dog Soldier villages now allied with Lakotas and Northern Arapahos bent on war. They became a third division of Cheyennes and carried increasing authority. Each treaty that the peace chiefs signed, and that White invaders and military authorities broke, meant that Cheyennes who had preached cooperation lost credibility. William Bent's own sons soon found violence more appealing than acquiescence.

William Bent's stockade and ranch stood at the southeastern end of the Cheyenne reservation, where he hoped to preserve his Cheyenne family empire along the Purgatoire River. Bent, along with the Cheyenne and Arapaho chiefs White Antelope, Left Hand, Black Kettle, Lean Bear, and Little Wolf, understood that to begin lives as ranchers, the Cheyenne and Arapaho needed water and firewood, grass to feed both horses and cattle, and bison to feed their people.

Only a few places on the southern Plains provided the landscape they needed, and the terrible Treaty of Fort Wise offered only a bit of that space. With a little luck, Bent hoped, he could buy time to reunite his family and his nation. But the ideas that Henry Schoolcraft and others had made into racial science and Indian policy left them with no luck and no time.[76]

In Colorado and the Pacific Northwest frontier settings, Indian war and gold rush migrations forced hard choices on mixed-descent people, often catching them in a dangerous middle. Found wanting by their Native kin when they translated bad treaties and bad news, their Indian blood made mixed families dangerous neighbors for new White residents. Many moved to reservations and became Indians. In Michigan and in Missouri River towns, however, peace had allowed mixed families to create lives with new mixtures of kin. But another war, begun over slavery, would upend every community.

=10=

Civil Wars in the West,
1860–1865

Abraham Lincoln's election in November 1860 electrified all three of William Bent's sons. Rumors flew through St. Louis, where George and Charles studied at Webster College. William wanted his sons to protect the family empire and its Cheyenne-Anglo partnership, and to avoid war. But when Southern states seceded from the Union and formed the Confederacy, and the first battles made headlines, the drama drew the Bent boys into the fight.

Mixed families, like others, got caught up in the Civil War. In Michigan, young men in the Johnston family went off to eastern battlefields. Felled by bullets and germs that invaded Union Army camps, few returned to their anxious families. In Kansas, Confederate guerrillas replaced Indian raiders as the threat mothers used to keep children inside. Mothers in the Drips family fled to reservations, where they plowed fields and protected them with guns, as Confederate raiders and their neighbors burned their homes, killed their horses, and stole their chickens. In Colorado, Indian war and civil war combined, splitting mixed families apart. Some Bent mothers and sons joined their Indigenous nations and went to war, while some sisters and fathers watched U.S. Army troops mow down their families. That era of war spared no one.

BATTLES: CIVIL WAR AND INDIAN WAR, 1860–1877

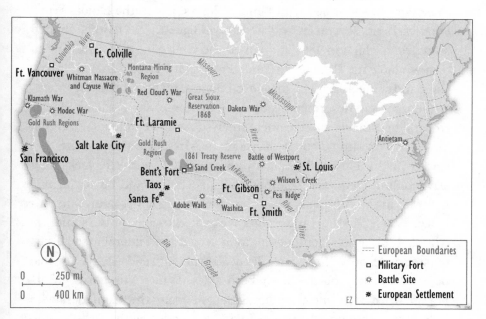

Fought over the issue of slavery's expansion into the West, the Civil War foregrounded ideas about race, citizenship, and manhood not only for Black Americans but also for Native people and their mixed-descent kin. White Americans had long used racial difference to justify Black slavery and Indian policy, including removal and war. For Native communities that crossed racial lines, such as the Bents' Colorado, the McKay family's Oregon, and Louise Geroux Drips's Great Nemaha Half-Breed Tract, those choices became uncomfortably visible in a war so freighted with race.[1]

George Bent's Confederate Civil War

George Bent began the war as a White man but ended it an Indian. Having spent several years among St. Louis's pro-Southern elite, including his Bent uncles and aunts who had households with many slaves, George joined the Confederates. His brother Robert, working on the family ranch near Fort Wise—formerly Bent's Fort and soon to be Fort Lyon—filled with Union soldiers, joined the Union Army. Charles Bent, seventeen and a year younger than George, slipped away from school in 1861 and joined the Cheyenne army forming in camps along the Republican and Smoky Hill rivers. In 1861 many sons, and some daughters, disobeyed their parents and joined armies.[2]

George Bent described his decision matter-of-factly: "I signed the roll and became part of Colonel Green's cavalry regiment." Nothing, however, was simple about decisions in Missouri, a slave state that stayed in the Union. Missouri's governor, Claiborne F. Jackson, a slaveholding Democrat, claimed that his state would be an "armed neutral" in the coming conflict, but personal loyalties spun into violence. When Missouri representatives voted to stay in the Union in March 1861, a pro-Confederate mob seized the Federal arsenal just outside St. Louis. The arms depot for the entire West, the arsenal became a deadly objective for both sides. When Missouri's governor guarded it using arms smuggled in from the Confederacy, a U.S. Army captain, Nathaniel Lyon, responded with ten thousand Federal troops. On May 10, 1861, he forced the badly outnumbered Missouri militia to surrender. Angry bystanders fired on the Federal soldiers, who then shot and killed twenty-eight people in the crowd. The Camp Jackson Massacre presaged the vicious fighting between neighbors that characterized the Civil War on this frontier.[3]

In those heated moments, just days before his eighteenth birthday, George Bent joined a volunteer ranger company. His commander was Sterling Price, a Missouri slaveholder, ex-governor, and executioner of the Taos rebels who killed George's uncle, Charles Bent. He now led the Missouri State Guard—not formally part of the Confederate Army but volunteers led by Confederate officers. The new soldiers wore their own uniforms, trained as hundred-day volunteers, and couldn't wait to find the war. George's horse and his Cheyenne riding skills distinguished him from the other recruits. Cheyenne fighters mounted horses on the run and shot when and how they pleased, unlike army soldiers who mounted and shot when ordered. However, few recruits had horses or guns at all, and professional army officers didn't trust them, calling them a "half-armed mob."[4]

Trained or not, war found these young men in August 1861 at the Battle of Wilson's Creek, known as the Bull Run of the West. And like Bull Run, everyone expected it to be quick, exciting, and decisive, but it wasn't. Two large armies, Confederate and Federal, marched toward each other through Missouri's oppressive summer heat. Union troops attacked first and drove the Confederate cavalry from their position just south of Springfield, Missouri. After retreating, the Confederate forces regathered to attack the Federal forces three times in one day, killing the Union general and forcing them to withdraw. No one could declare victory, and the war went on.[5]

Six months later George Bent fought at Pea Ridge in Arkansas, the largest Civil War battle west of the Mississippi and a terrible loss for the Confederacy. The Confederacy massed its Army of the West, approximately sixteen thousand strong, in northern Arkansas. This force included eight hundred Native troops from Indian Territory communities loyal to the Confederacy. They were led by Gen. Albert Pike, an Arkansas lawyer specializing in suing the U.S. government on behalf of Native nations. The Confederate troops routed the opposing Union forces, stampeding their horses and capturing their cannons. The Native troops—Cherokee, Creek, Choctaw, Chickasaw, and Seminole cavalry—marked that victorious moment by counting coup—the celebratory scalping of the wounded enemy—a breach of protocol that ended their formal participation in the war. George Bent remembered with some pride that "those Cherokee boys and their war cries and scalping gave old Pike more than he bargained for." Worse than counting coup, Confederate troops didn't chase the retreating Union Army, giving them time to regroup and win the battle decisively on the second day. Some 3,300 troops lost their lives at Pea Ridge.[6]

The western campaigns then turned south and east. George Bent's last fight came at Corinth, Mississippi, in the late summer of 1862, against Gen. Henry Halleck's 100,000-man Union Army. George served in a horse artillery among 66,000 Confederates. While retreating after weeks of fighting the massive Union force, George's artillery found itself surrounded by enemy soldiers. George recalled that he was out on a "scouting expedition" and fell "into the hands of the Union cavalry." His commanding officer reported that "Private

Bent had deserted" along with two hundred others in his company. However it transpired, George surrendered his weapon and got on a riverboat full of Confederate prisoners.[7]

On September 3, 1862, George arrived in St. Louis and was marched through the streets to a military prison. A classmate from his St. Louis school recognized him and also knew that Robert Bent happened to be in the city purchasing Indian trade goods. After Robert found out that George was indeed in federal prison, he went to see some Union officers who were "old friends of the Bents." They got George released from prison, but he had to promise to leave St. Louis immediately and to stay out of the war. He kept the first part of his agreement but failed entirely on the second. He and Robert left for home. George Bent remembered the moment as decisive: "From that time until today, fifty-one years, in war and in peace, I have been with the Cheyennes."[8]

George's White family connections got him out of prison, but White St. Louis no longer welcomed him. His Southern Cheyenne family, facing pressures to develop a new western life in the midst of war, didn't exactly welcome him either. He would have to prove himself as a kinsman, warrior, and translator when war spread over his southern Colorado homeland. Mixed-blood men still had choices to make, but their choices were increasingly limited by race and war.

Charles Drips and the Missouri Militia

Charles Drips, Andrew and Macompemay's oldest son, couldn't ride west to avoid the Civil War. He lived with his wife Eliza and their son Charles Andrew in the old river district of Kansas City. In December 1863 Charles was drafted into Missouri's Union Army. Men who wanted to avoid that service could pay a $300 fine, called a commutation fee, but Charles didn't have that much money. He worked as a riverboat pilot, an economic niche that supported many local Indians. By 1863, for a man nearing forty, the bloom of joining the Union Army had faded. He was listed as "colored" on his draft registration, a catchall term that meant simply not White. That label ensured that Charles would serve as a cook or mule tender rather than as a soldier.[9]

Charles's Civil War was the nasty guerrilla fighting of Missouri and Kansas, still driven by grudges from the Bleeding Kansas violence of the 1850s. The fighting was continuous, with little supervision by the regular army. Civilians joined renegade Union and Confederate troops in daily local battles.[10]

Kansas in the 1860s presented trouble beyond imagination. Neighbors torched each other's houses, killed each other's slaves and servants, and burned property records. More than five thousand residents of Indian Territory (now Oklahoma) fled north to Kansas to escape vicious intertribal war. Those Native refugees terrified White Kansans. The real danger, however, turned out to be non–Native bushwhackers—irregular guerrilla troops. Missouri River residents, White, Black and Native, slept in their clothes, ready to evacuate at any sound. They fastened bags of valuables around their children's necks so that in case of a nighttime raid, the children might escape with a little silver. Rumors about bushwhackers, army raiders, and wild Indians kept people armed and jumpy.[11]

Charles Drips served in a poorly trained and equipped Missouri and Kansas militia that had to chase bushwhackers, often their friends and neighbors. When the Confederate raider Gen. Sterling Price, George Bent's former leader, blasted through Missouri in September 1864, twenty Kansas and Missouri militia units, including the one that drafted Charles Drips, made a stand to keep Price from entering Kansas. That militia, hastily assembled to protect a region already burned several times by raiders, now faced a huge Confederate army. Led by officers who weren't army men and without enough bullets, the militia faded and then ran. Their failure enabled Sterling Price's force to pour into Kansas. Finally twenty-two thousand Federal troops arrived on October 23, 1864, and the Battle of Westport kept Kansas from falling into Confederate hands.[12]

After that battle, Charles Drips stayed in the army for two more hundred-day stints, likely digging holes, transporting the wounded, or cooking. Gen. Henry Halleck, who headed the Union's entire western command, refused to arm Native men, even in the extreme situation of Civil War Kansas. The exception to Halleck's goal of "keeping savages out of the war" was a regiment of a thousand Native men formed to retake Indian Territory, still under Confederate control. Creek and Seminole refugees who had fled north into Kansas created the Indian Home Guard. Two White officers—Col. John Ritchie and Col. William Weer—led those troops as they marched into Indian Territory armed with knives, some shotguns, and few supplies. They were accompanied by a Black regiment made up of former Cherokee slaves. The Indian Home Guard took the Cherokee capital and Fort Gibson in 1863, but lack of supplies and bad leadership ended their successful run. The specter of armed Native, Black, and mixed-blood troops led Union Army officials to decommission the Indian Home Guard, leaving Indian Territory and Kansas to endure Confederate raiding for several more years.[13]

Cousins and Cannon Fodder in Michigan

Michigan soldiers, with long fur trade pasts, fought to save mixed hearths and homes. John and Susan Johnston's (Ozhaguscoday-wayquay's) children still lived in Michigan and had large extended families with kin in Ojibwe, Potawatomi, and Odawa communities. Their Ojibwe relatives were "concentrated" onto a few reservations in Michigan, including La Pointe, Grand Traverse, and Sault Ste. Marie. These local bands—cousins, aunts, and uncles to the Johnstons—still fished and tapped maple trees in their homeland. It was a better situation than many Michigan Indian people faced, now removed to Minnesota, Kansas, or Indian Territory.[14]

The Johnston sons, George, John, and William, all watched their own sons fight in the Civil War. Fathers and sons hoped to protect an America that included Michigan's mixed-descent world. George Johnston, former translator and Indian Service employee, faced the coming Civil War as a struggling widower. In 1858, his second wife, Mary Rice Johnston, died, leaving him with six children still at home. George's eldest son, John George Johnston, mostly raised by his grandmother Ozhaguscodaywayquay, went into the Indian trade, a career still possible in Michigan in 1860. He made a living bringing in scarce beaver pelts but mostly raccoon and deer. He married a woman named Nancy and they settled into Sault Ste. Marie's blended world, living in a neighborhood, all Indian according to the census, filled with hunters and boatmen.[15]

The youngest of John and Susan's children, John McDougall Johnston, began the 1860s living in a similar enclave of households where many people still worked as voyageurs, paddling birchbark canoes still essential for transportation. John married French-Ojibwe Justine Piquette and they raised nine children. Justine's father, old Jean-Baptiste Piquette, spent a lifetime in the woods as a hunter and now lived with his daughter. Descended from esteemed Ojibwe leaders on both sides of his family, on cold winter nights Jean-Baptiste ate dried fish and pea soup, along with cornbread and maple syrup still harvested by Ojibwe hands.

Not everyone married. John and Justine's extended family also included Eliza Johnston, the second of John and Susan's daughters. Always strong and opinionated, she did a little trapping, trading, and sugaring to maintain her independence. In 1860 she lived in a small house next door to John and Justine.[16]

William Johnston, the man who orchestrated the lawsuit against his brother-in-law Henry Schoolcraft, was now a lawyer in Mackinac, a two-day canoe trip south of Sault Ste. Marie. Through the 1850s, he used marriage and property to build a life on the White side of Michigan's racial borders. William married a woman named Susan Davenport from an old trader family like the Johnstons. With his wife's land and his own success as a lawyer, William served as Mackinac County clerk and election supervisor. He became a respected old settler as Mackinac turned from a fur trade "curiosity" with "buildings like Indian lodges" to a bustling American town by 1860, with "three hotels, six boarding houses, eight dry-goods stores, and seven groceries," along with "a Court House, Jail, Custom House, Post Office." William and Susan had eight children, all named after Johnston relatives.[17]

These Michigan families, surviving and even thriving in 1860, didn't suffer the punishing neighbor's war unfolding in Kansas and Indian Territory. But their sons and fathers joined the Union Army as White men. In the spring and summer of 1861, when President Lincoln's call for troops reached the isolated communities of Michigan's Upper Peninsula, young men rushed to join the army. Organized entirely by states, companies and their makeup were haphazard. Local pride drew boys and men to form volunteer militias with their friends and neighbors. Rural boys grew up fighting and knew how to handle guns. The Johnstons did not join the First Michigan Sharpshooters, which included Native men—Ojibwes, Odawas, Hurons, and Potawatomis—who were segregated from their fellow Michiganders. In total, 16,475 young men from Michigan joined up as volunteers that first year. Those volunteers included three of George's sons, two of William's sons, and their cousin, Johnston Schoolcraft, Jane and Henry's son.[18]

Among those six young men, George and Louisa's son James died first, contracting "a sickness" in camp before the war even started. James' brother, Benjamin Johnston, joined a Michigan infantry unit, part of the Army of the Potomac. Writing to a friend, he described the horseplay of bored soldiers who took their dress hats "less than an hour after they were issued . . . and stuffed the hats and sewed them." The stuffed hats "made splendid footballs" until the killjoy colonel got involved and "they were all taken away." A month later Benjamin was dead, killed at Antietam in September 1862. William Miengun Johnston, William and Susan's eldest, died in December 1862, six days after he "received a rifle ball in the right breast" in the Battle of Fredericksburg. Samuel Johnston, George Johnston's third son, was only nineteen when he died. He succumbed to an unspecified disease on his way home from Tennessee in 1863. Samuel's cousin, Johnston Schoolcraft, Jane and Henry's son, joined the Union Army in June 1861. Wounded at Gettysburg, he died in April 1865 in a military hospital in Elmira, New York. Finally, Lewis Johnston, William's youngest son, joined the army in the summer of 1862, to fill Michigan's twelve-thousand-man quota. Conscripted and only seventeen, he alone among the Johnston family soldiers survived the Civil War.[19]

The Bent Family and the Colorado Citizens War

On the central Plains around Colorado, as in Kansas, entire families faced their neighbors in war. George Bent, sprung from military prison in St. Louis, returned to Colorado in 1862. He hadn't been home since a tornado of destructive change had whirled through the Bent family and the Southern Cheyenne after the 1858 Colorado gold rush. The bison disappeared in Colorado, replaced with thirty-five thousand Pikes Peak gold rushers, 97 percent of them young men. George missed the tornado's aftermath: seasons of hunger and sickness in the Cheyenne camps, the sale of Bent's Fort to the U.S. Army in January 1860, his father's move to the ranch on the Purgatoire. The new Colorado must have been a shock to George.[20]

The Bents' Purgatoire ranch was lonely. George's Cheyenne mothers had left, taking George's younger sister Julia with them. A drunken traveler had threatened to beat Julia "with a three-legged creepy"—a horsewhip with three metal spikes—because she wouldn't dance with him, the kind of threat White travelers regularly made to Native women. Robert Bent stayed at the ranch, managing the operation, and remained close to his father. The oldest Bent child, Mary, had married a White man named Robinson Moore in Kansas City in 1860. She brought her new family back to Colorado in 1862, imagining a safer haven from the chaos in Kansas.[21]

William Bent tried to keep George at home. He bought him a racehorse, took him to Denver to see the new city, and consulted him about business affairs. But George Bent drank, boasted about his Confederate experience, and got into fights. Soldiers threatened to throw him in the guardhouse as he "was a half-breed, a Noted Rebel, and ought to have been killed long ago." Such threats convinced George to head north to join his Cheyenne family along the Republican River. His sister Julia was there, along with Yellow Woman and Island, all in Black Kettle's camp. His brother Charles had joined a Dog Soldier society that hunted, fought, prayed, and died together. In this time of brewing war, George aspired to the same, but he didn't have the necessary battlefield credibility. He turned to Black Kettle, related to George through his grandfather White Thunder, for help in finding a place in the Cheyenne world.[22]

Black Kettle gave George Bent a new name, *Do-ha-no* or "Texan," because of his Confederate service, but he couldn't change George's personal history. Though he tried, Black Kettle couldn't change what was unfolding for the Cheyenne nation either. Black Kettle's position as "peace chief" in these years was controversial among the Cheyenne, but George Bent found a place as his translator. He assisted both Black Kettle and William Bent in talking to the Cheyenne as pressures between immigrants and Native villagers grew to a boiling point in Colorado.[23]

Colorado became an epicenter of trouble in the 1860s as Civil War and Indian War rolled over it. The U.S. Army called its effort to control powerful southwestern nations like the Comanche, Apache, and Navajo "pacification," but it ignited violence everywhere. Refugees fled north from that war into Colorado. Raiders stole army supplies and horses and then escaped into Colorado. William Bent's ranch and the Cheyenne villages clustered around it became part of this dangerous war economy. Other trouble came from the north, where enemy tribes—Sioux, Crow, and Pawnee—prevented the Cheyenne from hunting on the northern Plains where bison were still plentiful. Each summer, when Cheyennes hunted bison in the few places available to them, White travelers used the same routes. Immigrants' animals—horses, cattle, oxen, and mules—ate grass and destroyed buffalo wallows. Hungry and frustrated, the Cheyenne raided wagon trains and new communities along the Platte River in the summers of 1860 and 1861.[24]

Cattle stolen, horses run off, whiskey and guns liberated, all made White Coloradans mad with fear. And just as the U.S. Army started all those wars to conquer or pacify Native nations, most regular troops left the West's Indian War to go fight in the Civil War. Coloradans felt abandoned by their government as powerful Indian nations that hadn't appeared in travelers' guides and or gold rush accounts now threatened their hopes of wealth in the West.

John Evans, appointed territorial governor of Colorado in 1862, scrambled to figure out what to do. With no military support, and with information coming from mixed-descent translators and traders he didn't trust, he found it impossible to do even simple things like feed people and keep promises. Cheyenne and Arapaho villages began dividing into war camps and peace camps. Peace chiefs led their people to army posts and trading centers, hoping to be fed, but more often they just got trouble. William Bent complained about the situation around Fort Lyon, where soldiers took whiskey and went into Arapaho villages hoping "to trade the whiskey for a squaw to sleep with." Men scuffled over the whiskey and women. Sometimes people got shot, knifed, or raped, and Bent noted that such episodes cause "great confusion and the perpetrators are never identified."[25]

War chiefs, watching the peace chiefs deal with soldiers and hungry people, decided to make common cause with their old enemies, the Dakota and Lakota Sioux. These warriors and their villages, having fled the military onslaught against them in Minnesota and the Dakotas, had little to lose. Together the Cheyenne and the Lakota would bring war to the people now invading lands promised to them in treaties. Sometimes those invaders were other Native nations, and sometimes they were White soldiers, travelers, or farmers.[26]

The trouble came to a head in the summer of 1864, when Indian attacks increased on people and wagons streaming across the immigrant trails. White Coloradans feared a recurrence of the 1862 Minnesota Dakota uprising. After Federal officials refused that year to deliver food and payments that had been guaranteed to various Sioux nations, Dakotas decided war was their only alternative. The U.S. Army failed to control the well-orchestrated Dakota attacks on towns and roads, which finally left eight hundred White settlers dead by September and thirty-eight Dakota men swinging from gibbets by December. In June 1864, when Plains raiders killed a family of Colorado settlers, everyone in Denver believed it signaled the beginning of a Minnesota-scale outbreak. As the dead Hungate family was paraded through Denver's streets, residents from outlying areas poured into the city for protection. On June 15, 1864, the *Rocky Mountain News* published reports that a force of Indians "three thousand strong" stood poised to strike Denver. "Every bell in the city sounded," making everyone "all pale with fear," a young Denverite later remembered. She described men armed with axes "to cut away the stairs at the first sight of the red devils," and sobbing citizens hiding in the new U.S. Mint, waiting for an attack that never arrived. The next day the "army of hostiles" turned out to be cattle drovers, their animals and carts creating dust that looked like Indian campfires.[27]

As in Oregon after the 1847 Whitman massacre, and after the 1855 Cayuse and Yakima uprising, frightened men in Colorado joined citizen militias. The governor had originally called up Colorado's Volunteer Regiment, commanded by Maj. John Chivington, in 1861, to fight a Civil War emergency. A Confederate Army expedition had marched almost unopposed into New Mexico after army regular troops abandoned the West to fight farther east. The Colorado First handled the Confederate threat in New Mexico in two significant battles. That success gave Chivington credibility as a military leader as the Civil War ground on. Now that White Colorado demanded military action and Indian war seemed imminent, Chivington's Volunteers stepped in.[28]

That same summer of 1864, George and William Bent traveled among the Cheyenne to try to get them to move to the reservation on the Arkansas, where they might be safer. When Black Kettle took the peaceful villages south to the Arkansas, the Dog Soldiers, including George's brother Charles, made a permanent break from the Cheyenne camps, deciding that war was the only option. They headed north for a summer of raiding and killing.[29]

As that summer went on, citizens demanded more action from Governor Evans. They wanted Federal troops and local militia to kill Indians who made travel and trade impossible. Governor Evans knew, as did most military and civilian officials, that only a few Native people committed most of the violence. Evans issued his first "Proclamation of 1864" to distinguish between tribes that had kept the peace and those that hadn't. Now he relied on men like William Bent, White Coloradans experienced with Cheyenne or Arapaho families, to help him make this crucial distinction. He demanded that the Bent family notify the Cheyenne as to what they must do if they wanted safety. William and George went back to the camps and explained that there were now two categories of Indians: friendly and unfriendly. Unfriendly Indians would simply be killed. Friendly Indians had to prove their status by leaving unfriendly families and camps. They must turn themselves in to soldiers at Fort Lyon, who "would give them provisions and a place of safety." If they didn't do this immediately, "they might be killed through mistake."[30]

Mistakes had already been made. In May, Chivington's troops had three engagements with the Cheyenne, burned four of their villages, and killed leaders who had taken pride in their peaceful relations with Whites. The Colorado militia attacked the peace villages of Lean Bear and Black Kettle. They killed Lean Bear, who was wearing the peace medal he'd been given in Washington the year before. For people in the Dog Soldier camps, including Charles Bent, the killings proved that the only solution was war. The militant Dog Soldier societies now represented a large portion of the Cheyenne people. And if deciding to fight meant that all Cheyennes died in the effort, that price was worth paying. In their view, peace with Whites just meant a different kind of death. The Cheyenne nation that had survived so much had now split forever. George Bent decided to stay with Black Kettle and help the villages move south.[31]

Meanwhile in Denver, Colonel Chivington had convinced Governor Evans that the situation in Colorado was dire. With too few regular troops remaining in Colorado because of the war, Chivington insisted that Denver and the Platte River Road lay dangerously unprotected, and that Coloradans needed an immediate military solution. Evans ignored the advice of military officers in the region who wanted time to make treaties with "friendly" villages who were turning themselves in as Evans had demanded. Instead, Evans telegraphed Edwin Stanton, the U.S. secretary of war, describing his desperate circumstances: "murdered and scalped bodies, our troops near all gone." He demanded ten thousand troops to meet the united army of Indians he feared was gathering. Stanton couldn't send that many troops, but Evans quickly got permission to call up regiments of "mounted volunteers."[32]

In late August, a few regular army troops finally arrived. Eager to show their mettle, the Seventh Iowa Cavalry attacked the first Native people they saw—Black Kettle's peace village. The Cheyennes there were surprised but handily fought off the U.S. troops and took seven soldiers as prisoners. From this position of strength, Black Kettle decided it was time for his villages to turn themselves in. The Southern Cheyenne could exchange captive army soldiers in return for safe travel to the Arkansas Reservation. Black Kettle asked George Bent to write a letter requesting a meeting to discuss safe passage and returning soldiers. To deliver the letter, Black Kettle sent two elderly Cheyennes, Lone Bear and his wife, who had a daughter married to a trader. Alone and unarmed, they rode south to Fort Lyon.[33]

Hearing about the Cheyenne offer, Governor Evans and military leaders proposed a meeting in Denver. However, while the chiefs met in Denver, a large force of Colorado volunteer militias attacked their villages. Cheyenne warriors easily bested the militias, but it didn't make them more likely to trust soldiers or their leaders. When he returned from Denver, Black Kettle explained the deal Governor Evans had offered. If the villages stopped the raiding and if they surrendered to Maj. Edward Wynkoop, a man Black Kettle did trust, the war against Colorado Indians would stop. At Fort Lyon, under Major Wynkoop's protection, peaceful villages would receive rations and be safe from the Colorado militias. Few Cheyennes believed Evans's offer, and unlike Black Kettle, they had no trust in the military. Most villages decided not to move, but they kept their word about peace and made no attacks on White settlers or travelers that fall.[34]

A few reluctant leaders followed Black Kettle south toward Fort Lyon because their people were hungry and winter was coming. By late October, perhaps six hundred people had camped on Sand Creek, a tributary of the Arkansas. More than two thousand Cheyennes remained farther north, on the Smoky Hill River. George Bent and his sister Julia moved to Sand Creek with the Cheyenne lodges.[35]

As Cheyenne and Arapaho peace leaders moved their villages to Sand Creek, a new hundred-day volunteer militia marched out in search of "hostiles." Led by Colonel Chivington, they left Denver to gather up more seasoned members of the Colorado First who were patrolling the New Mexico border. Next, the troops traveled east along the Arkansas River. Chivington instructed soldiers to surround Bent's stockade. Not trusting the Bent family, he wanted to ensure that no one warned either the U.S. Army or Native villages that the militia had arrived. Soldiers kept the Bents under house arrest. Robert Bent, however, was told he could leave the ranch if he agreed to serve as Chivington's guide. His previous guide, James Beckwourth, a former Indian trader and Crow family man, claimed that during the long march east, the cold had taken too much of a toll on his old body and he couldn't go on. Chivington ordered Bent to take over as the expedition's scout, and Robert had no choice but to ride along. By the time Chivington's militia arrived at Fort Lyon in late November, the temporary army had 800 to 1,000 men.[36]

Chivington's arrival at Fort Lyon was a complete surprise. The troops, now with Robert Bent guiding them, marched into Fort Lyon and took it over, threatening to shoot any U.S. Army men who tried to leave. Chivington planned to attack the Cheyenne and Arapaho villages that had just surrendered at Fort Lyon, but he kept that plan secret from most of his own officers and from regular military at Fort Lyon. Chivington demanded that the commander at the fort issue him supplies, ammunition, and more soldiers, insisting that his militia were only hunting "hostiles" who had been active in summer raids.[37]

Robert Bent knew he was leading the U.S. Army and Colorado militia toward the surrendered Cheyenne villages. Reportedly he guided the troops and howitzers through shallow pools of water, hoping to dampen the ammunition and render it unusable. Chivington barked a reprimand. "I haven't had an Indian to eat for a long time," he said. "If you fool with me and don't lead me to that camp, I'll have you for breakfast." Bent led Chivington's troops in a ten-hour nighttime march over rough landscape until they reached the villages. The 120 lodges were mostly Southern Cheyenne, but Arapahos slept there too. Like all Cheyenne villages, the one gathered around Sand Creek housed families. Charles, Julia, and George Bent, as well as Robert's old friend and fellow translator, Edmund Guerrier, slept there.[38]

On November 29, 1864, Chivington and his soldiers arrived at the Cheyenne camp just as people were waking up. A Cheyenne woman and her child spotted them and sounded the alarm. Black Kettle immediately raised an American flag and a white flag, to indicate the village's peaceful status. George and Charles Bent rushed out of their tents to warn the soldiers away from the peace village. Edmund Guerrier and two White traders ran toward the soldiers lined up on the low bluff above the Cheyenne lodges. The soldiers fired on Guerrier, launching the attack.

Nothing could stop it. Chivington and his men—the U.S. regulars and Colorado volunteers both—had come to destroy villages. Black Kettle, hoping to draw fire to himself and to be killed for his role in bringing his people to this spot and allowing this slaughter, "stood in front of his lodge with his arms folded across his breast." He sang a death song: "Nothing lives long, Only the earth and the mountains." White Antelope, who had promised the Cheyenne that "the whites were good people and that peace was going to be made," immediately drew the fire of the soldiers, and "he fell dead in front of his lodge."[39]

After the initial volley and the first minutes of panic in the village, the soldiers kept shooting, at women, at children, at surrendering men. The troops shot from such a distance that their initial bullets missed, allowing people to scramble to the creek bank and dig holes for protection. As the troops closed in, positioning their mountain howitzers and raining artillery on the village, people still fled and hid. Trader John Smith and his wife Zarepta rescued their youngest child by sending her to run behind the troops. Black Kettle, shot at again and again, was never hit. He rescued his injured wives and took them to safety by the stream. The soldiers kept shooting.[40]

A few held back. Capt. Silas Soule refused to shoot and told his Fourth Colorado Cavalry to hold their fire. He was utterly shocked at what happened next. Later, in a cold rage, he reported the details to his commanding officer. He described the Cheyenne women and children as supplicants, "little children on their knees . . . having their brains beat out by men professing to be civilized," and mothers who fell to their knees "begging for their lives, of a dozen soldiers, within ten feet of them all firing." One mother, seeing the choice ahead, "took a knife and cut the throats of both children, and then killed herself." Jack Smith, mixed Cheyenne and old friend of the Bent brothers, surrendered, but soldiers shot him in the head. What happened after people were dead was worse. Soule described how "squaws' snatches were cut out for trophies," another woman "cut open, and a child taken out of her, and scalped." Then they burned the camp to the ground. Chivington's men never denied committing these atrocities. They displayed their trophies when they rode back to Denver in triumph.[41]

Robert Bent rode back to Fort Lyon along with a captured "hostile," his younger brother Charles. And just as he had saved his brother George from military prison, Robert now saved his other brother. As some Apaches rode by, Robert allowed them to "capture" Charles and take him down the river. Charles disappeared into New Mexico, and Robert went back to Fort Lyon.[42]

George Bent, shot twice in the thigh, survived by hiding in a pile of slowly freezing bodies. He would write about what happened next with a survivor's crystalline memory. "There we were," he recalled, "on that bleak, frozen plain, without any shelter whatever and not a stick of wood to build a fire." Burying their dead with dried grass, living Cheyennes and Arapahos staggered along the banks of Sand Creek, walking among "the naked and mutilated bodies of the dead," looking at "wives, husbands, children, or friends." Reliving it fifty years later, George wrote that "that night will never be forgotten as long as any of us who went through it are alive."[43]

The next morning, bitter cold, George Bent, his sister Julia, and other survivors traveled toward Little Robe's camp on the Smoky Hill River, fifty miles north. They feared soldiers would spot them on the open plain and come after them. The news had already reached the camps, and people rode out to meet the survivors with extra ponies and litters for the wounded. "Everyone was crying," Bent remembered, as "nearly everyone had lost relatives and friends."[44]

They also cried because Sand Creek presaged the future. The Dog Soldiers had been right all along. There was no peace option, no place of safety, and no hope of retaining any piece of their old lives. Cheyenne and Arapaho women—wives, mothers, sisters, daughters—saw no reason to follow peace chiefs and voted for war. Mixed-blood men could no longer choose to be part of two worlds or to make their own destinies; to the army they were "hostiles" and could choose only that life. George, Charles, and Robert Bent went to war, raiding and killing along the Platte, Republican, Arkansas, and Smoky Hill rivers with their Cheyenne kin.[45]

The Southern Cheyenne sent war pipes to the Brulé and Ogalala Sioux, to the Northern Arapaho, and even to their traditional enemies, the Pawnee. Thousands of warriors gathered in the winter of

1865, and as peace came to the eastern United States, war came to the West. Cheyenne and their allies killed people, burned farms and trading posts, attacked postal trains, and captured children. The violence was bloody and vengeful, and it severed the communication lines of the American West. The overwhelming and carefully orchestrated Indian raids terrified new residents in Colorado, Utah, Kansas, Nebraska, and New Mexico.[46]

In March 1865, after reading reports from army officers and Indian agents, President Lincoln began an investigation of what happened at Sand Creek. Congressional hearings of more than two months outlined the atrocities that Chivington and his men had committed. Governor Evans and Colonel Chivington lost their jobs, but no one was held accountable for Sand Creek. As White settlers demanded protection from the retributive rage sweeping the West, the U.S. Army finally arrived on the Platte in August 1865, but they found few Plains warriors. Smoking fires, slaughtered cattle, and empty fruit and oyster cans were the only evidence of the dangerous foe who had spoiled the dreams and eaten the supplies of gold rushers and settlers.[47]

Into the brewing disaster stepped the old traders with Cheyenne and Arapaho families. William Bent, Kit Carson, Jesse Chisholm, William McGaa, John Prowers, and John Smith insisted they could make peace with some Colorado Indians. In October 1865 Black Kettle, Little Raven, and six other leaders signed the Treaty of the Little Arkansas. But they represented only a small percentage of Cheyennes. Hundreds of lodges went north with the raiders, making the treaty that the peace leaders signed a failure from the beginning. The Cheyenne and Arapaho would receive a reservation south of the Arkansas River—but only when the raiding that plagued the central Plains stopped, hardly likely given how many lodges had joined the fight. William Bent insisted on another piece to the treaty: protection of the land along the Arkansas promised by the old Fort Wise treaty to mixed bloods of the tribe. Once again mixed people had been called out, named, and separated from their Native kin in the service of treaties that would never be signed or enforced. Nothing would make the Bents or any Native families safe in Colorado.[48]

The Great Nemaha Half-Breed Tract

Louise Geroux Drips, Andrew Drips's young widow, faced difficult choices in wartime Kansas. She had six children between the ages of two and ten and a house in Kansas City. After creditors were paid off, including the American Fur Company and several St. Louis merchants, only Andrew's four-dollar-a-month pension for his service in the War of 1812 remained. Andrew Drips's daughters with his Otoe wife Macompemay, Mary Jane and Catherine, owned houses, cattle, land, and slaves that their father had put in their names to avoid his creditors. But even with those resources, Kansas City wasn't safe during the war. As William Quantrill and other Confederate raiders burned out and murdered people across Missouri and Kansas, refugees poured into Kansas City for food and protection. Desperate, they broke into stores and homes and shot people who had horses or pigs. Like many others, Louise and Mary Jane left that chaos.[49]

Because Louise and her children had just been confirmed in their ownership of land on the Great Nemaha Half-Breed Tract in Nebraska, she took her three youngest children there in 1863. She joined Mary Jane Drips, who, seeking safety and hoping to protect family resources, had recently remarried, to a White man, Francis Barnes. They also took up land on the half-breed tract. Louise and Mary Jane would raise their children together on old Otoe reservation lands and the Great Nemaha Half-Breed Tract.[50]

A familiar mix of trade families pulled them to this spot, a day's paddle north from Kansas City. A considerable number of kin from Louise's French-Dakota world at Fort Pierre now lived around trading posts on half-breed tract lands. So Rouleau's trading post became the town of Rulo, Nebraska, and Michel and Antoine Barada's French-Omaha family compound became the town of Barada. Dozens of other families, Langdeaus and Gerouxes, Deroins and Goulets, now farmed and traded there.[51]

Louise's older children, Andrew Jackson, Walter, and Thomas, remained in Kansas City with Catherine Drips Mulkey, also crucial to the family support network. Because there were no schools in rural Nebraska, Mary Jane's son Leonard often lived with Catherine as well. Kansas City in those years was hardly a refuge. Indian and mixed people living on the Indian reservations surrounding Kansas City had no protection from illegal guerrillas or official Union and Confederate forces. Sometimes troops on the march forcibly "requisitioned" supplies and left letters promising repayment, but armed men often just took what they wanted from Native homes and stores.

One small accounting of the personal cost of these raids appears in Indian agency records. Details of hogs killed, horses and lumber stolen, and fields burned on the Shawnee reservation just south of Kansas City suggest the loss suffered by hundreds of Shawnees. Two sisters, Mrs. Pumpkin and Mrs. Hummingbird, aged seventy-two and seventy-seven, reported that raiders stole three mules and shot ten hogs, which they valued at forty-five dollars. The old Shawnee women had little else. "Can-chi-qua, a Shawnee," had his Indian ponies stolen in 1861, and then in August 1862 he lost his last three gray mares. Demonstrating the continuous nature of the terror in Kansas, "soldiers unknown" then broke into his house and took "clothing, beds, stove, and flooring." The next year, 1864, "soldiers" robbed him at gunpoint of oxen and two yearling steers. Finally in 1865 "persons unknown" torched his house.[52]

Nebraska's Civil War remained less chaotic than the devastation of Kansas and Missouri. In 1860 the non-Native population was less than twenty thousand, the Native population more than sixty thousand. The economy depended entirely on Indian annuities and the Indian trade.[53] As one land salesman crowed, millions of dollars of "annuity money is annually paid to the various tribes of Indians on our border." And, he promised, all that money went directly into the pockets and tills of merchants, "not a dollar of it is hid in the earth, or stowed away in old stockings." When Indians, unlike tightfisted White citizens, received any cash, "the Indian is on his pony and off to trade," not satisfied until "every last dollar is expended." Such promises drew new residents to Nebraska expecting to profit from cash-rich Indians or to swindle them out of land. The Great Nemaha Half-Breed Tract, bordered by Otoe reservations just to the west and the Iowa reservation to the south, lay right where land speculators could see it. These lands were finally in Drips family hands after thirty years of effort. They didn't intend to give them up.[54]

Intermarried families, with a century of experience, understood how to keep land in the community. Even though town builders and land speculators claimed that land along the Missouri River bluffs was superlatively fertile and easy to farm, it was steep and prone to flooding. The first towns in the half-breed tract were settled by French-Omaha mixed bloods who knew how to make a living on the river, such as Louis Neals, married to Susan Fontenelle, who received the first patent to own land there in 1860.

By 1861, many of the original land patents had already passed on to other owners, but not always by White opportunists stealing land from unsuspecting Indians. The land ended up in the hands of White men married to mixed or Native women: Indian traders, Indian agents, and a few White opportunists. Marriage could protect a woman's land and children by giving White or mixed-blood men a personal stake. Francis Barnes, Mary Jane Drips's husband, bought and sold his step-son's and wife's land to buy better pieces nearer the Otoe agency. To keep land in the family, Barnes had a local judge appoint him as legal guardian to Andrew Jackson Drips (Louise's eight-year-old son and Mary Jane's half-brother) to make sure no one stole the boy's land.[55]

When Louise moved to the Nemaha, she now lived among her Drips family relations and the French-Dakota people she had grown up with at Fort Pierre. It wasn't surprising that in 1863, when Henri Goulet lost his wife Pelagie, the widowed Louise Geroux Drips was an appeal-ing match. They both needed help managing their families, and they understood each other in French, in Dakota, and in hard life experi-ence. Marriage and remarriage was common in nineteenth-century families—Native, White, or mixed. People needed large families to cooperate in the hard work of living on the Plains. Soon Louise and Henri had two of Henri's older children living with them, four of Lou-ise's children from her marriage with Andrew Drips, and three chil-dren of their own. The family lived in two houses next door to each other. Using old strategies like marriage and adoption, women built new places where mixing blood might continue. Louise Geroux Drips Goulet used her family resources and cultural flexibility to find safety.[56]

Cheyenne Families After Sand Creek

William Bent hoped a half-breed tract in Colorado might provide his family with the tenuous safety it gave Andrew Drips's family in Nebraska. As war spread over the Plains, however, the danger increased. No matter what the peace chiefs and Indian agents negotiated, Dog Soldier bands expanded, military leaders ignored what Indian agents told them, new immigrants ignored all the rules, and Southern Cheyennes starved. For two years, Cheyenne raiders burned towns and telegraph poles while U.S. Army soldiers sought Dog Soldier camps and burned peace villages.[57]

Black Kettle still insisted peace was possible. George Bent, seeing that Native raiding and killing hadn't driven White settlers or soldiers away, began to agree. One night in October 1867, Black Kettle and George Bent, along with Little Raven of the Arapaho and Poor Bear of the Apache, headed 150 miles east to central Kansas to meet with U.S. officials at Fort Larned. The Dog Soldier societies, now controlling nearly half the Cheyenne villages and demanding war with Whites, threatened Black Kettle's life for attending. The old leader still carried the authority of bands willing to seek peace. Edmund Guerrier, the White and Cheyenne man who had been at Sand Creek and who would soon marry George's sister Julia, translated at the Fort Larned gathering.[58]

Neither traitors nor saviors, Black Kettle and Little Raven knew their people needed food, guns, and safety. Now, however, the choice was stark: a permanent move to Indian Territory or annihilation by the army. They couldn't stay in Colorado. The Medicine Lodge Treaty of 1867—concluded at a fort located on Medicine Lodge Creek—granted them the right to hunt, but not to live, along the Arkansas. Dog Soldier villages refused to consider that move. Instead, they imagined a new life living on the northern Plains with Crow, Lakota, and Northern Cheyenne. With nothing to keep them in Colorado, Cheyenne warriors joined those bigger villages and began new cycles of raiding. George Bent, a little wistfully, described those huge war villages far north on the Powder River as a "great circle of lodges . . . Each band singing its own songs, just like olden times."[59]

Returning to olden times cost the Bent family dearly. Charles Bent, youngest son and a Cheyenne warrior, became the exemplar of what happened when "Indian savagery mixed with white intelligence." Charles scared people for a reason: he and his Dog Soldiers targeted railroad camps, homesteads, and military posts, and the U.S. Army could not stop them. In the fall of 1867, while leading a group in a retaliatory attack, Charles took a bullet in the thigh and died of his wound a few weeks later.[60]

George, briefly, found peace in Black Kettle's village, located south of the Arkansas River on what is now the Kansas-Oklahoma line. William Bent and Black Kettle agreed on a marriage between Black Kettle's niece, Magpie Woman (Mo-hi-hy-wah), and George Bent (Ho-my-ike) that linked their families into a new generation. After a spring ceremony in which William Bent gave away fourteen wagonloads of goods, Magpie Woman and George Bent settled into village life. George remembered, simply, "These were happy days for us." George and Magpie often visited the Bent ranch on the Purgatoire, where George's siblings had homes, cattle, and children.[61]

Because they were visiting the Bent ranch, George and Magpie were not on the Washita River in the winter of 1868 when, once again, U.S. troops attacked Black Kettle's peaceful village. They killed more than thirty Cheyennes, none of them Dog Soldiers, and took fifty-three women and children as captives. They also took 875 horses and mules and burned three hundred lodges. Black Kettle, who had survived Sand Creek, was mown down, leaving the Cheyenne without a peace chief.[62]

Two decades of war and hundreds of broken treaties had driven Wichitas, Osages, Kiowas, Pawnees, Comanches, Cheyennes, and Arapahos off their homelands and into Indian Territory in dismal circumstances. George and Magpie, along with Black Kettle's shattered extended family, moved to Camp Supply along the Canadian River in what is now Oklahoma. Cheyennes and Arapahos agreed to find a reservation in this place, where government officials and military officers promised that "Indians" could live without being "molested by the whites."[63]

People can die of broken hearts. Watching his friends and family be rounded up and driven out of Colorado killed William Bent. He spent the last two years of his life rushing back and forth between his house in Kansas City and the Purgatoire River ranch. He wrote dozens of letters, testified in Congress, and served as translator and commissioner at treaty sessions, all in a futile effort to find a place in Colorado for an Indian reservation. Perhaps the travel and stress wore him down, or perhaps his new wife, Adaline, a White-Blackfoot woman, demanded too much. Bent worked his entire life to build a safe place for his family, where sharing lives and land with Native nations was possible and profitable. Now George and Julia were living with the Cheyenne hundreds of miles from Colorado in Indian Territory, not safe at all. Robert Bent and Mary Bent Moore still lived in Colorado but were at risk from soldiers and settlers. William died in Mary Bent Moore's care at the Purgatoire River ranch in May 1869.[64]

Many Johnstons, proud Ojibwe Michiganders, didn't live to see the post–Civil War West. George Johnston fell first. One cold January evening in 1861, he drank too much and wandered outside. When he didn't come back, his eldest daughter Louisa, who still lived at home, alerted neighbors, who found him frozen in a snowbank. At least he didn't have to watch his three sons die in the Civil War. Two more fathers fell. William Johnston lived long enough to see two of his nephews, his brother, and his son die. After those shocks he died in 1863, aged fifty-two, in Mackinac, leaving his wife Susan with a houseful of children and an estate of $350. Henry Schoolcraft, after suffering several debilitating strokes, died in 1864, a year before his son Johnston died, alone, in a New York hospital.[65]

Indian War and Civil War had racked up the dead in mixed-descent families. The Civil War wasn't supposed to be about Indians or mixed people in the West. But the Massacre at Sand Creek, the Dakota War, and the slaughter at Washita came out of the same cauldron of hate that fed the fight to maintain the enslavement of Black Americans. In that long moment, the Civil War created a West that could no longer risk mixing blood.

=11=

Reconstructing Race on Western Reservations, 1866–1885

One spring day in 1870, Dr. William Cameron McKay, physician on the Warm Springs Reservation in Oregon, went into town to vote. He had voted in many elections since the 1840s. But this time James Campbell, McKay's neighbor and a local election judge, stopped him. Campbell claimed that as a "half-breed Indian," McKay wasn't entitled to vote. Feeling confident of his status—he had been born in Oregon, elected to local office, and served in the U.S. Army—William McKay sued the election official for denying his rights as a citizen. The suit and several countersuits wound through the court system. For William, the issue was being refused the right to vote "on account of his being an Indian." Since he wasn't an Indian but a "half-breed," according to Oregon law he was entitled to vote and to own land. Given that legal status, McKay wanted to vote and to receive $500 for his trouble.[1]

William lined up experts to dispute his status as "Indian." He laid out his personal history to demonstrate his blended heritage. But his strategy backfired when the judge did some complicated racial math. The judge calculated that because William's father had a "half-breed" mother, and because William's mother was a "full-blooded" Chinook, he was "nine-sixteenths Indian, eight of which he gets from his Chinook mother and the other one from his Canadian father." Fractions of blood added up to make William "in legal contemplation an American Indian" and not "an American Half-Breed entitled to vote under the Donation Act of 1850."[2]

William appealed, and the district court agreed that the racial math didn't matter. Instead, the legal issue became that neither William McKay nor his father, Thomas McKay, "had ever been naturalized under the laws of the United States." Thomas had arrived in Oregon before it was a U.S. territory. A mixed-blood Canadian, he married a Chinook woman, and they had children in Oregon when it was controlled by Britain. So William, born in 1824, wasn't American. As an Indian and an alien one to boot, he could not vote in the state of Oregon. Nor could he ever be admitted to citizenship because he was "neither a white alien" nor a person of "African nativity or descent," the two categories of people who could become naturalized citizens under U.S. law.[3]

Indian Policy in the Reconstruction West

William McKay's citizenship case wound through the Oregon courts just as Reconstruction-era debates about the status of Black Americans were addressing race and citizenship. Native peoples entered into these crucial conversations through ongoing fights over the Civil Rights Act of 1866 and the Fourteenth Amendment. Western congressmen, including William McKay's own senator, George Williams, held up these rights measures until everyone had agreed that most Indians could never be citizens. Because citizenship had always been a promise of U.S. assimilation policy, and because many Native people already voted and paid taxes, some congressmen and reformers objected to such a blanket denial of rights.[4]

To break this impasse, Sen. Lyman Trumbull of Illinois, a contributing author of the Thirteenth Amendment abolishing slavery, introduced a distinction between Native people who lived in western communities—logging, mining, trading, and ranching—and those who remained within tribal nations. He invoked the category of

"Indians Not Taxed" in order to exclude members of Native nations from citizenship in the Civil Rights Act. As Trumbull put it in the Senate debates, "Our dealings with the Indians are with them as foreigners, as separate nations. We deal with them by treaty and not by law. . . . I should have no objection to changing [the legislation] so as to exclude the Indians. It is not intended to include them." Those Indians who were taxed—who lived in White communities and were no longer members of Native nations—could aspire to citizenship, but most could not. For Williams and other senators, only on these terms could the civil rights legislation proceed.[5]

Between 1868 and 1870, the Fourteenth Amendment guaranteeing citizenship to all persons "born or naturalized in the United States, and subject to the jurisdiction thereof," was ratified. Worried western senators asked the Senate Judiciary Committee to clarify if that language made all Indians into citizens. To their relief, the committee ruled that it did not. "Wild Indians" who hadn't signed treaties or paid taxes retained "their respective nationalities [and] . . . their separate political communities" and were not included in the circle of citizenship. But western politicians and others pushed further. With the brutal Plains Indian war making headlines, Indian service officials and military officers agreed with western leaders that it was dangerous to allow Native people any civil or property rights. In their view, no Indians, taxed or untaxed, under tribal jurisdiction or not, were covered under the Fourteenth Amendment. As uncivilized foreigners, they needed to be imprisoned on reservations where federal authorities could monitor them. Such sweeping views would apply as well to the world of trader families, mixed-descent marriages, and mixed-blood reserves.[6]

These were years in which the federal government was growing newly confident and powerful. The wartime Congress had used its muscle to pass the Homestead Act, the Railroad Act, and the Morrill Act, all aimed at promoting national development. The Reconstruction amendments all empowered Congress to enforce their constitutional guarantees. And it was the federal government that framed and enforced Indian policy. Commissions staffed by congressmen and church leaders traveled west to assess the Indian situation. The first, headed up by Sen. James Doolittle of Wisconsin in July 1865, returned to Washington utterly shocked. The commission found that Native people had made little progress toward becoming civilized farmers on land "reserved" for Native use by decades of treaties and land cessions. The loosely organized reservations set up in the 1850s, such as the ones where the Fontenelles lived in Nebraska and the McKays in Oregon, had failed. Too few Native people had become Christians or spoke English, and fewer still wanted to give up hunting or cede more of their land.

A new version of reservations, distant from White populations and policed by Federal troops, became the only solution. In 1868 Congress approved three new reservations that emerged from negotiations the year before by William Tecumseh Sherman's Peace Commission. The purpose was to "concentrate" all Plains Indians onto two reservations that would be far away from new settlers: the Great Sioux reservation in the Dakotas, and the Indian Territory reservation in what is now Oklahoma. (The third was the new Navajo reservation in New Mexico and Arizona.) Humanitarian reformers and western politicians both favored the new policy of forcing Native people onto reservations and keeping them there at gunpoint. The policy would protect Indigenous people from voracious settlers, while the military made sure those same White settlers and railroad builders could safely travel over Native lands. By the mid-1880s, the number of reservations in the West would double, and the amount of land in Native control fell by nearly 50 percent.[8]

Rebuilding Indian country on reservations became a joint project of the U.S. military and Christian reformers. A board of Indian commissioners, an umbrella group representing powerful mainline Protestant churches—Episcopalians, Methodists, Quakers, and Presbyterians—would now supervise U.S. Indian policy. After the brutalities of slavery and civil war, Christian citizens would have the chance to draw lines between modern, civilized behavior and backward, savage behavior—tasks shouldered by White men as their special burden. Reservations, properly managed by Christian reformers, would enable White and Black Americans to settle the West in segregated communities on lands taken from Indian people. It was a powerful, racist vision.[9]

As the federal government built reservations to house and reform Indigenous westerners while new westerners took their land, decisions about who was an Indian and should be on a reservation became central. Mixed-descent people had been called out, sometimes by name, in treaties that gave them land on half-breed tracts or required them to move with their tribal relatives. In this sense they were Indians. Because Indians were not citizens, federal officials intended to treat them like "paupers and criminals." A term used previously by President Andrew Jackson to justify removal, it now emphasized that Native people were dependents incapable of shouldering the duties of citizenship. The commissioner of Indian affairs who managed this moment was Francis Amasa Walker, an Amherst- and Harvard-trained statistician. He laid out his plans with chilling racial logic. Indians had to be incarcerated because "the supreme law of public safety" demanded it. He believed so deeply in Indians as a "beggarly, savage race . . . incapable of ambition" that he argued it was unjust and un-Christian for White men to make treaties with them.[10]

Crafted in a time of unending war, White reformers named these plans of military concentration and policed reservations a Peace Policy. That policy was calisthenic exercise for a newly ambitious federal government that used the West as a place to consolidate power and property along racial, ethnic, and class lines.[11] What this meant for intermarried families, people whose blood now made them a public danger, became a question of racial math, as William McKay had discovered.

In this dangerous time, George Bent, Mary Jane Drips Barnes, William McKay, and Joseph La Flesche worked at rebuilding Native homelands. Mixed-descent people often negotiated locations of new reservations and led their nations there, a terrible task that did not earn them admiration. Using old family strategies of connecting to new nations and clans, they wove protective webs, called *ganawendamaw* in Ojibwe or *tiyóspaye* in Lakota, around their kin. Sometimes they lost U.S. citizenship but became re-embedded in their Native communities. William Cameron McKay was hardly the only citizen to take his racial status to court. In Oregon, Nebraska, Kansas, Michigan, Wisconsin, and Minnesota, fur trade families sued over the right to vote, serve on juries, and own land. They no longer based their claims on education or social status but instead on fractions of race and blood.[12]

Cheyenne Oklahoma

Indian Territory was first created in 1828 as a loosely defined region to house Native nations driven from their eastern homelands. Its borders were redrawn in 1851, when Congress passed a bill appropriating funds to move Indigenous nations once they had ceded lands in other western territories. In 1868, in an era when blood was coming to matter so very much, that flexible space, Indian Territory, once again presented a solution. As they met in Washington, D.C., and in western forts, peace commissioners, Indian Service officials, and religious activists from eastern states created a fable about "the so-called Indian Territory" that they were establishing in Oklahoma (a name that means "red dirt" in Choctaw). They promised Native people that Oklahoma would be "preserved in its entirety for the future settlement of the nomadic tribes east of the Rocky Mountains." Next, with the help of reformers, they imagined that Oklahoma might one day "become a proposed Indian Commonwealth." In Oklahoma, the U.S. Army, the newly reformed Indian Service, and a phalanx of Christian missionaries intended to focus the full power of the federal government and God's will on Native people who had run out of choices. This place, home to the Osage and to removed Native nations from the East as well as Apaches, Comanches, Caddos, Kiowas, and Wichitas, would be the Bents' new residence.[13]

Witnesses at the birth of the new Indian country, the Cheyenne Bents suffered its trauma. After the raids following Sand Creek in 1865 and 1866, the Bents, and their Cheyenne and Arapaho kin, were pushed out of Colorado and away from roads, trails, rivers, and bison. By 1868, after two summers of raiding and two winters of hunger when treaty goods failed to appear, many Cheyennes decided to fight until death. George Bent, serving as interpreter, warned family friend Albert Boone, now an Indian agent for the Cheyenne, that Dog Soldier bands had gathered Indian ponies and "enough American horses for a cavalry regiment." Waves of Cheyenne, Sioux, and Pawnee warriors burned buildings, stole stock, killed people, and took children. Albert Boone and George Bent warned government officials about impending disaster and were fired. Now William Tecumseh Sherman and the U.S. Army stepped in. Indians had to be incarcerated or killed, pure and simple, or White America would have to give up settling the West.[14]

Southern Cheyennes and Arapahos tried to escape the spreading trouble. In that desperate moment in 1869, Cheyenne leaders sent George Bent to meet with the Utes and Jicarilla Apaches, ancient enemies who now lived in places distant from settlers, railroads, and Dog Soldier bands. But the Cheyennes could not find respite there. By the time George returned, he learned that his father had died and that the Cheyennes had agreed to move to Oklahoma. They would bring their villages to Fort Supply, opened as a temporary staging ground for the army late in 1868. Isaac Butterfield and John Smith, traders with Cheyenne wives and Cheyenne-White children, became "subagents" to supervise the move. Smith, who had lived in Cheyenne villages for thirty years, was shocked at the conditions at Fort Supply. Despite its name, no supplies had arrived except for wagons of liquor salesmen. The place was isolated and barren. Even the bison had abandoned it.[15]

As their Cheyenne families straggled into Fort Supply, the Bents gathered in Colorado for the last time to hear their father's will read. William Bent's creditors took the house in Kansas City, the Purgatoire River ranch, and the goods at his store at Fort Lyon. Robert and George got mules, a wagon, and seventy-eight head of cattle. Julia and Mary got the family furniture. Faced with no prospects in Colorado, Julia, Robert, and George sold their cattle to an old friend of William Bent, John Prowers. Married to a Cheyenne woman named Amache, Prowers had used his wife's access to Cheyenne lands and annuities to launch a cattle empire. In the fall of 1870, with a little cash in their pockets, George, Robert, and Julia Bent packed up a wagon and headed for Fort Supply to join the other Cheyennes.[16]

William Bent's children now made choices as adult Cheyennes

about how to survive. George, who had taken Kiowa Woman as a second wife in the chaos after the Washita massacre, needed work to support a growing family. He and his brother Robert saw no conflict in working for the government as interpreters and using the money they'd gotten from their father's cattle to join the liquor and gun trade. Along with their White partners, they sold guns, ammunition, and alcohol to anyone who could pay: Indians, soldiers, and missionaries. Julia married the Dakota-French man Edmund Guerrier, a longtime family friend who had lived at Bent's Fort and participated in Cheyenne efforts to save Colorado.[17]

In 1870, as a nation of Christian reformers looked on, Quaker missionaries took over for the army in managing Cheyennes in the new Indian Territory. On the fertile spiritual ground that was Indian country, the U.S. Christian Commission—organized to implement federal Indian policy—drew up western districts for each of the major Protestant denominations. Indian Territory would be managed by Quakers, Methodists, and Episcopalians. The first Quaker agent to arrive, Brinton Darlington, agreed with army officers who wanted the six thousand Cheyennes and Arapahos to move away from Fort Supply, liquor dealers, and potential Pawnee raiders. The agency site picked by Darlington and two missionaries had little wood, no traders, and bad water, so Cheyenne and Arapaho villages packed up to hunt.

Even though the army didn't like it, the right to hunt off the reservation was spelled out in clear treaty language, and Darlington had no better ideas about how to feed thousands of people. From his perspective as a trader and a Cheyenne father, George Bent wanted Cheyennes to hunt bison and sell hides for food and alcohol. He and Kiowa Woman stayed near the agency, but Magpie Woman left George and took their little daughter Ada to move with the hunting camps. In 1872 Cheyenne villages hunted and prepared nearly ten thousand bison hides for trade. Some Cheyennes had cash for a brief time, but it was all tied to debt at traders' stores.[18]

George Bent continued to work as an interpreter, giving everyone news they didn't want to hear. George warned that hunger, alcohol, and the army's inability to protect the reservation from non-Native thieves would lead to war. In May 1874 Kiowa and Comanche warriors struck an alliance by carrying war pipes to the Cheyenne. Though the chiefs tried to stop them, young men joined a united attack on Adobe Walls, a trading post once owned by William Bent in what is now the Texas Panhandle. The post was protecting thieves and their stolen Cheyenne horses. The allied raiders killed twenty-eight White, Mexican, and Indian hunters and teamsters but couldn't get to the horses inside. Native warriors then headed north into Kansas, attacking ranches, wagon trains, and mail carriers. They also rode up to the Cheyenne agency in August 1874 and shot Frank Holloway, son of the agency physician.[19]

The army had to respond. Even though Quaker agents and missionaries objected that most Cheyenne villages had stayed away from the raids, the army began the Red River War along the Texas border. Some Cheyenne leaders brought their villages into the agency for protection, but most went to war. Nearly two thousand warriors from Southern Cheyenne camps rode out to join the Kiowas and Comanches. Robert Bent went with them, but George Bent stayed to protect his position as interpreter. Staying close to the agency cost Bent many friends, but he needed his job. It was a long, terrible fall.[20]

The Indian War ground on through the winter of 1875. Finally in March, as supplies ran out and places to graze horses grew scarce, a large group of warriors surrendered. The remaining "hostiles" fled north, disappearing into Sioux and Northern Cheyenne camps in Montana and the Dakotas. The U.S. Army called the Red River War over. However, the two thousand Cheyennes who returned to the agency in the late spring had no food or hides to build lodges. With people starving, agent John Miles allowed "trusted Cheyennes," led by Robert Bent, to conduct a bison hunt along the Washita River. Bent set out with a large band, 650 men, women, and children, on a twenty-day hunt in June 1875. When they returned with 2,300 bison, meat kettles were full and hide sales were brisk.[21]

For the next few years, after this successful experiment, George Bent managed bison hunts to feed Cheyennes and Arapahos. Treading that line between aiding the enemy and supporting his family, Bent kept the agent and the army informed of who attended the hunts and how people behaved. The shocking news of General Custer's 1876 defeat by Northern Cheyennes at the Little Big Horn in what is now Montana slowly reached Fort Supply in newspapers delivered weeks later. Suddenly no one wanted to arm Southern Cheyennes, even for hunting, and army officials no longer trusted the Cheyenne interpreter George Bent. Trust became a moot point when the hunts failed in 1877 because so few bison remained on the southern Plains.[22]

Railroads made stripping the southern Plains of bison too easy. Transportation networks and quick profits created a bison-hide "rush." As bison hides became more commonly used for shoe leather, they did not require the elaborate scraping and curing needed for supple (and expensive) bison robes. A cheaper and easier tanning process could now be handled in East Coast cities. Anyone, male or female, White or Native, could hunt bison and ship hides east on railroads to distant tanneries.[23]

Throughout the 1870s, sensing easy profit, non-Native bison hunters had poured into Indian Territory, the place that was supposed to be forever sealed off from White America. Though this movement was illegal, the army did nothing to stop it. Non-Indian hunters aggravated already tense relations by stealing horses and selling alcohol on the side. They demanded sex, not marriage, from Indian women. Cheyenne women watched as the hides their men brought in were sold for whiskey instead of for food or horses. Julia Bent's husband, Edmund Guerrier, sent his string of ponies to Fort Supply so that his relatives wouldn't trade them to whiskey dealers. George joined up with some White merchants that he knew from Denver, Lee and Reynolds, and tried to cash in on both White and Native hunters. They paid Indian women three dollars per hide in credit at the traders' store. This was the end of the long partnership that required Indian hunters to take bison so their hides would be perfect, Indian women to turn rough hides into beautiful robes, and White or mixed traders to speak Native languages and marry Indian women.[24]

Then the cash and the bison were suddenly gone. No one could have predicted how quickly this happened. When hunters and traders headed north to repeat the same process on the northern Plains, Native traders like George Bent suffered like everyone else on the southern Plains. They begged at government forts and ate ponies that had died from disease. In that ugly situation, George sent Magpie and Kiowa Woman back to the agency, hoping they might get rations there. The U.S. government, much to the new Quaker agent's frustration and to the Cheyennes' sorrow, cut rations in half, insisting that the Indians should be providing their own food by now.[25]

The food crisis in Indian Territory worsened when another thousand Cheyennes arrived in 1877. The U.S. Army, in the wake of Custer's defeat, learned to fight in winter, when villages were camped together and ponies were hungry. Many Plains nations fled to Canada, but after two brutal winters, Northern Cheyenne leaders Dull Knife and Little Wolf surrendered to the U.S. Army. They led one thousand refugees on a seventy-day march south and arrived in Indian Territory at the Cheyenne-Arapaho agency. George Bent was in charge of finding them food and shelter when none was available. The northerners hated Oklahoma, which was hot and had too few bison and too many Cheyennes and Arapahos. A year later Dull Knife and 350 of his people fled north, stealing horses, provisions, and food and killing anyone who got in their way. The Northern Cheyennes who stayed behind included a young woman named Standing Out Woman who moved into George Bent's lodge and life. Making families in new places wasn't really a new beginning, but it healed some wounds and kept people alive.[26]

Fur Trade Mothers as Homesteaders

The nation's new beginning, charted in Civil War–era legislation, required two things: empty land and White settlers. The Homestead Act energized the old promise of open land for Americans and lured people west. When homesteaders arrived in distant western places, ready to create new lives after the war, they discovered that the region wasn't empty and the inhabitants weren't White. Homesteaders made their first claims in Kansas, in French-Indian communities that had briefly been abandoned during Civil War guerrilla raiding. The Ingalls family, who became characters in the widely read children's book series, made their own new beginning on Osage lands in Kansas in 1868.[27]

Mary Jane Drips Barnes struggled to manage homesteaders who threatened her Nebraska land on the Great Nemaha Half-Breed Tract. The intermarried Dripses and Barneses used Indian and Anglo-American family strategies to protect their land, heritage, and children. Mary Jane's mother's (Macompemay) Otoe people had lived there for generations, and now, she hoped, so would her children. Mary Jane's White husband, Francis Barnes, moved into her Native world in the 1860s. Even with a deed, a legal survey, and a non-Native husband, she found that hanging on to land was difficult. Her stepmother, Louise Geroux Drips Goulet, lost her land and didn't stay in Nebraska, but she still survived. Taken together, their two very different stories illustrate how mixed-descent families and Native nations persevered.[28]

To the new settlers of the West, Indian landownership, like citizenship, was apparently invisible. In the 1860s, when the Otoe reservation and the Great Nemaha Half-Breed Tract became Nebraska Territory, White men tried to create counties and administrative structures required by a new territory. They drew a proposed county around the Otoe reservation but learned that it couldn't become a county because it had "no settlers or citizens" among the hundreds of Otoes who lived there. Six White men arrived in a wagon from Kansas, but they failed to meet the sixty-day residency requirement. With no settlers to represent, Gage County nearly disappeared. Francis Barnes, Mary Jane's husband and a White resident by anyone's definition, formed a new townsite company and saved the new county. To preserve the fragile counties around the Nemaha tract, residents had to count their "half-breed neighbors" as "citizens" to get initial recognition, but refused to let them vote or serve in county offices.[29]

The Indigenous and trader worlds went underground. The first townsite in Nemaha County, named St. Deroin, was laid out by a French-Otoe man named Joseph Deroin, who ran a ferry across the

Missouri River. Deroin sold land lots to new settlers until one of them shot him when he came to collect money owed for that land. Although in their accounts White settlers from this era included tales of finding "Indian camps," going to "Indian dances" at the reservation, and locating the first county seat on an Indian reservation, the grand leather tome detailing the founding of Nemaha County insisted that "Nemaha had no Indians of its own." Those disappeared Native people, however, reappeared in 2010. Lorena Deroin, an Otoe elder descended from Joseph Deroin and living in Oklahoma, visited the old townsite to get some dirt from her ancestors' lands so she could be properly buried when the time came.[30]

Like Lorena Deroin, Mary Jane Drips Barnes refused to be written out of Otoe history. Knowing her rights as an Otoe woman and a U.S. citizen, she carried on an effective campaign of letters, court appearances, and lawsuits through the 1870s. She wanted Nebraska officials and the federal land office to recognize her ownership of land on the Great Nemaha Half-Breed Tract. That sliver of land on the Kansas-Nebraska border encompassed a long history of family connections between French-Canadian and Anglo-American trappers, traders, and military men, and women of several Indigenous nations. Now its future lay in the hands of mixed-descent women.[31]

Native landownership remained invisible to White men because, often, Native and mixed-blood women owned it. The Drips family, who received thousands of acres of land in the 1860 allotment, had almost no land on the Great Nemaha lands by 1870. The record shows rapid transfers of land and "half-breed scrip," with Drips family land ending up in the hands of local bankers. We know this story: the tragic loss of land for Indigenous people and Native women exploited by White land speculators, including their own husbands. Mary Jane's story, however, was different. She and her entire extended family used their connection to a White man, her husband Francis Barnes, to create a family compound on an Indian reservation.[32]

In 1870, with more options than the Cheyenne Bent family in Oklahoma, the Dripses and Barneses chose a reservation as the safest spot to make their lives visible and legal. Even as the Otoe agent warned that "1/4 or 1/8 bloods who had drawn lands on the half breed tract" were "defrauding the Otoe tribe by trying to regain tribal rights," Mary Jane did exactly that. Never considering that she wasn't Otoe, she spoke to her relatives and got a certificate stating that the chiefs of the Otoe tribe "do recognize Mary Jane Barnes, wife of Francis M. Barnes to be a member of our tribe." Now she could settle, along with Francis, on the Otoe reservation.[33]

Francis Barnes and Mary Jane's brother, the former Union soldier and riverboat pilot Charles Drips, became model farmers hired by the Indian Service to teach Indians to farm. Francis, like so many White men married into Native families, served as agent for the Otoe. In 1873 Barnes used a gun to threaten squatters who tried to settle on Mary Jane's kinfolk's Otoe lands. The Otoes had the only remaining large stands of timber along the Republican River; the rest had long since been chopped down by overland travelers for firewood. During cold winters, new settlers found Otoe trees the only fuel available. Barnes arrested several ax-wielding settlers but never managed to convict any.[34]

Louise Geroux Drips Goulet used a different strategy. Now married to Henri Goulet, also widowed with four children, they both had claims on the half-breed tract. Henri couldn't keep that land after his first wife's death. After he married Louise, they farmed Louise's land. By 1870, they had fourteen children living in their household. Like many settlers old and new, they risked losing that land to local storeowners who lent them money for seed and supplies. Worried about such loss and to protect the children of her first marriage, to Andrew Drips, Louise gave Francis Barnes control of her children's land.[35]

By 1875 a new wave of pressures beset the Dripses, Goulets, and Barneses along with the entire Otoe nation. According to their agents and Nebraska newspapers, Otoes clung to hunting and showed no interest in becoming American farmers. They held their good land in common, and raised corn in riverbeds. A series of corrupt agents ensured that the Otoes received no seeds, supplies, or farming tools, so they hunted bison. Otoes, Kaws, Shawnees, and Poncas all made more money selling hides than corn, which frustrated their agents.

However, the Otoes' horse population, a source of pride and wealth, was down to four hundred, not enough to mount a good hunt. Drought and economic hard times made corn hard to grow, and after 1873, many Otoes went hungry.[36]

Federal officials responded to this crisis in two ways. First, they insisted that the Otoe reservation be converted to individually titled plots of land. Second, they threatened that if the Otoes didn't sign away their rights to the reservation that remained after allotments, they would send them all to Oklahoma. Officials believed that these measures ensured that fine farmland would no longer lie unused and wasted. White Nebraskans could take "left over" land that was not part of Otoe individual allotments. Such leftovers included the land the Drips and Barnes family had settled and farmed.

Mary Jane Drips Barnes could see exactly what the future held. Having been educated in St. Louis at exclusive boarding schools, she wrote to her well-connected friends for help. Those friends included the St. Louisan Julia Boggs Dent, now married to Ulysses S. Grant, president of the United States. In 1875 Mary Jane wrote to Julia, "I know the President can make us a grant of our land." She explained that she and her family had worked hard and did not want to "leave our comfortable farms under duress and go south with the tribe to Oklahoma, which is surely their fate." When Mrs. Grant didn't respond, Mary Jane wrote to the commissioner of Indian affairs, demanding that he provide land titles to "deserving and industrious tribal members" like herself who had papers proving ownership and residency.[37]

A crucial piece of Mary Jane's strategy was to make use of family connections. When she and Louise Drips Goulet moved to Nebraska and became farmers, they made sure their children had options. Their sister and co-parent Catherine Drips Mulkey had never left Kansas City. Catherine bought the house that her father, Andrew Drips, had left to Louise and immediately sold her land on the Nemaha. She raised her younger half-siblings, Louise's children, and took care of Mary Jane's children when they attended school in Kansas City. Catherine never left her Otoe life behind. She labeled herself an Indian in her letters and in the census. Like other Kansans, Native and White, she and her husband, William Mulkey, invested in cattle.[38]

Catherine used her money and her fur trade connections to push her family into the new economies developing in the West. She went into business with an old friend from the convent school she had attended in St. Louis, a Wyandot woman named Sarah Pagne. Sarah had married Lucien Dagenett, a French-Odawa man who traded on the Wyandot reservation in southern Kansas. Long threads linked Catherine and Sarah's lives because of the Wyandots' surprising path through the fur trade and U.S. history. They started as Huron refugees from Canada called Wendats—a name that evolved into Wyandots—who settled in Odawa and Ojibwe villages around the Great Lakes in the early 1700s. Following the fur trade, Wyandots moved south into Michigan and Ohio and joined other Native groups. From there, in the 1830s they were removed to Kansas, where, like the Drips family, they were promised new land. And like most Kansas Indians, the Huron-Wendat-Wyandots were removed again after the Civil War, this time to Indian Territory. Sarah and Lucien Dagenett raised cattle on the Oklahoma-Kansas border, using Wyandot cowboys and drovers. When the business thrived, Catherine Drips Mulkey invested. She got Kansas City cattle merchants to pay better prices than the French-speaking Lucien had managed. These new linkages between the fur trade communities along the Missouri River to new Native communities in Oklahoma became a piece of Indian country's survival.[39]

Unlike Mary Jane and Catherine, Louise Drips Goulet lost her gamble to remain a Nebraska homesteader in the 1870s. Whether she and Henri failed because of drought, bad finances, speculators, or the terrible depression of 1873, we'll never know. The couple took Louise's four youngest children from her marriage to Andrew Drips and their six children from their own marriage and moved to Dakota Territory in 1873. They moved to the Sioux reservation just north of the Missouri River, where *tiyóspaye*, the all-encompassing web of social obligation that built family networks and kept the peace, still remained at the heart of Dakota life.[40]

The Goulets' move was a result of a Native victory. After fighting Lakota warriors for years, the U.S. government and military backed down and in 1868 agreed to end the war. The victorious Indians received the Great Sioux Reservation, about the same size as Kentucky, and retained the right to hunt outside that reservation. Because of that success, forty thousand Lakota, Dakota, and Yanktonai villages gathered there, the largest group of Native people living outside Indian Territory. Henri Goulet had Yankton Sioux cousins still hunting and raising children in the Great Sioux Reservation, and Louise had brothers and uncles in the mixed communities around Fort Pierre.[41]

Louise Drips Goulet listed her children as members of Yankton Sioux bands, hoping that they would be safe where people still danced and held pipe ceremonies to bind peoples together. However, only a year after moving to the Great Sioux Reservation, she died giving birth to her last child, also named Louise.[42]

Reconstruction's Reservations

Some mixed-descent women like Catherine Drips Mulkey stayed off reservations, but other women like Louise Drips Goulet looked to reservations for refuge. The McKays in the Pacific Northwest, as well as the La Flesches and Fontenelles, found work there as farmers, blacksmiths, teachers, scouts, and carpenters. As Native nations negotiated the conditions of life on reservations, discussions of who counted as Indian centered on blended families.[43]

William Cameron McKay, who sued the state of Oregon over his right to vote, had stayed in Oregon because he had options both as a man with fur trade roots and as an Indian. With his wife, the Canadian-Cree Margaret Campbell, in the 1860s he followed other fur trade families to Walla Walla, Washington, to raise sheep and cattle and to run trading posts along the busy Oregon Trail. He founded the community that became Pendleton, soon famous for Indian trade blankets and other wool products. However, a decade of Indian war left White Oregonians demanding that all Indians live on reservations, even long-resident families like William and Margaret. Because the McKays moved to the reservation, in 1868 the town was named after a failed U.S. vice-presidential candidate, George H. Pendleton, instead of its actual founder.[44]

William McKay spent the last three decades of his life on reservations, as reservation doctor, land owner, Indian, husband, and father. Although he couldn't vote, he was elected county coroner in several elections. Along with hundreds of other similar families, labeled "half-breeds" by Indian agents, he and Margaret moved back and forth between the Warm Springs Reservation and the Umatilla Reservation, both in isolated eastern Oregon.[45]

Mixed-descent people made up at least 20 percent of Oregon and Washington reservations. Those residents included old French families, with English and German names also sprinkled through the population rolls. Native women still provided a path to success for men from other nations—the United States or Canada or Germany—so the census showed many Indian women listed as "married to a white man." Many Native people had tended sheep and cattle since the 1830s for outfits like the Hudson's Bay Company. As the fur trade diminished in eastern Oregon and Washington, Umatilla, Spokane, and Nez Percé people added sheep to their lives, often partnering with local White people and creating new blended families to serve new purposes.[46]

Success created trouble. New immigrants sought control of sheep and the land they grazed on, but Native residents refused. Nez Percé and Shoshone leaders made several trips to Washington, D.C., to demand that treaties from 1855 and 1863 be upheld. In 1873 an executive order from President Ulysses Grant gave the Wallowa Valley, a small mountainous corner of northeastern Oregon, to the Nez Percé. However, new settlers demanded that grazing rights to that land be renegotiated, and in 1875 the Wallowa country was opened to non-Native settlement. After meeting with Nez Percé leaders in 1876, a commission recommended to Indian Service officials that all Nez Percé bands be moved to an Idaho reservation and that they be forced out by April 1, 1877.

When the U.S. Army came to remove the Nez Percé and Cayuse bands and their hundreds of families, one Nez Percé leader, Chief Joseph, or Hinmatoowyalaht'qit, refused to surrender and fled for Canada. As an example to Indians who left reservations, the U.S. Army decided to hunt down Chief Joseph and his desperate families. Months later in October 1877, after chasing them through the rugged northern Rockies, the army found the remaining bands only forty miles from the Canadian border. Afraid that they too would be dragged from their homes, Umatilla and Cayuse people guarded their reservation and shot at intruders, behavior described as a "rebellion." In 1878 Portland newspapers claimed that fifty Whites had been murdered, but authorities could find only three Cayuse whom they could label as killers, White Owl, Quit-a-Tumps, and Aps. They were hanged in the public square in Pendleton for their murder of White men and pronounced dead by the county coroner William McKay on February 4, 1879.[47]

To take advantage of White audiences who craved seeing captured Native warriors, William McKay's half-brother, the Cayuse Donald McKay, born in 1834, left the reservation to become a "show Indian" in 1876. Donald McKay's Indian shows featured "dangerous warriors" and included his daughter Minnie. Raised like many Cayuse children to ride horses, she became a trick rider, appearing in shows all over the Midwest until her death in 1884. After his daughter's death, and as the drama of the Indian wars faded in the short memories of eastern audiences, Donald found himself in a poorhouse in Boston. Local Oregonians, hearing of his situation, held a fundraiser horse race, with White and Cayuse riders vying for prizes. After returning from Boston, Donald McKay lived out his life on the Umatilla reservation.[48]

Reservations were thin protection in the era of war, removal, and racial segregation. In the history of the middle Missouri nations, the Omahas stand out because they negotiated a reservation on their homeland and stayed there. Other Native nations, no matter what treaties they signed, could not protect anything. Despite their businesses, educations, or military service, Kansas Indians lost every bit of tribal land to land speculators, railroads, and the federal government. Only the Omaha kept land in Nebraska. Every other tribe moved to small enclaves in Indian Territory and began the slow, bitter process of rebuilding lives in unfamiliar and destitute circumstances.[49]

The Omaha maintained some degree of traditional life. As an Omaha leader should, Joseph La Flesche maintained two large households. His two wives, the mixed-descent Mary Gale and the Omaha Tainne, did the work required in a chief's household. They stored food for feasts, housed guests, and organized hunts and planting. They also raised a large family. La Flesche's insistence on moving to the reservation and on sending children away had personal costs. Joseph's eldest son, Louis, died at age nine while attending the Presbyterian mission school at Bellevue. Their other nine children survived to adulthood. An exceptional family in many ways, they became prominent leaders and activists serving the Omaha. The oldest surviving La Flesche son, Francis, worked as an ethnologist for the Smithsonian, preserving Omaha traditions and histories. The daughters included a medical doctor, a journalist, and a financial manager for the tribe.[50]

Henry and Susan Fontenelle, the youngest of Lucien Fontenelle's and Mehubane's children, were the only ones to live full lives on the reservation. Their success depended on kin, marriage, and connections outside that reservation. Henry attended the Indian Manual Labor School near Bellevue. He hated school and ran away several times, traveling the 250 miles to the Omaha reservation, a distance made deadly by Sioux raiders and Civil War bushwhackers. He did meet a mixed Pawnee-Omaha woman, Emily Papin, with whom he made a life. Emily's father, like Henry Fontenelle's, was French and her mother was from an important Pawnee family, connections still crucial on reservations and in the Indian trade. In 1867 Henry became the official trader for the Omaha villages, making sure Omahas were paid fairly for their hides, furs, and produce, exactly the same position George and Robert Bent took on for the Cheyennes. Because such positions enabled lucrative under-the-table deals with local White merchants who paid for access to the Indian trade and annuity payments, mixed-descent men often benefited. With honest work and probably dishonest cash, Henry and Emily raised eight children who attended reservation schools.[51]

Susan Fontenelle, raised in the Drips household, married Louis Neals, who was French and Omaha. In 1862 they received the first allotment on the Great Nemaha Half-Breed Tract. Keeping that land, however, proved difficult in the churn of war and Reconstruction. Family troubles made the situation worse. Tecumseh Fontenelle, Susan's older brother, who never received land for his mixed status, worked as a blacksmith at the Great Nemaha agency. Soon after Susan and Louis Neals received their allotment, Louis killed Tecumseh. Whether it was a drunken tussle or a long-simmering feud, Louis served a prison sentence for that crime. Because Nebraska Territory had no penitentiary, he served in an Omaha jail.[52]

While Louis served his sentence, Susan Fontenelle Neals moved to Omaha to be near Omaha kin. The town had eighteen hundred people, only half the size of the Omaha villages that lay on its northern edge. Susan worked as a servant in a boardinghouse until Louis got out of prison and they could once again take up precarious lives farming on their Nemaha land. Again, we see the hands of the Drips family, linking families and using kin to save them. In 1870 the Neals household included one of Louise Drips Goulet's sons, George Washington Drips, aged eleven. Susan sometimes sent her own daughter to live with Catherine Drips Mulkey in Kansas City. Even as mixed-descent families challenged the racial borders that reservations were supposed to create, they also used them to protect territory and family. Firmly Omaha, the Fontenelles and La Flesches survived legal challenges over land and heritage.[53]

Louise Drips Goulet, Dakota and French, hoped the reservation would offer safety when times got tough. In 1874, as Louise was carrying her last child, White miners found gold in the Black Hills, the heart of the Great Sioux Reservation. In a too-familiar story, gold brought miners, settlers, and the U.S. Army. In 1876 a summer gathering of Lakota villages, surprised by Gen. George Armstrong Custer and 276 of his men, massacred every White soldier. The satisfying but illusory victory brought the full and concentrated power of the U.S. Army to the northern Plains in the winters of 1876 and 1877, obliterating any safety Louise imagined for her children. Many families fled to Canada, regrouped in Oklahoma, or died from starvation.[54]

After Louise died in 1875, Henri couldn't hold the family together through those terrible war years. His name showed up on the 1880 census as a hired farm laborer in Charles Mix County, the administrative entity surrounding the Yankton Sioux reservation. None of his children lived with him even though a few were still young, only six, nine, and ten. Louise and Henri's two older daughters, Mary and Maggie, appeared on the rolls at the Hampton Industrial Training School in Virginia in 1879, but the youngest children disappeared from view.[55]

Railroads, military posts, and mission schools reshaped the Sioux landscape and ended a life that had depended on bison. Mirroring what had happened in western Oklahoma and Texas on the southern Plains, Plains hunters, both non–Native and Native, killed hundreds of thousands of bison as the Northern Pacific Railroad gave White hunters easy access to eastern markets. Bison skinners and packers left rotting carcasses piled high near riverbanks. By 1883, a herd of 2 million had been reduced to a few dozen. Shocked by this sudden change, Native families clustered around Indian agencies to get away from gold rushers, hunters, and railroad builders, but the Indian Service wasn't prepared to meet the need. Facing starvation, families left the reservations.[56]

Charles Goulet, seventeen, and his little sister Louise, twelve, reappeared on the Yankton Sioux rolls in 1886. They lived with their recently married sister, Mary, who in her early twenties looked after them. None of this was the outcome Louise Drips Goulet had imagined when she left Nebraska. However, even with a vastly shrunken land base, the Sioux were still home in the Dakotas. At least they didn't have to move to Oklahoma, the federal government's ultimate threat.[57]

Oklahoma remained Indian Territory. With no gold, no more bison, and the black gold that would roil the twentieth century still undiscovered, it settled into its own peace. Sweet Medicine, the great prophet who had created the sacred arrows for the Cheyennes, also foretold the end of bison and the arrival of new animals, cattle, that would shape their lives. On his deathbed, he told people they would become great travelers in new lands. Other old stories warned them about the dangers of living too far apart. Life on reservations did magnify distinctions between Cheyennes, as Sweet Medicine predicted. Social status now derived from owning horses or cattle, living in a house or a tepee, where you sent children to school, where you gathered in the summer, and whether you used or gave away annuity goods.[58]

By 1878 George Bent appeared to be a Cheyenne leader. He provisioned his people, gave families meat, and translated trade deals. Cheyenne men developed influence through marriage. George had three wives from different sectors of the Cheyenne people, mirroring the divisions in Cheyenne villages. Magpie Woman, from a peacemaking faction of the tribe, hadn't lived with George since 1870. Kiowa Woman, who became part of George's household after the Washita Massacre, didn't like living near the agency with George. After 1880 she took her children to live in a traditional camp with a warrior named Buffalo Thigh. Standing Out Woman, from a Northern Cheyenne family who had fought the U.S. Army and resisted reservation life to the last, found life with George a challenge.[59]

George's employment with the Indian Service undermined his relationships with his wives and their extended families. His drinking, consorting with military men, and lavish spending made him unreliable. He bought and sold racehorses, organized betting schemes among Cheyenne men and U.S. soldiers, attended cowboy balls off the reservation, and traveled to Kansas, Texas, and Colorado buying supplies and drinking. At the same time, he had steady employment with the Indian Service as interpreter, trader, and sometimes cattle broker for the Cheyenne, all positions that required Cheyennes to trust him.[60]

Bent used his skills to contest "depredation claims" against the Cheyenne. These claims allowed U.S. citizens to demand restitution from the U.S. government for farm animals, supplies, and other goods lost in Indian attacks. If they lost items to White thieves, bad weather, or Mexican bandits, they had to accept those losses. If

"Indians" caused the loss, however, they were repaid out of annuity payments guaranteed to tribes. Native people lost millions to fraudulent depredation claims. George testified regularly that Cheyennes hadn't been at particular battles. George also argued that Cheyennes who had participated in raids hadn't taken the things that White immigrants claimed, because—like cows and pianos—they were impossible to carry. Over and over again, he saved Cheyennes from fraudulent claims.[61]

His efforts also caused resentment. When George gave Cheyenne cattle to the U.S. Army or leased grazing lands to White acquaintances, Cheyennes noticed. In 1884 an ugly scuffle ensued when a Texas drover took four hundred ponies illegally across Cheyenne lands and trampled the ripening gardens of a large summer camp. When the Indians fired guns to drive the horses away, and the Texans responded by shooting into the village, in the end an old warrior, Running Buffalo, lay dead. The Cheyennes wanted to kill the Texan who shot Running Buffalo, as a matter of simple justice, but George Bent stepped in and insisted that the killer be arrested. When Indian Service officials released the Texan, furious Cheyenne leaders shunned George for taking the side of a non-Cheyenne cattleman. It could have been worse. Influential Cheyenne leaders Stone Calf and Whirlwind arranged to have another mixed-descent man, Robert Poisal, killed for making bad cattle leases and arguing with the chiefs.[62]

George Bent created powerful enemies. The chiefs called mixed people *vehoe* or "white spiders" to their faces and threatened to ban them from the reservation. The most trouble came from Bent's efforts to send Cheyenne and Arapaho children to reservation schools. Few Cheyennes and Arapahos wanted to send their children away. When the children came home hungry and ill from long days in the dirty school, most parents refused to send them back. George insisted that his own children attend and threatened his neighbors that the agent would withhold food from families who kept their children away. By the 1880s, only about 25 percent of the tribes' children attended schools, and most were from a few leaders' families and from traders' White and Native families.[63]

When Magpie Woman died and Standing Out Woman kicked George out, it was an indication to many Cheyennes of his failure as a Cheyenne man. Now, without wives and with his children sent away to school, he had no standing in the Southern Cheyenne community. In the 1880s, he spent a lot of time away from the Cheyenne reservation, and from Oklahoma, living out a different Native future.[64]

George Bent's Many Families

George Bent wanted a living Indian world, not just memories. He wanted lodges and houses filled with wives and children, but he had seen too much to trust White people's ideas about how to get there. He had seen priests butcher babies, soldiers scalp captives, and mothers starve children, and he had no interest in that version of modernity. Rebuilding a Cheyenne homeland atop such atrocities seemed unlikely on the dry, treeless Cheyenne-Arapaho reservation. George's vision of a new Indian country was both intimate and expansive.

Searching for friends and space to rebuild, George Bent visited the Southern Ute reservation in 1880. He had been there earlier, in 1870, when the Cheyenne had considered moving to that southern Rockies landscape. The Utes, who had hunted and occasionally fought with Cheyennes on the Colorado plains, had resisted U.S. encroachments enough to protect their heritage but had also bent enough to escape annihilation. They lost their huge hunting range but retained some land in a familiar place. In 1880 Utes still had horses. They couldn't hunt bison as they had in the old days, but running sheep and cattle kept them Ute by enabling them to keep their horses. A trusted Cheyenne man who married a Ute wife could remind the Cheyennes of those possibilities. Bent began building the human bridges that a new Indian country required.[65]

About 1880, George Bent began a family with Vieage, a Ute woman from the Southern Ute reservation in southwestern Colorado. In 1890, 1900, and again in 1910, he showed up twice in the U.S. census: in Oklahoma and in Colorado. If this southern Colorado man is the George Bent we have followed—and the evidence is suggestive but not definitive—his story offers up many possibilities about mixing blood and Native life. Now he had four families: two with his Southern Cheyenne wives, Magpie and Kiowa Woman, one with the Northern Cheyenne Standing Out, and the last with Vieage.[66]

These marriages produced many children. He and Magpie Woman had had three: Ada, born in 1867, and two they lost as infants. He and Kiowa Woman produced Julia and George Bent, Jr. Standing Out Woman had six children with George: Charles in 1879, another George, Jr., in 1878, Mary in 1879, William in 1885, Daisy in 1888, and Lucy in 1895. Bent family names echoed again and again in this Native place. Vieage and George Bent appeared on the Ute reservation rolls and on the U.S. census. George was categorized as a "red man" but not a "ration Indian," meaning that he wasn't on the Ute Indian rolls and that he lived without government support raising cattle. He appeared to be an active father—at least he produced children regularly. He and Vieage had six children, neatly stair-stepped with children in Oklahoma, beginning with Ray in 1881, just when George fell out with the traditional Cheyennes. Amos, born in 1891, and twins Oscar and Sarah, born in 1892, arrived after Standing Out stopped living with George.[67]

Reservations meant to imprison became essential in a long, brutal era of enforced assimilation and hard racial categories. Cheyennes and Chinooks, Otoes and Dakotas, Ojibwes and Omahas were supposed to disappear in reservations. But traditional strategies of marriage, mixing blood, and making alliances enabled them to survive. George Bent, Louise Drips, Mary Jane Drips Barnes, and others like them left some reservations and went to others, seeking safety. Indigenous America and its mixed families used reservations to hide out, then to reappear when it was safer.[68]

=12=

"A Mighty Pulverizing Engine": Allotment Policy and Blood Quantum, 1880–1907

O n a hot, windy day in September 1880, nine-year-old Julia Bent got on a train in Arkansas City, Kansas. Already tired from the long buckboard ride from Colony, Oklahoma, dressed in white muslin and wearing new shoes, she tried to settle into the prickly cloth seats of the railroad car. She was traveling with her sister Ada, fourteen, and fifteen other Cheyenne and Arapaho children to the Carlisle Indian Industrial School. Julia and Ada were among the first of their nations to attend boarding school. In its second full year of operation, Carlisle bristled with the reform goals of its founder, the Civil War general, abolitionist, and prison director Richard Henry Pratt.[1]

By 1880, two centuries of treaty making and two decades of Indian War had left a legal morass of unfulfilled treaties and failed policy initiatives. The people who managed reservations—Christian reformers and federal officials—and the people who lived on them—Indigenous people and their friends and business partners—could not agree about how Native nations should join modern America. Where did Indigenous Americans fit into the evolving racial hierarchy? Did Native people, so recently at war with the United States and so recently pushed onto reservations, still threaten it?

FAMILIES TRAVEL: RESERVATIONS, RAILROADS, AND SCHOOLS

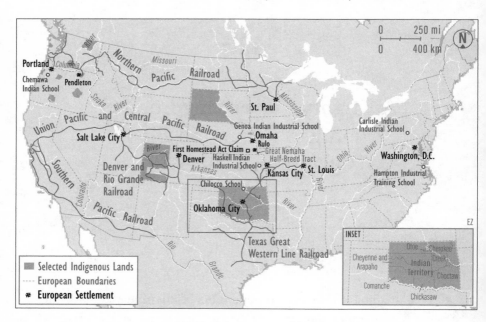

Native people faced their own questions about navigating modern conditions. How could gifts like land and water that had become "resources" be used in Indigenous ways? How could Ojibwe and Otoe women who now owned land obtain the needed legal protection? What about Cheyenne and Arapaho leaders who hired White cattlemen to manage land, or Yakima and Cayuse people who raised sheep and cattle so they could keep horses? This developing Indian modernity was, however, poisoned by reform ideas that came from nineteenth-century social science: blood quantum, land allotment, and marriage regulation.[2]

Schools and Trains

These policies paralyzed Indian country just when it needed to protect its sovereignty. And nations themselves were deeply divided about how best to provide that protection. Mixed-descent leader

Joseph La Flesche insisted that the Omaha nation could save itself only by traveling the path that American officials had laid out. He made his own children attend White-run schools so that they could build lives that were recognizably Omaha. But La Flesche's herd of fifty cattle and harvest of two thousand bushels of corn created a lot of talk among Omahas, and many turned their backs on his efforts. They refused to farm, learn English, or give up hunting. As they did on many other reservations, angry people moved to separate villages.[3]

Education, at the center of White reformers' agendas, caused deep divisions in reservation politics. White teachers taught reading and writing in old missions, warehouses, trading posts, and jails. Reformers who directed Indian policy demanded that their own definitions of Christian marriage and morality become essential lessons for Native students. Their goal was to abolish polygamous households like Joseph La Flesche's or George Bent's. Other lessons involved understanding the racial hierarchies evolving around them. Indian and mixed children should learn how to serve White America, while accepting a place outside it. Many Native parents, correctly, saw schools as places that killed and changed their children. Poorly built, crowded schools allowed diseases like measles and influenza to run rampant among Indian children. Schools provided inadequate clothing, and children were beaten for wearing "Indian blankets" or speaking Native languages.[4]

Most schools were initially located on reservations, where families foiled ambitions of reformers and federal policy makers. They spoke their own languages at home and took children to dances and hunts. Francis La Flesche, Joseph La Flesche's son, remembered years later the despair floating through school when students watched their Omaha families depart on a summer hunt. He described a "general depression among the remaining pupils at the school" as the colorfully bedecked horses and the happy people disappeared from sight. Building higher walls and enforcing stricter rules about visits would never solve the problems of heartache and loneliness.[5]

Ada and Julia's younger siblings attended reservation schools. School officials were proud of their efforts to gather up hundreds of Cheyenne, Arapaho, and Kiowa children "by day and night, traveling through storms and freezing weather." The director of Indian

Territory's Chilocco boarding school, located just south of the Kansas border, noted that after their arduous travels, children arrived "despondent and ill." Native leaders resented the tribal money used for building schools and paying teachers. The Cheyenne-Arapaho agent reported that one August "a scuffle had broken out" when Cheyennes discovered that much of their cattle herd had been sold to support education they believed was irrelevant or dangerous.[6]

Off-reservation boarding schools, where children could be entirely sequestered from their families, were expensive and even cruel. The case for these schools was made by wealthy members of influential Indian reform organizations—the Indian Rights Association, the Women's National Indian Association, and Friends of the Indian—who served as advisers to federal policy makers. They argued that only total immersion in English, manual labor, and Christianity could "leach Indian ways" from children. To accomplish this, Richard Henry Pratt and Samuel Chapman Armstrong, both Civil War heroes with sterling abolitionist credentials, included reeducating Indians in their great projects to turn former Black slaves into farmers and teachers.[7]

After watching Indian students at Armstrong's Hampton Normal and Agricultural School in Virginia, Pratt established the first all-Indian school, Carlisle, in 1879, in old military barracks in Pennsylvania. Military discipline, corporal punishment, and new names became part of Pratt's brand: "Kill the Indian: Save the Man." Carlisle became the model for twenty-six Bureau of Indian Affairs (BIA) boarding schools in fifteen states, and hundreds of private boarding schools sponsored by religious denominations. Between 1879 and 1918, more than ten thousand Native children from 140 tribes attended Carlisle, though only a few hundred graduated. Four La Flesche children attended Hampton, and four Bent children went to Carlisle. When the BIA opened Chemawa in Oregon to serve Native children from the entire Pacific Northwest in 1881, William McKay sent his youngest daughter, Leila.[8]

By pulling children away from their communities, off-reservation schools created new bonds between students but at an enormous cost. Amos Bent's sister died at the Haskell Indian Industrial School in Lawrence, Kansas. Louise Drips Goulet's daughter Maggie spent a year in a tuberculosis hospital after her stay at Hampton. By 1900, twenty-five thousand Native children attended off-reservation boarding schools each year, a number that increased until 1926.[9]

Reservation schools, mostly run by churches, served around forty thousand students each year. The Arapaho Boarding School in Darlington, Indian Territory, was headed up by a Quaker, James Duncan. Half his employees were White, but the staff included mixed-descent Shawnees, Winnebagos, Wyandots, and Cheyennes, all graduates of other boarding schools. Mirroring the racial hierarchies that evolved around them, students saw mixed employees working as seamstresses, laundresses, and cooks but rarely as teachers. The school educated boys and girls aged five to sixteen. George W. Bent, ten years old, attended the Arapaho school with his "1/4 white blood" carefully noted. Of the 122 students enrolled that year, a third had some fraction of White blood.[10]

Similar schools opened in Nebraska, where reformers ran into different challenges. An "industrial school," opened in Genoa, Nebraska, in 1884, used empty buildings on the Pawnee reservation, abandoned after Pawnee removal to Indian Territory. This school's primary goal was to teach Indians to work. The first sugar beet factory in the United States used twelve- to fourteen-year-old students from the Genoa Indian Industrial School as unpaid labor. This supposed "benefit" to local business backfired. Angry White workers, mostly Russian immigrants, had the Nebraska Knights of Labor pass a resolution barring the Native workers. They weren't anti-Indian but rather anti–unpaid work. The school opened too late for Mary Jane Drips Barnes's children to attend, but some of her grandchildren did. Mary Jane and her husband Francis used Genoa students to work on their farm and were criticized in the local paper.[11]

For students who endured the epidemics and other ordeals, schools had benefits. Students did learn English, enabling Native communities to challenge officials about payments or treaty rights. Boarding school students learned, too, that while many Indian nations shared the experience of land loss, some had weathered that loss better than others. Such information provided negotiators with powerful tools. Schools continued the cultural blending that had always been central to intermarried families. Boarding school students often built families with each other and with White supervisors and teachers, redefining what "Indian" meant to students and their kin.[12]

When Julia, Ada, and George Bent, Jr., or Maggie Goulet and Leila McKay returned from school in the 1880s, they stepped into communities that were struggling to survive. Ada Bent returned home after two years at Carlisle and lived with George and Standing Out Woman. She saw Cheyennes and Arapahos facing an impoverished reservation life and the end of Plains warfare. Those changes eroded traditional Cheyenne and Arapaho paths to leadership. Poverty meant that chiefs couldn't give enough gifts to maintain power. Without the opportunity to perform feats of bravery in battle, young men couldn't become adults. Without the means to give gifts and horses, poor parents couldn't celebrate sons or marry off daughters. Marriage or adoption, essential to redistributing wealth, no longer seemed worth it. People ended up without husbands, wives, children, or sisters. An old Cheyenne woman named Singing Grass lived all alone, a shocking situation in a Cheyenne community. She reported to the census taker that every one of her nine children had died, stark evidence of how difficult those years were.[13]

Amid poverty and change, cattle ranching offered a hopeful economic path. In the 1880s, a flurry of White cattle raids and violent Native responses forced the U.S. Army to protect Cheyenne borders from cattle thieves, so that Cheyennes, Arapahos, Comanches, and Kiowas could ranch safely. Sometimes they leased land to White ranchers, but they often ran the cattle themselves. Some blended trader families, able to make better deals because they had connections in the White world and spoke English, built up impressive herds on tribal common land.[14]

The Bent family benefited from this moment. Ada Bent had started at the Carlisle Indian School with Robert Burns, a Southern Cheyenne whose father had been killed at Sand Creek and whose mother had left her son to join the Northern Cheyennes. "Homesick and not thriving," Ada came home after two years, but Robert stayed at Carlisle for several more years and received a degree in accounting. After returning to the Cheyenne and Arapaho reservations, respectively, Ada and Robert married in 1890. Ada worked as a translator, and Robert managed the tribal cattle business and his father-in-law's herds. Success came from reaching across divides and linking Cheyenne families with White ranchers and Black or Mexican cowboys. However, when the Indian Service changed its goals yet again, mixed-descent families with large herds on tribal lands became a problem rather than a good example.[15]

Allotment and Blood

By 1885, impatient reformers like Herbert Welsh from the Indian Rights Association, and professional lobbyists who advised U.S. presidents and Indian commissioners, joined a chorus of Western land speculators and railroad builders who demanded access to Indian land. Reformers now supported taking reservation lands that had been guaranteed in treaties. They believed Indian emancipation could occur only when all Indians were divested of communally held land and water and forced into individual land-ownership. Allotment was also meant to remake families according to a precise recipe. Families should comprise a father who farmed and a mother who sewed, cleaned, and cooked. They would produce children who went to school, learned English, and became farm laborers, miners, or domestic servants. Living far away from White communities, they wouldn't drink and they would go to church. They would marry other Indians and create a separate Indian world that shadowed White America, happily serving it and staying out of its way.[16]

In 1887 Sen. Henry Dawes of Massachusetts, a long-serving Republican and devoted Indian reformer, introduced legislation that promised to move Native people toward that goal much faster. A huge and coercive federal effort, designed to end tribal control of land, the Dawes General Allotment Act did that and more—it destroyed Native families. President Theodore Roosevelt, declaring it a success in 1901, pronounced allotment as "a mighty pulverizing engine to break up the tribal mass." That engine, instead of freeing people, impoverished

American Indians, stripped them of their land, and made hidden qualities in their blood the sole determinant of their fates.[17]

As a means of ending tribal authority, the Dawes program divided tribal lands into plots allotted to individual Indians, the size of each plot determined by age, marital status, and quality of land. After up to twenty-five years of legal supervision, allottees would become landowning U.S. citizens. The bureaucracy arrayed around each Indian nation soon became efficient at working out the details of the program. Specially appointed allotment officers laid out forty- and eighty-acre plots (different from the 160 and 320 acres given to White settlers) and determined which Indians should be allotted those plots. As intended from the start, allotment made two-thirds of reservation land into "surplus"—thus available for White settlers, town builders, and railroad speculators. Between 1790 and 1880, Indigenous residents of the United States lost 1.5 billion acres in land exchanges, transfers, and treaty negotiations. That area, impossible to visualize, is more than double the size of the entire Louisiana Purchase.[18]

There was intense pressure on Native people from agents and new allotment officers to sign the Dawes rolls. Many refused, knowing the perils of signing any U.S. document. Officials threatened to take their cattle, reduce their rations, imprison them, burn their homes, and steal their children if they didn't sign. The process was riddled with error. To enter the rolls, someone had to remember who you were, and someone else had to write that down. If your history was not written down, or if your name, tribal connection, or blood quantum was listed incorrectly by people who spoke no Native language, you could lose tribal membership. Agents and their assistants wrote names, often made up or translated into English on the spot, in huge ledger books. Those ledgers reflected an incalculable loss. In 1880, when Native people were restricted to reservations, they had 138 million acres of land, including nearly all of what is now Oklahoma and big pieces of New Mexico, Arizona, and the Dakotas. By the 1920s, after allotment, less than 40 million acres remained in Native hands.[19]

Those signed onto the rolls had "sufficient" Native blood and family heritage to qualify as Indian. What *sufficient* meant was never settled and now is different for every Indigenous group. Notations like

"1/2 breed," "1/4 blood," "1/8 Cheyenne," "full blood" were entered in columns next to names. The relationship between blood and appearance—phenotype, in the language of scientists—is imperfect. Agents often guessed at how much Indian blood people had. Brothers and sisters of the same age and family circumstance were tagged differently. This guesstimate became their blood "quantum."

Blood quantum or "degree of Indian blood," carefully noted on Indian census forms and on the final Dawes rolls, became a criterion for allotting land. Blood also entered into discussions about "competency," a status that freed Indians from legal guardianship so they could sell land, cattle, or mineral rights. Having more White blood sometimes meant getting larger allotments; "full bloods" received less land and more supervision. As tribal land was divided up and allotted, local Indian Service officials, bankers, sheriffs, or lawyers were designated as "guardians" until Native landowners were deemed citizenship ready. Often those same "guardians" swooped in and simply took people's allotments. They demanded "payment" for having protected those acres, which was absolutely illegal but was viewed as a right of White men in Indian country. Just like people sentenced to prisons, insane asylums, and orphanages, allotted Indians were wards of the state and suffered when their wardens were corrupt or criminal.[20]

The Dawes Commission, the creators of those official rolls for each tribal nation, included several categories of Indian identity with corresponding rights. "Indians by blood" were those whose blood and family heritage qualified them as Indians. "Intermarried white citizens" included mixed families and White men who had Native wives or who did business with tribes. Many southern tribes had "freedmen," former slaves who had been freed after the Civil War. All these groups and their complicated blood reflected the long history of intermarriage in Native life.[21]

To tackle intermarriage, now a problem for the Bureau of Indian Affairs to manage, officials issued regulations intended to end racial mixing in Native communities. On the Cheyenne-Arapaho reservation, the local agent tried to stop marriages between White men and Indian women. Tellingly, he never included marriages between Indian women and mixed-descent men because those men were clearly not White. Indian women marrying White men, he explained, "ruined Indian women" and created "mixed blood paupers" who had to be fed and clothed at public expense. The local agent also created a regulation that prevented Indians or mixed-descent men from hiring White or Black men, a fact of Indian country life that broke rules about how White supremacy should work. Finally, the agent required that persons "not of Indian descent" register at the agency. Seventy-one men registered, but the agent complained that a hundred more "squaw men" remained "hidden" in Cheyenne lodges. These mostly White men, married to Indian women and living as Indians, lived in households that interrupted the march toward an ever-narrowing version of family. In contrast, hundreds of Indian women living just off the reservation in White men's houses as servants, cooks, and concubines were never a concern, much less considered perpetrators of a crime.[22]

To adjudicate issues like marriage, Cheyenne and Arapaho agents created a "court of Indian offenses." Allowing people to police themselves was supposed to make Cheyennes more willing to obey laws they hadn't created. Much to the agent's dismay, the Indian court's three judges, Wolf Face, Pawnee Man, and White Snake, simply refused to uphold such laws. The judges wouldn't convict anyone for marrying more than one wife, or allowing daughters to marry White men, labeled crimes by the Indian Service. These complex households were using marriage to link communities and protect people within circles of kin, the heart of Native life. After two sessions, the Cheyenne agent Charles Ashley disbanded the court.[23]

The business of allotment made everyone obsessed with blood. In 1890 and again in 1900, a Special Indian Census asked, "Has this Indian any white blood and if so, how much?" The census taker, generally the local Indian agent or his mixed-descent translator, guessed at the amount of blood in fractional quantities: one-half, one-quarter, one-eighth, one-thirty-second. The more Native blood you had, the higher your blood quantum. However, no one could tell by looking at you how much or what kind of ancestors' blood ran through your veins. Although scientists tried, they could never link skin color, hair, or other observable traits to blood.[24]

The U.S. courts upheld this flawed system. In 1900, in *Hadley v. United States*, a Washington district court ruled that "half-breeds" who received allotments were Indians. The logic applied was the "common knowledge" about two classes of "half-breeds": those with White fathers who abandoned them to be raised on reservations as Indians, and those whose fathers raised them as White men "under the laws of marriage and citizenship." In *Waldron v. United States* (1905), a U.S. circuit court focused on "Sioux mixed bloods" from influential fur trade families and on whether tribal governments could include them on the Dawes rolls. The court ruled that tribes had the authority to determine how much blood quantum enabled someone to enroll for an allotment. Indigenous nations have fought hard ever since to retain this power. Many people with mixed descent became Indian in this process—but Indians whose White blood made them legally competent but culturally suspect.[25]

As the Dawes rolls and allotment unfolded, the Chinook, Cree, and Canadian McKay brothers, now old men, watched their children move to the Yakima, Warm Springs, Colville, and Umatilla reservations. There they raised a few sheep, cattle, and horses and worked as farmers, translators, and teachers. The town of Pendleton annexed the part of the Umatilla reservation where the McKays ran cattle, and a legal battle spun up over cows, fences, and ownership. Allotment, however, would solve that problem.[26]

Before the Dawes Act of 1887, western states had experimented with local versions of allotment. At the Warm Springs and Umatilla reservations, in isolated, difficult-to-farm eastern Oregon and Washington, the Umatilla Allotment Act of 1885 gave small plots of land to individual Indian families. Timber and sheep interests then bought up the remaining reservation—nearly two-thirds of Umatilla land. White merchants and bankers in Umatilla and Wallowa counties served as guardians of Indian allottees, allowing non-Natives to pressure Native landholders for grazing and land leases, or for timber and fishing rights. Threats, bribes, and debt to store owners and bankers combined to extort land from Indian owners. The Umatilla reservation, once 6.4 million acres, dwindled to about 80,000 acres. Soon Native people worked for White employers off the reservation as herders, teamsters, and servants. They subsisted with tiny gardens and with fishing and hunting, which was both essential and illegal.[27]

The same process played out among the Otoe, though over a longer period. The Otoes had been removed to Indian Territory in 1882. The Drips and Barnes families stayed in Nebraska to manage remaining Otoe lands, about half of the original 320,000-acre Blue River Reservation. In the 1880s Otoe numbers, by the federal government's count, dropped to only eight hundred. By 1890, Otoes had recovered some population and had learned to scrape by in Oklahoma. To stabilize their position in Indian Territory, the Otoe tribal leaders decided to sell their Nebraska land and to use the proceeds to buy land from the Cherokee and Sac and Fox nations. Francis Barnes, Mary Jane Drips's husband, and her brother, Charles Drips, represented the Otoe as they bought a new reservation.[28]

That purchase, even with land surveyed and papers signed, didn't protect the Otoes from allotment. Two years later the Indian Service hired two of Mary Jane's sons, Emmet and William, mixed White and Otoe, to travel to Oklahoma and assist in dividing up Otoe land. Bureau of Indian Affairs officials hired boarding school graduates and mixed-descent people to negotiate with tribal governments. Emmet and William assisted Blackfeet Helen Clarke, who served as the Otoe allotment official, even though she spoke no Otoe. The commissioner of Indian affairs explained that because Clarke's blood quantum made her "Indian," she might "exert a greater influence with them than one who is not so identified." Young men with good educations, the Nebraska Barneses wanted their share of land, but they also wanted to mend relationships with their Otoe relatives. Indian Service bureaucrats called Indians who went along with allotment "progressive," and those who refused "traditional." These new words reflected old tribal divisions present in many nations, already made raw in the early reservation years. As mixed-blood Otoes—and as Dripses and Barneses—when they allied with White officials and didn't question the path to civilization forced by allotment, they made some enemies.[29]

The Otoes absolutely refused to allow allotment of the lands they had purchased. They had bought 129,000 acres of land outright; it was no treaty exchange or benevolent government donation. It was theirs. The U.S. government's position was that the Cherokees hadn't ever owned the land they sold to the Otoes. Not even Helen Clarke or the Barnes sons could explain how allotment and reducing the Otoe land base could improve Otoe fortunes. They worked for two years, and they all received death threats. Finally, after tribal leaders visited Washington and hired new lawyers, Helen Clarke prevailed. After years of painful political and personal decisions that would rend families for generations, the Otoes signed, reducing their holdings to a mere 38,000 acres, most of it without water. That loss, orchestrated by allotment policy, felt especially bitter because the particular effort to take Otoe land had been perpetrated by kin and neighbors.[30]

Marriage and Graft

The Dawes Act's focus on land did not change families fast enough. According to White reformers, Indian country presented two challenges: families that were multiracial in ways census takers couldn't capture, and household forms that shocked White observers. Lifelong heterosexual monogamy became a heroic symbol of modernity. Racially matched couples of men and women marched as if boarding Noah's Ark, two by two. Reformers, especially White women's organizations like the Women's National Indian Association, urged Congress to criminalize any form of marriage outside that narrow model. But the fur trade world and the communities that came out of it comprised a cornucopia of family types, including serial monogamy, polygamy, and men or women co-parenting. As divorce, annulment, "cohabitation" without a license, and miscegenation became illegal in Indian country, few relationships met the standards. White reformers had these common family arrangements in their own family closets, but now they needed to stay there.[31]

Western territories and states passed laws to define and control marriage. In Oklahoma, an entirely male territorial legislature passed a marriage law in 1897 that required Indian couples and White couples to get marriage licenses and required individuals to marry only one person. Few people—White, Native, or mixed—chose to get licenses to marry, and efforts to enforce the new law uncovered a sea of polygamous marriages and casual divorces made by White men.[32]

BIA officials called such common life choices adultery and abandonment. In 1900 the official at the Cheyenne agency made an example out of William Goodsell, a Southern Cheyenne and Carlisle graduate. After returning from school, he married two older widows, Day Woman and Curved Nose Woman, to show his community that he understood suitable Cheyenne behavior. If Goodsell was "properly punished," the agent wrote, it could "break up the nefarious practice of dual marriages among our Indians." The legal action failed because no one would testify against Goodsell. Like George Bent, and many White men, William Goodsell lived in several households. As a strategy of creating safety and connection in Oklahoma, such relationships would prove impossible to stop.[33]

In fact, these family arrangements just went underground. From the curated glimpses of families seen by census takers in Darlington, Oklahoma (and Warm Springs, Oregon, and Barneston, Nebraska), allotment and education appeared to have changed Indian life forever. Julia Bent, on the Dawes rolls as three-quarters-blood Cheyenne, built a family that, on its surface, would have made her Carlisle teachers proud. She married the Southern Cheyenne and Carlisle student Noble Prentiss in 1893 and made a family in the post-allotment Cheyenne world. Their first child, Lavinia, died in 1896, but by 1900 they had two living sons, aged one and three. Noble worked as a teamster, loading and unloading wagons and taking people and goods north to the train line.[34]

But Cheyenne choices rippled underneath that surface. Julia's mother, Kiowa Woman, lived with Julia and Noble too, and she still had two husbands: George Bent and Buffalo Thigh.[35] A range of families enabled Southern Cheyennes to outlast allotment. Three women could raise cattle, and two men could raise children. They did what Indigenous Americans had always done, which was to protect what was most important about being Cheyenne, Cayuse, Otoe, or Dakota—their families.[36]

George Bent faced these pressures as a man with no family. His brother Robert had just died, and his Cheyenne wives had kicked him out. He had served as government interpreter for twelve differ-ent agents, and he had a reputation as a man who carried "influence with traditional leaders." But now, without wives or brothers, he was a poor man. He moved between his sons' and daughters' house-holds or lived alone at the agency. Without a household of his own, he couldn't host visitors or new trading partners, or hold feasts, all vital aspects of Cheyenne life. Relying on the hospitality of others eroded his social and political position, already tenuous because of his drinking and duplicity. In 1890 Oklahoma, as in 1730 Michigan and 1840 Missouri, anyone without family had absolutely nothing.[37]

With allotment and family disaster bearing down, George Bent made his worst deal ever. Bent hoped that he and other Cheyennes might profit from the fact that no one knew how much land Cheyennes and Arapahos actually controlled. To make room for legal settlements in Oklahoma, U.S. officials had to force Cheyennes and Arapahos to sign away rights to the Cherokee Outlet, a 7 million–acre strip of land that formed the northern border of the Cheyenne-Arapaho res-ervation. In a typically murky Indian country situation, that chunk of what is now northern Oklahoma was part of the Cherokees' 1836 treaty land. In 1867 the Cherokees, threatened and bribed, agreed to lease that land as part of a new homeland for southern Plains nations. Now in July 1890, U.S. officials wanted Cheyenne leaders to partici-pate in a backroom deal that would put those Cherokee lands in U.S. hands. The officials needed three-quarters of all adult male Chey-ennes to agree to any land sale. Cheyenne leaders refused to partici-pate and then boycotted further sessions with U.S. officials. George thought this was foolish, believing that Cheyennes should learn to act like land speculators. He suggested to the leaders that they either demand more cash or insist on retaining rights to places that might have value as townsites. The leaders ejected him from their meeting.[38]

George complained about his treatment to his former White busi-ness partners, and they approached him with a deal. They would give him $10,000 if he gathered some Cheyenne and Arapaho chiefs who represented the "nation as a whole." Bent agreed, and by offer-ing the chiefs a little cash, he got them to go to the new town of Okla-homa City to sign papers that first claimed the Cherokee land and then sold it to the government. A consortium of speculators, including Bent's old partners, agency officials, and Bent himself, worked out a deal that gave the speculators 80 percent of any money that was paid by the U.S. government to Cheyennes and Arapahos. Such arrangements, explained as "fees paid for legal services" or other ruses, were common. The deal was corrupt in every way, and Bent knew it. But he was awash in debt, and $10,000 seemed an amount that would solve his problems. After lying to Cheyenne leaders about the heinous deal, he got them to sign. Next, the lawyers who had arranged the deal took him out for drinks. They had a notary present when he signed away his own payment. Back on the reservation, George Bent was investigated for corruption and fired from his post as interpreter.[39]

Although the Cheyennes lost nearly everything with allotment, they had no choice but to go on. George Bent, however, had lost his reputation. No traditional leaders would have anything to do with him after he certified that "three-quarters of the adult males" willingly relinquished their claim to the Cherokee Outlet. In the end, no matter who lied or cheated, Cheyennes lost their reservation as they signed away "all right, claim, and interest in lands in Indian territory," a grand total of 51 million acres. That paper, also signed by George Bent, meant that after 3,249 allotments, totaling about 529,000 acres, were made to Cheyennes who had signed the Dawes rolls, the rest of Cheyenne and Arapaho land was opened for sale. Thousands of reservation residents got nothing. George, his two remaining Cheyenne wives, and his nine living children were all allotted Indians, with their racial characteristics carefully noted in each Indian census: "1/4 white," "HB," "3/4 breed," "1/8 white." After allotment, however, none of them lived with George.[40]

Ghost Dancing and Rebuilding

Two decades of reservation life had devastated homelands and livelihoods. Mixed-descent people had taken cover as Indians, a category now defined by racial science. In the late 1880s, as trains carried children away to schools, agents cut government rations, and land was lost forever, Native peoples attended to their spiritual lives. As they had in other hard times, religious leaders like the Seneca dreamer Handsome Lake, or Tecumseh's brother, Tenskwatawa, the Shawnee prophet, offered up redemptive visions that helped people survive in a new world. During the reservation period, the Ghost Dance and other ceremonies like the Medicine Lodge Dance or the Buffalo Dance, became ways to see beyond the bitter years when Indigenous Americans became allotted Indians.[41]

The Ghost Dance, with its prophecy of renewal and Native power, emerged first in the 1870s in Rocky Mountain Shoshone and Bannock communities, located on the Oregon Trail and surrounded by U.S. troops. There holy men adapted old ceremonies to meet present needs. They used shirts with spiritual powers, including the power to hide Native people from White soldiers and agents. If people stayed away from troops and trails and instead danced, they would see a new world where living Native people, bison, and dead relatives would gather together outside the White world. Such messages appeared militant and frightening to Indian Service agents and Christian missionaries. In 1889 a Paiute man, Wovoka or Jack Wilson, preached a different version of a Ghost Dance. In that drought year, his dancing produced rain in the Nevada desert. By dancing, working hard at White man's jobs, and accepting Jesus as a new messiah, he promised that bison would return and water would flow. Schools and railroads quickly spread Wovoka's prophecy. By the fall of 1890, partly because Christian missionaries had already made the message familiar, people danced on thirty western reservations.[42]

Indians who wore American clothing, or who farmed, cut their hair, or went to school, didn't lose their Native identities but sharpened them. Dancing together, and praying for new things in old ways, offered redemption. Some versions of the message, like the Second Coming or the Rapture in evangelical Christianity, invoked a Supreme Being who could wipe out everyone on earth. Only true believers, in this case Native people, would return to a clean slate, where the Plains teemed with bison and the dead returned to protect the living. On the Great Sioux Reservation in 1890, drastically reduced in size and with rations cut, suspicious agents saw the Ghost Dance as a military threat.[43]

News of Wovoka's prophecy reached the Cheyenne reservation in 1890. It arrived just after George Bent sold out his people, and a wave of fifty thousand White "sooners" flooded the eastern part of their reservation in the 1889 land rush, the closing act of the homesteading era. In a single day, new arrivals who filled the six counties outnumbered the Cheyenne and Arapaho. To keep Indians away from the desperate land seekers, Cheyenne-Arapaho agents insisted that everyone stay near the agency. They withheld food, seeds, and animal feed from anyone who left the grim, waterless spot to hunt, graze cattle, or farm. Angry, two leaders of warrior societies, Young Whirlwind and Pawnee Man, seized the commissary building and held agency employees hostage while they loaded supplies onto wagons and drove away.[44]

Arapahos meanwhile were hearing rumors of a prophecy in Wyoming. In 1891 they sent two men, Black Coyote and Washee, both members of the new Indian police force, to investigate. Christ, it turned out, was an Indian and had appeared in Wyoming with a message. Young Arapahos who had studied at Carlisle took down the first written version of that message. Indians were to work hard, learn special songs, and wear special clothing. They shouldn't antagonize White people because if they did, God would remove them from the earth. God's message, although peaceful and redemptive, carried a hard edge.[45]

Resembling the prophetic religions preached and lived by other Americans such as Mormons, Shakers, and Baptists, Ghost Dancers offered a path to a new Native unity. In the summer of 1892, local Indian agency officials complained that most Indians had gone to the Ghost Dance camps, leaving few on their farms. However, in those years of terrible drought, no one was doing much farming. Corn, an unsuitable crop for western Oklahoma, lay dead in the fields by early June. Watching their own crops fail, the settlers who had rushed on to free land in 1889, 1891, and 1892 were gone by 1893. They moved on to greener pastures in other states or into small Oklahoma and Kansas towns. Perhaps God had stepped in.[46]

Those Whites who remained felt threatened by rumored gatherings of hundreds of "warriors." But Cheyennes were not gathering to plot revenge; they gathered to dance and recover. Indian agents tried to stop these large summer gatherings by getting Indian farmers, returned Carlisle students, and mixed-descent interpreters to explain to their kin that "dances and ceremonies" were now illegal. However, these same "trustworthy" Indians had become dancers themselves. In September 1894 five hundred Cheyennes ignored their agents' rules and visited the Otoe agency to dance and make new alliances.[47]

In 1896 the Oklahoma territorial legislature passed a bill making "the immoral practices of medicine men" illegal. But such laws had little effect as dance leaders just got more skilled at hiding their activities. At the Cheyenne agency, officials simply chose not to see who danced, who became leaders through new ceremonies, and who left the reservation. George Bent may have danced—we know his daughters and sons did—but we don't know about his own decision. He certainly left the reservation.[48]

Protecting Cheyenne History

After his betrayal of the Cheyennes, George reinserted himself once again into the Muache and Capote bands of Southern Utes, who were still living on the Southern Ute reservation in the 1890s. After a five-year gap in producing children, George returned to this Ute family. He raised horses and cattle and showed up in agency records when he raced horses illegally. Utes had faced their own troubles after a grisly 1879 episode in which Utes had killed their agent and eleven other Whites; local settlers and stock growers demanded that they be entirely removed. Even a decade later the demand that "the Utes must go" continued to eat away at their land base. A powerful group of White people who did business with Utes argued equally hard that they stay in Colorado. The Ute horse herd had been reduced a little, but few men or women used their animals to plow. Instead, they grazed their horses in the nearby mountains and took care of horses belonging to White residents. By the 1890s, the Bureau of Indian Affairs had built three dozen houses near the Southern Ute agency. Only three were occupied, including one where George Bent and his Ute wife Vieage lived with their six children.[49]

George Bent hoped to weave all his families safely into their new world. He needed money, wives, and a better reputation to help his children make their way into the physical and emotional landscape of twentieth-century Indian country. He needed to improve his own standing with Cheyenne leaders so that his daughters and sons could marry well. His opportunity came in a surprising form—White scholars suddenly appearing on reservations in the 1890s. Writers, anthropologists, and collectors wanted to find Indians before allotment and poverty made them disappear. They needed George, and George needed them, to achieve two goals. He wanted to ensure that White scholars recorded accurate histories of Plains Indians, putting the Cheyenne in their rightful place. And he wanted to rebuild his own relationships with elders.[50]

George worked with three scholars—James Mooney, George Bird Grinnell, and George Hyde—but they all failed to see the history that George laid out. What those writers wanted to hear and what George wanted to tell were entirely different. They wanted to hear stories of men on horseback, daring raids, and warrior societies that made the foe that the United States had vanquished and put on reservations savage and heroic. They didn't want to hear about women, men, kinship, and clans, a Cheyenne family history that George Bent had lived and gathered from his own kin.[51]

He met James Mooney first. Mooney worked for the Bureau of Ethnology, founded in 1879 by John Wesley Powell. The bureau was the first U.S. government entity to investigate North American Indians as research objects. Mooney, a self-trained Indian hobbyist-turned-linguist, developed ethnographic techniques that required living among Native people and learning their languages. He pushed against Henry Schoolcraft's view that all Native peoples could be lumped together into a single category, "savage." In the 1890s Mooney would develop a universalism that emphasized commonality rather than difference between human cultures.[52]

In his first ethnography expedition, Mooney traveled around Indian country just as the Ghost Dance on the Lakota reservations resulted in military action. In the fall of 1890, anxious officials at the Pine Ridge Agency and state leaders demanded protection from the "armed Sioux savages" who were gathering at huge Ghost Dance camps all over the Dakotas. To control the situation, Indian agents refused to deliver annuity rations or cattle to anyone who danced. The dance circles just grew in size until the U.S. Army's Seventh Cavalry fired on bands returning to Pine Ridge to turn themselves in. The Lakota were armed, but the result was a New Year's massacre at Wounded Knee, with three hundred Indians and twenty-five U.S. soldiers lying dead on the frozen ground. With national attention focused on the West, the Bureau of Ethnography sent Mooney to find out what had happened. After a season at Pine Ridge in 1891, he sought a fuller story in Indian Territory, where he met local informants—Jesse Bent, Carlisle returnee and George's nephew, and Grant Left Hand, Ada Bent's neighbor and a Ghost Dance evangelist. They accompanied Mooney to the Oklahoma dance grounds in 1892. He immediately joined in the dance and started taking pictures.[53]

Mooney's superiors were uninterested in Wovoka, the Paiute prophet, or in the religious qualities of the Ghost Dance. After the Wounded Knee Massacre, they wanted Mooney to interview and "capture" remaining "wild Indians"—Kiowas, Comanches, Cheyennes, and Arapahos. For that work, James Mooney needed a man like George Bent, who had worked as an interpreter among many Indian Territory nations and spoke the necessary languages. In 1895 George arranged interviews and informed Mooney about Cheyenne life and history. However, the anthropologist believed firmly that he should listen only to "the purest blooded and most conservative of that nation," a category that did not include his mixed-descent Cheyenne interpreter. Mooney never paid Bent and returned to Washington in 1896 to write up his research.[54]

Mooney did recommend George to another Cheyenne enthusiast, George Bird Grinnell. Grinnell, a publisher and outdoorsman, had been the editor of *Forest and Stream*, an icon of upper-class male sportsmen, since 1876. He believed that American Indians, and especially Cheyennes, needed publicity as the remaining great hunters of North America. Grinnell, his wife, and a retinue of assistants arrived in Colony, Oklahoma, in 1901. With George Bent as their guide, they set out to find Cheyennes living in camps and villages. The work gave Bent a way to talk to tribal elders, men and women who had shunned him for nearly a decade. Their conversations about the past instead of the more troublesome present gave George new purpose in life. Grinnell paid him a little for transcribing stories.[55]

As George Bent and George Bird Grinnell gathered stories for a book, a task that would take a dozen years, yet another scholarly George entered the picture. George Hyde (no relation to the author) would disappoint George Bent the most. Hyde was only twenty-three and still living with his mother when he first contacted Bent. Prematurely wizened, completely deaf, and nearly blind because of a bout with rheumatic fever when he was fourteen, he had dreamed about Indians his entire life.[56]

Hyde grew up in Omaha, where Indian country was not a distant memory. He went to school with the children of trader families and frontier soldiers. In 1898 the city of Omaha hosted the Trans-Mississippi and International Exposition, and George, then sixteen, attended the great Indian Congress there. Native people had been shipped in to entertain tourists. Assuring visitors that what they saw was authentic, the commissioner of Indian affairs promised them Indians "from all the principal tribes," camped in "tepees, wigwams, hogans etc.," conducting "their domestic affairs as they do at home." Young George Hyde couldn't get enough. He saw the famous Apache warrior Geronimo wearing a top hat, and Brulé Sioux and Northern Cheyennes dressed in spectacular war garb. He began collecting books and haunting the Omaha public library. By age twenty, he had decided to devote his life to studying Plains Indians.[57]

George Hyde was drawn to the warriors, the heroic and healthy men he longed to be. Unable to travel because of his physical limitations and lack of funds, he fired off letters to Indian agents and to teachers on Indian reservations. He also wrote to individual Indians, especially boarding school students, asking for information. He didn't call it ethnohistory, but he was determined adopt an Indian perspective, if an entirely male one. One of his letters crossed George

Bent's desk in 1902. George answered it, launching a sixteen-year correspondence of hundreds of letters.[58]

George Hyde would became a significant historian of Plains nations, but when he began writing to Bent, he was entirely unknown, unpublished, and defensive about his lack of credentials. To his credit, Hyde showed genuine interest in Bent's material. He had no preconceived notions of George's "position" as an authority and trusted him for details about battle sites and warriors. Early in their relationship, they wrote a series of articles together titled "Forty Years with the Cheyennes." George Hyde placed it in *The Frontier: A Magazine of the West*, published in Colorado Springs, Colorado, in 1905 and 1906.[59]

The *Frontier* series did not turn out as expected. George Bent got paid his share, $9.50, but he didn't think much of the magazine. "I think myself that the Frontier is gotten very poor," he wrote, noting the publication's cheap paper and low circulation. However, since he and Hyde had no other takers, "long as they pay us any thing, let them have writings." In April 1906 he reported that "people down here wanted more *Frontier Magazines* of this month." Cheyennes appreciated seeing their version of history. George wrote with evident pride that "they think our accounts in it were good."[60]

White readers in Denver did not agree. George Hyde and the publisher of *Frontier*, the geologist and amateur historian Francis Cragin, hoped Colorado residents were ready for a new story about Sand Creek. They had pitched the account as a retelling "written by one who witnessed the scenes described." George Bent's "Indian perspective," describing the brutal violence soldiers had inflicted on unarmed women and children, soon reached the veterans living in Denver. Furious, they called Bent a "cutthroat and killer." A lawyer named Jacob Downing took on the mantle of protecting the tale of White heroism at Sand Creek. He threw epithets at George in Denver newspapers, calling him "a liar, a scoundrel, but worst of all a halfbreed."[61]

George Bent, Downing declared, was "no pioneer." Such an accusation had enormous power in the early twentieth century. Pioneers were sacred as founders of western communities, land developers, lawyers, and streetcar builders like Downing. When they died, they left their papers to the historical societies they had founded so people could write histories about them. Downing left real estate records and letters, as well as a scalp lock taken from a warrior at Sand Creek. It was serious work to patrol the line between pioneers and people like the son of "renegade Col. Bent who married a squaw." George Bent's personal history, instead of making him a credible eyewitness, made him dangerous. In 1907 army veterans demanded that the state of Colorado erect a monument celebrating the brave soldiers at Sand Creek. A giant stone obelisk might balance the "scurrilous OUTRAGE on the reputations of the Colorado Third" contained in George Bent's words.[62]

Only certain histories, ones that relegated Indians to a nostalgic past, were possible at the time. In 1905 President Theodore Roosevelt visited Indian Territory on his way to San Antonio, Texas, for a reunion of his cavalry unit, the Rough Riders. Roosevelt made speeches as his train stopped in small Oklahoma communities. In the crowd in Frederick, he noticed the Comanche chief Quanah Parker, the most famous mixed-descent chief in the United States. Roosevelt invited him on a wolf hunt. Riding horses with his Rough Rider friends and hunting wolves with Quanah Parker gave Roosevelt a chance to relive his own Wild West.[63]

After Indian Territory became the modern state of Oklahoma in 1907, Roosevelt's final gift to the Comanches and Kiowas whose cattle lands had just been taken away was to remove two 8,000-acre tracts from the former reservation and turn them into the nation's first bison refuge. The nearest town, Cache, was Quanah Parker's home, and many Comanches, Kiowas, Cheyennes, and Apaches lived nearby. News of a train carrying fifteen hundred bison raised in a special paddock in New York's Central Park got everyone's attention. People rode into town, all dressed up to celebrate the bison's return and the final evolution of a bison-hunting past into a settler future. Old Comanches who remembered hunting bison watched the fenced-in animals inhale, bend their necks, and paw the earth. Their children and grandchildren, who didn't remember hunting and faced rebuilding Indian country after Roosevelt's "mighty pulverizing engine" had destroyed it, saw it differently. To them, the bison making wallows in a new place were modeling a path forward.[64]

EPILOGUE

The Twentieth Century

G eorge Bent knew how much the facts of his Cheyenne history challenged the frontier tales that Theodore Roosevelt
and White veterans of Sand Creek wanted to take into their
futures. Their modern West permitted neither Indians nor mixing
blood. Until the 1970s, main streets of western towns welcomed visitors with signs reading "No Indians or Breeds Allowed."[1]

Half-breed and *mixed-blood* became toxic words, racial slurs
aimed at denigrating and separating. They share history with words
like *mulatto* and *mestiza* that describe racial mixture but also carry
a painful edge. Like *boy* thrown at a Black man, the word *half-breed*
became poison intended to kill. Scrubbing U.S. history of that term
by removing *half-breed* from the names of places and people feels
right in the present. But renaming Half-Breed Lake in Minnesota
and Montana, or Half-Breed Road in Iowa and Nebraska, also covers
up a long history of intermarriage.[2]

The twentieth-century effort to erase that history began with the
1896 *Plessy v. Ferguson* case. That court decision enshrined White
supremacy, making racial distinctions central to everyday life in every
part of the United States. A powerful racial science, now discred-
ited, attempted to make race visible. Identifying people carrying any

327

non-White blood became the cultural and scientific key to protecting White citizenship. In the early twentieth century, the definition of *White*, now styled *Aryan* or *Anglo-Saxon*, became ever narrower. In 1910, the list of people excised from *White* included Jews, Irish, Syrians, Italians, Latvians, Blacks, Spanish, Mexicans, Chinese, Japanese, and Hindu. In an era when scientists argued about whether the French were really White or if Catholicism could be a genetic defect, American Indians were hardly American.[3]

Race determined who deserved education and pensions, or communities with roads, sewers, and telephone lines. The material benefits of Whiteness were sweetened by the most powerful advantage: the belief that your race made you superior. Securing that superiority required policing racial lines by jailing, beating, and lynching those outside the boundary, but mostly by legislating against them. In the early twentieth century, states passed hundreds of laws separating every aspect of daily life by race. Laws determined which race could use which textbook and sit in which classroom. To protect White blood, every U.S. state passed laws regulating marriage between races: Whites and Blacks, Whites and the "Mongolian Race," Whites and Indians, Indians and Blacks.[4]

Mixed-descent people, who could and did move between races, threatened that enormous cultural and legal effort. Laws never actually stopped people from loving and marrying. Just as White Americans feared, people sometimes left their "Indian" labels behind. Knowing that White America couldn't tolerate reminders of the racial mixing that anchored American history, people who made families across cultures developed strategies to survive an era that saw their heritage as malignant. To protect their children and histories, they hid, they passed, they traveled, and they denied family stories.[5]

Traveling and Passing

In the McKay family's Pacific Northwest, the White descendants of pioneers who fought Indian wars wanted certainty that their neighbors were not Indians. In that setting, Thomas McKay's descendants, products of a century of polygamy, serial marriage, racial mixing, and love, had to be either White or Native. His half-Chinook sons by Timmee, William and Alexander, became allotted Indians. Their children and grandchildren stayed near reservations, marrying Native people. To stay close to family, they tended sheep, logged, picked apples, and cleaned houses on land their families had once owned and traveled over. Thomas McKay's sons who had been born to Cree and French Isabelle Montour McKay decided it was safer to leave.[6]

George McKay, born to Isabelle just after Thomas's death in 1849, never appeared on Oregon's Indian rolls. Instead, he went east to become a cowboy and a miner. Like many mixed-descent men with fur trade heritages, he worked in the last years of the bison-hide trade in Montana, which continued booming until the early 1900s. Hudson's Bay Company names like McKay, McLoughlin, and Delarde peppered payrolls and city directories. When bison disappeared, men became miners or loggers, extractive industries now powering the economy of the West. By 1910, George was working as a quartz miner in Libby, Montana. His World War I draft card listed him as Indian, but the census recorded him as White.[7]

Another McKay option, taken by a third-generation Thomas McKay, born to William Cameron and Margaret Campbell McKay, was walking away from the reservation. Thomas lived at home and worked as a "laborer" on the Umatilla reservation, but after his father's death in 1893, he moved to a lumber camp. Now in his forties, he met and married a White woman named Asenath Pribble. She'd come from Kentucky to clean and cook in lumber camps surrounding the Oregon reservations. She and Thomas left the timber worker's hard life—and maybe Thomas's racial status—for new lives in Portland. They sold groceries and lived above their store. By 1910, the Portland McKays had another Thomas in the house. That year the census taker marked both Thomases, just like their neighbors, as White.[8]

Leila McKay, William and Margaret's youngest child, attended the Chemawa Indian School and then worked as a seamstress at the Umatilla agency school. She was listed as a "mixed blood" on the Umatilla reservation in 1892. After her parents' deaths, like her brother Thomas, she moved to Portland. She took up dressmaking and lived in Portland for more than thirty years—listed in every census as a single White woman. She took pride in her Oregon heritage and its Native roots. Representing "old Oregon," she offered a greeting in Chinook as she smashed a bottle of champagne to launch a new ship built at Astoria. That place, where Canadian McKays had first landed their ship in 1811, guided in by Leila's Chinook ancestors, had launched a story that was still unfolding. Stepping back over a racial line, as she approached old age Leila moved to the Yakima reservation to live with her younger McKay cousins.[9]

Staying and Rebuilding

Other families, in other places, held tight to their Native heritage. Among the Middle Missouri nations—Omahas, Otoes, and Dakotas—mothers and grandmothers like Mary Jane Drips Barnes and Emily Papin Fontenelle fought hard for land and to put their children on twentieth-century tribal rolls. Names, memories, and now blood protected them during dangerous times.

The Nebraska Dripses had many Otoe relatives living in Oklahoma, where there was a little money in postallotment Native communities. After tribal members received allotments and ceded their remaining land to the government, money from annuities or cattle or land sales sometimes accumulated in tribal accounts. As the last act of federal responsibility, government officials paid out any funds to tribal members, defined by who was listed on the Dawes rolls. Legal wrangling over allotment by local lawyers or merchants had usually drained any funds, leaving most tribes in debt. The Otoes, unusually, had a tidy sum: $333,201 in 1906.[10]

Now it got personal. That cash included money for land and cattle that the Drips and Barnes families had managed, money sitting in trust since the 1870s when most Otoes left Nebraska for Indian Territory. Mary Jane's son Frederick insisted that the Barnes-Drips family needed to be part of any monetary divisions. Using the new language of blood quantum, he explained that as one-quarter "breeds" who had always worked for the Otoe nation, they wanted their share. Oklahoma Otoes, seeing their funds winnowed down by people who weren't in Oklahoma, fought hard to stop them. After several hearings and a year of letter-writing and name-calling, the Nebraska Otoes got $1,800 each.[11]

Old political divisions, made deeper by anger over benefits that "half-breeds" had received during removal and allotment, came home to roost for the Barnes family. They had helped their people survive, but they also got land, money, and stability that few Otoes shared. In the early twentieth century, the Barnes and Drips children repaired some divisions using marriage. Four of Mary Jane Drips Barnes's sons—Charles, William, Emmet, and Frederick—moved to Oklahoma and took up residence near the Otoe reservation. Emmet and Frederick married into Otoe families. Breaking the rules of twentieth-century America, Frederick Barnes, like his relatives generations earlier, had two wives: one in Nebraska, and one in Oklahoma. Marriage couldn't and didn't solve every problem. But in the 1920s Otoe people allowed Andrew Drips and Macompemay's great-grandsons to build bridges, learning Otoe and raising horses.[12]

Mary Jane Drips Barnes knew that she had never stopped being part of an Otoe family. After her husband's death in 1917, Mary Jane needed help maintaining her farm. Frederick Barnes, now on the Otoe rolls and married into an Oklahoma Otoe family, came back to Nebraska to take care of his mother. Just as Macompemay had moved between Kansas City, Bellevue, and Otoe villages in the 1840s, her grandchildren moved between Otoe places in the 1910s and 1920s. Frederick took care of his ninety-year-old mother, the last remaining sibling of the Drips family so representative of the fur trade world. After Mary Jane's death in 1920, Frederick sold the house and moved back to Oklahoma.[13]

Omahas, unlike their Otoe neighbors, stayed in Nebraska. By the early twentieth century, Nebraska was a beacon for White settlement. Farmers from the Mississippi River Valley, Scandinavia, and Germany joined longtime residents like Omaha nation members Henry

Fontenelle and Emily Papin Fontenelle. The Fontenelles lived along the Missouri River among more than twenty-five hundred Omahas, Winnebagos, Pawnees, and Otoes. Despite the influx of White settlers, Nebraska remained Indian country. The Omaha leader Joseph La Flesche's daughter, Suzette La Flesche, attended boarding schools and returned home to write *Om-ah-ha-ta-tha: Omaha City* about the city's founders—Omaha elders. Eugene Fontenelle, Henry Fontenelle and Emily Papin's Omaha son, spent his life buying and selling land on the Omaha reservation. Like his father and his aunts, he attended Hampton Industrial School in Virginia. He married two women, first mixed-descent Omaha Mary Harvey and then White German immigrant Lena Mae Otteson. Families like the La Flesches and Fontenelles, mixed-descent and still powerful, survived the allotment era intact while many of their poorest kin lost their land and their lives.[14]

Eugene's eldest son, Logan Fontenelle, born in 1904, was named for his grandfather, the famous Omaha leader Logan Fontenelle, killed by Sioux raiders in 1855. Logan attended the Genoa Indian Industrial School, in central Nebraska, from 1914 to 1920. Aged thirteen and at school when the United States entered the Great War in 1917, Logan was too young to enlist. Seventy-four of his older classmates did, and Logan took over printing the school newspaper, which now included casualty lists from Europe. Logan then took those writing and accounting skills to work for the Indian Service in Montana. In 1928 he married a mixed-blood woman from Chouteau, Montana. The young couple, noted as "color: copper" on their marriage license, moved back and forth between Montana and Nebraska. After they had their own son, Logan Lucien Fontenelle, they chose Nebraska, where baby Logan would be surrounded by loving relatives who had settled in to stay.[15]

Writing and Marrying

George Bent and his family had struggled to rebuild lives after Cheyennes became war refugees in the 1870s. Thirty years later Oklahoma was a hard place where poverty, isolation, and allotment ate up families even in the midst of an oil boom. As oil wealth flowed to New York and Texas entrepreneurs and enriched a few families in the suddenly famous town of Tulsa, many who could leave Oklahoma in the 1910s and '20s, did. Black settlers who had immigrated from the South after the Civil War fled for Mexico and Canada. White settlers who had rushed into western and central Oklahoma trickled out as they learned how hard it was to live there, much less prosper. A world away from Tulsa's millionaires, on the Cheyenne-Arapaho reservation, few people farmed and even fewer lived on their allotments. With no equipment to cut hay, and no horses to pull wagons or threshers, most people depended on their families and did a little hunting and gardening. The Bent family, intermarried for generations, had endured, but barely.[16]

George Bent, with two wives and a three-room house in Seger, Oklahoma, lived on as his children went to work and married. Bent family names and histories echoed their way in the new Indian country: George, Charles, Mary, and William. Charles Bent, named for his uncle Charles, a Cheyenne Dog Soldier killed by U.S. soldiers in 1867, spent eight years at the Carlisle Indian Industrial School, a place meant to replace Native culture with U.S. culture. Charles, his Native roots intact, returned to Oklahoma and married a Southern Cheyenne woman named Walking in the Middle (Jessie Big Hawk) in 1905.[17]

Charles's brother William, named for his grandfather William Bent, who married Owl Woman and who built Bent's Fort, stayed in Oklahoma and attended the Cheyenne-Arapaho boarding school. Like his grandfather, William married a young Native woman, Ellen Adams, a Lakota from the Pine Ridge Reservation. They registered their marriage with the new state of Oklahoma. The registrar penciled in their "color" as "Chey. Ind. and Sioux Ind.," a mixed marriage if there ever was one. Ellen and William stayed in Oklahoma for a few years, but in 1914 they moved permanently to South Dakota to raise horses. William grew up hearing his Northern Cheyenne mother, Standing Out, describe the horses of her childhood. Ellen and William stayed there in that Native place where people still struggled but raised children and horses, gardened, and painted.[18]

Through this season of his children's marriages—the first decade of the twentieth century—George Bent recorded a history of his people. While working at the Seger Indian Agency as translator, accountant, and cattle trader, he kept writing to George Hyde, his co-author for the piece about Sand Creek that had caused so much fury in Denver. Detailed descriptions of famous battles, gathered from reservation elders, traveled in envelopes between Oklahoma and Omaha. Bent's technique was ethnographic and personal. If Hyde had a question about an event, Bent found an elder who had been there or who had heard stories about it as a child. He talked, asked questions, and wrote it down. Early in their correspondence, he told Hyde, "Whenever I see an old Indian I ask him about the old battles which may do to put in the book." His letters to Hyde consisted of direct quotes with authors clearly attributed, as in "Bull Hump said to me" or "I asked Twin Woman."[19]

As Bent and Hyde exchanged drafts of their Cheyenne history, George Bird Grinnell, the naturalist and editor, hired them both. Grinnell wanted to write a history of Indian warriors that didn't offend old White warriors or new pioneers. When Grinnell published his first book on the Cheyenne in 1915, *The Fighting Cheyennes*, he thanked George Hyde for "verifying the sources." Apparently, "verifying" meant taking Grinnell's rough notes, adding material from Hyde's own research and correspondence with Bent, and turning it into appealing, clear prose. Grinnell didn't mention George Bent.[20]

George Bent was unhappy when he read Grinnell's book. He didn't care if Grinnell took his words, but he did care that Grinnell got important details about Cheyenne history wrong, including the story of Sand Creek. Grinnell narrated the 1864 disaster as a tragic miscommunication in the fog of war. He laid the blame for the "so-called massacre" of peaceful Indians on a single cold-hearted killer, Chivington, not on Colorado volunteers who followed orders. Grinnell's army officials and soldiers admitted that mistakes were made in that confusing haze. George Bent's searing account of who shot whom, and when, sliced through any confusion.[21]

Grinnell's descriptions of the post–Sand Creek Indian raids as "heedless" violence also incensed Bent. Grinnell's account of "pure

Indian savagery" explained why American Indians had to be on reservations. According to Grinnell, Indians were so ignorant that when they broke into trading posts, they found "nothing but bundles of green paper" that "whirled away." Or when Indians attacked isolated homes, the "canned goods puzzled them" so they left them behind. Bent's version, sent to George Hyde, explained that Plains warriors knew what money, cans, and cows were. Moving quickly was the highest goal during the Great Raid and money or cans didn't help them shut down roads. Leaving out the stories and voices that George Bent provided, examples of family resilience and hard choices, simplified Grinnell's rendition.[22]

Frustrated with Grinnell's book, Bent pushed Hyde to recommit to writing a "true story" of life on the Plains. That true story would have to include men, women, and children, many still living. As Bent wrote hundreds of letters, filled with interviews, family stories, and memories, pieces of his own present life in modern Oklahoma crept in. He traveled to ceremonies, sponsored feasts and giveaways, and encouraged his children to do the same. He went deep into debt to give things away. After a lifetime, he knew that while money could whirl away in the wind, families anchored people in windy places.[23]

Before he could finish that history, the bitter bookend to World War I, the 1918 Spanish flu took George Bent. The flu took a terrible toll on the world but especially on Indian country, where people were hungry and vulnerable. Maybe that was, finally, the end of the story of the bison trade on the southern Plains. Born at Bent's Fort and raised in a Cheyenne lodge, George Bent died in Colony, Oklahoma, in a drafty wood-frame house. His words, and his family, lived on.

After Bent's death, George Hyde struggled to write Bent's history. In 1929 Hyde burned most of Bent's letters. He wrote to a friend that he'd been "temporarily discouraged." He had finished most of a book manuscript that he knew wrung the life out of Bent's accounts. Although some 340 letters remain, we will never see most of George Bent's words. After burning those letters, George Hyde began to succeed. Beginning in the 1930s, he published nine books that made him a respected historian of Plains Indian life. George Bent remained on his mind. After many false starts, George Hyde finally published

The Life of George Bent: Written from His Letters in 1968. He was eighty-five and died a year later. That published book was composed mostly of George Hyde's words, not Bent's oral histories of old men and women recalling wars on the Plains and battles on reservations and in courtrooms to protect their children. George Bent's story, of the flawed family man with an entwined history that intermarriage had created, remained untold.[24]

Surviving and Imagining

Marriage and family offered up surprising gifts. A McKay daughter, the Cayuse-Anglo Wenix, born to Thomas McKay's Cayuse partner in 1838, sued the city of Pendleton, Oregon, as an Indian. She owned a spring next to a house she built when the whole area was the Warm Springs Indian Reservation. In 1913, in an effort to control this water source, the town of Pendleton condemned her property. Wenix, nearing eighty, hired a lawyer but lost her suit. In the legal wrangling over the spring, her lawyer discovered she was owed a soldier's bounty promised to men who fought in the 1848 Cayuse War. Oregon lawyers knew to look for this benefit because there were so many Native widows of White men who had fought Indians and then married them in the 1850s and '60s. Because Wenix's mother, Thomas McKay's legal widow according to laws written by Oregon's founders, had never claimed the money, the bounty passed to her daughter. In 1915 Wenix lost her spring but found a small death benefit.[25]

There is a grimmer story of poverty and population loss to temper the redemptive stories of George Bent's marrying off his children or Wenix getting a soldier's bounty. The 1928 Meriam Report, commissioned by the U.S. government to assess Indian health and welfare after allotment, reported the stark costs of signing those Dawes rolls. Only 350,000 Indians remained in 1920. According to the investigators, who traveled to ninety-five communities, allotment had left Native people without land or any way to make a living in isolated regions. By any measure—infant mortality, education, calories, property ownership, bank accounts, literacy, disease rates—Indians suffered.[26]

Those statistics about how many children died in boarding schools and how many adults suffered from trachoma or tuberculosis were a warning that extinction was possible. Indigenous people knew that only their heritage and their hard-won wisdom could protect them. Facing such privation, people depended on families. Extended families—grandparents, aunts and uncles, and sometimes several husbands or many wives, though illegal—kept people fed.

John McDougall Johnston, the youngest of John Johnston and Ozhaguscodaywayquay's children, lived until 1896. As Ojibwe men always had, John Johnston created multiple families. His thirteen children lived on the Menominee reservation and in Sault Ste. Marie. Those two families included two different Mary Johnstons. One divorced her unfaithful husbands, opened a store, and raised eight Menominee daughters. The other stayed in Sault Ste. Marie and never married, but raised a dozen nieces and nephews to fish and make sugar camps. The two Marys carried the Johnstons into the twentieth century as mothers and respected members of their communities, living mixed-descent lives.[27]

Other branches of the family kept safe by moving. Charlotte Elizabeth Jane McMurray died in 1928 after spending her last years in a nursing home for elderly Church of England ladies in Quebec. Charlotte, named for her mother, Charlotte Johnston McMurray, and her two aunts Eliza Johnston and Jane Johnston Schoolcraft, was born in 1843. She lived with her parents in Ontario until she married an Irish immigrant named Hamilton Hartley Killaly. They moved to French-speaking Quebec City, the heart of the old fur trade even in the 1880s, and had six children. The Irish Episcopalian Killalys stood out in Quebec's French neighborhoods, but Charlotte passed as White. No census taker ever noted her as "part Indian" or "métis," common racial choices in twentieth-century Canada.[28]

Louise Geroux Drips Goulet, who gave Andrew Drips a new career and new family in the 1850s, died in 1875 on the Great Sioux Reservation. Her children stayed on the Yankton Sioux Indian rolls but traveled many places after the reservation years. Louise's youngest son, Charles Goulet, married a German immigrant woman. They put their twelve children on the Yankton Sioux rolls, starting with Christina in 1899 and finishing up with Ernest in 1929. After World War I, the family left South Dakota for Sioux City, Iowa, where Charles labored at the Hide House, turning cows into leather, just as his Dakota grandmothers had done fifty years earlier. This hard-working family, noted as Indian in the 1920 census, White in 1930, and Indian again in 1940, knew who they were and who they could count on. During the Depression, they sent children back to stay with relatives on the Yankton reservation. Their eldest son, Conrad Goulet, signed up to work for the Indian WPA in the 1930s. That work, building dams in the Black Hills, brought running water to Native and White communities in South Dakota. His family buried him, in 1955, in Charles Mix County, next to his Yankton Sioux Goulet uncles and aunts.[29]

Mixing Descent

These particular stories of mixing heritage began with the fur trade but spread far beyond, as frontier family making became part of every era of American history. In the fur trade's mix of commercial practice and human need, mixed-descent families readily emerged. Sometimes human need led to violence, as women were taken captive or raped, but for most women and men, mixing blood and sharing households was a means to stand fast and protect children and communities.[30]

Those choices rewove old strands of heritage and family into modern links of surprising strength. Diana McKay, born in 1936 on the Umatilla reservation, was the great-granddaughter of William Cameron McKay. Her parents, David McKay and Elsie Allen, gave her Cayuse and Nez Percé heritage along with her Scots-Canadian McKay name. She gathered roots each spring with her Cayuse aunts and raised horses as her Nez Percé family always had. Diana and her sister Laura were the first McKays to attend Pendleton High School, pioneers as reservation children to attend school with local White children. Diana joined the art club, the riding team, and the newspaper. In 1953 she was chosen Queen of the Pendleton Round-Up. The second Native girl chosen in the Round-Up's forty-year history, Diana McKay was feted as the "17-year old descendant of Dr. William Cameron McKay and Chief Joseph."[31]

In 1954, along with three other young Native Oregonians, Diana McKay traveled to Sheridan, Wyoming, to participate in the first Miss Indian America Pageant. The pageant had first been suggested by Lucy Yellow Mule, a young Crow woman frustrated with the violence between Native and White American residents in Sheridan. Like Diana McKay, she was selected as Rodeo Queen, but she faced such fierce and public discrimination from local merchants in the postwar Jim Crow era that both White and Indian community leaders were ashamed. Indian women, of course, were the diplomats. Lucy's efforts to improve relationships in Sheridan's complicated community ultimately won her, and the town of Sheridan, the George Washington Honor Medal from the Freedom Foundation. Their project, to promote better understanding between races, was a Cold War tactic to show that—contrary to Communist criticisms—American Indians were treated well in the United States.[32]

And trading on the beauty of Indian women seemed to be the only way to prove that. The result for Sheridan, Wyoming, was an All American Indian Day and the Miss Indian America Pageant, both established to preserve Indigenous rituals, art, language, and stories. In those years, land loss, reservation politics, and fights over blood had divided Native communities over how best to preserve a future. Such difficult rifts made choosing a good public relations representative for the Indian community deeply political. Miss Indian America must be someone "dedicated to the cultural well-being of [her] tribe" as well as having "the appearance, personality and poise to represent her people in the white community."[33]

Diana McKay didn't win, but the Oregon native of deeply rooted mixed heritage surely met the requirements as she rode into the future to serve her nation and family. Her Cree and Swiss ancestor, Marguerite Waddens McKay McLoughlin, had built similar bridges two centuries earlier. Like Marguerite and like Ozhaguscodaywayquay or Susan Johnston, both born about 1775, Diana McKay returned home from the beauty pageant and went about the tasks of her ordinary life, carrying extraordinary stories in her blood. She created a new family and tended to her horses. Building connections across bitter remnants of a colonial past continued to be hard, essential work. Horses and children still heal wounds.

ACKNOWLEDGMENTS

This book is a long advertisement for how important families are—made ones, born ones, chosen ones. While I thought about the risk and necessity of making kin, my families both sustained me and ignored me, as families should. While working on the book, I changed jobs, states, houses, time zones, and life stages, so it took a while to be born. The work started in Colorado and ended in Oklahoma, with a stint in Texas in between. My three children, Colin, Tim, and Grace, went off to college and built their own lives. I've welcomed new friends and new dogs and lost some old ones.

I gave talks about these particular families and the bigger questions of race, identity, and history in many, many places. Sometimes audiences challenged the words I used and the claims I made, but more important, they shared their own family stories. Oklahoma and the students I teach have offered lessons about descent, heritage, and listening. I carry that into what appears here, and I hope I honor such gifts. Two groups of people made scholarship possible: librarians and publishers. Without quiet space, access to materials, books, and expert help, I couldn't have found or told these stories. To trace them, I went to Washington, D.C., New Haven, Denver, Winnipeg, New York, Detroit, and Portland. Two monthlong stints at Chicago's Newberry Library, while I was still teaching at Colorado College, got me started. At the University of Oklahoma, Laurie Scrivener, Jackie Reese, Bridget Burke, and Lina Ortega taught me how to navigate western and Indigenous history.

A full year at the Clements Center for Southwest Studies at

Southern Methodist University in Dallas was a gift of time that I've never had before. I appreciated every second of it. In 2015–16 I wrote the book's center there and had it workshopped by Lucy Murphy, Elliott West, Dave Edmunds, Neil Foley, Ed Countryman, and Sherry Smith. A serious deadline and a stellar class of Clements fellows made my year in Dallas focused and productive. Thanks to Javier Rodriquez, David Romero, and Bryant Etheridge, along with Clements Center directors Andy Graybill and Sherry Smith and assistant director Ruth Anne Elmore.

In the fall of 2016, just as I started teaching at the University of Oklahoma and editing the *Western Historical Quarterly*, Sydelle Kramer and Susan Rabiner helped me get a book proposal into the hands of Steve Forman at W. W. Norton. Over the next year or so, I finished writing, but because the topic—race, family, fur trade, western violence—was big, the people endlessly absorbing, and the outside world too painful to watch, I produced an early draft that was, well, way too long. Four friends read that messy and monstrous version—Susan Johnson, Andy Graybill, Richard White, and Alex Finkelstein—and were honest about finding what mattered in the text. Then I got another gift of time—a one-month fellowship at the National Humanities Center in Durham, North Carolina. I spent June 2019 removing thousands of words, rethinking the structure of chapters, and getting to know my OU colleague Rilla Askew. In the fall of 2019, Sarah Pearsall and OU's monthly History Workshop read a draft of the book's beginning and sent me back to the drawing board.

Finally I had something that Steve Forman and I could work on together. After eighteen months, mostly in pandemic time, and a lot more drafts, cuts, and reworkings, it is ready to face the world. I'm grateful to Steve for his patience, clarity, and good eye. At Norton books, I'd also like to thank copyeditor Janet Biehl and project editor Rebecca Munro for paying very careful attention!

Ezra Zeitler, a wonderful mapmaker and geographer from Wisconsin, was endlessly patient as we worked together over several years to map these stories. The graduate fellows who work for the *Western Historical Quarterly* have an office tucked into Monnet Hall right next to mine; Curt Foxley, Abby Gibson, Louisa Brandt, Brendan Thomas, and Michael Baliff gave great advice. Ben Folger, an OU graduate student, fact-checked the manuscript. Even with all this help and all this time, my mistakes and hard choices about words appear in the text, evidence that flawed humans write history.

My kith and kin, both in Colorado and in Oklahoma, rarely asked why writing this book was taking so long. My husband, Jim McCall, did ask, but he mostly helped me find quiet places and taught me how to be an empty-nester, marveling at what life, and family, offer up.

NOTES

BHL	Bentley Historical Library, University of Michigan, Ann Arbor
BL	Bancroft Library, University of California, Berkeley
BRC-SF	Santa Fe Historical Collection
BRBM	Beinecke Rare Book & Manuscript Library, Yale University
Burton-DPL	Burton Historical Collection, Detroit Public Library
CCL	Colorado College Library, Colorado Springs
CHS	Colorado Historical Society, Denver
CSA	Colorado State Archives, Denver
CSPM	Colorado Springs Pioneer Museum
DCB	*Dictionary of Canadian Biography* (online)
HC	History Colorado, Denver
HL	Huntington Library, San Marino, Calif.
LOC	Library of Congress, Washington, D.C.
KSHS	Kansas State Historical Society, Topeka
MHS	Missouri Historical Society, St. Louis
NARA	National Archives and Records Administration, Washington, D.C.
NHS	Nebraska Historical Society, Lincoln
NMHML	New Mexico Historical Museum Library, Santa Fe

345

NYHS   New-York Historical Society

NYPL   New York Public Library

OHS   Oregon Historical Society, Portland

OKHS   Oklahoma Historical Society, Oklahoma City

PRC   Public Records of Canada, Winnipeg

SM   Southwest Museum, Los Angeles

WHC   Western History Collections, University of Oklahoma

Preface

1. European and Indigenous people made history on North American frontiers and what became the American West. In the last thirty-five years, scholars have staked new ground in understanding how those histories intersected. The books listed here, arranged chronologically, only sample the wealth of that scholarship. Patricia N. Limerick, *Legacy of Conquest: The Unbroken Past of the American West* (W. W. Norton, 1987); Albert L. Hurtado, *Indian Survival on the California Frontier* (Yale University Press, 1988); Richard White, *The Middle Ground: Indians, Empires, and Republics in the Great Lakes Region, 1650–1815* (Cambridge University Press, 1991); Colin Calloway, *One Vast Winter Count: The Native American West Before Lewis and Clark* (University of Nebraska Press, 2005); Kathleen DuVal, *The Native Ground: Indians and Colonists in the Heart of the Continent* (University of Pennsylvania Press, 2007); Coll Thrush, *Native Seattle: Histories from the Crossing-Over Place* (University of Washington Press, 2008); Brian DeLay, *War of a Thousand Deserts: Indian Raids and the U.S. Mexican War* (Yale University Press, 2009); Christina Snyder, *Slavery in Indian Country: The Changing Face of Captivity in Early America* (Harvard University Press, 2010); Brendan C. Lindsay, *Murder State: California's Native American Genocide, 1846–1873* (University of Nebraska Press, 2012); Elizabeth Fenn, *Encounters at the Heart of the World: A History of the Mandan People* (Hill and Wang, 2014); Claudio Saunt, *Unworthy Republic: The Disappearance of Native America and the Road to Indian Territory* (W. W. Norton, 2020). A generation of historians retold the western past with Native power and the brutality of conquest at its heart. More recently, Indigenous scholars have examined the violence of enslaving people and taking land, both to clarify the cost but also to explain how Indigenous Americans survived. So, Ned Blackhawk, *Violence over the Land: Indians and Empires in the Early North American West* (Harvard University Press, 2007); William J. Bauer, *We Were All*

Like Migrant Workers Here: Work, Community, and Memory on California's Round Valley Reservation, 1850–1941 (University of North Carolina Press, 2009); Michael Witgen, *An Infinity of Nations: How the Native New World Shaped North America* (University of Pennsylvania Press, 2012); Joshua L. Reid, *The Sea Is My Country: The Maritime World of the Makahs* (Yale University Press, 2016); Maurice Crandall, *These People Have Always Been a Republic: Indigenous Electorates in the U.S.-Mexico Borderlands, 1598–1912* (Yale University Press, 2019), offer up powerful examples of rethinking conquest and its consequences.

2. Kimberlé Crenshaw, *On Intersectionality: Essential Writings* (New Press, 2019); Karen Vieira Powers, "Conquering Discourses of 'Sexual Conquest': Of Women, Language, and Mestizaje," *Colonial Latin American Review* 11, no. 1 (2002): 7–32; Jennifer M. Spear, "Colonial Intimacies: Legislating Sex in French Louisiana," *William and Mary Quarterly* 60, no. 1 (2003).

3. Ann Laura Stoler, "Tense and Tender Ties: The Politics of Comparison in North American History and (Post) Colonial Studies," *Journal of American History* 88, no. 3 (2001): 829–865; Susan Sleeper-Smith, ed., *Rethinking the Fur Trade: Cultures of Exchange in an Atlantic World* (University of Nebraska Press, 2009); Jennifer Spear, *Race, Sex and Social Order in Early New Orleans* (Johns Hopkins University Press, 2009); Brenda Macdougall, *One of the Family: Metis Culture in Nineteenth-Century Saskatchewan* (University of British Columbia Press, 2010); Nicole St. Onge, Carolyn Podruchny, and Brenda Macdougall, eds., *Contours of A People: Metis Mobility, Family, and History* (University of Oklahoma Press, 2012); Lucy E. Murphy, *Great Lakes Creoles: A French Indian Community on the Northern Borderlands* (Cambridge University Press, 2014); Michel Hogue, *Metis and the Medicine Line: Creating a Border and Dividing a People* (University of North Carolina Press, 2015).

4. Tiya Miles, *The House at Diamond Hill: A Cherokee Plantation Story* (University of North Carolina Press, 2010), 31–34; Andrew Jackson, Message to Congress "On Indian Removal," December 6, 1830, *Records of the United States Senate, 1789–1990*, RG 46, NARA.

5. Circe D. Sturm, *Race, Culture, and Identity Politics in the Cherokee Nation of Oklahoma* (University of California Press, 2002); Anton Treuer, *Everything You Wanted to Know About Indians But Were Afraid to Ask* (University of Minnesota Press, 2012); Melissa L. Meyer, *Thicker Than Water: The Origins of Blood as Symbol and Ritual* (Routledge, 2005); Katherine Ellinghaus, *Blood Will Tell: Native Americans and Assimilation Policy* (University of Nebraska Press, 2017).

6. David E. Wilkins and Shelley Wilkins, *Dismembered: Native Disenrollment and the Battle for Human Rights* (University of Washington Press, 2017); Alaina Roberts, *I've Been Here All the While: Black Freedom on Native*

Land (University of Pennsylvania Press, 2021); Norbert Hill and Kathleen Ratteree, eds., *The Great Vanishing Act: Blood Quantum and the Future of Native Nations* (Fulcrum, 2017); Mark Walker, "Cherokee Nation Addresses Bias Against Descendants of Enslaved People," *New York Times*, February 24, 2021.

7. Nancy Cott, *Public Vows: A History of Marriage and the Nation* (Harvard University Press, 2002); Sarah Carter, *The Importance of Being Monogamous: Marriage and Nation Building in Western Canada to 1915* (Athabasca, 2008); Mark Rifkin, *When Did Indians Become Straight? Kinship, the History of Sexuality, and Native Sovereignty* (University of North Carolina Press, 2011); Peter Boag, *Redressing America's Frontier Past* (University of California Press, 2013); Rachel Hope Cleves, *Charity and Sylvia: A Same-Sex Marriage in Early America* (Oxford University Press, 2014); Laurel Thatcher Ulrich, *A House Full of Females: Plural Marriage and Women's Rights in Early Mormonism, 1835–1870* (Knopf, 2017); Sarah M. S. Pearsall, *Polygamy: An Early American History* (Yale University Press, 2019).

Prologue: Seasons of Marriage and War

1. Vernon Bailey and J. Kenneth Soutt, "Two New Beavers from Labrador and New Brunswick," *Journal of Mammalogy* 23, no. 1 (1942): 86–88; Sylwester Kaszowski, Charles C. Rust, and Richard M. Shackelford, "Determination of Hair Density in the Mink," *Journal of Mammalogy* 61, no. 1 (1970): 27–34.

2. Jennifer S. H. Brown and Robert Brightman, eds., *The Orders of the Dreamed: George Nelson on Cree and Northern Ojibwa Religion and Myth* (University of Manitoba Press, 1988); Richard Preston, "Cree," *Canadian Encyclopedia* (McClelland & Stewart, 1999); Deanna Broughton, *Hide, Wood, and Willow: Cradles of the Great Plains Indians* (University of Oklahoma Press, 2019), 113.

3. Susan Sleeper-Smith, *Indigenous Prosperity and American Conquest: Indian Women of the Ohio River Valley* (University of North Carolina Press, 2018), 67–70; Fenn, *Encounters*, 31–36.

4. Lyle Campbell, *American Indian Languages: The Historical Linguistics of Native America* (Oxford University Press, 1997); R. Cole Harris, ed., *Historical Atlas of Canada: From the Beginning to 1800* (University of Toronto Press, 1987), chaps. 9, 33–36; Jan Ulrich, *New Lakota Dictionary* (Lakota Language Consortium, 2008), 1–12; Daniel K. Richter, *Facing East from Indian Country: A Native History of Early America* (Harvard University Press, 2001), 1–17.

5. Michael A. McDonnell, *Masters of Empire: Great Lakes Indians and the Making of America* (Hill and Wang, 2015), 12–13; Ann Marie Plane, *Colo-*

nial Intimacies: Indian Marriage in Early New England (Cornell University Press, 2000), 22–24.

6. Timothy Pauketat, *Cahokia: Ancient America's Great City on the Mississippi* (Viking, 2009); Kathleen DuVal, *Independence Lost: Lives on the Edge of the American Revolution* (Random House, 2017), xxi, xxv, 12–14; Robbie Ethridge, *From Chicaza to Chickasaw: The European Invasion and the Transformation of the Mississippian World, 1540–1715* (University of North Carolina Press, 2013), 16–21.

7. Barbara A. Mann and Jerry L. Fields, "A Sign in the Sky: Dating the League of the Haudenosaunee," *American Indian Culture and Research Journal* 21, no. 2 (1997): 105–63; Edward Countryman, "Toward a New Iroquois History," *William and Mary Quarterly* 69, no. 2 (2012): 347–60.

8. Jacques Cartier, "First Relation, 1534," in *Early English and French Voyages, Chiefly from Hakluyt, 1534–1608*, ed. Henry S. Burrage (Scribner's, 1906), 3–31; Robert Juett and Georg Michael Asher, "The Third Voyage of Henry Hudson," *Henry Hudson the Navigator, The Original Documents in Which His Career Is Recorded* (Hakluyt Society, 1860), 18.

9. Peter C. Mancall, *Fatal Journey: The Final Expedition of Henry Hudson* (Basic Books, 2009).

10. William W. Warren, *History of the Ojibways, Based Upon Traditions and Oral Statements* (n.p., 1885), 80–81; Witgen, *Infinity of Nations*, 40–41.

11. Heidi Bohaker, "*Nindoodemag*: The Significance of Algonquin Kinship Networks in the Eastern Great Lakes Regions, 1600–1701," *William and Mary Quarterly* 63, no. 1 (2006): 23–52; Andrew J. Blackbird, "Earliest Possible Known History of Mackinac Island," in Blackbird, *History of the Ottawa and Chippewa Indians of Michigan* (n.p., 1887).

12. Edmund Jefferson Danziger, *The Chippewas of Lake Superior* (University of Oklahoma Press, 1979), 6–8; Witgen, *Infinity of Nations*, 40–46.

13. Warren, *History of Ojibways*, 105.

14. Bohaker, "*Nindoodemag*," 27–29; Witgen, *Infinity of Nations*, 16, 29–33, 69–80; Keith R. Widder, *Beyond Pontiac's Shadow: Michilimackinac and the Anglo-Indian War of 1763* (Michigan State University Press, 2013), 31–35; Lalemant, "1626," in Reuben Gold Thwaites, ed., *The Jesuit Relations and Allied Documents, 1610–1791*, 73 vols. (1899; reprint LeMoyne College, 1998), 4:203.

15. Warren, *History of Ojibways*, 95.

16. Harold Hickerson, "The Feast of the Dead Among the Seventeenth Century Algonkians of the Upper Great Lakes," *American Anthropologist* 62, no. 1 (1962): 81–107.

17. Richard A. Rhodes, "Ojibwe Politeness and Social Structure," in *Papers of the Nineteenth Algonquian Conference*, ed. William Cowan (University of Toronto Press, 1988), 165–74; Heidi Bohaker, "Reading Anishinaabe Iden-

tities: Meaning and Metaphor in *Nindoodem* Pictographs," *Ethnohistory* 57, no. 1 (2010): 11–33; Nicolas Perrot, *The Indian Tribes of the Upper Mississippi Valley and Region of the Great Lakes*, trans. Emma Helen Blair (Arthur H. Clark, 1911).

18. Snyder, *Slavery in Indian Country*, 30–37; "Letter by Reverend Father Étienne de Carheil to Monsieur Louis Hector de Callières, Governor," in Thwaites, *Jesuit Relations*, 65:241.

19. Kathleen DuVal, "Indian Intermarriage and Métissage in Colonial Louisiana," *William and Mary Quarterly* 65, no. 2 (2008): 267–304; Plane, *Colonial Intimacies*, 23–27; Nancy Shoemaker, *A Strange Likeness: Becoming Red and White in Eighteenth-Century North America* (Oxford University Press, 2006), 14–16.

20. McDonnell, *Masters of Empire*, 27–28; Bohaker, "Reading Anishinaabe Identities," 13–15.

21. Samuel de Champlain, *Récits de voyages en Nouvelle-France 1603–1632*, ed. Mathieu d'Avignon (Lavalle University, 2018); Marcel Trudel, "Champlain, Samuel de," DCB.

22. Daniel K. Richter, *The Ordeal of the Longhouse: The Peoples of the Iroquois League in the Era of European Colonization* (University of North Carolina Press, 1992), 60–62.

23. Hans M. Carlson, *Home Is the Hunter: The James Bay Cree and Their Land* (University of British Columbia Press, 2008), 48–55; Flora Beardy and Robert Coutts, eds., *Voices from Hudson's Bay: Cree Stories from York Factory* (McGill University Press, 1996), 7, 10.

24. Thomas White, York Factory Journals, 1727/folio 2, Hudson's Bay Company Archives, PRC.

25. Victor P. Lytwyn, *Muskekowuck Athinuwick: Original People of the Great Swampy Land* (University of Manitoba Press, 2002), 98–105.

26. Ibid., 98–99; John S. Milloy, *The Plains Cree: Trade, Diplomacy and War, 1790 to 1870* (University of Manitoba Press, 1988), 5–7.

27. Harris, *Historical Atlas of Canada*, 1:4–7; David G. Mandelbaum, *The Plains Cree: An Ethnographic, Historical, and Comparative Study* (1940; reprint Canadian Plains Research, 1979), 14–16.

28. Thwaites, *Jesuit Relations*, 47:151–53; Julie Cruikshank, *Life Lived Like a Story: Life Stories of Three Yukon Elders* (University of British Columbia Press, 1992), 339.

29. Radisson and Greseliers quoted in Mandelbaum, *Plains Cree*, 18; Thwaites, *Jesuit Relations*, 53:58–92, 61:148–217.

30. Georges-Émile Giguère, "Albanel, Charles," DCB.

31. Kenneth Warren Chase, *Firearms: A Global History to 1700* (Cambridge University Press, 2003), 32; David J. Silverman, *Thundersticks: Firearms and the Violent Transformation of Native America* (Harvard University Press, 2016), 27–36; White, *Middle Ground*, 44–47.

32. Kathryn M. LaBelle, "The Wendat Feast of the Souls, 1636," in *French and Indians in the Heart of North America,1630–1815*, ed. Robert Englebert and Guillaume Teasdale (Michigan State University Press, 2013), 1–20.

33. Allan Greer, *Mohawk Saint: Catherine Tekakwitha and the Jesuits* (Oxford University Press, 2005), 5–8.

34. Bruce Trigger and William Swagerty, "Entertaining Strangers: North America in the Sixteenth Century," in *The Cambridge History of the Native Peoples of the Americas*, ed. Bruce G. Trigger and Wilcomb E. Washburne (Cambridge University Press, 1996), vol. 1, pt. 1, 325–98; Thwaites, *Jesuit Relations*, 13:219; Dean Snow and William A. Starna, "Sixteenth-Century Depopulation: A View from the Mohawk Valley," *American Anthropologist* 91, no. 1 (2009): 142–49; Paul Kelton, *Cherokee Medicine, Colonial Germs: An Indigenous Nation's Fight Against Smallpox, 1518–1824* (University of Oklahoma Press, 2015), 29–31.

35. Jon Parmenter, *The Edge of the Woods: Iroquoia, 1534–1701* (Michigan State University Press, 2010), 46; Thwaites, *Jesuit Relations*, 15:41; Scott Stevens, "Historiography of New France and the Legacy of Iroquois Internationalism," *Comparative American Studies* 11, no. 2 (2013): 148–65.

36. Roger M. Carpenter, *The Renewed, the Destroyed, and the Remade: The Three Thought Worlds of the Iroquois and the Huron, 1609–1650* (Michigan State University Press, 2004), 44–67; Thwaites, *Jesuit Relations*, 8:299.

37. Kathryn M. LaBelle, *Dispersed But Not Destroyed: A History of Seventeenth-Century Wendat People* (University of British Columbia Press, 2013), 15–23; Chrestien Le Clercq, *New Relation of Gaspesia: With the Customs and Religion of the Gaspesian Indians*, ed. William F. Ganong (University of Toronto Press, 1910), 122; Snyder, *Slavery in Indian Country*, 86–91.

38. Danziger, *Chippewas of Lake Superior*, 24; Greer, *Mohawk Saint*, 26–28.

39. White, *Middle Ground*, 24; McDonnell, *Masters of Empire*, 40–44.

40. Parmenter, *Edge of Woods*, 48–49.

41. Carpenter, *Renewed*, 22–23; Sleeper-Smith, *Indigenous Prosperity*, 44–48; Leslie P. Choquette, *Frenchmen into Peasants: Modernity and Tradition in the Peopling of French Canada* (Harvard University Press, 1997), 251.

42. Grace Lee Nute, "Chouart des Groseilliers, Médard," DCB; Carolyn Podruchny, *Making the Voyageur World: Travelers and Traders in the North American Fur Trade* (University of Nebraska Press, 2007), 18–19; Samuel Champlain, *The Works of Samuel de Champlain*, ed. H. P. Biggar (University of Toronto Press, 1925), 2:82; Francois Le Mercier quote in Thwaites, *Jesuit Relations*, 43:85; Parmenter, *Edge of Woods*, 82–84, 167–71, 270–73.

43. Sleeper-Smith, *Indigenous Prosperity*, 26–28, 55; Witgen, *Infinity of Nations*, 132–33.

44. Bruce M. White, "Encounters with Spirits: Ojibwa and Dakota Theories About the French and Their Merchandise," *Ethnohistory* 4, no. 1 (1994):

369–405; McDonnell, *Masters of Empire*, 41–43; A. Irving Hallowell, "Concordance of Ojibwa Narratives in the Published Works of Henry R. Schoolcraft," *Journal of American Folklore* 59, no. 232 (1946): 150.

45. White, *Middle Ground*, 29–30; Parmenter, *Edge of Woods*, 156–57; Witgen, *Infinity of Nations*, 186.

46. Henry Lewis Morgan, *The American Beaver and His Works* (Lippincott, 1868); Harris, *Historical Atlas of Canada*, vol. 1, chaps. 36–38.

47. Duncan Halley, Frank Rosell, and Alexander P. Savljev, "Population and Distribution of Eurasian Beaver (*Castor fiber*)," *Baltic Forestry* 18, no. 1 (2012): 168–75; David Corner, "The Tyranny of Fashion: The Case of the Felt-Hatting Trade in the Late Seventeenth and Eighteenth Centuries," *Textile History* 22, no. 2 (1991): 153–78; Fiona Clark, *Hats* (Anchor Press, 1992), 10, 82–84; Samuel Pepys, *Diary*, entry for April 26, 1662, https://www.gutenberg.org/files/4200/4200-h/4200-h.htm.

48. White, *Middle Ground*, 99–101; W. J. Eccles, *France in America* (Harper & Row, 1972), 35–41; Podruchny, *Making the Voyageur World*, 12–16.

49. Parmenter, *Edge of Woods*, 222–27; Greer, *Mohawk Saint*, 107–9.

Chapter 1: Ozhaguscodaywayquay and John Johnston

1. John Johnston to Henry Schoolcraft, June 10, 1828, Box 7, Henry Rowe Schoolcraft Papers, LOC; George Nelson, *My First Years in the Fur Trade: The Journals of 1802–1804*, ed. Laura Peers and Theresa Schenck (Minnesota Historical Society Press, 2002), 43–47; Brenda J. Child, *Holding Our World Together: Ojibwe Women and the Survival of Community* (Viking, 2012), 43–44.

2. Bernard Bailyn, *The Barbarous Years: The Peopling of North America: The Conflict of Civilizations, 1600–1675* (Knopf, 2012), 97–117; Catherine M. Cameron, "The Effects of Warfare and Captive-Taking on Indigenous Mortality in Postcontact North America," in *Beyond Germs: Native Depopulation in North America*, ed. Catherine M. Cameron, Paul Kelton, and Alan C. Swedlund (University of Arizona Press, 2015).

3. Jon Parmenter, "After the Mourning Wars: The Iroquois as Allies in Colonial North American Campaigns, 1676–1760," *William and Mary Quarterly* 64, no. 1 (2007): 39–76.

4. Robert Livingston, Journal, February 9, 1689–90, Livingston Papers, NYHS; Lieutenant Governor Leisler to Bishop of Salisbury, March 21, 1690, in *Documents Relative to the Colonial History of the State of New-York*, ed. Edmund Bailey O'Callaghan and Fernow Berthold (Weed, Parsons, 1853), 3:700.

5. Witgen, *Infinity of Nations*, 120–126; Sleeper-Smith, *Indigenous Prosperity*, 16–18, 37–40.

6. Harold A. Innis, *The Fur Trade in Canada: An Introduction to Canadian Economic History*, abridged ed. (Yale University Press, 1962).

7. E. E. Rich, *The History of the Hudson's Bay Company 1670–1870* (Hudson's Bay Society, 1958), vol. 1; Wesley Frank Craven, *The Virginia Company of London, 1606–1624* (Virginia Company, 1957).

8. John M. Bumsted, *The Peoples of Canada: A Pre-Confederation History*, 2nd ed. (Oxford University Press, 2009), 13, 41–48.

9. Ernest Voorhis, *Historic Forts and Trading Posts of the French Regime and of the English Fur Trading Companies* (n.p., 1930); "The Royal Charter of the Hudson's Bay Company," 1670, HBC Heritage, http://www.hbcheritage.ca/things/artifacts/the-royal-charter.

10. Jennifer S. H. Brown, *Strangers in Blood: Fur Trade Company Families in Indian Country* (University of British Columbia Press, 1980), 86–91; Heather R. Driscoll, "'A Most Important Chain of Connection': Marriage in the HBC," in *From Rupert's Land to Canada: Essays in Honour of John E. Foster*, ed. Theodore Binemma et al. (University of Alberta Press, 2001), 81–87; Rich, *History of Hudson's Bay Company*, 1:xi–xvi.

11. Gilles Havard, *The Great Peace of Montreal of 1701: French-Native Diplomacy in the Seventeenth Century*, trans. Phyllis Aronoff and Howard Scott (McGill University Press, 2001), 88; Robert Michael Morrissey, *Empire by Collaboration: Indians, Colonists, and Governments in Colonial Illinois Country* (University of Pennsylvania Press, 2015), 52–57.

12. Governor Callière, September 18, 1700, quoted in Havard, *Great Peace*, 26; Francis Jennings, *The Ambiguous Iroquois Empire: The Covenant Chain Confederation of Indian Tribes with English Colonies* (W. W. Norton, 1984), 44–46.

13. Havard, *Great Peace*, 18, 25; White, *Middle Ground*, 347–55.

14. Claude-Charles Le Roy de la Potherie, *Histoire de l'Amérique septentrionale* (n.p., 1722), 4:194; Louise Dechêne, *Habitants and Merchants in Seventeenth-Century Montreal*, trans. Liana Vardi (McGill University Press, 1992), 7–10.

15. Havard, *Great Peace*, 134–37; Potherie, *Histoire de l'Amérique septentrionale*, 4:234–36, 241.

16. Havard, *Great Peace*, 362; Witgen, *Infinity of Nations*, 118–20; Matthew Dennis, *Cultivating a Landscape of Peace: Iroquois-European Encounters in Seventeenth-Century America* (Cornell University Press, 1995), 76–118.

17. Silverman, *Thundersticks*, 45, 119–20; Pekka Hämäläinen, "The Shapes of Power: Indians, Europeans, and North American Worlds from the Seventeenth to the Nineteenth Century," in *Contested Spaces of Early America*, ed. Juliana Barr and Edward Countryman (University of Pennsylvania Press, 2014), 31–68.

18. David Thompson, *David Thompson's Narrative of His Explorations in Western America, 1784–1812*, ed. J. B. Tyrrell (Champlain Society, 1916), vol. 12;

Governor Fullartine, 1713, quoted in Rich, *History of Hudson's Bay Company*, 1:491.

19. Jan de Vries, "Between Purchasing Power and the World of Goods: Understanding the Household Economy in Early Modern Europe," in *Consumption and the World of Goods*, ed. John Brewer and Roy Porter (Routledge, 1993), 85–132; Arthur J. Ray and Donald Freeman, *"Give Us Good Measure": An Economic Analysis of the Relations Between Indians and the Hudson's Bay Company Before 1763* (University of Toronto Press, 1978), 154–65.

20. *James Isham's Observations on Hudson's Bay, 1743*, ed. E. E. Rich (Champlain Society, 1949).

21. "Present State of the Northern Indians in the Department of Sir William Johnston, Comprehended in 1763," in O'Callaghan and Berthold, *Documents of Colonial History of New-York*, 7:641.

22. W. Stewart Wallace, ed., *The Encyclopedia of Canada* (University Associates of Canada, 1948), 6:249; "Statement of David McLoughlin" (1902), quoted in T. C. Elliott, "Marguerite Wadin McKay McLoughlin," *Oregon Historical Quarterly* 36, no. 4 (1935): 339; W. Stewart Wallace, ed., *Documents Relating to North West Company* (Champlain Society, 1934), app. A.

23. J. I. Cooper, "Waddens, Jean-Étienne," DCB; Wallace, *Documents Relating to North West Company*, 4.

24. *Minutes of the Hudson's Bay Company 1671–1684*, ed. E. E. Rich and A. M. Johnson (Champlain Society, 1948), 2:xiv–xv; Charles A. Bishop, *The Northern Ojibwa and the Fur Trade: An Historical and Ecological Study* (Holt, Rinehart & Winston of Canada, 1974), 310–12; Innis, *Fur Trade in Canada*, 42–49.

25. Cooper, "Waddens, Jean-Étienne"; Paul W. Thistle, *Indian-European Trade Relations in the Lower Saskatchewan River Region* (University of Manitoba Press, 1986), 25–28.

26. Joseph Robson, *Account of Six Years Residence in Hudson's Bay, from 1733 to 1736, and 1744 to 1747* (1752, reprint Dodo Press, 2009), 6, 37.

27. Carter, *Importance of Being Monogamous*, 114; Mandelbaum, *Plains Cree*, 294; Thistle, *Indian-European Trade Relations*, 17; Toby Morantz, "Northern Algonquian Concepts of Status and Leadership Reviewed: A Case Study of the Eighteenth-Century Trading Captain System," *Canadian Review of Sociology* 30, no. 4 (1993): 482–501.

28. Child, *Holding Our World Together*; John Mack Faragher, "The Custom of the Country: Cross-Cultural Marriage in the Far Western Fur Trade," in *Western Women: Their Lives, Their Land*, eds. Lillian Schlissel, Vicki L. Ruiz, and Janice Monk (University of New Mexico Press, 1991), 199–215; Susan E. Gray, "Miengun's Children: Tales from a Mixed-Race Family," *Frontiers: A Journal of Women Studies* 29, no. 2 (2008): 146–49.

29. Jacqueline Peterson, "Prelude to Red River: A Social Portrait of the Great Lakes Metis," *Ethnohistory* 25, no. 1 (1978): 41–67.

30. Gabriel Franchère, *Journal of a Voyage on the North West Coast of North America During the Years 1811, 1812, 1813 and 1814*, ed. W. Kaye Lamb, trans. Wessie Tipping Lamb (Champlain Society, 1969); Daniel Williams Harmon, *Sixteen Years in the Indian Country: The Journal of Daniel Williams Harmon, 1800–1816* (Champlain Society, 1957); Carter, *Importance of Being Monogamous*, 113–21; Pearsall, *Polygamy*, 63–79.

31. Kenneth E. Kidd, *Blackfoot Ethnography: Being a Synthesis of the Data of Ethnological Science with the Information Concerning the Blackfoot Indians . . .* (Archaeological Survey of Alberta, 1937); Mandelbaum, *Plains Cree*, 19–24, 29–30, 77–78.

32. Edward Umfreville, *The Present State of Hudson's Bay, Containing a Full Description of That Settlement . . .* (Charles Stalker, 1790); Adolph M. Greenberg and James Morrison, "Group Identities in the Boreal Forest: The Origin of the Northern Ojibwa," *Ethnohistory* 29, no. 2 (1982): 75–102.

33. Podruchny, *Making the Voyageur World*, 166–71; Peter Pond, "Narrative of Peter Pond," in *Five Fur Traders of the Northwest*, ed. Charles M. Gates (Minnesota Historical Society, 1933), 47; Alexander Ross, *The Fur Hunters of the Far West: A Narrative of Adventures in the Oregon and Rocky Mountains* (Smith, Elder, 1855), 2:236–37.

34. Andrew Graham, "Remarks on Hudson's Bay Trade, After 25 Years in the Company's Service in 1769," HM 1720, HL.

35. Fred Anderson, *The War That Made America: A Short History of the French and Indian War* (Viking, 2007), 22–48; Alan Taylor, *The Divided Ground: Indians, Settlers, and the Northern Borderland of the American Revolution* (Knopf, 2006), 8–17; Brenda Macdougall, "Speaking of Metis: Reading Family Life into Colonial Records," *Ethnohistory* 61, no. 1 (2014): 27–56.

36. Innis, *Fur Trade in Canada*, 390–403; Bruce M. White, *Grand Portage as a Trading Post: Patterns of Trade at "The Great Carrying Place"* (University of Minnesota Press, 2005), 27–29, 85–86.

37. Carter, *Importance of Being Monogamous*, 105–7; Harmon, *Sixteen Years in Indian Country*, 54.

38. Henry Rowe Schoolcraft, "Memoir of John Johnston," *Historical Collections* (Michigan Pioneer and Historical Society, 1908), 36:53–94; Theresa M. Schenck, *The Voice of the Crane Echoes Afar: The Sociopolitical Organization of the Lake Superior Ojibwa, 1640–1855* (Garland, 1997), 18–19.

39. Fred M. Anderson, *The Crucible of War: The Seven Years' War and the Fate of British North America, 1754–1766* (Vintage, 2001), 457–59, 519–23.

40. Widder, *Beyond Pontiac's Shadow*, 141–54; McDonnell, *Masters of Empire*, 216–22.

41. "Winter Count of Battiste Goode, Brule Sioux," cited in Mari Sandoz, *The Beaver Men: Spearheads of Empire* (University of Nebraska Press, 1964), 159; Elizabeth A. Fenn, *Pox Americana: The Great Smallpox Epidemic of 1775–82* (Hill and Wang, 2002), 215–17, 219.

42. Warren, *History of Ojibways*, 160–61; Witgen, *Infinity of Nations*, 310–14.

43. Marjorie Cahn Brazer, *Harps upon the Willows: The Johnston Family of the Old Northwest* (Historical Society of Michigan, 1993), 12–15; U.S. and Canada, Passenger and Immigration Lists, Index New York Ship Arrivals, 1789, Ancestry.com.

44. Schoolcraft, "Memoir of John Johnston," 57–58; Brazer, *Harps upon the Willows*, 17–19.

45. Theresa M. Schenck, *William W. Warren: The Life, Letters, and Times of an Ojibwe Leader* (University of Nebraska Press, 2007), 33–36, 45.

46. Warren, *History of Ojibways*, 66–69; Robert Englebert, "Diverging Identities and Converging Interests: Corporate Competition, Desertion, and Voyageur Agency, 1815–1818," *Manitoba History* 55 (2007): 18–25.

47. Podruchny, *Making the Voyageur World*; John Johnston to Henry Schoolcraft, June 10, 1828, Box 7, Schoolcraft Papers, LOC.

48. Alan Knight and Janet E. Chute, "In the Shadow of the Thumping Drum: The Sault Metis—The People In-Between," in *Lines Drawn upon the Water: First Nations and the Great Lakes Borders and Borderlands*, ed. Karl S. Hele (Wilfred Laurier, 2008), 253; Warren, *History of Ojibways*, 372.

49. Child, *Holding Our World Together*, 43–44.

50. Deidre Stevens Tomaszewski, *The Johnstons of Sault Ste. Marie: An Informal History of the Northwest as Portrayed Through the Experiences of One Pioneer Family* (n.p., 1993), 3–4; Warren, *History of Ojibways*, 178.

51. Tomaszewski, *Johnstons of Sault Ste. Marie*, 4–5; Anna Brownell Jameson, *Winter Studies and Summer Rambles in Canada* (Saunders & Ottley, 1838), 214–15; Susan Sleeper-Smith, *Indian Women and French Men: Rethinking Cultural Encounter in the Western Great Lakes* (University of Massachusetts Press, 2001), 34–38.

52. Brazer, *Harps upon the Willows*, 49–54; Schoolcraft, "Memoir of John Johnston," 51–53; Jane Johnston Schoolcraft, Poem Transcription, 1829, Box 44, Schoolcraft Papers, LOC.

53. Jameson, *Winter Studies and Summer Rambles*, 214–15; Jacqueline Peterson, "Women Dreaming: The Religiopsychology of Indian-White Marriages and the Rise of Metis Culture," in *Sexual Borderlands: Constructing an American Sexual Past*, ed. Kathleen Kennedy and Sharon Rena Ullman (Ohio State University Press, 2003), 27–44.

Chapter 2: Wintering Families and Corporate War, 1770–1810

1. Alexander Mackenzie, *Journals and Letters of Sir Alexander Mackenzie*, ed. W. Kaye Lamb (Hakluyt Society, 1970), 8, 75–76; Gloria Fedirchuk, "Peter Pond: Map Maker of the Northwest (1740–1807)," *Arctic* 43, no. 2 (1990): 184–86.

2. David L. Preston, *The Texture of Contact: European and Indian Settler Communities on the Frontiers of Iroquoia, 1667–1783* (University of Nebraska Press, 2012), 50–56; Linda Gordon, "Internal Colonialism and Gender," in *Haunted by Empire: Geographies of Intimacy in North American History*, ed. Ann Laura Stoler (Duke University Press, 2006), 427–51; John Filson, *The Discovery, Settlement and Present State of Kentucke* (n.p., 1784).

3. Peter Silver, *Our Savage Neighbors: How Indian War Transformed Early America* (W. W. Norton, 2009), 45–59; Gregory Evans Dowd, *War Under Heaven: Pontiac, the Indian Nations, and the British Empire* (Johns Hopkins University Press, 2004), 22–24; "A Farmer on Juniata," *Pennsylvania Packet*, November 7, 1782.

4. Claudio Saunt, *West of the Revolution: An Uncommon History of 1776* (W. W. Norton, 2014), 20–24.

5. Anthony Hendry, *York Factory to the Blackfeet Country: The Journal of Anthony Hendry, 1754–1755*, ed. Lawrence J. Burpee (Royal Society of Canada, 1908), 13:352–55; Arthur J. Ray, *Indians in the Fur Trade: Their Role as Trappers, Hunters, and Middlemen in the Lands Southwest of Hudson Bay, 1660–1870* (University of Toronto Press, 1998), 72–76.

6. Brown, *Strangers in Blood*, 12–14; Allan Greer, *Property and Dispossession: Natives, Empires, and Land in Early Modern North America* (Cambridge University Press, 2018), 298–301.

7. Governor and Committee Fur Sales Books, Price Lists, York Factory, 1742, 1782, Records of Northern Department, Hudson's Bay Company Archives, PRC; E. E. Rich, *The Fur Trade and the Northwest to 1857* (Champlain Society, 1967), 108–10.

8. Lawrence J. Burpee, *The Search for the Western Sea: The Story of the Exploration of North-Western America* (Musson, 1908), 2:325–53; E. E. Rich, *Montreal and the Fur Trade* (McGill University Press, 1966), xi, xvi; W. Stewart Wallace, *The Pedlars from Quebec and Other Papers on the Nor'westers* (Champlain Society, 1954), 19–26.

9. Mackenzie, *Journals and Letters*, 8, 75–76; Harold A. Innis, "Peter Pond in 1780," *Canadian Historical Review* 9, no. 4 (1928): 308–21; David Chapin, *Freshwater Passages: The Trade and Travels of Peter Pond* (University of Nebraska Press, 2014), 193–97.

10. Brown, *Strangers in Blood*, 84–91; King's Bench Warrant, District of Montreal, "For summoning Joseph Fagniant to attend as witness against Peter

Pond for murder," March 11, 1785, in "Some Further Material on Peter Pond," *Canadian Historical Review* 16 (1935): 61–64; Henry Raup Wagner, *Peter Pond: Fur Trader and Explorer* (Yale University Press, 1955), 9–11.

11. Fenn, *Pox Americana*, 170–81; Hugh Faries, "The Diary of Hugh Faries," in *Five Fur Traders of the Northwest*, ed. Charles M. Gates (Minnesota Historical Society, 1933), 192–95; Alexander Mackenzie, *Mackenzie's Voyages*, ed. Milo Milton Quaife, 2 vols. (Lakeside Press, 1931), 1:35; Ray, *Indians in the Fur Trade*, 104–7.

12. Rich, *History of Hudson's Bay Company*, 1:558–61; Eric W. Morse, *The Canoe Routes of the Voyageurs: The Geography and Logistics of the Canadian Fur Trade* (Minnesota Historical Society, 1962).

13. Theodore Catton, *Rainy Lake House: Twilight of Empire on the Northern Frontier* (Johns Hopkins University Press, 2017), 117–20; John Jennings, *Bark Canoes: The Art and Obsession of Tappan Adney* (Firefly Books, 2004), 41.

14. Franchère, *Journal of a Voyage*, 192–95; Sylvia Van Kirk, *Many Tender Ties: Women in Fur-Trade Society, 1670–1870* (University of Oklahoma Press, 1983), 92–95.

15. Louis Rodrigue Masson, ed., *Les bourgeois de la Compagnie du Nord-Ouest: Récits de voyages, lettres et rapports inédits relatifs au Nord-Ouest canadien*, 2 vols. (1889; reprint Antiquarian Press, 1960), 1:19–21; Marjorie Wilkins Campbell, *The North West Company* (Clarke, Irwin, 1957), 55–61.

16. Janet Guildford, "MacKay, Alexander Howard," DCB; Masson, *Les bourgeois de la Compagnie*, 1:17–19, 22–26.

17. Mackenzie, *Journals and Letters*, ix–xvi.

18. W. A. Sloan, "Aw-Gee-Nah," DCB; T. H. McDonald, ed., *Exploring the Northwest Territory: Sir Alexander Mackenzie's Journal of a Voyage by Bark Canoe from Lake Athabasca to the Pacific Ocean in the Summer of 1789* (University of Oklahoma Press, 1966).

19. Thomas Douglas Selkirk, *A Sketch of the British Fur Trade in North America; with Observations Relative to the North-West Company of Montreal* (n.p., 1816), 55–60; Mackenzie, *Journals and Letters*, 1:211–24.

20. Podruchny, *Making the Voyageur World*, 118; Harry W. Duckworth, ed., *English River Book: A North West Company Journal and Account Book of 1786* (McGill-Queens University Press, 1990), 10–15.

21. Harmon, *Sixteen Years in Indian Country*, 23–24, 118–19.

22. Alexander Henry and David Thompson, *New Light on the Early History of the Greater Northwest: The Manuscript Journals of Alexander Henry and David Thompson, 1799–1814*, ed. Elliott Coues (F. P. Harper, 1897), 553–54.

23. North West Company Post Reports: English River 1815, Rainy River 1799, and Norway House 1796, B60/E1 and 3, Hudson's Bay Company Archives, PRC; Podruchny, *Making the Voyageur World*, 150–52.

24. Deanna Christensen, *Ahtahkakoop: The Epic Account of Plains Cree Head Chief and His People* (Starblanket, 2000), 47–55; Duncan McGillivray, *The Journal of Duncan McGillivray of the North West Company at Fort George on the Saskatchewan, 1794–1795*, ed. A. S. Morton (Macmillan of Canada, 1929).

25. T. C. Elliott, "Marguerite Wadin McKay McLoughlin," *Oregon Historical Quarterly* 36, no. 4 (1935): 338–47; Mackenzie, *Journals and Letters*, 1:82; Selkirk, *Sketch of British Fur Trade*, 140–43.

26. Child, *Holding Our World Together*, 8–9, 23–24; Murphy, *Great Lakes Creoles*, 148–53.

27. Grace Lee Nute, *Lake Superior* (Bobbs-Merrill, 1944).

28. Alexander Henry, *Alexander Henry's Travels and Adventures in the Years 1760–1776*, ed. Milo Milton Quaife (University of Chicago Press, 1921), 1:47–57; David A. Armour, "Cadot, Jean-Baptiste," DCB; William Johnson, "Account of Johnson's Indian Department Expenses to September 25, 1767" and "Speismacher's Indian Transactions, December 8, 1767–July 18, 1768," Fur Trade Miscellany, Burton-DPL; Knight and Chute, "In the Shadow of the Thumping Drum," 85–114.

29. William Johnson quoted in Henry, *Travels and Adventures*, 1: 237; St. Anne's Parish Church Records, "Marriages at Mackinac," *Wisconsin Historical Collections* 18 (1908): 484–87; "Mackinac Baptisms," *Wisconsin Historical Collections* 19 (1910): 21–57; Wallace, *Pedlars from Quebec*, 35–41; Schenck, *Voice of the Crane*, 78–80.

30. Brazer, *Harps upon the Willows*, 92–94; Nute, *Lake Superior*, 45–48.

31. Basil Johnston, *Moose Meat and Wild Rice: Rollicking Tales About Life on a Modern Day Indian Reserve* (McClelland & Stewart, 1978), 9–11, 18–19, 47.

32. Juliette A. Kinzie, *Wau-Bun: The "Early Day" in the North-West* (Caxton Club, 1901), 21–22; Susan Johnston, Ledger Book 1818–1828, Records of Michigan Superintendency, RG 75, NARA.

33. Johnston, Ledger Book; Henry Rowe Schoolcraft, *Personal Memoirs of a Residence of Thirty Years with the Indian Tribes on the American Frontiers* (n.p., 1851); Thomas L. McKenney, *Sketches of a Tour to the Lakes, of the Character and Customs of the Chippeway Indians, and of Incidents Connected with the Treaty of Fond du Lac* (Fielding Lucas, Jr., 1827), 181–82.

34. Brazer, *Harps upon the Willows*, 73–80; Maureen Konkle, *Writing Indian Nations: Native Intellectuals and the Politics of Historiography, 1827–1863* (University of North Carolina Press, 2004).

35. Campbell, *North West Company*, 76–79; Joseph Frobisher, secretary of Beaver Club, "Agreeable to the Resolve at our last Meeting, Mr. John Johnston was balloted for and unanimously elected Member of this Club," December 19, 1807, *Minutes of the Beaver Club, 1807–1827* (Minnesota Historical Society, 1899).

36. Child, *Holding Our World Together*, 77–81; Warren, *History of Ojibways*, 175; Bruce M. White, "The Woman Who Married a Beaver: Trade Patterns and Gender Roles in the Ojibwa Fur Trade," *Ethnohistory* 46, no. 1 (1999): 109–47.

37. Brazer, *Harps upon the Willows*, 77; John Johnston to R. Mackenzie, November 11, 1807, and John Johnston to George Johnston, September 7, 1809, Box 1, George Johnston Papers, Burton-DPL.

38. Schoolcraft, "Memoir of John Johnston," 36:53–94; Marjorie Wilkins Campbell, *McGillivray, Lord of the Northwest* (Clarke, Irwin, 1962), 33, 109.

39. Murphy, *Great Lakes Creoles*, 148–53; Widder, *Beyond Pontiac's Shadow*, 41–43, 53–54.

40. Another fur trade father, Daniel Harmon, expressed those fears. Harmon, *Sixteen Years in Indian Country*, 164, 199–200, 219.

41. Donald McKay, Day Book of Trade, 1799–1806, File 1719, Colin Rankin Papers, University of Waterloo Archives; Brown, *Strangers in Blood*, 156–58; Jean Morrison, "MacKay, Alexander Howard," DCB.

42. Morrison, "MacKay, Alexander Howard."

43. Kirk, *Many Tender Ties*, 50–51, 133–38; Alice M. Johnson, *Saskatchewan Journals and Correspondence: Edmonton House 1795–1800, Chesterfield House 1800–1802* (Hudson's Bay Record Society, 1987); Carter, *Importance of Being Monogamous*, 30–31; "Honorable Roderick McKenzie, Being Chiefly a Synopsis of Letters from Sir Alexander Mackenzie," in Masson, *Les bourgeois de la Compagnie*, 1:8–31.

44. Brown, *Strangers in Blood*, 91–104; Agnes C. Laut, *Lords of the North* (William Briggs, 1910), 71–78.

45. Campbell, *North West Company*, 156–57; North West Company, Minutes, Fort William, July 9, 1804, in Wallace, *Documents Relating to North West Company*.

46. Harmon, *Sixteen Years in Indian Country*, 230–31; Van Kirk, *Many Tender Ties*, 98–119; Adele Perry, *Colonial Relations: The Douglas-Connolly Family and the Nineteenth-Century Imperial World* (Cambridge University Press, 2015), 74–80.

Chapter 3: Fur Trade Migrants

1. Brown, *Strangers in Blood*, 96–99; Laut, *Lords of the North*, 71–78; John Lambert, *Travels Through Lower Canada, and the United States of North America in the Years 1806, 1807, and 1808* (Richard Phillips, 1810), 2:92–94.

2. North West Company, Minutes, Fort William, July 18, 1809, in Wallace, *Documents Relating to North West Company*.

3. Washington Irving, *Astoria, Or Anecdotes of an Adventure Beyond the Rocky,*

ed. Richard Dilworth Rust (University of Nebraska Press, 1976), 14–18; James P. Ronda, *Astoria and Empire* (University of Nebraska Press, 1990), 6–9.

4. Peter J. Kastor, "'What Are the Advantages of the Acquisition?': Inventing Expansion in the Early American Republic," *American Quarterly* 60, no. 4 (2008): 1003–35; Bethel Saler, *The Settlers' Empire: Colonialism and State Formation in America's Old Northwest* (University of Pennsylvania Press, 2015), 42–43.

5. Walter N. Sage, "The Appeal of the Northwest Company to the British Government to Forestall John Jacob Astor's Columbian Enterprise," *Canadian Historical Review* 17 (1936): 304–11; Susan Smith-Peter, "A Class of People Admitted to the Better Ranks: The First Generation of Creoles in Russian America, 1810s–1820s," *Ethnohistory* 60, no. 3 (2013): 363–84.

6. K. W. Porter, *John Jacob Astor, Business Man* (Cambridge University Press, 1933), 1:165–74; Ronda, *Astoria and Empire*, 46–57.

7. Henry and Thompson, *New Light on Early History*, 3:18; David Thompson, *The Writings of David Thompson*, ed. William E. Moreau (McGill-Queens University Press, 2009), 1:xxxiv, 320.

8. Alexander Ross, *Adventures of the First Settlers on the Oregon or Columbia River; Being a Narrative of the Expedition Fitted Out by John Jacob Astor* (Smith, Elder, 1849), 11–12; Ronda, *Astoria and Empire*, 88–90, 93–94; Franchère, *Journal of a Voyage*, 45.

9. Helen Hornbeck Tanner, ed., *Atlas of Great Lakes Indian History* (University of Oklahoma Press, 1986), 66; Saler, *Settlers' Empire*, 121–28.

10. Thomas Jefferson, Second Inaugural Address (1805), in James D. Richardson, ed., *A Compilation of the Messages and Papers of the Presidents* (Bureau of National Literature, 1896), vol. 1, pt. 3, 380; Thomas Jefferson, Annual Message of the President (December 1801), ibid., 352; Claudio Saunt, "Financing Dispossession: Stocks, Bonds, and the Deportation of Native Peoples in the Antebellum United States," *Journal of American History* 106, no. 2 (2019): 315–37.

11. Jay Gitlin, *The Bourgeois Frontier: French Towns, French Traders, and American Expansion* (Yale University Press, 2010), 39–43.

12. Duncan Cameron, "The Nipigon Country" (1805), in Masson, *Les bourgeois de la Compagnie*, 239–54; Reuben Gold Thwaites, ed., *Mackinac Register: 1725–1821* (State Historical Society of Wisconsin, 1908), 18–19.

13. Katherine Grandjean, *American Passage: The Communications Frontier in Early New England* (Harvard University Press, 2016), 92–105; Susan Johnston, Ledger Book 1818, RG 75, NARA; Waishkey quoted in Henry and Thompson, *New Light on Early History*, 1:86.

14. Charles McKenzie to Roderick McKenzie, January 8, 1809, in E. Arthur, "Charles McKenzie, l'homme seul," *Ontario History* 70 (1978): 39–62.

15. C. H. Chapman, "The Historic Johnston Family of the 'Soo,'" *Historical Collections* (Michigan Pioneer and Historical Society, 1903), 23:305–53; Warren, *History of Ojibways*, 242–46; John Johnston to Henry Schoolcraft, April 28, 1828, Box 7, Schoolcraft Papers, LOC.

16. Brazer, *Harps upon the Willows*, 82–83.

17. John Morgan Gray, *Lord Selkirk of Red River* (Michigan State University Press, 1963); Janet Lewis, *The Invasion: A Narrative of Events Concerning the Johnston Family of St. Mary's* (Harcourt Brace, 1932), 128.

18. Brazer, *Harps upon the Willows*, 85–87.

19. "Notes of a Memoir of Mrs. Henry Rowe Schoolcraft," Scrapbook 1, 1842, Box 41, Schoolcraft Papers, LOC.

20. Schoolcraft, "Memoir of John Johnston," 36:53–94.

21. Wilson Price Hunt, *Voyage of Mr. Hunt and His Companions from St. Louis to the Mouth of the Columbia by a New Route Across the Rocky Mountains* (Eyries & Malte-Brun, 1821), 9–10.

22. Ross, *Adventures of First Settlers*, 23–24, 44–45; Nancy Shoemaker, *Native American Whalemen and the World: Indigenous Encounters and the Contingency of Race* (University of North Carolina Press, 2015), 8–9; Irving, *Astoria*, 33–40.

23. Ross, *Adventures of First Settlers*, 65–68; Irving, *Astoria;* Ronda, *Astoria and Empire*, 112–14.

24. Ross, *Adventures of First Settlers*, 72; Coll Thrush, "Vancouver the Cannibal: Cuisine, Encounter, and the Dilemma of Difference on the Northwest Coast," *Ethnohistory* 58, no. 1 (2011): 1–35.

25. Gray H. Whaley, *Oregon and the Collapse of Illahee: U.S. Empire and the Transformation of an Indigenous World, 1792–1859* (University of North Carolina Press, 2010), 25–26; Reid, *Sea Is My Country*, 19–30; Robert H. Ruby and John A. Brown, *Indian Slavery in the Pacific Northwest* (Arthur H. Clark, 1993), 39–47.

26. Stephen Reynolds, *The Voyage of the New Hazard to the Northwest Coast, Hawaii and China, 1810–1813*, ed. Frederick Holway (Peabody Museum, 1938).

27. Ross, *Adventures of First Settlers*, 81.

28. Franchère, *Journal of a Voyage*, 123–26; Frederic W. Howay, "The Loss of the *Tonquin*," *Washington Historical Quarterly* 8, no. 2 (1922): 83–92.

29. Ross, *Adventures of First Settlers*, 85; Campbell, *North West Company*, 179–85; Ronda, *Astoria and Empire*, 232–35; T. C. Elliott, ed., "Journal of David Thompson," *Quarterly of the Oregon Historical Society* 15, no. 2 (1914): 104–25.

30. Henry and Thompson, *New Light on Early History*, 3:748, 850; Franchère, *Journal of a Voyage*, 155.

31. Whaley, *Oregon and the Collapse of Illahee*, 55–57; Franchère, *Journal of a Voyage*, 155.

32. Wilson Price Hunt, *The Overland Journal Diary of Wilson Price Hunt*, trans. Hoyt C. Franchère (Oregon Book Society, 1973).

33. Ronda, *Astoria and Empire*, 263–66.

34. Lawrence Hatter, *Citizens of Convenience: The Imperial Origins of American Nationhood on the U.S.-Canadian Border* (University of Virginia Press, 2016), 213–17; Richter, *Facing East from Indian Country*, 255–57.

35. Campbell, *North West Company*, 189–92; Brazer, *Harps upon the Willows*, 97–99; Gen. Isaac Brock to Capt. Charles Roberts, July 12 and 17, 1812, *Historical Collections* (Michigan Historical and Pioneer Society, 1890), 15:101–2, 108; Alan Taylor, *The Civil War of 1812: American Citizens, British Subjects, Irish Rebels, and Indian Allies* (Knopf, 2011), 152–53.

36. Taylor, *Civil War of 1812*, 161–66; Ann Durkin Keating, *Rising Up from Indian Country: The Battle of Fort Dearborn and the Birth of Chicago* (University of Chicago Press, 2012), 153–61.

37. Frederick Cook, ed., *Journals of the Military Expedition of Major John Sullivan Against the Six Nations of Indians in 1779 . . .* (New York State, 1887), 8.

38. John Johnston to George Johnston, October 18, 1813, John Johnston to George Johnston and family, November 3, 1813, and John Johnston to George Johnston and William Johnston, January 1, 1814, all in Box 7, George Johnston Papers, Burton-DPL; Duncan Smythe to George Johnston, June 18, 1851, Box 3, Johnston Papers, Burton-DPL.

39. Brazer, *Harps upon the Willows*, 107; "John Johnston of Sault Saint Marie: An Episode in the War of 1812," *Rose-Belford Canadian Monthly Review*, July 1881, 4–6.

40. John Johnston, "Memoir," Box 1, Schoolcraft Papers, LOC.

41. Schoolcraft, "Memoir of John Johnston," 36:18–22.

42. Brazer, *Harps upon the Willows*, 108–12; John Johnston to George Johnston, August 8, 1814, Box 1, George Johnston Papers, Burton-DPL.

43. John Johnston to "Dear Boys," November 12, 1814, Box 1, George Johnston Papers, Burton-DPL; Brazer, *Harps upon the Willows*, 115; White, *Middle Ground*, 514–18.

44. Taylor, *Civil War of 1812*, 265–67; Lewis Cass to James Monroe, September 4, 1814, in Clarence Edwin Carter, ed., *The Territorial Papers of the United States*, 28 vols. (USGPO, 1934–75), 10:482–83.

45. Sandy Antal, *A Wampum Denied: Procter's War of 1812* (McGill-Queens University Press, 2011), xix, 339–42, 390; Colin Calloway, "End of an Era: British-Indian Relations in the Great Lakes Region After the War of 1812," *Michigan Historical Review* 12, no. 2 (1986): 1–20.

46. W. R. Manning, ed., *Diplomatic Correspondence of the United States: Canadian Relations, 1784–1860* (Carnegie Endowment, 1940), 2:221, 233, 261; R. David Edmunds, *The Shawnee Prophet* (University of Nebraska Press, 1985), 112–16; Robert M. Owens, *Mr. Jefferson's Hammer: William Henry Harrison*

and the Origins of American Indian Policy (University of Oklahoma Press, 2007).

47. Theodore Catton, *Rainy Lake House: Twilight of Empire on the Northern Frontier* (Johns Hopkins University Press, 2017), 107–11; Henry and Thompson, *New Light on Early History*, 2:757–60.

48. Shoemaker, *Native American Whalemen*, 5; "Liste des bourgeois, commis, éngagés, et voyageurs, 1804, 1810," in Masson, *Les bourgeois de la Compagnie*, v. 2, app.; Henry and Thompson, *New Light on Early History*, 2:835–40, 872.

49. Robert Alexander Innes, *Elder Brother and the Law of the People: Contemporary Kinship and Cowessess First Nation* (University of Manitoba Press, 2013), 83–87.

50. George Colpitts, *Pemmican Empire: Food, Trade and the Last Bison Hunts on the North American Plains, 1780–1882* (Cambridge University Press, 2015), 7–9; Brenda Macdougall and Nicole St. Onge, "Rooted in Mobility: Metis Buffalo-Hunting Brigades," *Manitoba History* 71 (Winter 2013): 21–32; George Bryce, *The Romantic Settlement of Lord Selkirk's Colonists: The Pioneers of Manitoba* (Barse & Hopkins, 1910), 28.

51. Hogue, *Metis and the Medicine Line*, 22–25; Gerald Friesen, *The Canadian Prairies: A History* (University of Toronto Press, 2010), 80; Bryce, *Romantic Settlement*, 28.

52. Alexander Ross, *The Red River Settlement: Its Rise, Progress, and Present State* (Smith, Elder, 1856), 16; John M. Bumsted, *Lord Selkirk: A Life* (University of Manitoba Press, 2009), 58–60.

53. Rich, *History of Hudson's Bay Company*, 2:255–59; Bumsted, *Lord Selkirk*, 171–73, 182–87; John Johnston, "Memoir," Box 1, Schoolcraft Papers, LOC; John Johnston to George Johnston, November 9, 1816, Box 1, George Johnston Papers, Burton-DPL.

54. Quoted in Bryce, *Romantic Settlement*, 47, 88–89; Hogue, *Metis and Medicine Line*, 24–25.

55. Campbell, *North West Company*, 203–6; Bumsted, *Lord Selkirk*, 214, 229; Ross, *Red River Settlement*, 21–26.

56. Joseph James Hargrave, *Red River* (John Lovell, 1871), 167–68; Bryce, *Romantic Settlement*, 92–93; Bumsted, *Lord Selkirk*, 256–60; Masson, *Les bourgeois de la Compagnie*, 1:70–72.

57. Hartwell Bowsfield, "Grant, Cuthbert," DCB; Ross, *Red River Settlement*, 28–29; David Ricardo, ed., *Report of the Proceedings Connected with the Disputes Between the Earl of Selkirk and the North-West Company . . .* (Lane & Mower, 1819).

58. Robert Coutts and Richard Stewart, eds., *The Forks and the Battle of Seven Oaks in Manitoba History* (University of Manitoba Press, 1994), 12–18.

59. John Pritchard quoted in "Depositions Relating to Certain Transactions at

the Selkirk Settlement, 1815–1817," *Journal of the North Dakota Historical Society* 4 (1915): 369–436.

60. Deposition of Daniel McKenzie and Robert McRobb (1816), in *A Narrative of Occurrences in the Indian Countries of North America . . .* , ed. Samuel Wilcocke (B. McMillan, 1817), 82–87; Bumsted, *Lord Selkirk*, 311.

61. Bumsted, *Lord Selkirk*, 306–12.

62. John McLoughlin, *Letters of Dr. John McLoughlin: Written at Fort Vancouver, 1829–1832*, ed. Burt Brown Barker (Binfords & Mort, 1948), 1:xvi, xxiii–xxvii; Rich, *History of Hudson's Bay Company*, 2:385–89.

63. Gerhard J. Ens and Joe Sawchuk, *From New Peoples to New Nations: Aspects of Métis History and Identity from the Eighteenth to the Twenty-First Centuries* (University of Toronto Press, 2018), chap. 3; Hogue, *Metis and Medicine Line*, 25–26.

64. Pierre Chrysologue Pambrum, *Red River Report* (n.p., 1818); Frederick Merk, ed., *Fur Trade and Empire: George Simpson's Journal* (Harvard University Press, 1931), xxiii, xxxvi–xxxix, 37–40; Richard S. Mackie, *Trading Beyond the Mountains: The British Fur Trade on the Pacific, 1793–1843* (University of British Columbia Press, 1997), 64–66, 112–14; Ens, "Battle of Seven Oaks," 109–12.

65. David Peterson del Mar, "Intermarriage and Agency: A Chinookan Case Study," *Ethnohistory* 42, no. 1 (1995): 1–30; Robert Boyd, *People of the Dalles: The Indians of Wascopam Mission* (University of Nebraska Press, 2004), 319–21.

Chapter 4: "This Kind of Business Will Make Trouble"

1. John Francis McDermott, ed., *The Early Histories of St. Louis* (Missouri Historical Society, 1952); Thomas J. Scharf, *History of Saint Louis City and County from the Earliest Periods to the Present Day; Including Biographical Sketches of Representative Men* (Louis H. Everts, 1883), 1:83–87, 108–14.

2. U.S. Census, Donegal Township, Westmoreland County, Pa., 1800, Roll 41, p. 1038, Ancestry.com; "Riddle's First Ohio Militia, 1812–18," Reel 61, War of 1812 Service Records, Ancestry.com Operations, 1999; *Missouri Gazette*, June 10, 1815; James Monroe to Auguste Chouteau, March 11, 1815, Papers of the St. Louis Fur Trade, Part 1, MF 3057, Chouteau Collection, MHS.

3. Book of Baptisms, 4:36b, St. Louis Basilica Archives, New Orleans; Alan C. Trottman, "Lucien Fontenelle," in *Trappers of the Far West: Sixteen Biographical Sketches,* ed. LeRoy R. Hafen (University of Nebraska Press, 1983), 123–41.

4. Frederic L. Billon, ed., *Annals of St. Louis in Its Early Days Under the French and Spanish Dominations* (n.p., 1886); *Missouri Gazette*, July 26, 1808.

5. Troy Bickham, *The Weight of Vengeance: The United States, the British Empire, and the War of 1812* (Oxford University Press, 2012).

6. Charles R. Geisst, *Beggar Thy Neighbor: A History of Usury and Debt* (University of Pennsylvania Press, 2013), 139–48; Murray N. Rothbard, *The Panic of 1819: Reactions and Policies* (Columbia University Press, 1962), 14–47.

7. William K. Klingaman and Nicholas P. Klingaman, *The Year Without Summer: 1816 and the Volcano That Darkened the World and Changed History* (St. Martin's Press, 2013), 14–18, 338; Gregory Kushman, "Humboldtian Science, Creole Meteorology, and the Discovery of Human-Caused Climate Change in Northern South America," *Osiris* 26, no. 1 (2011): 19–44.

8. Klingaman and Klingaman, *Year Without Summer*, 133–39; William F. Gray, *Virginia Farmers' Almanack for 1817* (n.p., 1817).

9. Stephen Aron, *American Confluence: The Missouri Frontier from Borderland to Border* (Indiana University Press, 2006), 198–200.

10. Murphy, *Great Lakes Creoles*, 44–47; Jeffrey S. Adler, *Yankee Merchants and the Making of the Urban West: The Rise and Fall of Antebellum St. Louis* (Cambridge University Press, 1991), 14, 23–25.

11. Gitlin, *Bourgeois Frontier*, 133–36.

12. Patricia Cleary, *The World, the Flesh, and the Devil: A History of Colonial St. Louis* (University Missouri Press, 2011), 119; William E. Foley and David C. Rice, *The First Chouteaus: River Barons of Early St. Louis* (University of Illinois Press, 1983), 94; Carl J. Ekberg and Sharon K. Person, *St. Louis Rising: The French Regime of Louis St. Ange de Bellerive* (University of Illinois Press, 2015), 38–45.

13. Nicholas de Finiels, *An Account of Upper Louisiana*, ed. Carl J. Ekberg and William E. Foley (University of Missouri Press, 1989), 85–86.

14. Ora Brooks Peake, *A History of the United States Indian Factory System, 1795–1822* (Sage, 1954), 27–29; David A. Nichols, *Engines of Diplomacy: Indian Trading Factories and the Negotiation of American Empire* (University of North Carolina Press, 2016), 27–29, 132.

15. Tanis C. Thorne, *The Many Hands of My Relations: French and Indians on the Lower Missouri* (University of Missouri Press, 1996), 121–25; Emma S. Norman, *Governing Transboundary Waters: Canada, the United States, and Indigenous Communities* (Routledge, 2014), 36.

16. John D. Haeger, "Business Strategy and Practice in the Early Republic: John Jacob Astor and the American Fur Trade," *Western Historical Quarterly* 19, no. 2 (1988): 183–202; Adler, *Yankee Merchants*, 13–16.

17. Harvey L. Carter, "Andrew Drips," in *Mountain Men and Fur Traders of the Far West: Biographical Sketches*, ed. LeRoy R. Hafen, 10 vols. (Arthur H. Clark, 1963–73), 2:331–45; Hiram M. Chittenden, *The American Fur Trade of the Far West* (University of Nebraska Press, 1986), 1:149; Trottman, "Lucien Fontenelle," in Hafen, *Mountain Men*, 2:81–82; "Labor

Contract Between the Missouri Company and Thomas James, 1811," in Thomas James, *Three Years Among the Indians and Mexicans* (1845; reprint n.p., 2016), 270–75.

18. "Journal of Truteau on the Missouri River, 1794–1795," in *Before Lewis and Clark: Documents Illustrating the History of the Missouri, 1785–1804,* ed. A. P. Nasatir, 2 vols. (Missouri Historical Society, 1952), 1:260; Pierre Menard to Pierre Chouteau, April 21, 1810, in Chittenden, *American Fur Trade,* 3:897

19. James Monroe to John Calhoun, November 1, 1818, in Chittenden, *American Fur Trade,* 2:563; *St. Louis Enquirer,* October 17, 1818; Edwin James, *Account of an Expedition Under the Command of Major Stephen Long* (H.C. Carey & Lea, 1823), 1:18, 22–25.

20. Ann Fabian, *The Skull Collectors: Race, Science and America's Unburied Dead* (University of Chicago Press, 2010), 38–41; James, *Account of an Expedition,* 1:60–63.

21. J. C. Kammerer, "Largest Rivers in the United States," U.S. Geological Survey, rev. 1990, https://pubs.usgs.gov/of/1987/ofr87-242; Scharf, *History of Saint Louis,* 1:313; Phil E. Chappell, *A History of the Missouri River: Early Navigation and Craft Used; The Rise and Fall of Steamboating* (n.p., 1905), 18, 71.

22. Jeffrey N. Ostler, *Surviving Genocide: Native Nations and the United States from the American Revolution to Bleeding Kansas* (Yale University Press, 2019), 215–28; William Clark, "Estimate of the Indians, Fort Mandan Miscellany," in *The Definitive Journals of Lewis and Clark,* ed. Gary E. Moulton, 7 vols. (Bison Books, 2002), 3:404.

23. *Missouri Gazette,* April 23, 1810; *Missouri Gazette,* June 7, 1819.

24. Timothy Flint, *Recollections of the Last Ten Years, Passed in Occasional Residences and Journeying in the Valley of the Mississippi* (Cummings, Hilliard, 1826), 184; Gov. William Clark to Nicholas Boilvin, May 14, 1808, in Carter, *Territorial Papers of the United States,* 14:217.

25. Tai S. Edwards, *Osage Women and Empire: Gender and Power* (University of Kansas Press, 2018), 64–67; John Mack Faragher, *Daniel Boone: The Life and Legend of an American Pioneer* (Henry Holt, 1992), 313.

26. James, *Account of an Expedition,* 1:105, 128.

27. Ibid., 1:134–36; Robert J. Willoughby, *The Brothers Robidoux and the Opening of the American West* (University of Missouri Press, 2012), 46–63.

28. Chittenden, *American Fur Trade,* 2:573.

29. David J. Wishart, *The Fur Trade of the American West, 1807–1840: A Geographical Synthesis* (University of Nebraska Press, 1979), 42–46.

30. "Account of James Mackay, Trader 1798" and "John Evans Journal," in Nasatir, *Before Lewis and Clark,* 1:485–96; Walter B. Douglas, "Manuel Lisa," *Missouri Historical Society Collections* 3, no. 4 (1911): 393–97.

31. Alice C. Fletcher and Francis La Flesche, *The Omaha Tribe* (University of Nebraska Press, 1972), 40–46.

32. "Journal of Truteau on the Missouri River," in Nasatir, *Before Lewis and Clark*, 174–80; Richard Oglesby, *Manuel Lisa and the Opening of the Missouri Fur Trade* (University of Oklahoma Press, 1963), 153–55, 166–67; Thomas Biddle to Col. H. Atkinson, October 29, 1819, *American State Papers*, Senate, 16th Cong., 1st sess., Indian Affairs, 2:201–3.

33. Mary C. Wright, "Economic Development and Native American Women in the Early Nineteenth Century," *American Quarterly* 33, no. 5 (1981): 525–36; James, *Account of an Expedition*, 1:244–45, 247–49.

34. Thomas Forsyth to Lewis Cass, "Character of the Traders and History of the Trade" (report), October 24, 1833, Forsyth Papers, Box 2, MHS; Francis La Flesche, *The Osage Tribe: Rite of the Chiefs; Sayings of the Ancient Men* (USGPO, 1932), 61–67; Pekka Hämäläinen, *Lakota America: A New History of Indigenous Power* (Yale University Press, 2019), ix, 60–65.

35. Thorne, *Many Hands*, 46–47, 96–98; DuVal, *Native Ground*, 19, 78–79; Fletcher and La Flesche, *Omaha Tribe*, 201.

36. George E. Hyde, *The Pawnee Indians* (University of Oklahoma Press, 1951), 111–15; "Stephen Long," in *Early Western Travels, 1748–1846: A Series of Annotated Reprints . . .*, ed. Reuben Gold Thwaites (Arthur H. Clark, 1904–7), 15:94–95; William Whitman, *The Oto* (Columbia University Press, 1937), 18.

37. Zenas Leonard, *Narrative of the Adventures of Zenas Leonard* (D. W. Moore, 1839), 25–28; Richard E. Jensen, ed., "A Description of the Fur Trade in 1831 by John Dougherty," *Nebraska History* 56 (1975): 108–20.

38. Sarah White Smith, "1838 Diary, June 9," in *First White Women over the Rockies: Diaries, Letters, and Biographical Sketches*, ed. Clifford Drury (Arthur H. Clark, 1963), 3:84; Anna Lee Walters, *Talking Indian: Reflections on Survival and Writing* (Cornell University Press, 1985), 168–69; Alanson Skinner, "Ethnology of the Ioway Indians," *Bulletin of the Public Museum of Milwaukee* 5, no. 4 (1926): 208.

39. Thorne, *Many Hands*, 51–53, 60–62; Alice C. Fletcher, "The Sacred Pole of the Omaha Tribe," *American Antiquarian* 17, no. 5 (1895), 262–64; Hyde, *Pawnee Indians*, 172–77.

40. Alice C. Fletcher, *Tribal Structure; A Study of the Omaha and Cognate Tribes*, ed. Franz Boas and F. W. Hodge (G. E. Steichert, 1909); R. David Edmunds, *The Otoe-Missouria People* (University of Arizona Press, 1976), 3–6.

41. Clyde A. Milner, *With Good Intentions: Quaker Work Among the Pawnees, Otos and Omahas in the 1870s* (University of Nebraska Press, 1982), 120–21.

42. White, "The Woman Who Married a Beaver"; Lucy Eldersveld Murphy, "Women, Networks, and Colonization in Nineteenth-Century Wisconsin,"

in *Contours of a People: Metis Family, Mobility, and History*, ed. Nicole St. Onge, Carolyn Podruchny, and Brenda Macdougall (University of Oklahoma Press, 2012), 230–64.

43. James, *Account of an Expedition*, 1:184.

44. Ibid., 1:176–77.

45. Ibid., 1:189.

46. Mark William Kelly, *Lost Voices on the Missouri: John Dougherty and the Indian Frontier* (Sam Clark, 2013); Wishart, *Fur Trade of the American West*, 44–49.

47. George Catlin, *Letters and Notes on the Manners, Customs, and Condition of the North American Indians*, 2 vols. (Wiley & Putnam, 1844), 2:11, 122.

48. Murphy, *Great Lakes Creoles*, 41–46; Collette Hyman, *Dakota Women's Work: Creativity, Culture, and Exile* (Minnesota Historical Society, 2012), 23–27.

49. Landon Y. Jones, *William Clark and the Shaping of the West* (Oxford University Press, 2004), 221–29, 275; Jay H. Buckley, *William Clark, Indian Diplomat* (University of Oklahoma Press, 2008), 59.

50. Nichols, *Engines of Diplomacy*, 7–9, 11; Edward E. Hill, *The Office of Indian Affairs, 1824–1880* (Clearwater Publishing, 1974), 151–54.

51. Buckley, *William Clark*, 130–35; William Clark to John C. Calhoun, May 8, 1821, and May 28, 1822, Letters Received, Central Missouri Agency, RG 75, NARA; J. M. Opal, *Avenging the People: Andrew Jackson, the Rule of Law, and the American Nation* (Oxford University Press, 2017), 201–6.

52. An Act to Revise Trade and Intercourse Act, May 6, 1822, *U.S. Statutes at Large*, 3:678–80, Office of Federal Register, NARA.

53. *Missouri Gazette and Public Advisor*, January 18, 1823; Thomas Hempstead to Joshua Pilcher, February 12, 1823, in *The West of William H. Ashley, 1822–1838*, ed. Dale L. Morgan (Old West, 1964), 20–21.

54. Roger L. Nichols, "Backdrop for Disaster: Causes of the Arikara War of 1823," *South Dakota History* 14, no. 2 (1984): 93–113; William Ashley, letter, *Missouri Republican*, June 4, 1823; William Ashley to Benjamin O'Fallon and Henry Leavenworth, June 4, 1823, in Morgan, *West of Ashley*, 25–29.

55. William R. Nester, *The Arikara War: The First Plains Indian War* (Mountain Press, 2001), 129–47.

56. Thomas Jefferson to William Clark, August 17, 1808, in Carter, *Territorial Papers of the United States*, 14:220–25; Christopher Steinke, "'Here Is My Country': Too Né's Map of Lewis and Clark in the Great Plains," *William and Mary Quarterly* 71, no. 4 (2014): 589–610.

57. Charles Gratiot to John Jacob Astor, December 17, 1821, and February 8, 1823, MF 3059, Chouteau Collection, MHS.

58. Gitlin, *Bourgeois Frontier*, 101–2; Chittenden, *American Fur Trade*, 1:280–85.

59. David Lavender, *Fist in the Wilderness* (Doubleday, 1964), 347; Gen. William Clark, List of Claims, January 12, 1826, St. Louis Superintendency, Office of Indian Affairs, RG 75, NARA.

60. "Trading License," House Doc. no. 118, 1827, 19th Cong., 1st sess., Serial 136; Whitman, *Oto*, 14, 78; Fletcher and La Flesche, *Omaha Tribe*; Richard E. Jensen, "Bellevue: The First Twenty Years, 1822–1842," *Nebraska History* 56, no. 3 (1975): 339–74.

61. Charles Dunham, "Charles Bent," in Hafen, *Mountain Men*, 2:21; Grace Lee Nute, "The Papers of the American Fur Company: A Brief Estimate of Their Significance," *American Historical Review* 32, no. 3 (1927): 519–38.

62. Frances Fuller Victor, ed., *River of the West: The Adventures of Joe Meek* (R. W. Bliss, 1870), 50–51; Jon T. Coleman, *Here Lies Hugh Glass: A Mountain Man, a Bear, and the Rise of the American Nation* (Hill and Wang, 2012), 5–7.

63. James Kennerly, "James Kennerly Diary," ed. Edgar B. Wesley, *Missouri Historical Society Collections* 6, no. 1 (1928): 76–91; Lucien Fontenelle to Andrew Drips, 1828, Box 1, Drips Family Papers, MHS.

64. Chittenden, *American Fur Trade*, 1:262–67; Jacob Ferris, *The States and Territories of the Great West: Including Ohio, Indiana, Illinois, Missouri, Michigan, Wisconsin, Iowa, Minesota [sic], Kansas and Nebraska . . .* (E. F. Beadle, 1856).

65. William R. Swagerty, "Marriage and Settlement Patterns of Rocky Mountain Trappers and Traders," *Western Historical Quarterly* 11, no. 2 (1980): 159–80; Faragher, "Custom of the Country," 199–215; Warren Angus Ferris, *Life in the Rocky Mountains, 1830–1835*, ed. Paul C. Phillips (Old West, 1940), 7–10; Lucien Fontenelle to William Laidlaw, July 31, 1833, Box 1, Andrew Drips Papers, MHS.

66. Dale L. Morgan, *Jedediah Smith and the Opening of the West* (University of Nebraska Press, 1953), 188–92; *Missouri Observer and St. Louis Advertiser,* October 31, 1827.

67. Ramsay Crooks to Lewis Cass, November 19, 1830, Crooks-Astor Letterbooks, 1:202, American Fur Company Papers, NYPL; John D. Haeger, "Business Strategy and Practice in the Early Republic: John Jacob Astor and the American Fur Trade," *Western Historical Quarterly* 19, no. 2 (1988): 183–202.

68. J. P. Cabanne to Pierre Chouteau, Jr., October 14, 1828, MF 3063, Chouteau Collection, MHS; William J. Shallcross, *Romance of a Village: The Story of Bellevue* (Roncka Bros., 1954), 30.

69. Laura Ishiguro, "Northwestern North America to 1900," in *The Routledge Handbook of the History of Settler Colonialism*, ed. Edward Cavanagh and Lorenzo Veracini (Routledge, 2016), 125–28; James Belich, *Replenishing the Earth: The Settler Revolution and the Rise of the Anglo-World, 1783–1939* (Oxford University Press, 2009), 90–99.

Chapter 5: From the Sault to Oregon Country

1. John Johnston to Gov. Lewis Cass, October 20, 1819, Box 1, Schoolcraft Papers, LOC; Adam Bowett, *Woods in British Furniture-Making, 1400–1900: An Illustrated Historical Dictionary* (Royal Botanic Gardens, 2012).

2. Matthew Crow, "Atlantic North America from Contact to the Late Nineteenth Century," in Cavanagh and Veracini, *Routledge Handbook of History of Settler Colonialism*, 99–105; Saler, *Settlers' Empire*, 69–82.

3. Lavender, *Fist in the Wilderness*, 61–70; John Johnston to Peter Hager, November 14, 1817, Box 1, Schoolcraft Papers, LOC; John Johnston to George Johnston, July 11, 1818, Box 1, George Johnston Papers, Burton-DPL.

4. Edmund Jefferson Danziger, "'We Have No Spirit to Celebrate with You': Aboriginal Peoples of the Great Lakes Respond to Canadian and United States Policies During the Nineteenth Century," in *Lines Drawn upon the Water: First Nations and the Great Lakes Borders and Borderlands*, ed. Karl S. Hele (Wilfred Laurier University Press, 2008), 1–20.

5. Ramsay Crooks to George Johnston, December 10, 1818; and John Johnston to George Johnston, February 27, 1819, both in Box 1, George Johnston Papers, Burton-DPL.

6. John Johnston to George Johnston, January 15, 1817, Box 1, George Johnston Papers, Burton-DPL; Samuel Fletcher Cook, *Drummond Island: The Story of the British Occupation, 1815–1828* (Robert Smith, 1896) 79–81.

7. Invoice of Sundry Merchandise sold John Johnston Esq. at Michilmackinac, August 1, 1818, and John Johnston to George Johnston, December 27, 1819, both in Box 1, George Johnston Papers, Burton-DPL; Marriage Records, 1822–30, Chippewa County, Mich.; Jane Johnston to George Johnston, September 18, 1822; and John Johnston to family, November 1822, both in Box 1, George Johnston Papers, Burton-DPL.

8. Theresa M. Schenck, "The Cadots: The First Family of Sault Ste. Marie," *Michigan History* 72 (1988): 36–43; George's Coat of Arms, 1822, George Johnston Letterbook, University of Michigan, BHL.

9. "Lawrence Schoolcraft," in *Appleton's Cyclopaedia of American Biography*, ed. John Fiske and James Grant Wilson (D. Appleton, 1900), 5:442; "Henry Schoolcraft Insolvency Papers," Oneida County Records Center, Utica, N.Y.; Schoolcraft, *Personal Memoirs*, 39–44; William Ficklin to Henry Schoolcraft, March 21, 1820, Box 1, Schoolcraft Papers, LOC.

10. Henry Schoolcraft, Ledger Book, April 1820, Box 1, Schoolcraft Papers, LOC; Academy of Natural Sciences in Philadelphia to Henry Schoolcraft, April 28, 1820, Box 1, Schoolcraft Papers, LOC; Henry Rowe Schoolcraft, *Journal of a Tour into the Interior of Missouri and Arkansaw, from Potosi*

(Sir Richard Phillips, 1821), 7, 14, 43–45; Lewis Cass to John C. Calhoun, November 18, 1819, in *American State Papers* (USGPO, 1834), 2:31.

11. Schoolcraft, *Personal Memoirs*, 49; 40–59; David S. Heidler and Jeanne T. Heidler, eds., *Encyclopedia of the War of 1812* (ABC-CLIO, 1997), 83–84; Andrew C. McLaughlin, *Lewis Cass* (Houghton Mifflin, 1891), 345–46.

12. Richard G. Bremer, "Henry Rowe Schoolcraft: Explorer," *Michigan Historical Review* 12, no. 1 (1986): 40–59.

13. Henry Rowe Schoolcraft, *Narrative Journal of Travels Through the Northwestern Regions of the United States Under Governor Cass in the Year 1820* (E. and E. Hosford, 1821), xxi–xxx; Saler, *Settlers' Empire*, 110–18.

14. Phil Bellfy, "Cross-Border Treaty-Signers: The Anishnaabeg of the Lake Huron Borderlands," in Hele, *Lines Drawn upon the Water*, 21–42; Schoolcraft, *Narrative Journal*, 130–32.

15. David Bates Douglass, *American Voyageur: The Journal of David Bates Douglass*, ed. Sydney W. Jackman and John F. Freeman (Northern Michigan University Press, 1969), 21, 61–64; Schoolcraft, *Narrative Journal*, 139–40.

16. Lewis Cass to secretary of war, June 17, 1820, in Carter, *Territorial Papers of the United States*, 11:36–37.

17. Bremer, "Henry Rowe Schoolcraft," 48–50; John C. Calhoun to Henry Schoolcraft, January 20, 1820; and Henry Schoolcraft to William H. Crawford, January 18, 1820, both in Box 1, Schoolcraft Papers, LOC.

18. Francis Paul Prucha, *American Indian Policy in the Formative Years: The Indian Trade and Intercourse Acts, 1790–1834* (University of Nebraska Press, 1970), 52–56; Kyhl Lyndgaard, "Landscapes of Removal and Resistance: Edwin James' Cross-Cultural Collaborations," *Great Plains Quarterly* 30, no. 1 (2010): 37–52.

19. Lewis Cass to Henry Schoolcraft, October 24, 1821, Box 1, Schoolcraft Papers, LOC; Schoolcraft, *Personal Memoirs*, 70–81, 87; Robert E. Bieder, *Science Encounters the Indian, 1820–1880: The Early Years of American Ethnology* (University of Oklahoma Press, 1986), 149–50.

20. Richard G. Bremer, *Indian Agent and Wilderness Scholar: The Life of Henry Rowe Schoolcraft* (Clarke Historical Library, 1987), 12–24.

21. Andrew McNab to Henry Schoolcraft, December 14, 1821; Maria Schoolcraft to Henry Schoolcraft, February 11, 1822; and Henry Schoolcraft to John Johnston, July 6, 1822, all in Box 2, Schoolcraft Papers, LOC; Schoolcraft, *Personal Memoirs*, 100.

22. Robert Dale Parker, *The Sound the Stars Make Rushing Through the Sky: The Writings of Jane Johnston Schoolcraft* (University of Pennsylvania Press, 2007), 18–22; John Johnston to David Trimble, June 12, 1822, Box 2, Schoolcraft Papers, LOC; Anna M. Johnstone, "Recollections of One of the Old Houses of the Soo," Founders and Pioneers, Bayliss Public Library, Sault St. Marie, Mich.; Henry Schoolcraft to Jane Johnston, January 9, 1823; Jane

Johnston to Henry Schoolcraft, January 9, 1823; and Henry Schoolcraft to C. C. Trowbridge, December 18, 1822, all in Box 2, Schoolcraft Papers, LOC; Maria Eliza Schoolcraft to Henry Schoolcraft, April 20, 1823, Box 3, Schoolcraft Papers, LOC; Konkle, *Writing Indian Nations*, 169–75.

23. "Notes on the Ojibwe language," in Henry Schoolcraft to Lewis Cass, November 1822, Box 2, Schoolcraft Papers, LOC; Schoolcraft, *Personal Memoirs*, 109.

24. Thomas Jefferson to Hendrick Apaumut, December 21, 1808, Founders Online, https://tinyurl.com/f43xmnas; John Demos, *The Heathen School: A Story of Hope and Betrayal and the Early Republic* (Knopf, 2014); Nicholas Guyatt, *Bind Us Apart: How Enlightened Americans Invented Racial Segregation* (Basic Books, 2016), 145–58.

25. George M. Marsden, *Fundamentalism and American Culture* (Oxford University Press, 2006), 49–50; Jeremiah Porter, "A Missionary in Early Sault Ste. Marie: Journal of Jeremiah Porter," ed. Lewis Beeson, *Michigan History Magazine* 38 (1954).

26. Keith R. Widder, "The Convergence of Native Religion, Roman Catholicism, and Evangelical Protestantism at Mackinaw Mission, 1823–1837," *Journal of Presbyterian History* 77, no. 3 (1999): 167–80; Jane Schoolcraft, "The Contrast, A Splenetic Effusion" (1823), Box 70–1, Schoolcraft Papers, LOC; Theresa M. Schenck, "Who Owns Sault Ste. Marie?," *Michigan Historical Review* 28, no. 1 (2002): 108–20.

27. James Doty to Henry Schoolcraft, October 22, 1822; Henry Schoolcraft to Lewis Cass, February 15, 1822; and Jane Johnston to Henry Schoolcraft, January 12 and February 9, 1823, all in Box 2, Schoolcraft Papers, LOC.

28. Schoolcraft, *Personal Memoirs*; James Doty to Henry Schoolcraft, October 25, 1822, Box 1, Schoolcraft Papers, LOC; Maria Schoolcraft to Henry Schoolcraft, March 24, 1823; Henry Schoolcraft to Jane Schoolcraft, April 24, 1824; Lewis Cass to Henry Schoolcraft, October 19, 1823; and B. F. Stickman to Henry Schoolcraft, January 1, 1824, all in Box 3, Schoolcraft Papers, LOC.

29. Jane Schoolcraft, "Pensive Hours" and "Lines to a Friend Asleep," Box 65, and R. M. Laird to Henry Schoolcraft, May 20, 1824, Box 3, all in Schoolcraft Papers, LOC; "Jane Johnston Schoolcraft," in Karen L. Kilcup, *Native American Women's Writing 1800–1924: An Anthology* (Blackwell, 2000), 57–69.

30. Jane Schoolcraft, "Absence No. 2, Neezhicka" (1825), Box 70–1, Schoolcraft Papers, LOC.

31. Brazer, *Harps upon the Willows*, 189; R. M. Laird to Henry Schoolcraft, May 20, 1824, Box 3, Schoolcraft Papers, LOC; Jeremy Mumford, "Mixed-Race Identity in a Nineteenth-Century Family: The Schoolcrafts of Sault Ste. Marie, 1824–27," *Michigan Historical Review* 25, no. 1 (1999): 1–23.

32. Theresa M. Schenck, *All Our Relations: Chippewa Mixed Bloods and the*

Treaty of 1837 (Centre for Rupert's Land Studies, 2010), 2; Carter, *Territorial Papers of the United States,* 11:256; Murphy, *Great Lakes Creoles,* 137–47.

33. Lewis Cass to Henry Schoolcraft, December 21, 1824, Box 4, Jane Schoolcraft to Henry Schoolcraft, January 12, 1825, Box 4, and John Johnston to Henry Schoolcraft, February 9, 1825, Box 5, all in Schoolcraft Papers, LOC.

34. Henry Schoolcraft to Samuel Conant, January 20, 1825, Box 4, and Lewis Cass to Henry Schoolcraft, February 1, 1825, Box 5, both in Schoolcraft Papers, LOC.

35. James Schoolcraft to Henry Schoolcraft, February 22, 1825, Box 5, Schoolcraft Papers, LOC; John Johnston to George Johnston, March 26, 1827, Box 2, George Johnston Papers, Burton-DPL.

36. Henry Schoolcraft to Lewis Cass, August 28, 1825, Box 6, Schoolcraft Papers, LOC; Letterbook, Sault Ste. Marie Agency, September–December 1825, Office of Indian Affairs, RG 75, NARA.

37. Schoolcraft, *Personal Memoirs,* 225–28; Letterbook, Sault Ste. Marie Agency, August–December 1826, Office of Indian Affairs, RG 75, NARA.

38. T. D. Bonner, *The Life and Adventures of James P. Beckwourth: Mountaineer, Scout, and Pioneer, and Chief of the Crow Nation of Indians* (Harper & Bros., 1856), 75; Victor, *River of the West,* 50–51.

39. Victor, *River of the West,* 50–51; Ferris, *Life in the Rocky Mountains,* 18.

40. Victor, *River of the West,* 81–86; Ferris, *Life in the Rocky Mountains,* 72–77.

41. William Benemann, *Men in Eden: William Drummond Stewart and Same-Sex Desire in the Rocky Mountain Fur Trade* (University of Nebraska Press, 2012), 189–203; Lois Halliday McDonald, *Fur Trade Letters of Francis Ermatinger* (Arthur H. Clark, 1980).

42. Peter Boag, *Re-Dressing America's Frontier Past* (University of California Press, 2011), 59–67; Bernard DeVoto, *Across the Wide Missouri* (Bonanza Books, 1947), 32–33.

43. Victor, *River of the West,* 67–69, 32–33; Andrew Drips to John P. Sarpy, July 27, 1832, Box 1, Andrew Drips Papers, MHS.

44. Washington Irving, *Adventures of Captain Bonneville* (1837), chap. 6; Ferris, *Life in the Rocky Mountains,* 141–42; 154–55; Victor, *River of the West,* 112–15.

45. Trottman, "Lucien Fontenelle," 123–41; Lucien Fontenelle to William Laidlaw, July 31, 1833, Box 1, Andrew Drips Papers, MHS.

46. Maximilian of Wied quoted in Hermann Josef Roth, "Maximilian Prinz zu Wied: Jaeger, Reisender, Naturforscher," *Fauna und Flora in Rheinland-Pfalz* (Gesellschaft für Naturschutz und Ornithologie, 1995); Paul Schach, "Maximilian, Prince of Wied (1782–1867): Reconsidered," *Great Plains Quarterly* 14, no. 1 (1994): 5–20.

47. John Dougherty to William Clark, September 20, 1832, Letters Received, Upper Missouri Agency, Office of Indian Affairs, RG 75, NARA.

48. Joseph B. Herring, *The Enduring Indians of Kansas: A Century and a Half of Acculturation* (University of Kansas Press, 1990), 2–3.

49. Henry Fontenelle, "Memories," *Bellevue Trader*, November 19, 1875; Charles J. Kappler, ed., *Indian Affairs: Laws and Treaties* (USGPO, 1904), 2:479; Judith A. Boughter, *Betraying the Omaha Nation, 1790–1916* (University of Oklahoma Press, 1998), 40–41.

50. John McLoughlin to governor and committee of HBC, October 6, 1825, in McLoughlin, *Letters of McLoughlin*, 1:1–8; Mackie, *Trading Beyond the Mountains*, 64–66, 112–14.

51. Merk, *Fur Trade and Empire*, xxi, xxxii.

52. T. C. Elliott, ed., "Journal of Alexander Ross—Snake Country Expedition, 1824," *Quarterly of the Oregon Historical Society* 14, no. 4 (1913): 366–85; T. C. Elliott, ed., "Peter Skene Ogden's Snake Country Journal," *Quarterly of the Oregon Historical Society* 10, no. 4 (1909): 331–65; Gloria Griffen Cline, *Peter Skene Ogden and the Hudson's Bay Company* (University of Oklahoma Press, 1980), 29; John Work, *The Snake Country Expedition of 1830–1831: John Work's Field Journal* (University of Oklahoma Press, 1971), xxi–xxii.

53. Robert Boyd, *The Coming of the Spirit of Pestilence: Introduced Infectious Diseases and Population Decline Among Northwest Coast Indians, 1774–1874* (University of Washington Press, 1999), 86–94; Rich, *History of Hudson's Bay Company*, 2:471–73, 658–59; Melinda Marie Jetté, *At the Hearth of the Crossed Races: A French-Indian Community in Nineteenth-Century Oregon, 1812–1859* (Oregon State University Press, 2015), 18–19.

54. Whaley, *Oregon and the Collapse of Illahee*, 83–87; John McLoughlin to deputy governor, August 10, 1828, in McLoughlin, *Letters of McLoughlin*, 1:68–70.

55. U.S. Census, 1850, Oregon Territory, Marion County, at 106; Hubert Howe Bancroft, "History of the Pacific Coast," in *The Works of Hubert Howe Bancroft*, 39 vols. (Bancroft, 1874–90), 27:571; John K. Townsend, "Narrative of a Journey Across the Rocky Mountains to the Columbia River, 1839," in Thwaites, *Early Western Travels*, vol. 21.

56. Rich, *History of Hudson's Bay Company*, 2:658–68; Townsend, "Narrative of a Journey," 21:148, 155; Nathaniel Wyeth to John McLoughlin, May 5, 1836, in Nathaniel Wyeth, *The Correspondence and Journals of Captain Nathaniel J. Wyeth*, ed. Frederick George Young (Oregon Historical Society, 1899), 176.

57. Alexandra Harmon, *Indians in the Making: Ethnic Relations and Indian Identities Around Puget Sound* (University of California Press, 2000); Cornelius J. Brosnan, *Jason Lee, Prophet of the New Oregon* (Macmillan, 1932), 2–5; "Letter—no. 48," in Catlin, *Letters and Notes on Manners*, 2:108–15.

58. Whaley, *Oregon and the Collapse of Illahee*, 99–103.

59. Daniel Lee and Joseph H. Frost, *Ten Years of Methodist Missions in Oregon 1834–1844* (J. Collard, 1844), 110–15; Brosnan, *Jason Lee*, 88.

60. Cyrus Shepherd, letter, *Zion's Herald* 6, October 28, 1835, 170.

61. Brosnan, *Jason Lee*, 68–72; Whaley, *Oregon and the Collapse of Illahee*, 108–9; Lee and Frost, *Ten Years*, 126–31; Robert J. Loewenberg, "New Evidence, Old Categories: Jason Lee as Zealot," *Pacific Historical Review* 47, no. 3 (1978): 343–36.

62. Jason Lee, "Diary of Rev. Jason Lee," *Quarterly of the Oregon Historical Society* 17 (June 1916): 91–93.

63. *Christian Advocate and Journal* 13, January 4, 1839, 77; *Zion's Herald* 9, December 19, 1838, 202.

64. Brosnan, *Jason Lee*, 103–7.

65. Robert Stuart to Henry Schoolcraft, August 20, 1826, Box 6, Schoolcraft Papers, LOC.

66. Henry Schoolcraft to George Johnston, September 30, 1826, Box 2, George Johnston Papers, Burton-DPL.

67. Henry Schoolcraft to Lewis Cass, April 28, 1827, Box 7, Schoolcraft Papers, LOC.

68. Jane Schoolcraft, "Sweet Willy," Box 66, Schoolcraft Papers, LOC; Schoolcraft, *Personal Memoir*, 262.

69. U.S. Indian Office, Michigan, 1836 Census of Ottawa and Chippewa Mixed Breeds; Henry Schoolcraft to Jane Schoolcraft, June 1828; and George Johnston to Henry Schoolcraft, May 22, 1827, both in Box 7, Schoolcraft Papers, LOC.

70. Henry Schoolcraft to George Johnston, May 23, 1829, Box 2, George Johnston Papers, Burton-DPL.

71. Henry Schoolcraft to Lewis Cass, September 1830, Box 9, Schoolcraft Papers, LOC.

72. George Johnston to Jane Schoolcraft, June 18, 1830; and George Johnston to William Johnston, September 9, 1830, both in Box 2, George Johnston Papers, Burton-DPL.

73. Henry Schoolcraft to Lewis Cass, October 10, 1828; and Petition of Susan Johnston to the Committee of Claims, March 2, 1830, both in Box 9, Schoolcraft Papers, LOC.

74. Saler, *Settlers' Empire*, 110–18; *The Life, Letters, and Speeches of Kah-Ge-Ga-Gah-Bowh, or G. Copway, Chief, Ojibway Nation* (S. W. Benedict, 1856); John P. Bowes, *Land Too Good for Indians: Northern Indian Removal* (University of Oklahoma Press, 2016), 11–13, 40–49; Saunt, *Unworthy Republic*, 63–80.

75. Anne F. Hyde, "The Blue Flower and the Account Book: Writing a History of Mixed-Blood Americans," *Pacific Historical Review* 85, no. 1 (2016): 1–22; Kappler, *Indian Affairs*, passim; Michael Witgen, "A Nation of Settlers: The Early American Republic and the Colonization of the Northwest Territory," *William and Mary Quarterly* 76, no. 3 (2019): 391–98.

76. Treaty with the Otoe and Missouri Tribe 1825, in Kappler, *Indian Affairs,* 2:256–57; Treaty with the Chippewa, etc., 1833, in Kappler, *Indian Affairs,* 2:403–5; "Testimony of Michel Cadotte, Jr.," January 4, 1841, File 4, Box 1, Charles F. X. Goldsmith Papers, Wisconsin Historical Society, Madison; Sarah A. Curtis, *Civilizing Habits: Women Missionaries and the Revival of French Empire* (Oxford University Press, 2010), 171–72.

77. Jacob van der Zee, "The Sac-Fox Half Breed Tract," *Iowa Journal of History and Politics* 13 (1915): 151–65; Schenck, *All Our Relations.*

78. Isaac Galland, "Dr. Galland's Account of the Half-Breed Tract," *Annals of Iowa* 10 (1912): 450–66; Kappler, *Indian Affairs,* 1:260–70.

Chapter 6: Forging Peace on the Southern Plains, 1821–1840

1. Sami Lakomäki, *Gathering Together: The Shawnee People Through Diaspora and Nationhood, 1600–1870* (Yale University Press, 2014), 6–8, 167–79; George Bird Grinnell, *The Cheyenne Indians: Their History and Ways of Life* (Yale University Press, 1923), 1:3–4.

2. Francis D. Haines, *The Buffalo: The Story of American Bison and Their Hunters from Prehistoric Times to the Present* (University of Oklahoma Press, 1995), 13, 47, 66–68; Dan Flores, *American Serengeti: The Last Big Animals of the Great Plains* (University of Kansas Press, 2016), 115–19; J. M. Baltimore, "In the Prime of the Buffalo," *Overland Monthly and Out West Magazine* 14, no. 83 (1889): 515–20.

3. Allen H. Bent, The Bent Family in America (D. Clapp & Son, 1900); "Relief to Citizens U.S. for Indian Depredations," House Doc. 38 [1832], 22nd Cong., 1st sess., Serial 217, at 29–31; Coleman, *Here Lies Hugh Glass,* 6, 45–48.

4. Lauren Brand, " 'Great Conceptions of Their Own Power': Native and U.S. Diplomacy in the Old Southwest," *Western Historical Quarterly* 47, no. 1 (2016): 261–81; Alice Baumgartner, "Massacre at Gracias a Dios: Violence on the Lower Rio Grande, 1821–1856," *Western Historical Quarterly* 52, no. 1 (2021): 35–58.

5. David D. Smits, "The Frontier Army and the Destruction of the Buffalo: 1865–1883," *Western Historical Quarterly* 25, no. 3 (1994): 312–38; Isaac Slater, *Slater's Royal National Commercial Directory of Manchester and Salford, with Their Vicinities* (Slater, 1879), 80, 103, 126; Donald Jackson, ed., *The Journals of Zebulon Montgomery Pike, with Letters and Related Documents* (University of Oklahoma Press, 1966), 2:343.

6. Waldo R. Wedel, "Environment and Native Subsistence Economies in the Central Great Plains," *Smithsonian Miscellaneous Collections* 101, no. 3 (USGPO, 1941), 15–18; Frederick C. Marryat, *The Travels and Adventures*

of Monsieur Violet, in California, Sonora, and Western Texas (George Routledge, 1843), 24.

7. Tom D. Dillehay, "Late Quaternary Bison Population Changes on the
Southern Plains," *Plains Anthropologist* 19, no. 65 (1974): 180–96; DeLay,
War of a Thousand Deserts, 54–60.

8. Kate L. Gregg, ed., *The Road to Santa Fe: The Journal and Diaries of George
Champlin Sibley, 1825–26* (University of New Mexico Press, 1952), 30–35;
Alpheus Hoyt Favour, *Old Bill Williams, Mountain Man* (University of
North Carolina Press, 1936), 69–71.

9. Ross Frank, *From Settler to Citizen: New Mexican Economic Development
and Creating a Vecino Society, 1750–1820* (University of California Press,
2000), 138–45; Josiah Gregg, *The Commerce of the Prairies*, ed. Max Moor-
head (University of Oklahoma Press, 1926), 10–15; Stephen G. Hyslop,
*Bound for Santa Fe: The Road to New Mexico and the American Conquest,
1806–1848* (University of Oklahoma Press, 2002), 109–12.

10. David Lavender, *Bent's Fort* (Doubleday, 1954), 104–106; Philip St. George
Cooke, *Scenes and Adventures in the Army; or, Romance of Military Life*
(Lindsay & Blakiston, 1859), 47–49.

11. Otis E. Young, *First Military Escort on the Santa Fe Trail, 1829* (Arthur H.
Clark, 1952), 173–84.

12. John Cabanne to Pierre Chouteau, Jr., September 16, 1825, in Morgan, *West
of Ashley*, 155–56; David Beyreis, *Blood in the Borderlands: Conflict, Kinship,
and the Bent Family* (University of Nebraska Press, 2020), 11–13.

13. Jose Agustin de Escudero, "Decree," in H. Bailey Carroll and J. Villasana
Haggard, eds., *Three New Mexico Chronicles* (Quivara Society, 1942), 19;
David J. Weber, *The Taos Trappers: The Fur Trade in the Far Southwest,
1540–1846* (University of Oklahoma Press, 1971), 57–58.

14. George Bird Grinnell, *The Fighting Cheyennes* (Charles Scribner's Sons,
1915), 74–78; Susan L. Johnson, *Writing Kit Carson: Fallen Heroes in a
Changing West* (University of North Carolina Press, 2020), 40–43; George
Bent to George Hyde, May 11, 1917, Folder 37, George Bent Letters, BRBM.

15. "List of Persons Naturalized, January 1, 1831, to November 30, 1831," Mexican Archives of New Mexico, New Mexico State Library, Santa Fe; *Missouri
Intelligencer*, September 29, 1832; Bent, *Bent Family in America*, 57–59.

16. Lavender, *Fist in the Wilderness*, 398–411; Janet LeCompte, "Gantt's Fort
and Bent's Picket Post," *Colorado Magazine* 41, no. 2 (1964): 111–26.

17. Elliott West, *The Contested Plains: Indians, Goldseekers, and the Rush to Colorado* (University of Kansas Press, 1998), 65–79; Pekka Hämäläinen, "The
Western Comanche Trade Center: Rethinking the Plains Indian Trade System," *Western Historical Quarterly* 29, no. 4 (1998): 485–513; Phyllis S. Morgan, *As Far as the Eye Could Reach: Accounts of Animals Along the Santa Fe
Trail, 1821–1880* (University of Oklahoma Press, 2015), xv, 11–13.

18. Edward Adamson Hoebel, *The Cheyenne Way: Conflict and Case Law in Primitive Jurisprudence* (University of Oklahoma Press, 1941), 99–100; Jerome A. Greene, *Washita: The U.S. Army and the Southern Cheyennes* (University of Oklahoma Press, 2004), 9, 27.

19. John H. Moore, *The Cheyenne* (Blackwell, 1996), 104–107; George Bird Grinnell, *The Cheyenne Indians, Their History and Ways of Life*, 2 vols. (Yale University Press, 1915), 1:38–39, 2:8–11; George Bent to George Hyde, October 18, 1908, Folder 10, George Bent Letters, BRBM.

20. James F. Brooks, *Captives and Cousins: Slavery, Kinship, and Community in the Southwest Borderlands* (University of North Carolina Press, 2002), 211–21; Jacob Fowler, *The Journal of Jacob Fowler*, ed. Elliott Coues (University of Nebraska Press, 1970), 65.

21. Joaquín Rivaya-Martínez, "A Different Look at Native American Depopulation: Comanche Raiding, Captive Taking, and Population Decline," *Ethnohistory* 61, no. 3 (2014): 391–418; Grinnell, *Cheyenne Indians*, 1:268–70.

22. John Stands In Timber and Margot Liberty, *Cheyenne Memories* (Yale University Press, 1998), 87; Peter J. Powell, *Sweet Medicine: Continuing Role of the Sacred Arrows, the Sun Dance, and the Sacred Buffalo Hat in Northern Cheyenne History* (University of Oklahoma Press, 1998), 4–5, 19–20; Silverman, *Thundersticks*, 11.

23. Anne F. Hyde, *Empires, Nations, and Families: A New History of the North American West, 1800–1860* (Ecco, 2012), 147–53; Beyreis, *Blood in the Borderlands*, 23–30.

24. LeCompte, "Gantt's Fort and Bent's Picket Post," 111–26; Pekka Hämäläinen, *The Comanche Empire* (Yale University Press, 2008), 161–65; William S. Kiser, *Borderlands of Slavery: The Struggle over Captivity and Peonage in the American Southwest* (University of Pennsylvania Press, 2017), 17–19, 31–38.

25. George E. Hyde, *Life of George Bent: Written from His Letters*, ed. Savoie Lottinville (University of Oklahoma Press, 1968), 60–62.

26. George Bent to George Hyde, February 15, 1905, Box 1, George Bent Letters, HC; Hyde, *Life of George Bent*, 50–51.

27. Hyde, *Life of George Bent*, 51–53; Donald J. Berthrong, *The Southern Cheyennes* (University of Oklahoma Press, 1963), 76–80; George A. Dorsey, "How the Pawnee Captured the Cheyenne Medicine Arrows," *American Anthropologist* 5, no. 4 (1903): 644–58.

28. Douglas C. Comer, *Ritual Ground: Bent's Old Fort, World Formation, and the Annexation of the Southwest* (University of California Press, 1996), 19–20; DeLay, *War of a Thousand Deserts*, 55–59; Hämäläinen, *Comanche Empire*, 167.

29. LeCompte, "Gantt's Fort and Bent's Picket Post," 111–26.

30. David Fridtjof Halaas and Andrew E. Masich, *Halfbreed: The Remarkable*

True Story of George Bent—Caught Between the Worlds of the Indian and the White Man (Da Capo Press, 2004), 25–26.

31. Lavender, *Bent's Fort*, 188; Grinnell, *Cheyenne Indians*, 1:131–45.

32. Halaas and Masich, *Halfbreed*, 26–27; Elliott West, *The Way to the West: Essays on the Central Plains* (University of New Mexico Press, 1995), 107–10; H. L. Lubbers, "William Bent's Family and the Indians of the Plains," *Colorado Magazine* 13, no. 1 (1936): 19–23.

33. LeRoy R. Hafen, ed., "The W. M. Boggs Manuscript About Bent's Fort, Kit Carson, the Far West and Life Among the Indians," *Colorado Magazine* 7, no. 2 (1930): 45–69.

34. Hyde, *Life of George Bent*, 71–73; "Medicine Arrows," Folder 459, George Bird Grinnell Papers, SM.

35. Dorsey, "How the Pawnee," 57–58; Hyde, *Life of George Bent*, 31–40.

36. Comer, *Ritual Ground*, 121; Silverman, *Thundersticks*, 222–23, 244–46; Richard Irving Dodge, *Our Wild Indians: Thirty-Three Years of Personal Experience Among the Red Men of the Great West* (A. D. Worthington, 1882), 36–45.

37. Grinnell, *Cheyenne Indians*, 1:71–74; West, *Contested Plains*, 88–90.

38. Alexander Barclay to Mary Barclay, February 13, 1836, and Alexander Barclay to George Barclay, July 20, 1838, both in George P. Hammond, ed., *The Adventures of Alexander Barclay, Mountain Man* (Old West, 1976).

39. Alexander Barclay to George Barclay, July 20, 1838, ibid.

40. W. S. Fitzpatrick, ed., *Treaties and Laws of the Osage Nation, as Passed to November 26, 1890* (Cedar Vale Commercial, 1895), 12–18; DuVal, *Native Ground*, 184–90; Louise Barry, "William Clark's Diary, May 1826–February 1831," *Kansas Historical Quarterly* 14, no. 1 (1948): 1–39; Kristen Tegtmeier Oertel, *Bleeding Borders: Race, Gender, and Violence in Pre–Civil War Kansas* (Louisiana State University Press, 2009), 16–17.

41. Moses Merrill to Henry Schoolcraft, January 23, 1833, Box 11, Schoolcraft Papers, LOC; Moses Merrill to Baptist Friends Association, April 10, 1833, and Moses Merrill to Rev. Lucius Bolles, September 2, 1834, both in MSS S-2189, Moses Merrill Papers, BRBM.

42. Moses Merrill to Rev. Lucius Bolles, September 2, 1834, and Moses Merrill to Rev. Lucius Bolles, April 1835, both in Moses Merrill Papers, BRBM.

43. John Montgomery, *Methodist Committee Report, Kaws, 1853*, Series A, File 4, Indian Mission Schools Collection, KSHS.

44. Kathryn Cook, *Hand in Hand: A Missionary Family Struggles to Develop Schools for American Indians* (Trafford, 2004), 37–40; Christiana Polke McCoy, "Account and Memoir, 1842," William Polke Family Papers, Lilly Library, Indiana University.

45. George Schultz, *Indian Canaan: Isaac McCoy and the Vision of an Indian*

State (University of Oklahoma Press, 1972), 108–12; Isaac McCoy, *History of Baptist Indian Missions: Embracing Remarks on the Former and Present Condition of the Aboriginal Tribes* (W. M. Morrison, 1832).

46. Lakomäki, *Gathering Together*, 177–80; Isaac McCoy, *The Annual Register of Indian Affairs Within the Indian (or Western) Territory* (n.p., 1835), 199.

47. McCoy, *Annual Register of Indian Affairs*, 58, 77; Ostler, *Surviving Genocide*, app. 2.

48. McCoy, *Annual Register of Indian Affairs*, 74–75; C. A. Harris, January 9, 1837, in *Report of the Commissioner of Indian Affairs, 1837* (USGPO, 1837).

49. "A Brief Sketch of Abelard Guthrie," in *The Provisional Government of Nebraska Territory*, ed. William E. Connelley (Nebraska State Historical Society, 1899), 101–52.

50. Supt. Lewis Cass to Comms. Stokes, Carroll, and Vaux, July 14, 1832, in Letterbook 9:32–35, Office of Indian Affairs, RG 75, NARA; Lt. Col. James B. Many to Colonel Arbuckle, July 4, 1833, quoted in Grant Foreman, *Fort Gibson: A Brief History* (Arthur H. Clark, 1936), 34.

51. DeLay, *War of a Thousand Deserts*, 65–68; Catlin, *Letters and Notes on Manners*, 2:466.

52. Dodge quoted in *Niles Weekly Register* 48 (1834): 74; Fred S. Perrine, ed., "The Journal of Hugh Evans, Covering the First and Second Campaigns of the United States Dragoon Regiment in 1834 and 1835," *Chronicles of Oklahoma* 3 (September 1925): 175–215.

53. James Mooney, *Calendar History of the Kiowa Indians* (Smithsonian, 1898), 273–74; DeLay, *War of a Thousand Deserts*, 78–79; Beyreis, *Blood in the Borderlands*, 38–43.

54. Comm. Hugh McLeod, *Report of the Council House Fight, March 1840*, Journal, Fifth Legislature, Republic of Texas, cited in H. W. Brands, *Lone Star Nation: The Epic Story of the Battle for Texas Independence* (Doubleday, 2004), 490; Hämäläinen, *Comanche Empire*, 216.

55. Rupert Norval Richardson, *The Comanche Barrier to South Plains Settlement* (Arthur H. Clark, 1933); 85–97, app. 2.

56. Gary Clayton Anderson, *The Conquest of Texas: Ethnic Cleansing in the Promised Land, 1820–1875* (University of Oklahoma Press, 2005), 181–85; Powell, *Sweet Medicine*, 1:54.

57. Hämäläinen, *Comanche Empire*, 165–66; West, *Contested Plains*, 77; Stan Hoig, *The Western Odyssey of John Simpson Smith, Frontiersman, Trapper, Trader, and Interpreter* (Arthur H. Clark, 1974), 40–44.

58. Joyce Szabo, *Howling Wolf and the History of Ledger Art* (University of New Mexico Press, 1994); Janet Lecompte, "Bent and St. Vrain Among the Kiowa and Comanche," *Colorado Magazine* 49, no. 4 (1972): 282–85.

Chapter 7: Rivers of Trouble in Indian Country, 1831–1843

1. David J. Wishart, *An Unspeakable Sadness: The Dispossession of the Nebraska Indians* (University of Nebraska Press, 1994), 78–79; Moses Merrill, "Extracts from the Diary of Rev. Moses Merrill, Missionary to the Otoe Indians, 1832–1840," *Nebraska Historical Society Transactions* 4 (1892): 157–91; Clyde D. Dollar, "The High Plains Smallpox Epidemic of 1837–38," *Western Historical Quarterly* 8, no. 1 (1977): 15–38.

2. Orville Dewey, *A Sermon on the Moral Uses of the Pestilence, Denominated Asiatic Cholera: Delivered on Fast-Day, August 9, 1832* (Benjamin T. Congdon, 1832); Ramon Powers and James N. Leiker, "Cholera Among the Plains Indians: Perceptions, Causes, Consequences," *Western Historical Quarterly* 29, no. 3 (1998): 317–40.

3. Dollar, "High Plains Smallpox Epidemic," 22–25; Fenn, *Pox Americana*, 16–19; John Dougherty to William Clark, October 9, 1837, William Clark Papers, Records of the Superintendent of Indian Affairs, vol. 6, KSHS.

4. Lucille H. Campey, *Ignored but Not Forgotten: Canada's English Immigrants* (Dundurn, 2014), 28–29, 55; Marjorie Kohli, *The Golden Bridge: Young Immigrants to Canada, 1833–1939* (Natural Heritage, 2003), 13–18.

5. James Joseph Buss, *Winning the West with Words: Language and Conquest in the Lower Great Lakes* (University of Oklahoma Press, 2011), 53–61; Stephen Kantrowitz, "White Supremacy, Settler Colonialism, and the Two Citizenships of the Fourteenth Amendment," *Journal of the Civil War Era* 10, no. 1 (2020): 29–53.

6. Thorne, *Many Hands*, 196–204; William Unrau, *Indians, Alcohol, and the Roads to Taos and Santa Fe* (University of Kansas Press, 2013), 13–18, 44–61, 101; John Dougherty to William Clark, September 22, 1830, William Clark Papers, Records of the Superintendent of Indian Affairs, vol. 6, KSHS; William Clark to John Dougherty, June 6, 1836, Letters Received, Council Bluffs Agency, Office of Indian Affairs, M234, R215, RG 75, NARA.

7. William L. Sublette to Robert Campbell, November 2, 1835, Robert Campbell Family Papers, MHS; Merrill J. Mattes, "The Sutler's Store at Fort Laramie," *Annals of Wyoming* 18, no. 2 (1946): 102–13; Hugh M. Lewis, *Robidoux Chronicles: French-Indian Ethnoculture of the Trans-Mississippi West* (Trafford, 2004), 136.

8. Marilyn Irvin Holt, "Joined Forces: Robert Campbell and John Dougherty as Military Entrepreneurs," *Western Historical Quarterly* 30, no. 2 (1999): 183–202; Alfred Jacob Miller quoted in DeVoto, *Across the Wide Missouri*, 313.

9. Marriage Records, 1856–67, Falls City, Neb.; J. Sterling Morton, *Illustrated History of Nebraska: A History of Nebraska from the Earliest Explorations of the Trans-Mississippi Region*, 3 vols. (University of Nebraska Press, 1911),

1:71–72; DeSmet, *Life, Letters and Travels,* 5:14, 157; Trottman, "Lucien Fontenelle," 2:123–41.

10. William R. Swagerty, "A View from the Bottom Up: The Work Force of the American Fur Company in the 1830s," *Montana: Magazine of Western History* 43, no. 1 (1993): 18–33.

11. Andrew Drips to John Sarpy, July 1832, Box 1, Andrew Drips Papers, MHS; Sarpy's Ledger Book 1832–1837, American Fur Company, MHS; Morton, *Illustrated History of Nebraska,* 1:71–72; Receipt for tuition, St. Joseph's Academy 1841, Box 3, Andrew Drips Papers, MHS.

12. Edmunds, *Otoe-Missouria People,* 3–7; Treaty of Prairie du Chien (1830) in Kappler, *Indian Affairs,* 2:305; William and Ann Cluck to Catherine Drips, "40 Acres of Land for $300," May 10, 1841, Folder 1819–1859, Drips Family Papers, BL.

13. An Act to Regulate Trade and Intercourse with the Indian Tribes, *U.S. Statutes at Large, 1834,* 4:729, Office of Federal Register, NARA.

14. Hyde, *Empires, Nations, and Families,* 31–50; "Noel pere and of Tonpapai," baptismal register, St. Ferdinand's Church, Florissant, Mo.

15. Craig Miner and William Unrau, *The End of Indian Kansas: A Study of Cultural Revolution, 1854–1871* (University of Kansas Press, 1977), 4–14; Franklin G. Adams, ed., "Reminiscences of Frederick Chouteau," *Transactions of the Kansas State Historical Society* 8 (1904): 428.

16. James A. Hanson, "The Myth of the Silk Hat and the End of the Rendezvous," in Sleeper-Smith, *Rethinking the Fur Trade,* 420–38.

17. Tiya Miles, *The Dawn of Detroit: A Chronicle of Slavery and Freedom in the City on the Straits* (New Press, 2017), 6–15, 75–78; M. Lilliana Owens, "The Early Work of the Lorettines in Southeastern Kansas," *Kansas Historical Quarterly* 15, no. 3 (1947): 263–76; Margaret Jackson Drips and Andrew Jackson Drips, 1841, Marriage Records, 1841–1900, Missouri State Archives, Jefferson City; Andrew Drips to Peter Sarpy, August 3, 1844, Box 1, Andrew Drips Papers, MHS; Jane Drips to Catherine Drips, Bill of sale for "Frank," July 18, 1843, Drips Family Papers, BL.

18. Charles C. Spaulding, *Annals of the City of Kansas: Embracing Full Details of the Trade and Commerce of the Great Western Plans* (Van Horn & Abeel, 1858), 20.

19. Willoughby, *Brothers Robidoux,* 184.

20. Amanda Raster and Christina Gish Hill, "The Dispute over Wild Rice: An Investigation of Treaty Agreements and Ojibwe Food Sovereignty," *Agriculture and Human Values* 34, no. 2 (2017): 267–81; Edward Ermatinger and Francis Ermatinger, *Fur Trade Letters of Francis Ermatinger: Written to His Brother Edward During His Service with the Hudson's Bay Company, 1818–1853* (Arthur H. Clark, 1980).

21. Maureen Konkle, "Recovering Jane Schoolcraft's Cultural Activism in the

Nineteenth Century," *The Oxford Handbook of Indigenous American Literature*, ed. James H. Cox and Daniel Heath Justice (Oxford University Press, 2014), 81–100; Samuel L. Longley to Henry Schoolcraft, December 2, 1830, Box 10, Schoolcraft Papers, LOC; Schoolcraft, *Personal Memoirs*, 341.

22. Anna Maria Johnston to James Schoolcraft, January 6, 1831; and Henry Schoolcraft to James Schoolcraft, February 2, 1831, both in Box 10, Schoolcraft Papers, LOC.

23. Robert Stuart to Henry Schoolcraft, January 31, 1831; Henry Schoolcraft to James Schoolcraft, February 2, 1831; and Jane Schoolcraft to Henry Schoolcraft, February 16, 1831, all in Box 10, Schoolcraft Papers, LOC; Christine R. Cavalier, "Jane Johnston Schoolcraft's Sentimental Lessons: Native Literary Collaboration and Resistance," *MELUS* 38, no. 1 (2013): 98–118.

24. James Schoolcraft to James Allen, January 5, 1832, Box 10, Schoolcraft Papers, LOC.

25. U.S. Census, 1830, Chippewa County, Michigan Territory; Baptism and Marriage Records, St. Ann Parish, 1691–1834, Mackinac, Mich.; Jane Schoolcraft, Elmwood Diary, June 1829, Box 8, and Jane Schoolcraft to Henry Schoolcraft, February 16, 1831, Box 10, both in Schoolcraft Papers, LOC; Jane Schoolcraft, "The Contrast," in *The Sound the Stars Make Rushing Through the Sky: The Writings of Jane Johnston Schoolcraft*, ed. Robert Dale Parker (University of Pennsylvania Press, 2007).

26. Saunt, *Unworthy Republic*, 53–65; Saler, *Settlers' Empire*, 116–18; Bowes, *Land Too Good for Indians*, 123–31.

27. Schoolcraft, *Personal Memoirs*, 244–48.

28. Henry Schoolcraft, "Chart of the Trading Posts for the Chippewa, Within the Limits of the Agency of Sault St. Marie," November 1, 1832, Box 11, Schoolcraft Papers, LOC; Flatmouth's Speech, July 17, 1832, quoted in Warren, *History of Ojibways*, 478–81; Schoolcraft, *Personal Memoirs*, July 20, 1832; Gary Clayton Anderson, *Kinsmen of Another Kind: Dakota-White Relations in the Upper Mississippi Valley, 1650–1862* (University of Nebraska Press, 1984), 385–87.

29. Andrew R. Graybill, *The Red and the White: A Family Saga of the American West* (Liveright, 2013), 81–84; George Johnston to Rev. Henry Kearney, September 1832; and George Johnston to Henry Schoolcraft, May 22, 1832, both in Box 2, George Johnston Papers, Burton-DPL; Henry Schoolcraft to Jane Johnston Schoolcraft, June 15, 1832, Box 10, and William Johnston to Jane Johnston Schoolcraft, July 18, 1833, Box 11, both in Schoolcraft Papers, LOC.

30. Articles Purchased by E. S. Trowbridge for Mrs. Henry Schoolcraft, October 4, 1832, Box 10; Jane Schoolcraft to Henry Schoolcraft, September 22, 1833, Box 11, both in Schoolcraft Papers, LOC.

31. Jane Schoolcraft to Henry Schoolcraft, March 12, 1834, Box 13, School-

craft Papers, LOC; A. Irving Hallowell, *Contributions to Ojibwe Studies: Essays, 1934–1972*, ed. Jennifer S. H. Brown and Susan E. Gray (University of Nebraska Press, 2010), 452–56; Christopher Vecsey, *Traditional Ojibwa Religion and Its Historical Changes* (American Philosophical Society, 1983), 121, 138.

32. Anna Maria Johnston to Jane Schoolcraft, January 4, 1834; and James Schoolcraft to Henry Schoolcraft, February 9, 1834, both in Box 13, Schoolcraft Papers, LOC.

33. William McMurray to Jane and Henry Schoolcraft, February 11, 1834; James Schoolcraft to Henry Schoolcraft, March 1, 1834 ; James Schoolcraft to Henry Schoolcraft, February 27, 1834; William McMurray to Henry Schoolcraft, March 10, 1834; and Jane Schoolcraft to Charlotte McMurray, March 4, 1834, all in Box 13, Schoolcraft Papers, LOC.

34. Lewis Cass to Henry Schoolcraft, April 15, 1833; George Johnston, Report for Quarterly Supplies from Fort Brady, January 1–March 31, 1833, Box 12, Schoolcraft Papers, LOC.

35. George Johnston to Henry Schoolcraft, July 2 and 18, 1834, Box 13, Schoolcraft Papers, LOC; George Johnston, "Statement of Particulars of Occurrences at the Office of Indian Affairs, 4th October, 1834 Michilimackinac," Box 3, George Johnston Papers, Burton-DPL.

36. James Schoolcraft to Henry Schoolcraft, August 23 and November 2, 1834, Box 13, Schoolcraft Papers, LOC; George Johnston to Irish relative, January 8, 1834, Box 3, George Johnston Papers, Burton-DPL; James Schoolcraft to George Johnston, December 30, 1834, Box 13, Schoolcraft Papers, LOC.

37. James R. Gibson, *Farming the Frontier: The Agricultural Opening of the Oregon Country, 1786–1846* (University of Washington Press, 1986), 78.

38. Sarah Ogden to Eva Maria Dye, 1890, Eva Emery Dye Papers, OHS; Jack Nisbet, *The Mapmaker's Eye: David Thompson and the Columbia Plateau* (Washington State University Press, 2005), 36–38; "Arrangements of the Proprietors, Clerks, Interpreters, and etc. in 1799 for the Northwest Company," in Masson, *Les bourgeois de la Compagnie*, 1:62; "Umfreville/Umphreville . . . ," Red River Métis Genealogies, n.d., *Mothers of the Resistance 1869–1870*, https://resistancemothers.wordpress.com/about/umfreville.

39. John B. Horner, *Days and Deeds in the Oregon Country* (Binfords & Mort, 1928); Hubert Howe Bancroft, *History of Oregon* (Bancroft, 1886), 318; Francis Norbert Blanchet, *Historical Sketches of the Catholic Church in Oregon, During the Past Forty Years* (n.p., 1878), 37–39.

40. U.S. Census, Marion County, Oregon Territory, 1850, Roll M432, at 101B; Fort Nisqually Journal of Occurrences, January 20, 1846–April 30, 1847, Hudson's Bay Collection, HL.

41. Herman J. Viola, "The Wilkes Expedition on the Pacific Coast," *Pacific Northwest Quarterly* 80, no. 1 (1989): 21–31.

42. John McLoughlin to governor and committee, HBC, June 1839 and November 1840, in McLoughlin, *Letters of McLoughlin*, 2d ser.; Sam Walter Haynes, *James K. Polk and the Expansionist Impulse* (Oxford University Press, 2002), 15–22.

43. J. Q. Thornton, *History of the Provisional Government of Oregon* (E. M. Waite, 1874); Jetté, *At the Hearth*, 139–43, 229.

44. J. C. Frémont, *Report of the Exploring Expedition to the Rocky Mountains in the Year 1842 andd to Oregon and North California in the Years 1843–44* (USGPO, 1845), 9–11; T. Hartley Crawford to Andrew Drips, Letter of Commission, September 8, 1842, Office of Indian Affairs, War Department, RG 75, NARA; Unrau, *Indians, Alcohol*, 62–68.

45. An Act to Regulate Trade and Intercourse with the Indian Tribes, Section 10, Section 30, *U.S. Statutes at Large, 1834*, Office of Federal Register, NARA; Branko Milanovic, Peter H. Lindert, and Jeffrey G. Williamson, "Pre-Industrial Inequality," *Economic Journal* 121, no. 551 (2011): 255–72; "Prices, Incomes, and Economic Wellbeing Around the World Before 1950," Global Price and Income History Group, University of California–Davis, http://gpih.ucdavis.edu.

46. "Articles of Agreement Between John Jewett and Drips, Interpreter at Fort Pierre," September 5, 1843, Drips Family Papers, BL.

47. T. Hartley Crawford to Andrew Drips, Letter of Commission, September 8, 1842, Office of Indian Affairs, War Department, RG 75, NARA; D. D. Mitchell to Maj. Andrew Drips, October 6, 1842, St. Louis Superintendency, Office of Indian Affairs, War Department, RG 75, NARA.

48. James Illingsworth to Andrew Drips, February 1, 1842; H. Picotte to Andrew Drips, March 25, 1842; and Andrew Drips to Maj. D. D. Mitchell, January 2, 1843, all in Box 2, Andrew Drips Papers, MHS; Andrew Drips to D. D. Mitchell, January 22, 1844, Drips Family Papers, BL; Unrau, *Indians, Alcohol*, 67–68, 74.

49. Miner and Unrau, *End of Indian Kansas*, 4–14; Thorne, *Many Hands*, 149–59; Berlin Basil Chapman, *The Otoes and Missourias: A Study of Indian Removal and the Legal Aftermath* (University of Oklahoma Press, 1965), 40–47.

50. Bethany R. Berger, "Red: Racism and the American Indian," *UCLA Law Review* 56, no. 3 (2009): 591–656; Stephanie Gamble, "Capital Negotiations: Native Diplomats in Washington," Johns Hopkins Ph.D. diss., 2014, 105–9; Faye Yarbrough, *Race and the Cherokee Nation: Sovereignty and the Nineteenth Century* (University of Pennsylvania Press, 2008), 30–38; Saunt, *Unworthy Republic*, 67–70.

51. George Fitzhugh, "Acquisition of Mexico-Filibustering," *De Bow's Review* 25, no. 6 (1858); Rachel St. John, "Contingent Continent: Spatial and Geographic Arguments in the Shaping of the Nineteenth-Century United States," *Pacific Historical Review* 86, no. 1 (2017): 18–49.

52. Theodore J. Karamanski, *Fur Trade and Exploration: Opening the Far Northwest, 1821–1852* (University of Oklahoma Press, 1983), 144; Margaret Arnett MacLeod, "Dickson the Liberator," *Beaver,* no. 287 (Summer 1956): 4–7.

53. George Johnston to Rev. Henry Kearny, November 15, 1835; and William Johnston to George Johnston, July 6, 1836, both in Box 3, George Johnston Papers, Burton-DPL.

54. M. E. Arthur, "General Dickson and the Indian Liberating Army in the North," *Ontario History* 62 (1970): 151–62.

55. Gen. Robert Dickson to Col. George Johnston, September 6, 1836, Box 3, George Johnston Papers, Burton-DPL; William Nourse to John Siveright, September 15, 1836, quoted in Grace Lee Nute, "James Dickson: A Filibuster in Minnesota in 1836," *Missouri Valley Historical Review* 10, no. 2 (1923): 127–40.

56. William McMurray to George Johnston, July 30, 1836, Box 3, George Johnston Papers, Burton-DPL.

57. Gen. Robert Dickson to Col. George Johnston, September 6, 1836, Box 3, George Johnston Papers, Burton-DPL.

58. Ibid.; Nute, "James Dickson," 134.

59. Grace Lee Nute, ed., "Diary of Martin McLeod," in *Minnesota History Bulletin* 4 (1921–22): 351–439.

60. Entries for October 10 and 12, 1836, ibid.; *Detroit Daily Advertiser,* August 23, 1836.

61. William Johnston to George Johnston, December 20, 1836; James Schoolcraft to George Johnston, October 7, 1836, Box 3, George Johnston Papers, Burton-DPL.

62. John Dougherty to William Clark, August 8, 1837, John Dougherty to Pierre Chouteau, July 7, 1837, Box 1, 1823–1849, John Dougherty Papers, RG 3902, AM, NHS.

63. Warren, *History of Ojibways,* 483–84; Schoolcraft, *Personal Memoirs,* 592, 604; Hogue, *Metis and the Medicine Line,* 44–47.

64. Michel Ducharme, "Closing the Last Chapter of the Atlantic Revolution: The 1837–38 Rebellions in Upper and Lower Canada," in *Proceedings of the American Antiquarian Society* 116, no. 2 (2006): 413–25; Andrew Bonthius, "The Patriot War of 1837–1838: Locofocoism with a Gun?," *Labour/Le Travail* 52 (Fall 2003): 9–43; Schoolcraft, *Personal Memoirs,* 580.

65. Henry Schoolcraft to Major Cobbs, October 33, 1837, Box 15, Schoolcraft Papers, LOC.

66. Henry Schoolcraft to George Johnston, December 8, 1836; and Henry Schoolcraft to George Johnston, February 7, 1837, both in Box 3, George Johnston Papers, Burton-DPL; Jane Johnston Schoolcraft to Henry Schoolcraft, December 1837, Box 15, Schoolcraft Papers, LOC; Schoolcraft, *Personal Memoirs,* 581–82.

67. Bremer, *Indian Agent*, 153; Henry Schoolcraft, *Personal Journals, 1833–1841*, Box 60; Jane Schoolcraft to Henry Schoolcraft, May 11, 1836, Box 15; and Jane Schoolcraft to Charlotte McMurray, June 17, 1837, Box 15, all in Schoolcraft Papers, LOC.
68. Schoolcraft, *Personal Memoirs*, 632–34; Jane Schoolcraft, "On Leaving My Children John and Jane," Box 16, Schoolcraft Papers, LOC.

Chapter 8: *"Marked for Slaughter"*

1. James Bennett quoted in Thomas R. Hietala, *Manifest Design: Anxious Aggrandizement in Late Jacksonian America* (Cornell University Press, 1985), 133; Amy S. Greenberg, *A Wicked War: Polk, Clay, Lincoln, and the 1846 U.S. Invasion of Mexico* (Knopf, 2012), 55–58, 76–77; Peter Guardino, *The Dead March: A History of the Mexican War* (Harvard University Press, 2018), 91–97; 106–10.
2. Murphy, *Great Lakes Creoles*, 187–93; Sleeper-Smith, *Rethinking the Fur Trade*, 13–15, 544–46.
3. Louis F. Burns, *Turn of the Wheel: A Genealogy of the Burns and Tinker Families* (n.p., 1980), 193; Francis La Flesche, "Francis La Flesche (Omaha)," in *Recovering Native American Writings in the Boarding School Press*, ed. Jacqueline Emery (University of Nebraska Press, 2017), 157–77.
4. "Statement of Indian Manual Labor School, 1844," Letters Received, Fort Leavenworth Agency, M234, Roll 302; and Letters Received, Great Nemaha Agency, M234, Roll 309, both in Office of Indian Affairs, RG 75, NARA.
5. Morton, *Illustrated History of Nebraska*, 1:72–73; Henry Fontenelle, "History of the Omaha Indians," *Transactions of the Nebraska Historical Society* 1 (1885): 76–83; BIA Rosters of Field Employees 1848–1850, Materials from Quartermaster, Council Bluffs Agency, Office of Indian Affairs, E974, RG 75, NARA.
6. Charles Charvat, *Logan Fontenelle: An Indian Chief in Broadcloth and Fine Linen* (American Print Co., 1961); Thorne, *Many Hands*, 153.
7. Hämäläinen, *Lakota America*, 186–90; James Gatewood to George R. Manypenny, October 16, 1853, in *Annual Report of the Commissioner of Indian Affairs, 1853* (USGPO, 1853), 106–10; John Miller to Commissioner Harvey, December 1846, Letters Received, Council Bluffs Agency, Office of Indian Affairs, RG 75, NARA.
8. J. A. MacMurphy, "Some Frenchmen of Early Days on the Missouri River," *Nebraska State Historical Society* 5 (1893): 43–63; Robert A. Trennert, Jr., "The Mormons and the Office of Indian Affairs: The Conflict over Winter Quarters, 1846–1848," *Nebraska History* 53 (1972): 381–400; Juanita Brooks,

ed., *On the Mormon Frontier: The Diary of Hosea Stout, 1844–1861*, 2 vols. (University of Utah Press, 1964), 188–89.

9. U.S. Census, 1860, Omaha Indian Reservation, Nebraska Territory; Individual Allotments According to the Treaty of Prairie du Chien, July 1830, and an Act of Congress, July 31, 1854, Office of Indian Affairs, E401, RG 75, NARA.

10. Kappler, *Indian Affairs*, 2:450–51; Henry Schoolcraft to Jane Johnston Schoolcraft, March 25, 1836, Box 13, Schoolcraft Papers, LOC.

11. Anna Maria Schoolcraft to George Johnston, July 6, 1839, Box 2, George Johnston Papers, Burton-DPL; James Schoolcraft to Henry Schoolcraft, July 15, 1839, Box 15, Schoolcraft Papers, LOC.

12. Henry Schoolcraft to Jane Schoolcraft, June 29, 1840, Box 16, Schoolcraft Papers, LOC; T. Hartley Crawford to Joel Poinsett, July 29, 1840, Letters Received, Michigan Superintendency, Office of Indian Affairs, RG 75, NARA; Schoolcraft, *Personal Memoirs*, 686.

13. Richard White, "Ethnohistorical Report on the Grand Traverse Ottawas, Prepared for the Grand Traverse Tribe of Ottawa and Chippewa Indians" (unpublished paper, in author's personal collection); Carol Devens, *Countering Civilization: Native American Women and Great Lakes Missions* (University of California Press, 1992), 127–37.

14. Jane Schoolcraft to Janee Schoolcraft, January 28, 1838, and Henry Schoolcraft to Jane Schoolcraft, May 27, 1839, both in Box 16, Schoolcraft Papers, LOC.

15. Regna Darnell, *Invisible Genealogies: A History of Americanist Anthropology* (University of Nebraska Press, 2001), 9; Hans F. Vermeulen, *Before Boas: The Genesis of Ethnography and Ethnology in the German Enlightenment* (University of Nebraska Press, 2015), 7, 18, 41.

16. Bremer, *Indian Agent*, 251–55; T. Hartley Crawford to Henry Schoolcraft, September 19, 1840, Box 59, Schoolcraft Papers, LOC; Vermeulen, *Before Boas*, 7.

17. James Schoolcraft to Henry Schoolcraft, February 1, 1842, Box 17; George Johnston to Jane Schoolcraft, December 8, 1841, Box 16; and W. L. Shearman to Henry Schoolcraft, December 15, 1841, Box 16, all in Schoolcraft Papers, LOC.

18. William McMurray to Henry Schoolcraft, March 22, 1842, Box 17, and Henry Schoolcraft to Jane Schoolcraft, June 1, 1842, Box 18, both in Schoolcraft Papers, LOC.

19. William Merrill Decker, *Epistolary Practices: Letter Writing in America Before Telecommunications* (University of North Carolina Press, 1998); Henry Schoolcraft to Janee Schoolcraft, June 16, 1842, Box 18, Schoolcraft Papers, LOC.

20. Janee Schoolcraft to Henry Schoolcraft, March 18, March 25, and June 9, 1843, all in Box 20, Schoolcraft Papers, LOC.

21. Jack Abbott to Henry Schoolcraft, December 30, 1845, Box 22; Janee Schoolcraft to Henry Schoolcraft, March 5 and June 18, 1845, Box 21; and Henry Schoolcraft to Mary Howard, August 1845, Box 22, all in Schoolcraft Papers, LOC.

22. Brooks, *Captives and Cousins*, 175–79; Rivaya-Martínez, "Different Look," 396; James E. Sherow, "Workings of the Geodialectic: High Plains Indians and Their Horses in the Region of the Arkansas River Valley, 1800–1870," *Environmental History Review* 16, no. 2 (1992): 61–84; Andrés Reséndez, The *Other Slavery: The Uncovered Story of Indian Enslavement in America* (Mariner Books, 2016), 224–30; Butler and Lewis to W. Medill, August 8, 1846, in *Annual Report of the Commissioner of Indian Affairs, 1846* (USGPO, 1846).

23. DeLay, *War of a Thousand Deserts*, 93–94; *Missouri Republican*, May 19, 1842, and November 1, 1843; David Charles Beyreis, "Business in the Borderlands: Bent, St. Vrain & Co., 1830–1849," Ph.D. diss., University of Oklahoma, 2012, 175–78.

24. Hafen, "Boggs Manuscript About Bent's Fort," 52–53; Lewis H. Garrard, *Wah-To-Yah and the Taos Trail: The Classic History of the American Indians and the Taos Revolt* (H. W. Derby, 1850), 55.

25. Alexander Barclay to George Barclay, May 1, 1840, Alexander Barclay Papers, 1823–1858, BANC MSS P-E 238, BL.; Ann Hafen, "Lancaster P. Lupton," in Hafen, *Mountain Men*, 213–15; William Lupton to Lancaster Lupton, December 1850, Lupton Papers, CHS.

26. Lavender, *Bent's Fort*, 17; George Bird Grinnell, "Notes on Bents Fort," 32–33, MS 5 Folder, Southwest Museum, Los Angeles; M. Inez Hilger, *Arapaho Child Life and Its Cultural Background* (USGPO, 1952), 102; Hyde, *Life of George Bent*, 40.

27. Comer, *Ritual Ground*, 171; Janet LeCompte, "The Mountain Branch: Raton Pass and Sangre de Cristo Pass," in *The Santa Fe Trail: New Perspectives* (Colorado Historical Society, 1987), 56; Charles Bent to Manuel Alvarez, January 30, 1841, Folder 46, Box 1, BRC-SF; Bent to Alvarez, December 25, 1842, Folder 60, Box 2, BRC-SF.

28. DeLay, *War of a Thousand Deserts*, 129–38; Lavender, *Bent's Fort*, 228–35; Beyreis, "Business in the Borderlands," 110–12, 304–8.

29. Harmon, *Indians in the Making*, 40–42; George Simpson to governor and committee of HBC, March 10 and 24, 1842, in Joseph Schafer, ed., "Letters of Sir George Simpson, 1841–1843," *American Historical Review* 14, no. 1 (1908): 70–94.

30. George Simpson to governor and committee of HBC, November 21, 1841, in Schafer, "Letters of Sir George Simpson"; "List of items traded in October

1835," *Fort Nisqually Journal of Occurrences,* vols. 1 and 5, February 4 and April 7, 1846, FN1234, HL.

31. *Fort Nisqually Journal,* vol. 1, June 11, 1834; vol. 2, September 20, 1843; and vol. 6, May 1 and May 14, 1849, FN1234, HL.

32. Stephen Dow Beckham, ed., *Oregon Indians: Voices from Two Centuries* (Oregon State University Press, 2006), 60–61; Bancroft, *History of Oregon,* 1:11; Peter Skene Ogden to George Simpson, March 20, 1847, in John S. Galbraith, *The Hudson's Bay Company as an Imperial Factor, 1821–1860* (University of California Press, 1957), 267–68.

33. John McLoughlin, "Report to Governor and Committee," June 1, 1844, and James Douglas, "Report to Governor and Committee," April 30, 1845, both in McLoughlin, *Letters of McLoughlin,* vol. 2; Caleb Cushing, "Supplemental Report on the Oregon Territory to the Committee on Foreign Affairs," February 16, 1839, House Report no. 101, 25th Cong., 3rd sess.

34. *Oregonian,* September 7, 1846; *Oregon Spectator,* March 18 1847; Bancroft, *History of Oregon,* 1:530; William Barlow and Mary S. Barlow, "History of the Barlow Road," *Oregon Historical Quarterly* 3, no. 1 (1902): 71–81.

35. Julie Roy Jeffrey, *Converting the West: A Biography of Narcissa Whitman* (University of Oklahoma Press, 1991).

36. Narcissa Whitman to Sister Jane, March 1, 1842, in Clifford M. Drury, *Marcus and Narcissa Whitman, and the Opening of the Old Oregon,* 2 vols. (Arthur H. Clark, 1973).

37. Larry Cebula, *Plateau Indians and the Quest for Spiritual Power, 1700–1850* (University of Nebraska Press, 2007), 61–68; 221–58; Melanie J. Norton and John Booss, "Missionaries, Measles, and Manuscripts: Revisiting the Whitman Tragedy," *Journal of the Medical Library Association* 107, no. 1 (2019): 108–13.

38. William A. Mowry, *Marcus Whitman and the Early Days of Oregon* (Silver Burdett, 1901), 217–23; William McBean to James Douglas, November 30, 1847, in Beckham, *Oregon Indians,* 63–64.

39. Cline, *Peter Skene Ogden,* 187; Jeffrey, *Converting the West,* 193–99; William McBean to the Presbyterian Board of Supervisors, November 30, 1847, reprinted in *Oregon Spectator,* December 10, 1847.

40. Young Chief as reported by Peter Skene Odgen to E. Walker, Letter to governor and committee of HBC, December 27, 1847; *Oregon Spectator,* December 30, 1847; *Oregon Spectator,* December 10, 1847.

41. Joel Palmer, "Report on the War, Oregon Territory, 1848," in *Annual Report of the Commissioner of Indian Affairs, 1848* (USGPO, 1848), app. K; Eva Emery Dye, *McLoughlin and Old Oregon, a Chronicle* (A. C. McClurg, 1900), 221.

42. Lavender, *Bent's Fort,* 252–55.

43. DeLay, *War of a Thousand Deserts,* 238–45; Annexation of Texas, *Congressional Globe,* 28th Cong., 1st sess., April 26, 1844.

44. Matt Field, letter, *New Orleans Picayune*, November 17, 1844; Guardino, *Dead March*, 116–19; Hietala, *Manifest Design*, 138–44.

45. Greenberg, *Wicked War*, 76–78; *El Siglo Diez y Nueve*, November 30, 1845, quoted in Gene M. Brack, *Mexico Views Manifest Destiny, 1821–1846* (University of New Mexico Press, 1975), 143.

46. Greenberg, *Wicked War*, 89–90, 101–6; *New York Tribune*, May 1, 1846; *Charleston Mercury*, May 11, 1846.

47. Lavender, *Bent's Fort*, 252–55; Charles Bent, "Charles Bent to Manuel Alvarez, March 2, June 11, 1846," *New Mexico Historical Review* 30 (October 1955): 344–48; Charles Bent, "Bent Letters," *New Mexico Historical Review* 31 (April 1956): 164; Stephen Watts Kearny, *Winning the West: General Stephen Watts Kearny's Letter Books, 1846–1847* (Pekitanoui, 1998), 140–47; Beyreis, *Blood in the Borderlands*, 70–71.

48. K. Jack Bauer, *The Mexican War, 1846–1848* (Macmillan, 1974), 125–28; Guardino, *Dead March*, 87–94, 317.

49. Charles Montgomery, *The Spanish Redemption: Heritage, Power, and Loss on New Mexico's Upper Rio Grande* (University of California Press, 2002), 40; Charles Bent to Manuel Alvarez, May 3, 1846, Benjamin Read Collection, 87, NMHML.

50. Greenberg, *Wicked War*, 115–16; Hyde, *Life of George Bent*, 85; George Ruxton, *Adventures in Mexico and the Rocky Mountains* (John Murray, 1847), 290–92.

51. Gen. Stephen W. Kearny to Brig. Gen. David R. Jones, July 31, 1846, in Letterbook, Kearny Collection, MHS.

52. William A. Keleher, *Turmoil in New Mexico, 1846–1848*, 2nd ed. (University of New Mexico Press, 1982), 12–14; Dwight L. Clarke, *Stephen Watts Kearney, Soldier of the West* (University of Oklahoma Press, 1961), 150–52; Marc Simmons, *Kit Carson and His Three Wives: A Family History* (University of New Mexico Press, 2011), 68–69; Thomas E. Chávez, *Manuel Alvarez, 1794–1856: A Southwestern Biography* (University Press of Colorado, 1990), 107–9.

53. Charles Bent to Manuel Alvarez, May 3, 1846, Folder 86, Box 2, BRC-SF; Stephen G. Hyslop, "Courtship and Conquest: Alfred Sully's Intimate Intrusion at Monterey," *California History* 90, no. 1 (2012): 4–62; Alexander Barclay, "Diary," entries for August 7, August 24, and September 23, 1847, Barclay Papers, CHS; Charles Bent to Manuel Alvarez, June 11, 1846, Bent Papers, Western History Collection, Denver Public Library.

54. Col. Sterling Price, "Report to Adjutant General," February 15, 1847, in *Insurrection Against the U.S. Government in New Mexico and California, 1847–1848*, Senate Doc. no. 442, 56th Cong., 1st sess.; Morris F. Taylor, "A New Look at an Old Case: The Bent Heirs' Claim in the Maxwell Grant," *New Mexico Historical Review* 43, no. 3 (1968): 213–28.

55. Beyreis, *Blood in the Borderlands*, 73–75; Michael McNierney, ed., *Taos 1847:*

The Revolt in Contemporary Accounts (Johnson Publishing, 1980); James A. Crutchfield, *Tragedy at Taos: The Revolt of 1847* (Republic of Texas Press, 1995), 40–46; Teresina Bent, "Account of Her Father's Death," *New Mexico Historical Review* 8 (1933): 121–23.

56. Price, "Report to the Adjutant General"; Howard Louis Conard, *Uncle Dick Wootton: The Pioneer Frontiersman of the Rocky Mountain Region*, ed. Milo Milton Quaife (R. R. Donnelley & Sons, 1957), 159.

57. Simmons, *Kit Carson and His Three Wives*, 74, 83–85; Price, "Report to the Adjutant General"; McNierney, *Taos 1847*, 43–48.

58. Hyslop, *Bound for Santa Fe*, 385–87; *St. Louis Union*, March 9, 1847; *Niles National Register*, March 20, 1847; Allan Nevins, ed., *Polk: The Diary of a President, 1845–1849* (Longmans, Green, 1952), 218.

59. H. L. Lubers, "William Bent's Family and the Indians of the Plains," *Colorado Magazine* 13, no. 1 (1936): 19–23; Garrard, *Wah-To-Yah*, 117–21; Quantrille D. McClung, *Carson-Bent-Boggs Genealogy* (Colorado Historical Society, 1962), 100–102; Ralph Emerson Twitchell, *The History of the Military Occupation of the Territory of New Mexico from 1846 to 1851 by the Government of the United States* (Smith Brooks, 1909); 127–31; *St. Louis Weekly Reveille*, December 27, 1847.

60. Beyreis, "Business in the Borderlands," 371–72, 391; Richard L. Rieck, "A Geography of Death on the Oregon-California Trail, 1840–1860," *Overland Journal* 9, no. 1 (1991): 13–21; Sarah Keyes, "'Like a Roaring Lion': The Overland Trail as a Sonic Conquest," *Journal of American History* 96, no. 1 (2009): 19–43; George Bent to George Hyde, February 10, 1915, Box 4:35, BRBM.

61. Route advertised in *Oregon Spectator*, February 12, 1848.

62. Bancroft, *History of Oregon*, 2:44–45; David McLoughlin, "Pioneer Reminiscences," *Morning Oregonian*, May 3, 1901, clippings file, Oregon Historical Society; Ronald B. Lansing, *Juggernaut: The Whitman Massacre Trial, 1850* (Ninth Judicial Circuit Historical Society, 1993).

Chapter 9: Surviving War and Peace in the 1850s

1. Joel Palmer to Supt. George Manypenny, May 24, 1855, in *Annual Report of the Commissioner of Indian Affairs, 1855* (USGPO, 1856), 18; Isaac I. Stevens, *Reports of Explorations and Surveys for a Railroad Route from the Mississippi River to the Pacific Ocean* (U.S. War Department, 1855).

2. R. R. Thompson to Supt. Joel Palmer, October 25, 1855, in *Oregon Superintendency Records*, 23:60, Office of Indian Affairs, RG 75, NARA; Robert H. Ruby and John A. Brown, *Cayuse Indians: Imperial Tribesmen of Old Oregon* (University of Oklahoma Press, 1972), 193–95.

3. Alvin M. Josephy, Jr., *The Nez Perce Indians and the Opening of the Northwest*

(Yale University Press, 1971), 319–20; Lawrence Kip, *The Indian Council at Walla Walla, May and June 1855* (n.p., 1855); William C. McKay, "Statement," Box 1, William McKay Papers, OHS.

4. Andrew R. Graybill, "Rangers, Mounties, and the Subjugation of Indigenous Peoples, 1870–1885," *Great Plains Quarterly* 24, no. 2 (2004): 83–100; Thomas W. Dunlay, *Wolves for the Blue Soldiers: Indian Scouts and Auxiliaries with the U.S. Army, 1860–1890* (University of Nebraska Press, 1982).

5. William Novak, *The Legal Transformation of Citizenship in the Nineteenth Century* (American Bar Association, 2002), 87–93; Martha Jones, *Birthright Citizens:A History of Race and Rights in Antebellum America* (Cambridge University Press, 2018), 12.

6. Ann McGrath, *Illicit Love: Interracial Sex and Marriage in the United States and Australia* (University of Nebraska Press, 2015), 35–48.

7. Henry R. Schoolcraft, *Notes on the Iroquois* (New York State Senate, 1845), 10, 136, 199; Henry Rowe Schoolcraft, "Our Indian Policy," *Democratic Review* 14 (1844): 169–84; Bieder, *Science Encounters the Indian*, 172–74.

8. Henry Schoolcraft to Lewis Cass, March 7, 1845, Box 22, Schoolcraft Papers, LOC; Vermeulen, *Before Boas*, 407–8; George W. Stocking, "The Turn-of-the-Century Concept of Race," *Modernism/Modernity* 1, no. 1 (1994): 4–16; Henry Schoolcraft, "Draft of Speech to the Ladies Society of New York," October 12, 1845, Box 22, and Henry Schoolcraft to William Medill, July 28, 1846, Box 23, both in Schoolcraft Papers, LOC; Bremer, *Indian Agent*, 282–83.

9. U.S. Census, 1850, St. Luke's Parish, South Carolina, Slave Schedules and Agricultural Schedules, Howard Family and Moultrie Family; Henry Schoolcraft to Mary Howard, September 15, 1846, Box 23, Schoolcraft Papers, LOC.

10. Henry Schoolcraft to Mary Howard, October 5, 1846, Box 23; Mary Howard to Henry Schoolcraft, November 3, 1846, Box 23; and Jane Schoolcraft to Henry Schoolcraft, April 12, 1844, Box 21, all in Schoolcraft Papers, LOC.

11. Johnston Schoolcraft to Henry Schoolcraft, April 27, 1847, July 20, 1848, November 22, 1849, and January 3 and April 11, 1851, all in Box 25, Schoolcraft Papers, LOC; Johnston Schoolcraft to George Johnston, September 6, 1848, and September 8, 1849, Box 3, George Johnston Papers, Burton-DPL.

12. Henry Schoolcraft to Janee Schoolcraft, November 18, 1849, Box 24, Schoolcraft Papers, LOC.

13. Henry Schoolcraft to Jane Schoolcraft, November 18, 1849, Box 24, Schoolcraft Papers, LOC; Schoolcraft, *Personal Memoirs*, 645–46; John Schoolcraft to George Johnston, October 12, 1849, and July 29, 1850, Box 3, George Johnston Papers, Burton-DPL.

14. "Expenses of Collecting and Digesting Statistics of the Indian Tribes," *Abstract of Expenditures of the United States*, 5:183, 1854, Records of Account-

ing Officers, RG 217, NARA; Henry Schoolcraft to George Manypenny, February 10, 1857, Box 28, Schoolcraft Papers, LOC.

15. Mary Howard Schoolcraft to Miss Cass, February 26, 1857, Box 28, Schoolcraft Papers, LOC.

16. Mary Howard Schoolcraft, *The Black Gauntlet: A Tale of Plantation Life in the South* (J. B. Lippincott, 1860).

17. Nancy Shoemaker, "Race and Indigeneity in the Life of Elisha Apes," *Ethnohistory* 60, no. 1 (2013): 27–50; Nancy Shoemaker, "An Alliance Between Men: Gender Metaphors in Eighteenth-Century American Indian Diplomacy East of the Mississippi," *Ethnohistory* 46, no. 2 (1999): 239–63; K. Tsianina Lomawaima and T. L. McCarty, *To Remain an Indian: Lessons in Democracy from a Century of Native American Education* (Teachers College Press, 2006), 18, 31; "List of Persons Employed in the Indian Department," in *Annual Report of the Commissioner of Indian Affairs, 1850* (USGPO, 1850), 138–39.

18. Michael Witgen, "Seeing Red: Race, Citizenship and Indigeneity in the Old Northwest," *Journal of the Early Republic* 38, no. 4 (2018): 607–10; Blackbird, *History of the Ottawa and Chippewa*, 56, 59; Child, *Holding Our World Together*, 63; George W. Manypenny, *Our Indian Wards* (R. Clarke, 1880), 129–30; "Chippaway Chiefs to Superintendent Luke Lea," November 6, 1851, Commissioner of Indian Affairs, Letters Received, Office of Indian Affairs, M234, Roll 149, RG 75, NARA; "Treaty with the Chippewa" (1854) in Kappler, *Indian Affairs*, 2:648–52.

19. Child, *Holding Our World Together*, 75–78; Bruce M. White, "The Regional Context of the Removal Order of 1850," in *Fish in the Lakes, Wild Rice, and Game in Abundance: Testimony on Behalf of Mille Lacs Ojibwe Hunting and Fishing Rights*, ed. James M. McClurken (Michigan State University Press, 2000), 194–95.

20. Bancroft, *History of Oregon*, 2:66–88; J. P. Dunn, *Massacres of the Mountains: A History of the Indian Wars of the Far West* (Harper & Bros., 1886), 195; J. Ross Brown, "The Coast Rangers," *Harper's Monthly* 23 (1861): 306.

21. "The Donation Land Claim Act, 1850," An Act to Create the Office of Surveyor-General of the Public Lands in Oregon, and to Provide for the Survey, and to Make Donations to Settlers of the Said Public Lands, U.S. Statute 9 Stat. 496, 497 (1850).

22. Jetté, *At the Hearth*, 211; 1850–1856, Clippings File, Rogue River Wars, Eva Emery Dye Papers, OHS.

23. Joel Palmer to Supt. George Manypenny, June 23, 1853, *Annual Report of the Commissioner of Indian Affairs, 1853* (USGPO, 1854), 207–11; Stevens, *Reports of Explorations*, 12:108.

24. William C. McKay, "Statement," William McKay Papers, OHS; Ruby and Brown, *Cayuse Indians*, 206–11; "Special Report of the Secretary of War, 1855–1856," Senate Doc. no. 26, 34th Cong., 1st sess., Serial 819, at 34–36.

25. Stephen Dow Beckham, *Requiem for a People: The Rogue Indians and the Frontiersmen* (University of Oklahoma, 1971), 128–30.

26. Clifford E. Trafzer and Richard D. Scheuerman, *Renegade Tribe: The Palouse Indians and the Invasion of the Inland Pacific Northwest* (Washington State University Press, 1986), 64–66; Muster Roll, Fort Dalles, August 1855, Returns from U.S. Military Posts, 1800–1916, Bureau of Indian Affairs, M617, Roll 285, RG 75, NARA.

27. *Pioneer and Democrat* (Oregon), February 27, 1856; Joel Palmer to George Manypenny, January 8, 1856, Oregon Superintendency, Letterbook E:10, Bureau of Indian Affairs, MF Roll 6, RG 75, NARA; Andrew Pambrun, *Sixty Years on the Frontier in the Pacific Northwest* (Galleon Press, 1978), 140.

28. Walter R. Echo-Hawk, "Foreword," in Mark van de Logt, *War Party in Blue: Pawnee Scouts in the U.S. Army* (University of Oklahoma Press, 2010), xii, xiv.

29. Durwood Ball, *Army Regulars on the Western Frontier, 1848–1861* (University of Oklahoma Press, 2001), xii, xx; Robert Utley, *Frontiersmen in Blue: The United States Army and the Indian, 1848–1865* (Macmillan, 1967), 188–93; Lindsay, *Murder State*, 199–203.

30. Dunn, *Massacres of the Mountains*, 209–11; Gen. John E. Wool to secretary of war, January 27, 1856, in *Annual Report of the Commissioner of Indian Affairs, 1856* (USGPO, 1856), 50–51, 56; *Pioneer and Democrat* (Oregon), February 17, 1856; *Oregonian*, April 14, 1856.

31. W. J. Betts, "From Red River to the Columbia, the Story of a Migration," *Beaver* 301 (Spring 1971): 50–55; John V. Campbell, "The Sinclair Party— An Emigration Overland Along the Old Hudson Bay Company Route from Manitoba to the Spokane Country in 1854," *Washington Historical Quarterly* 7, no. 3 (1916): 187–201.

32. Frances Fuller Victor, *The Early Indian Wars of Oregon* (F. C. Baker, 1891), 421; William McKay, "Reminiscences," William McKay Papers, OHS.

33. Utley, *Frontiersmen in Blue*, 199–201; Supt. John Mullan to J. W. Denver, September 5, 1858, in *Annual Report of the Commissioner of Indian Affairs, 1858* (USGPO, 1858), 277–84; Howlish Wampoo quoted in Robert H. Ruby and John A. Brown, *The Spokane Indians: Children of the Sun* (University of Oklahoma Press, 2006), 114.

34. U.S. Census, 1860, Champoeg, Marion County, M653, at 38.

35. Jetté, *At the Hearth*, 191, 217.

36. Sub-Agent G. H. Abbot to Supt. Edward Geary, October 1, 1860, in *Annual Report of the Commissioner of Indian Affairs, 1860* (USGPO, 1860), 175; William C. McKay to Agent William Logan, September 4, 1862, in *Annual Report of the Commissioner of Indian Affairs, 1862* (USGPO, 1862), 399; Wil-

liam C. McKay, Report, August 1, 1863, in *Annual Report of the Commissioner of Indian Affairs, 1863* (USGPO, 1863), 78.

37. Agent William H. Barnhart to superintendent, Oregon, July 20, 1864, in *Annual Report of the Commissioner of Indian Affairs* (USGPO, 1864), 86–90.

38. James A. Hanson, "A Forgotten Fur Trade Trail," *Nebraska History* 68 (1987): 2–9; Pierre Chouteau, Jr., & Co., Fort Pierre, Ledger Book 1842–48, reel 11, 2:270–451, Chouteau Collection, MHS; Charles Edmund DeLand, ed., "Fort Tecumseh and Fort Pierre: Journal and Letter Books, February 27, 1848," *South Dakota Historical Society* 9 (1918): 93–239.

39. J. G. Bruff, *Gold Rush: The Journals, Drawings, and Other Papers of J. Goldsborough Bruff, Captain, Washington City and California Mining Association, April 2, 1849–July 20, 1851* (Columbia University Press, 1949), 1:32.

40. Amos E. Oneroad and Alanson B. Skinner, *Being Dakota: Tales and Traditions of the Sisseton and Wahpeton*, ed. Laura L. Anderson (University of Minnesota Press, 2003), iv, 21–22; Marriage Records, May 4, 1848, Missouri State Archives, Jefferson City.

41. "Leonard Benoist," Findagrave.com; U.S. Census, 1850, Jackson County, Mo.; John S. Gray, "Honoré Picotte, Fur Trader," *South Dakota Historical Society* 6, no. 2 (1976): 186–202; General Land Office plats and notes, Clay County, 1849–1855, Missouri State Archives, Jefferson City.

42. Francis Parkman, *The Oregon Trail: Sketches of Prairie and Rocky-Mountain Life* (Little, Brown, 1872), 21–28; Charles P. Deatherage, *Early History of Greater Kansas City, Missouri and Kansas* (n.p., 1927), 1:340–46.

43. Gregory J. Johansen, " 'To Make Some Provision for Their Half-Breeds': The Nemaha Half-Breed Reserve, 1830–66," *Nebraska History* 67 (1986): 8–29; George Manypenny, Speech on Indian Affairs, *National Intelligencer* (Washington, D.C.), May 1 and 15, 1855; Berlin Basil Chapman, "The Nemaha Half-Breed Reservation," *Nebraska History* 38 (1957): 1–23; Records Relating to the Nemaha Half-Breed Reserve, Lists of Allotted and Unallotted Mixed-Bloods, Office of Indian Affairs E402, RG 75, NARA.

44. Register of Traders Licenses, Records of the Miscellaneous Division, 1847–1873, 1:163, E94, NARA; Miner and Unrau, *End of Indian Kansas*, 139–41.

45. Carter, "Andrew Drips," 159–60; *A Memorial and Biographical Record of Kansas City and Jackson County, Mo.* (Lewis Publishing, 1896), 522–23.

46. Marriage Records, 1851, Missouri State Archives, Jefferson City; U.S. Census, 1860, Kansas City, Jackson County; Chapman, "Nemaha Half-Breed Reservation"; U.S. Census, 1900, Richardson, Neb.; Chapman Brothers, *Portraits and Biographical Album of Gage County, Nebraska* (n.p., 1888), 760.

47. U.S. Census, 1860, Jackson County, Slave Schedules, 1, Ancestry.com, 2004.

48. Henry Lewis Morgan, *The Indian Journals*, ed. Leslie A. White (University of Michigan Press, 1959), 26; Robert A. Trennert, *Alternative to Extinction:*

Federal Indian Policy and the Beginning of the Reservation System, 1846–1851 (Temple University Press, 1975), 49–52.

49. C. Joseph Genetin-Pilawa, *Crooked Paths to Allotment: The Fight over Federal Indian Policy After the Civil War* (University of North Carolina Press, 2012), 20–23.

50. Francis Paul Prucha, *American Indian Treaties: The History of a Political Anomaly* (University of California Press, 1994), 226–34; Manypenny, *Our Indian Wards*, 130–33; Boughter, *Betraying the Omaha*, 49, 62–64; Henry Fontenelle, "History of Omaha Indians," *Nebraska Burtonian*, August 18, 1884.

51. Paul Wallace Gates, *Fifty Million Acres: Conflicts over Kansas Land Policy, 1854–1890* (Cornell University Press, 1954), 3–10; James C. Malin, *The Nebraska Question, 1852–1854* (University of Kansas Press, 1953), 51–55; Michael Woods, *Bleeding Kansas: Slavery, Sectionalism, and Civil War on the Missouri-Kansas Border* (Routledge, 2016), 9–11, 17–22; Tony Mullis, *Peacekeeping on the Plains: Army Operations in Bleeding Kansas* (University of Missouri Press, 2004), 44–48.

52. James Gatewood to Col. A. Cumming, "Report of the Council Bluffs Agency, 1853," in *Annual Report of the Commissioner of Indian Affairs, 1853* (USGPO, 1853), 105–6; Miner and Unrau, *End of Indian Kansas*, 7–13; Daniel Vanderslice, Account Book 1853–1877, Ayer Manuscripts, Newberry Library, Chicago; Great Nemaha Agency, Letters Received, June 1859–April 1860, Office of Indian Affairs, RG 75, NARA.

53. James McLaughlin, *My Friend the Indian* (Houghton Mifflin, 1910), 83, 91–99; *Missouri Republican* (St. Louis), August 18, 1852, and July 19, 1853; Vanderslice, Account Book 1853–1877, entry for March 30, 1860; Miner and Unrau, *End of Indian Kansas*, 25–29.

54. Melvin Randolph Gilmore, "The True Logan Fontenelle," *Nebraska State Historical Society Journal* 19 (1919): 64–71; Fletcher and La Flesche, *Omaha Tribe*, 100–101; George Manypenny, in *Annual Report of the Commissioner of Indian Affairs, 1855* (USGPO, 1855), 69–70.

55. Peter A. Sarpy to George Manypenny, November 28, 1855, Letters Received, Council Bluffs Agency; "Proceedings of a Council Held at Joseph La Flesche's House," January 20, 1860, Letters Received 1856–1861, Council Bluffs Agency, R604; and O. H. Irish to H. B. Branch, September 29, 1861, Letters Received 1859–1864, Omaha Agency; all in Office of Indian Affairs, RG 75, NARA; Boughter, *Betraying the Omaha*, 68–75.

56. Rosters of Field Employees, 1848–1850, Materials from quartermaster (Logan Fontenelle), Council Bluffs Agency, Bureau of Indian Affairs, E974, RG 75, NARA.

57. Prucha, *American Indian Treaties*, 140–41; "Great Indian Council on the Plains," *North American and U.S. Gazette*, July 30, 1851; D. D. Mitchell,

"Report of Treaty with Prairie Tribes," November 11, 1851, in *Annual Report of the Commissioner of Indian Affairs, 1851* (USGPO, 1851), 27–29.

58. Hyde, *Life of George Bent*, 91; DeSmet, *Life, Letters and Travels*, vol. 2; Donald L. Fixico, ed., *Indian Treaties in the United States: An Encyclopedia and Documents Collection* (ABC-CLIO, 2018), 140–41.

59. Kappler, *Indian Affairs*, 2:593–97; Charles D. Bernholz and Brian L. Pytlik Zillig, "The *Treaty of Fort Laramie with Sioux, Etc., 1851:* Revisiting the Document Found in Kappler's *Indian Affairs: Laws and Treaties*," n.d., American Indian Treaties Portal, http://treatiesportal.unl.edu/treatyoffortlaramie1851/; Stuart Banner, *How the Indians Lost Their Land: Law and Power on the Frontier* (Harvard University Press, 2005), 228–43.

60. Comm. Luke Lea, November 27, 1851, in *Annual Report of the Commissioner of Indian Affairs, 1851* (USGPO, 1851), 3–13.

61. Unrau, *Indians, Alcohol*, 132–34, 143–46; Mark J. Stegmaier and David H. Miller, eds., *James F. Milligan: His Journal of Frémont's Fifth Expedition, 1853–1854* (Arthur H. Clark, 1988), 180–85.

62. Halaas and Masich, *Halfbreed*, 72; Nellie McCoy Harris, "Memories of Old Westport," *Annals of Kansas City* 1, no. 4 (1947): 470–74; Nathan Scarritt, "Reminiscences of the Methodist Shawnee Mission: And Religious Work Among That Tribe," *Missouri Valley Historical Society: The Annals of Kansas City* 1 (1924): 437.

63. Hyde, *Life of George Bent*; George Bent to George Hyde, May 29, 1906, Box 1, Folder 10, George Bent Letters, BRBM; "Catalog of the Officers and Students of Webster College Family Boarding School for Boys for the Annual Session, 1858–1859," 6–7, MHS.

64. Lavender, *Bent's Fort*, 349–51.

65. Spaulding, *Annals of the City of Kansas*, 21–24; "Historic Context Study of the Purgatoire River Region," Colorado Preservation, December 30, 2011, https://issuu.com/coloradopreservation/docs/historic-context-study-ranching.

66. West, *Contested Plains*, 91–93; Hyde, *Life of George Bent*, 105–8; William Bent to William Hafferday, 1857, in LeRoy R. Hafen, *Overland Routes to the Gold Fields, 1859, from Contemporary Diaries* (Arthur H. Clark, 1942), 317.

67. D. W. Working, "The Hicklins on the Greenhorn," *Colorado Magazine* 4, no. 5 (1927): 183–88; Janet LeCompte, *Pueblo, Hardscrabble, Greenhorn: The Upper Arkansas, 1832–1856* (University of Oklahoma Press, 1978) 157–68.

68. U.S. Census, 1850, Kansas Territory; U.S. Census, 1861, Boggsville and Julesburg, Colo.; C. W. Hurd, *Boggsville: Cradle of the Colorado Cattle Industry* (Boggsville Committee, 1950); Christina Gish Hill, *Webs of Kinship: Family in Northern Cheyenne Nationhood* (University of Oklahoma Press, 2017).

69. William Bent to Supt. A. M. Robinson, December 17, 1858, Letters Sent, Upper Platte Agency, Office of Indian Affairs, RG 75, NARA.

70. West, *Contested Plains*, 147–51; William Bent's Report, October 5, 1859, in *Annual Report of the Commissioner of Indian Affairs, 1859* (USGPO, 1859), 137–39.

71. Luke Tierney, *A History of the Gold Discoveries on the South Platte River and a Guide of the Route* (Pacific City, 1859), 13–27; Margaret Coel, *Chief Left Hand: Southern Arapaho* (University of Oklahoma Press, 1981), 103–108; *Rocky Mountain News*, April 18, 1860.

72. Althea Bass, *The Arapaho Way: A Memoir of an Indian Boyhood* (C. N. Potter, 1966), 127–28; Ronald Becher, *Massacre Along the Medicine Road: A Social History of the Indian War of 1864 in Nebraska Territory* (Caxton, 1999), 50–51; Hill, *Webs of Kinship*, 108–12.

73. A. B. Greenwood, "Report," in LeRoy R. Hafen, ed., *Reports from Colorado: The Wildman Letters, 1859–1865* . . . (Arthur H. Clark, 1961); John Sedgwick, *Correspondence of John Sedgwick, Major-General* (Carl and Ellen Battelle Stoeckel, 1903), 2:18, 24.

74. Coel, *Chief Left Hand*, 118–19; William Unrau, "A Prelude to War," *Colorado Magazine* 41, no. 4 (1964): 299–319; Hyde, *Life of George Bent*, 107–108.

75. A. B. Greenwood, "Special Report on the Cheyennes and Arrapahoes," October 25, 1860, in *Annual Report of the Commissioner of Indian Affairs, 1860* (USGPO, 1860), 228–31; Unrau, "Prelude to War," 303–5; Stan Hoig, *Peace Chiefs of the Cheyennes* (University of Oklahoma Press, 1980), 47–49, 85–87.

76. John H. Moore, *The Cheyenne Nation: A Social and Demographic History* (University of Nebraska Press, 1987), 171–76; West, *Contested Plains*, 280–83.

Chapter 10: Civil Wars in the West, 1860–1865

1. Adam Arenson and Andrew Graybill, eds., *Civil War Wests: Testing the Limits of the United States* (University of California Press, 2015); Laura E. Free, *Suffrage Reconstructed: Gender, Race, and Voting Rights in the Civil War Era* (Cornell University Press, 2015), 9–33.

2. Lea VanderVelde, *Mrs. Dred Scott: A Life on Slavery's Frontier* (Oxford University Press, 2009), 181; Christopher Phillips, *Damned Yankee: The Life of General Nathaniel Lyon* (University of Missouri Press, 1990), 15–154.

3. Hyde, *Life of George Bent*, 111; William Garrett Piston and Richard W. Hatcher, III, *Wilson's Creek: The Second Battle of the Civil War and the Men Who Fought It* (University of North Carolina Press, 2000), 8; Thomas C. Reynolds, *General Sterling Price and the Confederacy*, ed. Robert G. Schultz (University of Chicago Press, 2009), 78, 166–68.

4. Piston and Hatcher, *Wilson's Creek*, 166–68; Hyde, *Life of George Bent*, 11; Brig. Gen. Ben McCulloch quoted in Jeffrey L. Patrick, *Campaign for Wilson's Creek: The Fight for Missouri Begins* (McWhiney Foundation Press, 2011), 88.

5. James G. Downhour, "Nathaniel Lyon," in *Encyclopedia of the American Civil War*, ed. David S. Heidler and Jeanne T. Heidler (Oxford University Press, 2000); George Bent to George Hyde, April 3, 1904, Box 1, George Bent Letters, HC.

6. William L. Shea and Earl J. Hess, *Pea Ridge: Civil War Campaign in the West* (University of North Carolina Press, 1992); Carl Moneyhon, "Albert Pike," *Encyclopedia of Arkansas*, https://encyclopediaofarkansas.net/entries/albert-pike-1737/; George Bent to George Hyde, October 1909, Box 1, George Bent Letters, HC.

7. Hyde, *Life of George Bent*, 112; *Compiled Service Records of Confederate Soldiers Who Served in Organizations from the State of Missouri*, War Department Collection of Confederate Records, RG 109, M380, Roll 1, NARA.

8. *Daily Missouri Democrat*, September 3, 1862; Hyde, *Life of George Bent*, 112.

9. U.S. Civil War Draft Registrations, 6th Cong. District, Missouri, 1863–65, https://www.ancestry.com/search/collections/1666/.

10. Matthew M. Stith, *Extreme Civil War: Guerrilla Warfare, Environment, and Race on the Trans-Mississippi Frontier* (Louisiana State University Press, 2016), 36–44.

11. Michael Fellman, *Inside War: The Guerrilla Conflict in Missouri During the American Civil War* (Oxford University Press, 1990), ix; Samuel J. Crawford, *Kansas in the Sixties* (A. C. McClurg, 1911), 92–94, 143–55; Stith, *Extreme Civil War*, 40–43.

12. "Outrages by Bushwacker," *Daily Missouri Democrat*, September 16, 1863; Fellman, *Inside War*, 25–26; Thomas W. Cutrer, *Theater of a Separate War: The Civil War West of the Mississippi River, 1861–1865* (University of North Carolina Press, 2017), 411–17.

13. Gen. James W. Denver to Gen. Henry Halleck, April 8, 1862, in U.S. War Department, *The War of the Rebellion: A Compilation of the Official Records of the Union and Confederate Armies*. Pub. under the Direction of the Secretary of War, 12 vols. (USGPO, 1901), 8:665–679; Annie Heloise Abel, *The American Indian as Participant in the Civil War* (Arthur H. Clark, 1919), 68–70, 131–46; Mary Jane Warde, *When the Wolf Came: The Civil War in Indian Territory* (University of Arkansas Press, 2013), 180–83.

14. Child, *Holding Our World Together*, 77–78; Rebecca Kugel, *To Be the Main Leaders of Our People: A History of Minnesota Ojibwe Politics, 1825–1898* (Michigan State University Press, 1998), 122.

15. Susan E. Gray, *The Yankee West: Community Life on the Michigan Frontier* (University of North Carolina Press, 1996), 76–78; George Johnston to

George Moffatt, October 17, 1847, George Johnston Letterbook, Johnston Family Collection, BHL; A. D. P. Van Buren, "Indian Reminiscences of Calhoun and Van Buren Counties," *Historical Collections* (Michigan Pioneer and Historical Society, 1908), 10:164–65; U.S. Census, 1860, Sault Ste. Marie, Chippewa County, Mich.

16. *Lake Superior News and Mining Journal*, February 19, 1860; U.S. Census, 1860, Sault Ste. Marie, Chippewa County, Mich., 22.

17. Schenck, *All Our Relations*, app.; W. P. Strickland, *Old Mackinaw; or, The Fortress of the Lakes and Its Surroundings* (Lippincott, 1860), 65; U.S. Census, 1860, Mackinac Island, Mich., 88.

18. Laurence Hauptmann, *Between Two Fires: American Indians During the Civil War* (Free Press, 1995), 128–33; National Park Service, *American Indians and the Civil War* (Eastern National, 2013).

19. Benjamin S. Johnston to William P. Spaulding, August 21, 1862, Box 2, William Spaulding Collection, BHL; National Park Service, "Soldier Details: Johnston, Samuel," *The Civil War*, https://www.nps.gov/civilwar/search -soldiers.htm; John Robertson, ed., *Michigan in the War* (W. S. George, 1882); *Detroit Free Press*, March 19, 1863; "John J. Schoolcraft," *Findagrave. com*.

20. U.S. Census, 1860, Kansas Territory, Colo.; "Population of Colorado State," 2016, http://population.us/co/; Walker D. Wyman, "Freighting: A Big Business on the Santa Fe Trail," *Kansas Historical Quarterly* 1, no. 1 (1931): 17–27; Beyreis, *Blood in the Borderlands*, 109–12.

21. LeRoy R. Hafen, *Broken Hand: The Life of Thomas Fitzpatrick, Mountain Man, Guide and Indian Agent* (Old West, 1981), 105; Stan Hoig, *The Sand Creek Massacre* (University of Oklahoma Press, 1961), 16; U.S. Census, 1860, Westport Township, Jackson County, Mo.

22. George Bent to George Hyde, April 25, 1906, and Bent to Hyde, May 4, 1906, both in Folder 8, George Bent Letters, BRBM; George Bent to George Hyde, September 23, 1913, and Bent to Hyde, April 9, 1909, both in Box 2, George Bent Letters, HC; Halaas and Masich, *Halfbreed*, 105–108; Major B. S. Henning to Maj. C. S. Charlot, December 7, 1863, in *War of Rebellion*, 41:796–97.

23. Hoig, *Sand Creek*, 23–25; Coel, *Chief Left Hand*, 170–73; Loretta Fowler, *Wives and Husbands: Gender and Age in Southern Arapaho History* (University of Oklahoma Press, 2010), 83–85.

24. Andrew E. Masich, *Civil War in the Southwest Borderlands, 1861–1867* (University of Oklahoma Press, 2017), 98–104; Berthrong, *Southern Cheyennes*, 168.

25. John Evans to Commissioner Dole, November 19, 1863, in *Annual Report to the Commissioner of Indian Affairs, 1863* (USGPO, 1863), 420–42; William

Bent, testimony, "The Chivington Massacre," in *Report of the Joint Committee on the Conduct of the War,* 3 vols. (1865), Senate Report no. 142, 38th Cong., 2nd sess., 2:93.

26. Loretta Fowler, "Arapaho and Cheyenne Perspectives: From the 1851 Treaty to the Sand Creek Massacre," *American Indian Quarterly* 39, no. 4 (2015): 364; Berthrong, *Southern Cheyennes,* 168; Hoig, *Peace Chiefs,* 106–7.

27. Gary Clayton Anderson, *Massacre in Minnesota: The Dakota War of 1862, the Most Violent Ethnic Conflict in American History* (University of Oklahoma Press, 2019), 135–48; John Evans to William P. Dole, July 2, 1864, Letters Received 1861–1880, Colorado Superintendency, Office of Indian Affairs, M243, RG 75, NARA; *Rocky Mountain News,* June 12 and 14, 1864; Susan R. Ashley, "Reminiscences of Colorado in the Early Sixties," *Colorado Magazine* 13 (November 1936): 219–30.

28. Reginald Craig, *Fighting Parson: Biography of Col. John M. Chivington* (Westernlore Press, 1959), 66; Ned Blackhawk et al., *Report of the John Evans Study Committee* (Northwestern University, May 2014), 5; Maj. Jacob Downing to Col. John Chivington, May 3, 1864, in *War of Rebellion,* 34:907–8.

29. Blackhawk et al., *Evans Report,* 63–64; Gov. John Evans to Gen. Samuel Curtis, June 12, 1864, Outgoing, 1863–1865, Territorial Governor's Collection, CSA.

30. *Rocky Mountain News,* June 28, 1864; Gov. John Evans to Major Colley, June 28, 1864, Outgoing, 1863–1865, Territorial Governor's Collection, CSA; Halaas and Masich, *Halfbreed,* 123–31.

31. Hoig, *Sand Creek,* 53–53; Grinnell, *Fighting Cheyennes,* 138, 146–48; Major Eayre to Colonel Chivington, April 15, 1864, in *War of Rebellion,* 34:101.

32. John Evans to Sec. Stanton, June 14, 1864, in *War of Rebellion,* 34:330; ibid., 41:694; Hoig, *Sand Creek,* 56, 60.

33. Becher, *Massacre Along Medicine Road;* "Black Kettle and Other Chiefs to Maj. Colley," August 29, 1864, Sand Creek File, Special Collections, CCL.

34. Coel, *Chief Left Hand,* 251–56.

35. Hyde, *Life of George Bent,* 144–46.

36. William Bent, testimony, appendix to "Massacre of the Cheyenne Indians," in *Report of the Joint Committee on the Conduct of the War,* 3 vols. (1865), Senate Report no. 142, 38th Cong., 2nd sess., 93. Julia S. Lambert, "Plain Tales of the Plains," *Trail* 8 (1916): 6–11; Robert Bent, sworn statement, January 1865, in John M. Carroll, *The Sand Creek Massacre: A Documentary History* (Sol Lewis, 1985), 95–96.

37. Blackhawk et al., *Evans Report,* 75, 85; Hoig, *Sand Creek,* 140, 144.

38. Coel, *Chief Left Hand,* 275.

39. Hyde, *Life of George Bent,* 151–55.

40. James Beckwourth, sworn statement, March 3, 1865, in Carroll, *Sand Creek Massacre,* 241.

41. Gary L. Roberts and David Fridtjof Halaas, "Written in Blood: The Soule-Cramer Sand Creek Massacre Letters," *Colorado Heritage* (Winter 2001): 22–32; Col. John Chivington to Maj. Gen. Samuel Curtis, November 29, 1864, in *War of Rebellion*, 41:948, 951; Lynn Perrigo, ed., "Major Hall Sayre's Diary of the Sand Creek Campaign," *Colorado Magazine* 15 (1928): 333.

42. Robert Bent, sworn statement, in Carroll, *Sand Creek Massacre*, 185; George Bent to George Hyde, April 2, 1906, Folder 7, George Bent Letters, BRBM.

43. Ari Kelman, *A Misplaced Massacre: Struggling over the Memory of Sand Creek* (Harvard University Press, 2013), 39; Hyde, *Life of George Bent*, 157–59; Jerome A. Greene and Douglas D. Scott, *Finding Sand Creek: History, Archeology, and the 1864 Massacre Site* (University of Oklahoma Press, 2004), 20, 40–41; "Massacre of the Cheyenne Indians," i–vi, 3:147–203.

44. Hyde, *Life of George Bent*, 158.

45. Ibid., 168–72; Hoig, *Peace Chiefs*, 111–12; Blackhawk et al., *Evans Report*, 76–78.

46. Hyde, *Life of George Bent*, 181; Larry C. Skogen, *Indian Depredation Claims, 1796–1920* (University of Oklahoma Press, 1996), 156–64; Becher, *Massacre Along Medicine Road*, 187–91.

47. Doolittle to U.S. president, May 27, 1865, in *Annual Report of the Commissioner of Indian Affairs, 1865* (USGPO, 1865), 319.

48. George Bent to George Hyde, May 22, 1906, and October 12, 1905, Folder 6, George Bent Letters, BRBM; Berthrong, *Southern Cheyennes*, 254–57; Treaty with Cheyenne and Arapaho (1865), in Kappler, *Indian Affairs*, 2:887–92.

49. Andrew J. Drips, Probate Records, Kaw County, Mo., June 28, 1861.

50. Margaret Jackson Drips, Marriage Records, Kaw County, Mo., 1842, Missouri State Archives, Jefferson City; U.S. Census, Kaw County, Mo., 1850; Hugh Jackson Dobbs, *History of Gage County, Nebraska: A Narrative of the Past* (Western, 1918), 1004–5.

51. Adeline S. Gnirk, *The Saga of Sully Flat* (Gregory Times-Advocate, 1977); Albert Green, "The Oto Indians," *Nebraska Historical Society Proceedings* 21 (1917): 175–209; Special surveyor for Nemaha, Letterbook 57, M234, Roll 36, Office of Indian Affairs, RG 75, NARA.

52. Agent Abbot, testimony taken April–August 1866, "Ledger Book of Testimony and Claims of Shawnee Indians for Indemnity for Losses by Theft, Robbery, and Otherwise During the Continuance of the Late Rebellion," November 25, 1866, Shawnee Mission Agency, E961, RG 75, NARA.

53. David J. Drozd and Jerry Deichert, "Nebraska Historical Population Report," *Publications Since 2000* (2007), 37 https://digitalcommons .unomaha.edu/cgi/viewcontent.cgi?article=1302&context=cparpublicati ons; Loretta Fowler, *The Columbia Guide to American Indians of the Great Plains* (Columbia University Press, 2005), 201; Kingsley M. Bray, "Teton

Sioux: Population History, 1655–1881," *Nebraska History* 75, no. 2 (1994): 165–88.

54. "Andrew J Dripps Jr Probate Notice," *Nebraska Advertiser,* March 3, 1865; Daniel W. Overton, "Spending the Indians' Money: A Quantitative Case Study of Oto-Missouri Trust Fund Disbursements, 1855–1881," *Nebraska History* 75 (1993): 72–81; Berlin Basil Chapman, "Testimony on the History of the Otoe and Missouria Lands Before the Indian Claims Commission," October 1950, 34–35, Indian Claims Commission, Oto Files, WHC.

55. U.S. Census, 1860, Manuscript Census, Richardson County, Neb.; Sarah Carter, *Imperial Plots: Women, Land, and the Spadework of British Colonialism on the Canadian Prairies* (University of Manitoba Press, 2016), 22–26; Francis Barnes, Charles Drips, Purchases, Rulo, Neb., Land Transfer Ledger: Richardson County, 1859–66, Richardson County Historical Society, Falls, Neb.

56. Greene, *Washita,* 35–38; Jill St. Germain, *Broken Treaties: United States and Canadian Relations with the Lakotas and the Plains Cree, 1868–1885* (University of Nebraska Press, 2009).

57. Henry M. Stanley, "A British Journalist Reports the Medicine Lodge Peace Councils of 1867," *Kansas Historical Quarterly* 33, no. 3 (1967): 249–320.

58. Berthrong, *Southern Cheyennes,* 290–95; Robert G. Athearn, *William Tecumseh Sherman and the Settlement of the West* (University of Oklahoma Press, 1995), 171–77; Hyde, *Life of George Bent,* 259, 267–68.

59. Theodore R. Davis, "A Summer on the Plains," *Harper's New Monthly Magazine* 36 (February 1868): 306; Hyde, *Life of George Bent,* 212–15.

60. Agent E. W. Wynkoop, "Arapahoe, Cheyenne, and Apache Agency," September 14, 1867, in *Annual Report of the Commissioner of Indian Affairs, 1867* (USGPO, 1867), 310–19; Hyde, *Life of George Bent,* 112.

61. Stan Hoig, *The Battle of the Washita: The Sheridan-Custer Indian Campaign of 1867–69* (University of Nebraska Press, 1979); Mari Sandoz, "Introduction," in George Bird Grinnell, *The Cheyenne Indians: Their History and Ways of Life* (reprint, Yale University Press, 1962), 2:vi.

62. Kerry R. Oman, "The Beginning of the End: The Indian Peace Commission of 1867–1868," *Great Plains Quarterly* 22, no. 1 (2002): 35–51.

63. O. H. Browning to President Andrew Johnson, January 16, 1868, in *Annual Report of the Commissioner of Indian Affairs, 1867* (USGPO, 1867), 1–18.

64. Lesley Wischmann, *Frontier Diplomats: Alexander Culbertson and Natoyist-Siksina' Among the Blackfeet* (University of Oklahoma Press, 2004), 141–43; Lavender, *Bent's Fort,* 366; *Missouri Republican,* May 25, 1869.

65. *St. Joseph Traveler,* January 16, 1861, Clipping File, George Johnston Papers, Burton-DPL; William M. Johnston, Michigan Wills and Probate Records 1784–1980, Chippewa County, 1865, Ancestry.com, 2015; Obituary, Henry

Schoolcraft, *Atlanta Constitution*, December 19, 1864; Karl Hele, "Odd Couple Overcame the Odds," *Sault Star* (Michigan), September 10, 2017.

Chapter 11: Reconstructing Race on Western Reservations, 1866–1885

1. U.S. Census, 1870, Wasco County, East Dalles Precinct, Ore., 431A; *McKay v. Campbell*, Case No. 8840, District Court, D. Oregon, July 1, 1870.
2. *McKay v. Campbell*, September 26, 1870.
3. Ibid., November 7, 1871.
4. Richard G. White, *The Republic for Which It Stands: The United States During Reconstruction and the Gilded Age, 1865–1896* (Oxford University Press, 2017); Steven Hahn, *A Nation Under Our Feet: Black Political Struggles from Slavery to the Great Migration* (Harvard University Press, 2003), 377–85; Khal Schneider, "Distinctions That Must Be Preserved: On the Civil War, American Indians, and the West," *Civil War History* 62, no. 1 (2016): 36–61.
5. Senator Trumbull, statement, January 30, 1866, *Congressional Globe*, 39th Cong., 1st sess., at 498, 572; Stephen Kantrowitz, "Jurisdiction, Civilization, and the Ends of Native American Citizenship," *Western Historical Quarterly* 52, no. 2 (2021): 189–208; Deborah Rosen, *American Indians and State Law: Sovereignty, Race, and Citizenship, 1790–1880* (University of Nebraska Press, 2007), 87–99.
6. Kantrowitz, "Jurisdiction, Civilization," 89–93; *Report on the Effect of the 14th Amendment upon Indian Tribes*, December 14, 1870, Senate Report no. 268, 41st Cong., 3rd sess., at 2.
7. Kantrowitz, "White Supremacy, Settler Colonialism"; Banner, *How Indians Lost Their Land*, 231–44.
8. Donald Chaput, "Generals, Indian Agents, Politicians: The Doolittle Survey of 1865," *Western Historical Quarterly* 3, no. 3 (1972): 269; *Condition of the Indian Tribes*, Joint Special Committee Report no. 156 (1867), 39th Cong., 2nd sess., Serial 1279, at 3; Klaus Frantz, *Indian Reservations in the United States: Territory, Sovereignty, and Socioeconomic Change* (University of Chicago Press, 1999), 18–31; Robert Lee, "Accounting for Conquest: The Price of the Louisiana Purchase of Indian Country," *Journal of American History* 103, no. 4 (2017): 921–42.
9. Comm. Eli S. Parker, December 23, 1869, in *Annual Report of the Commissioner of Indian Affairs, 1869* (USGPO, 1869), 4–18; William J. Novak, "The Myth of the 'Weak' American State," *American Historical Review* 113, no. 3 (2008): 752–72.
10. Comm. F. A. Walker, November 1, 1872, in *Annual Report of the Commissioner of Indian Affairs, 1872* (USGPO, 1872), 3–5; Francis Amasa Walker,

"The Indian Question," *North American Review* (April 1873): 337, 347–48, 375. John R. Wunder, *Retained by the People: A History of American Indians and the Bill of Rights* (Oxford University Press, 1993), 17–19.

11. Cathleen D. Cahill, *Federal Fathers and Mothers: A Social History of the U.S. Indian Service, 1869–1933* (University of North Carolina Press, 2011), 26–33; White, *Republic for Which It Stands*, 113–16.

12. Murphy, *Great Lakes Creoles*, 145–46; Saler, *Settlers' Empire*, 226–31; Catherine J. Denial, *Making Marriage: Husbands, Wives, and the American State in Dakota and Ojibwe Country* (Minnesota Historical Society Press, 2013), 68–74.

13. Francis Paul Prucha, *American Indian Policy in Crisis: Christian Reformers and the Indian, 1865–1900* (University of Oklahoma Press, 2014); U.S. Board of Indian Commissioners, *Third Annual Report to the President of the United States, 1871* (USGPO, 1872), 9–12.

14. George Bent to Albert Boone, June 4, 1868, Letters Received, Upper Arkansas Agency, Office of Indian Affairs, RG 75, NARA; Berthrong, *Southern Cheyennes*, 308; William Sherman to Samuel Tappan, September 6, 1868, Samuel Tappan Papers, BRBL.

15. Berthrong, *Southern Cheyennes*, 303–6; John Smith to Agent Murphy, February 1, 1868, Letters Received, Upper Arkansas Agency, Office of Indian Affairs, RG 75, NARA; "Camp Supply, Indian Territory," *Harper's Weekly*, February 27, 1869, 140.

16. Beyreis, *Blood in the Borderlands*, 142–44; William Bent Personal Property Distribution, July 26, 1869, File no. 18, Bent's Fort Collection, CHS; Bent Family Genealogy File, Missouri Valley Room, Kansas City Public Library, Kansas City; John W. Prowers to George Bent, October 15, 1870, Patents, Cheyenne and Arapaho Agency Records, American Indian Archives, OKHS.

17. Brinton Darlington to Eli Parker, August 13, 1869, Letters Received, Upper Arkansas Agency, Office of Indian Affairs, RG 75, NARA; Fowler, *Wives and Husbands*, 111–14; Indian Census Rolls, 1888–1940, Special Census Cheyenne and Arapaho, June 3, 1887, at 5, Ancestry.com, 2007.

18. Prucha, *American Indian Policy in Crisis*, 14–43; Brinton Darlington to commissioner, August 12, 1870, in *Annual Report of the Commissioner of Indian Affairs, 1870* (USGPO, 1870), 267; Brinton Darlington to Enoch Hoag, November 9, 1870, Letters Received, Upper Arkansas Agency, Office of Indian Affairs, RG 75, NARA.

19. Halaas and Masich, *Halfbreed*, 280–83; Berthrong, *Southern Cheyennes*, 383–89; J. T. Marshall, *The Miles Expedition of 1873–1875: An Eyewitness Account of the Red River War* (Encino Press, 1971).

20. T. H. Barrett to General Miles, April 24, 1873, Depredations: 1868–1927, Cheyenne and Arapaho Agency Records, American Indian Archives, OKHS.

21. Berthrong, *Southern Cheyennes*, 393–98; John H. Seger, *Early Days Among*

the *Cheyenne and Arapahoe Indians* (University of Oklahoma Press, 1934); "Orders, Ben Clark to Visit Cheyenne and Arapaho Agency," June 20, 1875, Folder 4, Benjamin H. Clark Collection, WHC.

22. George Bent to J. D. Miles, November 4, 10, and 15, 1876, George Bent Family, Cheyenne and Arapahoe Agency Records, American Indian Archives, OKHS.

23. Andrew Isenberg, *The Destruction of the Bison: An Environmental History, 1750–1920* (Cambridge University Press, 2001), 120–23; Joseph W. Snell, ed., "Diary of a Dodge City Buffalo Hunter, 1872–1873," *Kansas Historical Quarterly* 32, no. 4 (1965): 345–95.

24. C. J. Jones, *Buffalo Jones' Forty Years of Adventure* (Crane, 1899); Snell, "Diary of a Dodge City Buffalo Hunter"; William Nicholson to commissioner of Indian affairs, June 20, 1876, Letters Received, Office of Indian Affairs, M234, R61, RG 75, NARA.

25. William Nicholson to commissioner of Indian affairs, June 20, 1876, Letters Received, Office of Indian Affairs, M234, R61, RG 75, NARA; Donald J. Berthrong, *The Cheyenne and Arapaho Ordeal: Reservation and Agency Life in the Indian Territory, 1875–1907* (University of Oklahoma Press, 1992), 10–11.

26. James N. Leiker and Ramon Powers, *The Northern Cheyenne Exodus in History and Memory* (University of Oklahoma Press, 2011), 13–15.

27. Caroline Fraser, *Prairie Fires: The American Dreams of Laura Ingalls Wilder* (Henry Holt, 2017).

28. U.S. Census, 1860, Richardson County, Nebraska Territory; U.S. Census, 1870, Barneston, Neb.; Chapman, "Nemaha Half-Breed Reservation," 12–20; Miner and Unrau, *End of Indian Kansas*, 12–20.

29. Dobbs, *History of Gage County*, 38–41; James E. Potter, *Standing Firmly by the Flag: Nebraska Territory and the Civil War, 1861–1867* (University of Nebraska Press, 2013); Ralph Tennal, *History of Nemaha County, Kansas* (University of Kansas Press, 1916), 46–47; Paige Raibmon, "Obvious but Invisible: Ways of Knowing Health, Environment, and Colonialism in a West Coast Indigenous Community," *Comparative Studies in Society and History* 60, no. 2 (2018): 241–73.

30. John McCoy, *Andreas' History of the State of Nebraska: Nemaha County* (1882), pt. 15, http://www.usgennet.org/usa/ne/topic/resources/andreas/nemaha/nemaha-p1.html; Tennal, *History of Nemaha County*, 63–68; Chelcey Adami, "Lorena Deroin Is Walking History Book for Otoe-Missouria," *Stillwater News Press* (Oklahoma), March 17, 2010.

31. Wishart, *Unspeakable Sadness*, 34; Ronald D. Parks, *The Darkest Period: The Kanza Indians in Their Last Homeland, 1846–1873* (University of Oklahoma Press, 2014), 233–35.

32. Berlin Basil Chapman, "The Barnes Family of Barneston," *Nebraska History* 47 (1966): 57–83; Joseph Sharp to Comm. George Manypenny, February 24, 1857, Great Nemaha, Office of Indian Affairs, S323, RG 75, NARA.

33. Certificate of Tribal Special Case, September 11, 1871, Special Case 95, L. 11715–1892, Office of Indian Affairs, RG 75, NARA; Lucy E. Murphy, "Public Mothers: Native American and Metis Women as Creole Mediators in the Nineteenth-Century Midwest," *Journal of Women's History* 14, no. 4 (2003): 142–66.

34. Jesse Griest, "Report on Oto-Missouria," in *Annual Report of the Commissioner of Indian Affairs, 1877* (USGPO, 1877), 95–98; Chapman, "Barnes Family of Barneston," 61; "Narrative of Major Albert Lamborn Green," in Dobbs, *History of Gage County*, 89–110; *Beatrice Express* (Nebraska), July 1871.

35. Wishart, *Unspeakable Sadness*, 217–22; Michael E. Dickey, *The People of the River's Mouth: In Search of the Missouria Indians* (University of Missouri Press, 2011), 115–20; U.S. Census, 1860, Rulo, Neb., 9; U.S. Census, 1870, Richardson County, Neb., Township No. 3, at range 16, 17.

36. Agent Barclay White to commissioner, October 23, 1874, in *Annual Report of the Commissioner of Indian Affairs, 1874* (USGPO, 1874), 201–4.

37. Mary J. Barnes to Mrs. U. S. Grant, January 25, 1875, Special Case 95, Otoe B. 155–1875, Office of Indian Affairs, RG 75, NARA; Mary J. Barnes to commissioner, December 9, 1875, Letters Received, Special Case 95, Otoe B. 155–1875, Office of Indian Affairs, RG 75, NARA.

38. U.S. Census, 1860, 1870, Jackson County, Mo.; Newspaper clippings file, Box 3, Folder 7, Drips Family Papers, BL.

39. *Wyandotte Gazette* (Kansas), September 23, 1881; *Baxter Springs Gazette* (Kansas), September 30, 1893; Perl Wilbur Morgan, *History of Wyandotte County, Kansas, and Its People* (Lewis, 1911), 1:33–38; James W. Tyner and Alice Tyner Timmons, eds., *Our People, and Where They Rest* (University of Oklahoma Press, 1972).

40. U.S. Census, 1870, Richardson County, Neb.; Richardson County, Rulo Township, Land Records, vol. 2, 1870, 1872, 1874; Ella Deloria, *Speaking of Indians* (reprint, University of Nebraska Press, 1998), 24–25.

41. Hämäläinen, *Lakota America*, 294–99; Michael M. Casler and W. Raymond Wood, eds., *Fort Tecumseh and Fort Pierre Chouteau: Journal and Letter Books* (South Dakota Historical Society, 2017), 216.

42. Raymond J. DeMallie, "The Sioux to 1850," in William Sturtevant, ed., *Handbook of American Indians*, 17 vols. (USGPO, 1978), 13:760; Paul L. Hedren, *After Custer: Loss and Transformation in Sioux Country* (University of Oklahoma Press, 2011), 5–8.

43. Paige Raibmon, *Authentic Indians: Episodes of Encounter from the Late-Nineteenth-Century Northwest Coast* (Duke University Press, 2005).

44. U.S. Census, 1860, 1870, Oregon; Jetté, *At the Hearth*; Pioneer Ladies Club, *Reminiscences of Oregon Pioneers* (n.p., 1937); Lewis A. McArthur and Lewis L. McArthur, *Oregon Geographic Names* (n.p., 1928), 626–27.

45. "County Election Results," *Umatilla Times*, June 6, 1882; U.S. Census, 1870, Wasco County, Ore., M593, at 431A; U.S. Census, 1880, Umatilla County, Ore., M1084, at 54A.

46. "Census of the Mixed Bloods on Umatilla Reservation, June 30, 1886," Records of the Oregon Superintendency, M2, 1886 report at 13; Indian Census Rolls, 1885, Cayuse, Umatilla, Shoshoni; David G. Lewis, "Four Deaths: The Near Destruction of Western Oregon Tribes and Native Lifeways, Removal to the Reservation, and Erasure from History," *Oregon Historical Quarterly* 115, no. 3 (2014): 414.

47. Elliott West, *The Last Indian War: The Nez Perce Story* (Oxford University Press, 2011); David Peterson del Mar, *Beaten Down: A History of Interpersonal Violence in the West* (University of Washington Press, 2002), 30; *Daily Oregonian*, February 4, 1879.

48. Indian Census Rolls, 1881, 1883, Warm Springs Reservation; Indian Census Rolls, 1889, 1896, Umatilla Reservation; Alfred Meacham, *Wi-Ne-Ma (The Woman-Chief) and Her People* (American Publishing, 1876).

49. Boughter, *Betraying the Omaha*, 68–69; Secretary of the Interior, *Report of the Secretary of the Interior, 1872* (USGPO, 1872), 460–61.

50. Robin Ridington, "Omaha Survival: A Vanishing Indian Tribe That Would Not Vanish," *American Indian Quarterly* 11, no. 1 (1987): 37; Sherry L. Smith, "Francis La Flesche and the World of Letters," *American Indian Quarterly* 25, no. 4 (2001): 579–603; Sarah Pripas-Kapit, "'We Have Lived on Broken Promises': Charles A. Eastman, Susan La Flesche Picotte, and the Politics of American Indian Assimilation During the Progressive Era," *Great Plains Quarterly* 35, no. 1 (2015): 51–78.

51. Thomas P. Barr, "The Pottawatomie Baptist Manual Labor Training School," *Kansas Historical Quarterly* 43, no. 4 (1977): 377–431; Francis La Flesche, *The Middle Five: Indian Schoolboys of the Omaha Tribe* (reprint, University of Nebraska Press, 1978); Norma Green, *Iron Eye's Family: The Children of Joseph La Flesche* (Nebraska State Historical Society, 1969), 26–28.

52. Thorne, *Many Hands*, 115; Elizabeth A. Grobsmith, *Indians in Prison: Incarcerated Native Americans in Nebraska* (University of Nebraska Press, 1994), 11, 13; Thurston County, Neb., Blackbird Precinct, Special Schedules of the Eleventh Census (1890) Enumerating Union Veterans and Widows of Union Veterans of the Civil War, M123, Ancestry.com, 2014.

53. U.S. Census, 1860, Omaha, Nebraska Territory; U.S. Census, 1870, Richardson County, Neb.

54. Jerome A. Greene, *American Carnage: Wounded Knee, 1890* (University of Oklahoma Press, 2014), 14–18; Hedren, *After Custer*, 21–24.

55. Jon L. Brudvig, comp., "Hampton Normal & Agricultural Institute: American Indian Students, 1878–1923" (1994, 1996), http://www.twofrog.com/hampton.html; U.S. Census, 1880, Charles Mix County, Dakota Territory, at 234D.

56. Isenberg, *Destruction of Bison*, 140–41; Comm. E. A. Hayt, in *Annual Report of the Commissioner of Indian Affairs, 1878* (USGPO, 1878), 22–25.

57. Hedren, *After Custer*, 148–49; Indian Census Rolls, 1886, Yankton Sioux, Crow Creek Agency, at 21; U.S. Census, 1890, Lake Traverse, Charles Mix County, S.D.

58. Grinnell, *Cheyenne Indians,* 1:370.

59. Standing Out Bent, interview by Louise Barnes, 1938, Indian-Pioneer Papers Collection, WHC; Walter Campbell to Dorothy Gardner, December 5, 1939, Box 18, Walter Campbell Papers, WHC.

60. *Arkansas City Traveler,* August 29, 1883; Standing Out Bent interview, 1938.

61. George Bent to Agent G. D. Williams, April 27 and May 24, 1887, Letterbooks vol. 20, Cheyenne and Arapahoe Agency Records, American Indian Archives, OKHS.

62. Berthrong, *Cheyenne and Arapaho Ordeal,* 100–101; Henry Tall Bull and Tom Weist, *Cheyenne Legends of Creation: Stories of the Northern Cheyenne* (Montana State University Press, 1972), 11–13, 23.

63. Berthrong, *Cheyenne and Arapaho Ordeal,* 84–88; John D. Miles, *Report of the Superintendent of Indian Affairs, 1883* (USGPO, 1883); Mary Jane Warde, "George Washington Grayson and the Creek Nation, 1843–1920," Ph.D. diss., Oklahoma State University, 1991, at 207–12.

64. Ada Bent, Julia Bent, George Bent, Student Record Cards, Carlisle School Records, Office of Indian Affairs, RG 75, NARA; *Cheyenne Transporter,* September 15 and October 10, 1884.

65. Eddie Bent Box, letter to author, June 21, 2017; Charles S. Marsh, *People of the Shining Mountains: The Utes of Colorado* (Pruett, 1982); Blackhawk, *Violence,* 280–83.

66. U.S. Census, La Plata County, Colo., 1880, 1890; U.S. Census, Oklahoma 1910, Darlington Township, Cement, Okla.; U.S. Census, Colorado Special State Census, 1885, Ancestry.com, 2006; Indian Census Rolls, 1884, 1887, 1891, Cheyenne.

67. U.S. Census, 1890, La Plata County, Colo.; U.S. Census, 1900, Southern Ute Reservation, La Plata, Colo., 3A; Indian Census Rolls, 1884, 1887, 1891, Cheyenne; Census of the Allotted Southern Utes, Ignacio Subagency, 1886, 1891, 1898.

68. James F. Brooks, *Mesa of Sorrows: A History of the Awat'ovi Massacre* (W. W. Norton, 2016), 217–22.

Chapter 12: "A Mighty Pulverizing Engine"

1. *Cheyenne Transporter*, August 25, 1880; Julia Bent, Student File, Carlisle School Records, 1880–1893, Office of Indian Affairs, RG 75, NARA; Ada Bent, Student File, Carlisle School Records, 1880–1882, Office of Indian Affairs, RG 75, NARA.

2. Heather Cox Richardson, *West from Appomattox: The Reconstruction of America After the Civil War* (Yale University Press, 2008), 78–82; Genetin-Pilawa, *Crooked Paths to Allotment*, 112–17.

3. Wishart, *Unspeakable Sadness*, 122–25; David J. Carlson, "'Indian for a While': Charles Eastman's Indian Boyhood and the Discourse of Allotment," *American Indian Quarterly* 25, no. 4 (2001): 604–25.

4. Indian Rights Association and Historical Society of Pennsylvania, *Indian Rights Association Papers, 1864–1973* (Indian Rights Association, 1974), xii–xv.

5. Andrew Woolford, *This Benevolent Experiment: Indigenous Boarding Schools, Genocide, and Redress in Canada and the United States* (University of Nebraska Press, 2015), 65–77; La Flesche, *Middle Five*, 123.

6. K. Tsianina Lomawaima, *They Called It Prairie Light: The Story of Chilocco Indian School* (University of Nebraska Press, 1995), 3–5; *Chilocco: The School of Opportunity for Indians* (n.p., 1933); *Cheyenne Reporter*, September 17, 1880.

7. Indian Rights Association, *Brief Statement of the Nature and Purpose of the Indian Rights Association: With a Summary of Its Work for the Year 1882* (USGPO, 1882).

8. David Wallace Adams, *Education for Extinction: American Indians and the Boarding School Experience, 1875–1928* (University of Kansas Press, 1995), 23–27; Jacqueline Fear-Segal and Susan D. Rose, *Carlisle Indian Industrial School: Indigenous Histories, Memories, and Reclamations* (University of Nebraska Press, 2016); Margaret Jacobs, *White Mother to a Dark Race* (University of Nebraska Press, 2009), 4–6, 132–37; "The Indian School at Chemawa," *West Shore* 13, no. 1 (1887): 5–12; William McKay to Eva Emery Dye, 1893, Box 2, Eva Emery Dye Papers, OHS.

9. Donald J. Berthrong, "From Buffalo Days to Classrooms: The Southern Cheyennes and Arapahos in Kansas," *Kansas History* 12, no. 2 (1989): 100–109; Myriam Vučković, *Voices from Haskell: Indian Students Between Two Worlds, 1884–1928* (University of Kansas Press, 2008), 120–21; Indian Census Rolls, 1885, 1887, Yankton, Dakota, at 680; Indian Census Rolls, 1894, 1897, Southern Ute, Colo.

10. Henrietta Mann, *Cheyenne-Arapaho Education, 1871–1982* (University Press of Colorado, 1998); U.S. Census, 1890, Canadian County, Reno, Indian Territory, at 4B.

11. Wilma A. Daddario, "'They Get Milk Practically Every Day': The Genoa Indian Industrial School, 1884–1934," *Nebraska History* 73 (Spring 1992): 2–11; Chapman, "Barnes Family of Barneston," 57–83; "Report of Superintendent of Indian Schools," in *Annual Report of the Commissioner of Indian Affairs, 1894* (USGPO, 1894), 344; Henry Oxnard to J. M. Rusk, May 13, 1891, in *Annual Report of the Commissioner of Indian Affairs, 1891* (USGPO, 1891), 151–53; Robert M. Harveson, "The First Successful Sugar Beet Factory in the United States?," *Farm and Ranch*, February 21, 2016.

12. Adams, *Education for Extinction*, 58–59; Kevin Whalen, *Native Students at Work: American Indian Labor and the Sherman Institute's Outing Program* (University of Washington Press, 2016), 18–31.

13. George E. Hyde, *A Sioux Chronicle* (University of Oklahoma Press, 1956), 209–13; Loretta Fowler, *Arapahoe Politics, 1851–1978: Symbols in Crises of Authority* (University of Nebraska Press, 1986), 297; U.S. Census, 1890, Darlington, Canadian County, Indian Territory.

14. Thomas L. Hedglen, "Cheyenne-Arapaho Cattle Company," *Encyclopedia of Oklahoma History and Culture*, OKHS; *Evening Star* (Kansas City), August 1 and 5, 1885; J. M. Lee to commissioner of Indian affairs, August 18, 1885, Letterbooks 8:304–5, Cheyenne and Arapaho Agency Records, American Indian Archives, OKHS.

15. Ada Bent Student Information Card (1880), Carlisle School Records, Series 1329, Box 4, RG 75, NARA; Berthrong, *Cheyenne and Arapaho Ordeal*, 116–18, 174; Indian Census Rolls, 1888, Cheyenne and Arapaho, M595, at 27; U.S. Census, 1890, 1900, Canadian County, Darlington, Indian Territory; John Truden, "Where Cowboys and Indians Meet: A Southern Cheyenne Web of Kinship and the Transnational Cattle Industry, 1877–1885," *Western Historical Quarterly* 50, no. 4 (2019): 263–90.

16. Henry Dawes, "Have We Failed with the Indian?," *Atlantic Monthly*, August 1899, 280–85; Laura Wexler, *Tender Violence: Domestic Visions in an Age of U.S. Imperialism* (University of North Carolina Press, 2001), 22, 52–53; William T. Hagan, *The Indian Rights Association* (University of Arizona Press, 1985), 50–56.

17. Genetin-Pilawa, *Crooked Paths to Allotment*, 134–38; Theodore Roosevelt, "First Annual Message," December 3, 1901, https://tinyurl.com/25ujy2xc; Louis S. Warren, *God's Red Son: The Ghost Dance Religion and the Making of Modern America* (Basic Books, 2017), 158–59; William T. Hagan, *Taking Indian Lands: The Cherokee (Jerome) Commission, 1889–1893* (University of Oklahoma Press, 2011), 80–84; Peter C. Mancall, ed., *Encyclopedia of Native American History*, 3 vols. (Facts on File, 2011), 3:271–72, 340–43.

18. Melissa L. Meyer, *Thicker Than Water: The Origins of Blood as Symbol and Ritual* (Routledge, 2005), 110–18; Paul Spruhan, "A Legal History of Blood Quantum in Federal Indian Law to 1935," *South Dakota Law Review* 51, no.

1 (2006): 1–50; Jennifer L. Hochschild and B. M. Powell, "Racial Reorganization and the United States Census, 1850–1930: Mulattoes, Half-Breeds, Mixed Parentage, Hindoos, and the Mexican Race," *Studies in American Political Development* 22, no. 1 (2008): 1–65; Doug Kiel, "Bleeding Out: Histories and Legacies of 'Indian Blood,'" in Hill and Rattereee, *Great Vanishing Act,* 80–97.

19. Banner, *How Indians Lost Their Land,* 257–65; Saunt, *Unworthy Republic,* 17–19, 187–89; Angie Debo, *And Still the Waters Run: The Betrayal of the Five Civilized Tribes* (Princeton University Press, 1940), 44–47.

20. U.S. Census, 1890, 1900; Special Indian Census, 1880; Paul Schor, *Counting Americans: How the U.S. Census Classified the Nation* (Oxford University Press, 2017), 118–24; Pamela D. Palmater, *Beyond Blood: Rethinking Indigenous Identity* (University of British Columbia Press, 2011); Mikaela M. Adams, "Residency and Enrollment: Diaspora and the Catawba Indian Nation," *South Carolina Historical Magazine* 13, no. 1 (2012): 24–49; Redbird Smith, "Testimony," U.S. Congress, *Annual Report to the Civilized Tribes Commission,* 1902, 31–32.

21. Department of the Interior, "Circular of the Secretary of the Interior, September 17, 1887," Records of the Indian Division, RG 48.5, NARA; Graybill, *Red and White,* 171–81; Rose Stremlau, "Allotment, Jim Crow, and the State: Reconceptualizing the Privatization of Land, the Segregation of Bodies, and the Politicization of Sexuality in the Native South," *Native South* 10, no. 1 (2017): 60–75.

22. Marriages 1841–1927, Cheyenne and Arapahoe Agency Records, American Indian Archives, OKHS; Department of the Interior, "Rules for the Court of Indian Offences," Kiowa, Comanche, and Wichita Reservation, 1883, and Cheyenne and Arapahoe, 1889, Office of Indian Affairs, American Indian Archives, OKHS; J. M. Lee to commissioner of Indian affairs, March 7, 1886, Letterbooks 10:499; and notices signed by J. M. Lee, June 13, 1886, Letterbooks 14:241–43, both in Cheyenne and Arapaho Agency Records, American Indian Archives, OKHS; Kendra Taira Field, *Growing Up with the Country: Family, Race, and Nation After the Civil War* (Yale University Press, 2018), 8, 60–63.

23. C. F. Ashley to commissioner of Indian affairs, October 1, 1889, and June 3, 1890, Letterbooks 27:30, Cheyenne and Arapaho Agency Records, American Indian Archives, OKHS.

24. U.S. Census, 1890, 1900; Special Indian Census, 1880; D. L. Beaulieu, "Curly Hair and Big Feet: Physical Anthropology and the Implementation of Land Allotment on the White Earth Chippewa Reservation," *American Indian Quarterly* 8, no. 4 (1984): 281–314.

25. Harry H. Anderson, "The Waldron-Black Tomahawk Controversy and the Status of Mixed Bloods Among the Teton Sioux," *South Dakota History*

21, no. 1 (1991), 69–76; Alexandra Harmon, "Tribal Enrollment Councils: Lessons on Law and Indian Identity," *Western Historical Quarterly* 32, no. 2 (2001): 175–200; Spruhan, "Legal History of Blood Quantum," 38–39; U.S. v. Hadley, 99 F. 437 (C.C.D. Wash. 1900).

26. U.S. Indian Service, "Umatilla Reservation, Employees Listed, 1881, 1883, 1891," *U.S. Register of Civil, Naval and Military Service, 1863–1959*, Department of Commerce and Labor, Bureau of the Census, 77 vols., Ancestry.com; U.S. Census, Umatilla County, Pendleton, Ore., 1880, at 54A; Enumeration District 112; Indian Census Rolls, 1883, 1889, 1891, Umatilla; Indian Census Rolls, 1880, 1884, 1888, Warm Springs Reservation.

27. Michelle M. Jacob, *Yakama Rising: Indigenous Cultural Revitalization, Activism, and Healing* (University of Arizona Press, 2014), 17–19, 38; Robert H. Ruby, John Brown, and Cary C. Collins, *A Guide to the Indian Tribes of the Pacific Northwest* (University of Oklahoma Press, 2010).

28. Chapman, *Otoes and Missourias*, 385–92.

29. Ibid.; Emmet Barnes, Indian Claims Commission Hearings, Transcript of Proceedings, January 28, 1948, 63620–1939—Pawnee—054, Office of Indian Affairs, RG 75, NARA; Schedule of Tribes Occupying Reservations, in *Annual Report of the Commissioner of Indian Affairs, 1891* (USGPO, 1891), 116–17.

30. Graybill, *Red and White*, 171–77; Otoe-Missouria Tribe, *The Otoe-Missouria Elders: Centennial Memoirs* (n.p., 1981); Chapman, *Otoes and Missourias*, 215–18; "Report on Otoe Subagency," in *Annual Report of the Commissioner of Indian Affairs, 1892, 1894* (USGPO, 1892, 1894), 398–401.

31. Carter, *Imperial Plots*, 33–36; Rose Stremlau, " 'To Domesticate and Civilize Wild Indians': Allotment and the Campaign to Reform Indian Families, 1875–1887," *Journal of Family History* 30, no. 3 (2005): 265–86; Julie L. Reed, *Serving the Nation: Cherokee Sovereignty and Social Welfare, 1800–1907* (University of Oklahoma Press, 2016), 198–203; Valerie Matthes, *The Women's National Indian Association: A History* (University of New Mexico Press, 2015), 64–84.

32. "Self Control," *Indian Advocate* (Oklahoma) 9, no. 4 (1897);. Reed, *Serving the Nation*, 230–35.

33. "Report of Mary McCormick," May 1900, Field Matrons, 1897–1915, CAA 81; and G. W. H. Stouch to George Coleman, April 9, 1900, CAA 6, Letter Press Book, both in Cheyenne and Arapahoe Agency Records; American Indian Archives, OKHS; Rose Stremlau, *Sustaining the Cherokee Family: Kinship and the Allotment of an Indigenous Nation* (University of North Carolina Press, 2011), 69; David A. Chang, *The Color of the Land: Race, Nation, and the Politics of Land Ownership in Oklahoma, 1832–1929* (University of North Carolina Press, 2010).

34. Indian Census Rolls, 1885–1940, Seger Colony, 1887–89, Cheyenne Bands

at Cantonment 1891; U.S. Census, 1890, 1900, Reno Township, Canadian County, Indian Territory; Julia Bent, Returned Student Reports, Carlisle School Records, RG 75, NARA.

35. Indian Census Rolls, 1885–1940, Cheyenne and Arapaho, 1890, 1891, 1900; U.S. Census, 1890, 1900, Reno Township, Canadian County, Indian Territory, 363–90.

36. Sarah M. S. Pearsall, "Native American Men—and Women—at Home in Plural Marriages in Seventeenth-Century New France," *Gender and History* 27, no. 3 (2015): 591–610.

37. "The Rush to Oklahoma," *Harper's Weekly*, May 18, 1889; Berthrong, *Cheyenne and Arapaho Ordeal*, 149; *Oklahoma Gazette*, May 23, 1892; Hagan, *Taking Indian Lands*, 62–68; J. W. Morris and Edwin C. McReynolds, *Historical Atlas of Oklahoma* (University of Oklahoma Press, 1967).

38. George Bent, testimony, January 7, 1890, and J. W. Noble to commissioner of Indian affairs, February 5, 1890, Letters Sent, Bureau of Indian Affairs, RG 75, NARA; C. C. Painter, *Cheyennes and Arapahoes Revisited and a Statement of Their Contract with Attorneys* (Indian Rights Association, 1893), 27–44, 49–51, 53–62.

39. *Eleventh Report of the Board of Indian Commissioners* (USGPO, 1890); Seger Agency, Oklahoma, Cheyenne Annuity Payment Rolls, October 23, 1902, Bureau of Indian Affairs, RG 75, NARA; Indian Census Rolls, 1891, Cheyenne, Darlington, Indian Territory; Hagan, *Taking Indian Lands*, 80–82; Mary Jane Warde, "Fight for Survival: The Indian Response to the Boomer Movement," *Chronicles of Oklahoma* 67 (Spring 1989): 30–51.

40. Gregory N. Smoak, *Ghost Dances and Identity: Prophetic Religion and American Indian Ethnogenesis in the Nineteenth Century* (University of California Press, 2008), 3; Louis S. Warren, "Wage Work in the Sacred Circle: The Ghost Dance as Modern Religion," *Western Historical Quarterly* 46, no. 2 (2015): 141–68.

41. Warren, *God's Red Son*, 131–35; Smoak, *Ghost Dance*, 160–66.

42. Jeffrey D. Anderson, *One Hundred Years of Old Man Sage: An Arapaho Life* (University of Nebraska Press, 2007), 62–65.

43. Berthrong, *Cheyenne and Arapaho Ordeal*, 141–45; Hagan, *Taking Indian Lands*, 166–71; Berlin Basil Chapman, *Federal Management and Disposition of the Lands of the Oklahoma Territory, 1866–1907* (Arno Press, 1979), 277.

44. Warren, *God's Red Son*, 56–58; James Mooney, *The Ghost-Dance Religion and the Sioux Outbreak of 1890* (University of Nebraska Press, 2012), 26, 158; Donald J. Berthrong, "Struggle for Power: The Impact of Southern Cheyenne and Arapaho 'Schoolboys' on Tribal Politics," *American Indian Quarterly* 16, no. 1 (1992): 1–16.

45. Gregory James Brueck, "Breaking the Plains: Indians, Settlers, and Reform-

ers in the Oklahoma Land Rush," Ph.D. diss., University of California, Davis, 2012; Standing Out Bent interview, 1938.

46. Frank D. Healy, "Notice," 1901, 86, Microfilm Roll 2, M840; *Interior Department Territorial Papers: Oklahoma, 1889–1912*, Records of the Office of the Secretary of the Interior, 28 vols., RG 48, NARA; Smoak, *Ghost Dance*, 171–72.

47. Warren, *God's Red Son*, 308–10; Mooney, *Ghost-Dance*, 159.

48. David Rich Lewis, *Neither Wolf nor Dog: American Indians, Environment, and Agrarian Change* (Oxford University Press, 1994), 26–29, 44–48; M. Wilson Rankin, *Reminiscences of Frontier Days; including an Authentic Account of the Thornburg and Meeker Massacre* (Old West, 1938), ix–xx; U.S. Census, 1900, Southern Ute Reservation, La Plata, Colo., Roll 130, at 3A; Indian Census Rolls, 1891, 1902, Southern Ute Reservation, Ignacio Subagency.

49. George Bent to William Reynolds, January 13, 1898, Box 3, George Bent Papers, CHS.

50. L. G. Moses, *The Indian Man: A Biography of James Mooney* (University of Nebraska Press, 2002), 28–33, 51–55.

51. Neil M. Judd, *The Bureau of American Ethnology: A Partial History* (University of Oklahoma Press, 1967), 11–12.

52. Mooney, *Ghost-Dance*, 172; Warren, *God's Red Son*, 197–202, 209, 288–94, 308–15.

53. Moses, *Indian Man*, 99–103; James Mooney, "Indian Shield Heraldry," *Southern Workman* 30, no. 9 (1901): 500–4; John C. Ewers, introduction to James Mooney, *Calendar History of the Kiowa Indians* (USGPO, 1898), xii; Mooney quoted in Moses, *Indian Man*, 22.

54. Sherry L. Smith, "George Bird Grinnell and the 'Vanishing Plains Indians,'" *Montana: Magazine of Western History* 50, no. 13 (2000): 18–31; George Bird Grinnell to Maj. G. W. H. Stouch, May 11, 1901, Box 4, George Bent Letters, BRBM.

55. John Dishon McDermott, "A Dedication to the Memory of George E. Hyde, 1882–1968," *Arizona and the West* 17, no. 2 (1975): 103–106.

56. W. A. Jones to Indian agents, September 1897, as reported in *Omaha Bee*, April 4, 1898.

57. Lincoln B. Faller and George Bent, "Making Medicine Against 'White Man's Side of Story': George Bent's Letters to George Hyde," *American Indian Quarterly* 24, no. 1 (2000): 64–90.

58. Halaas and Masich, *Halfbreed*, 335–37; Faller and Bent, "Making Medicine," 68–70.

59. George Bent and George Hyde, "Forty Years with the Cheyennes," *Frontier*, October 1905, 3–22; Bent to Hyde, November 27, 1905, Folder 4, and Bent to Hyde, February 28, 1906, Folder 6, both in George Bent Letters, BRBM; Bent to Hyde, November 30, 1905, Box 1, George Bent Letters, HC.

60. George Bent to George Hyde, April 12, 1906, Folder 8, George Bent Letters, BRBM.

61. Francis Cragin, "Memoir" (1915), Cragin Collection, CSPM; *Denver Times*, November 5, 1905.

62. Object E1748.1, Jacob Downing Collection, Colorado Historical Society, Denver; *Colorado Republican*, March 22, 1906; *Colorado News and Free Press*, July 5, 1907; *Summit County Journal* (Colorado), July 6, 1907.

63. John R. Abernathy, *In Camp with Theodore Roosevelt; or, The Life of John R. (Jack) Abernathy* (Oklahoma Times-Journal, 1933); Foster Harris, "T.R. and the Great Wolf Hunt," *Oklahoma Today* 8 (Fall 1958); Theodore Roosevelt, "Wolf Hunt in Oklahoma," *Scribner's Magazine* 38, no. 5 (1905): 513–32.

64. Tom McHugh, *The Time of the Buffalo* (Bison Books, 1979), 3–4, 275.

Epilogue: The Twentieth Century

1. Vine Deloria, Jr., *Custer Died for Your Sins: An Indian Manifesto* (Macmillan, 1969), 62. The signs from Lander, Wyo., Pendleton, Ore., Sisseton, S.D., and Lamar, Colo., are from the photo collection of the Western History Center, Laramie, Wyo., and the digital collection of the Denver Public Library; Philip J. Deloria, *Indians in Unexpected Places* (University Press of Kansas, 2004), 7–9.

2. Mary Divine, "This Washington County Lake Had a Derogatory Name," *Twin Cities Pioneer Press*, May 11, 2017; Peter Salter, "History and Hurt on Half Breed Drive," *Lincoln Journal Star*, February 15, 2015.

3. Matthew Frye Jacobson, *Whiteness of a Different Color: European Immigrants and the Alchemy of Race* (Harvard University Press, 1999), 1–12; Lauren L. Basson, *White Enough to Be American?: Race Mixing, Indigenous People, and the Boundaries of Race and Nation* (University of North Carolina Press, 2008), 123–38; Russell Thornton, "Who Counts? Indians and the U.S. Census," in Hill and Ratteree, *Great Vanishing Act*, 142–58.

4. Kelly Lytle Hernandez, *City of Inmates: Conquest, Rebellion and the Rise of Human Caging in Los Angeles, 1771–1965* (University of North Carolina Press, 2017), 12–16, chap. 3; Peggy Pascoe, *What Comes Naturally: Miscegenation Law and the Making of Race in America* (Oxford University Press, 2009), 94–109.

5. Ellinghaus, *Blood Will Tell*, 115–18; Mara Loveman, *National Colors: Racial Classification and the State in Latin America* (Oxford University Press, 2014); Allyson Hobbes, *A Chosen Exile: A History of Racial Passing in the United States* (Harvard University Press, 2014).

6. U.S. Census, 1880, 1890, Umatilla County, Pendleton, Ore.; U.S. Census, 1890, 1900, 1910, Douglas County, Canyonville, Ore.; Indian Census Rolls,

1891, 1894, 1901, Umatilla, Grande Ronde, Warm Springs Reservation; Bauer, *We Were All Like Migrant Workers*, 106–28.

7. U.S. Census, 1850, Multnomah County, Oregon Territory; U.S. Census, 1870, Dalles County, Ore.; Hogue, *Metis and the Medicine Line*, 60–62; Philip Rand, "Incidents in the Life of Thomas Pambrun, as Taken from Men Who Knew Him," Pambrun Family Collection, OHS; U.S. Census, 1890, Chouteau, Mont.; U.S. Census, 1900, Libby, Mont.

8. U.S. Census, 1860, Marion County, Ore.; U.S. Census, 1870, Dalles County, Wasco, Ore.; U.S. Census, 1880, Pendleton, Ore.; U.S. Census, 1900, Umatilla Reservation; U.S. Census, 1910, Multnomah County, Portland, Ore.; Portland City Directories, 1903, 1911, 1914.

9. Indian Census Rolls, 1892, Umatilla Agency, at 7 on "Mixed Bloods on the Umatilla Reserve"; *Official Register of the United States, Containing a List of the Officers and Employees in the Civil, Military, and Naval Service* (USGPO, 1885), 1:728; *East Oregonian*, September 19, 1917; *Oregon Daily Journal*, August 31, 1919; Portland City Directories, 1907, 1913; U.S. Census, 1900, 1910, 1920, Multnomah County, Portland, Ore.; Indian Census Rolls, 1936, Yakima Reservation.

10. Debo, *And Still the Waters Run*, 61–90; Chapman, "Barnes Family of Barneston," 25–28; Agent Larrabee to secretary of interior, June 30, 1906, A. Letterbook, 550:28–30, Office of Indian Affairs, RG 75, NARA.

11. F. J. Barnes to Representative Hinshaw, February 8, 1906, F. 13732–1906, Office of Indian Affairs, RG 75, NARA; Chief Whitehorse to Francis E. Leupp, Petition, January 22, 1907, in *Annual Report of the Commissioner of Indian Affairs, 1908* (USGPO, 1908), 318.

12. Indian Census Rolls, 1900, 1904, 1907, 1912, Otoe and Ponca; U.S. Census, 1900, 1910, 1930, Ponca City, Okla.; U.S. Census, 1880, 1890, 1910, Barneston, Neb.

13. Kansas State Census, 1905; Marriage Records, Jackson County, Kansas City, Kans., 1899; U.S. Census, 1920, Barneston, Neb.; U.S. Census, 1930, Ponca, Okla.

14. Jeffrey D. Means, "'Indians Shall Do Things in Common': Oglala Lakota Identity and Economics During the Early Reservation Era, 1868–1889," *Montana: Magazine of Western History* 60, no. 3 (2011): 3–21; Susette La Flesche, *Om-ah-ha-ta-tha: Omaha City* (University of Nebraska Press, 1898); Hampton Normal and Agricultural Institute, *Annual Report of the Principal to the Board of Trustees, 1888* (Hampton Institute Press, 1888), 10–21; Indian Census Rolls, 1880, 1887, 1901, Omaha and Winnebago; U.S. Census, 1910, Burt County, Decatur, Neb., at 21.

15. Sidney Byrd, "Rabbit Runners and Indian Boarding Schools," pt.1, *Genoa Leader-Times* (Nebraska), March 28, 1991; *Indian News* 1, no. 8 (1913); *Indian News* 19, no. 1–2 (1917); Indian Census Rolls, 1907, Omaha and Win-

nebago; U.S. Census, 1910, Decatur, Burt County, Neb.; Marriage Records, 1928, Forsyth, Rosebud County, Mont.; U.S. Census, 1940, Decatur, Burt County, Neb.

16. Field, *Growing Up with the Country*, 140–43; Muriel H. Wright, *Our Oklahoma* (Coop Publishing, 1939); Patricia Nelson Limerick, "Land, Justice, and Angie Debo Telling The Truth to—and About—Your Neighbors," *Great Plains Quarterly* 21, no. 4 (2001): 261–73; Harold Martin Troper, "The Creek-Negroes of Oklahoma and Canadian Immigration, 1909–11," *Canadian Historical Review* 53, no. 3 (1972): 272–88.

17. U.S. Census, 1910, Cement Township, Darlington Village, Okla.; Charles Bent, Student Information Card, 1897–1905, Carlisle School Records, RG 75, NARA.

18. Bethany R. Berger, "Red: Racism and the American Indian," *UCLA Law Review* 56, no. 3 (2009): 591–656; Marriage Records, 1910, Blaine County, Okla.; U.S. Census, 1920, Pine Ridge Reservation, S.D.; George Bent to George Hyde, September 25, 1913, Folder 25, George Bent Letters, BRBM; Debo, *And Still the Waters Run*; Philip Deloria, *Becoming Mary Sully: Toward an American Indian Abstract* (Washington State University Press, 2019).

19. George Bent to George Hyde, February 20, 1905, Folder 3; Bent to Hyde, March 26, 1906, Folder 7; and Bent to Hyde, August 2, 1911, Folder 13, all in George Bent Letters, BRBM.

20. George Bent to George Hyde, April 2, 1906, Folder 7, George Bent Letters, BRBM; McDermott, "Dedication to the Memory of Hyde," 105; Grinnell, *Fighting Cheyennes*, vi.

21. Bent to Hyde, November 10, 1915, Box 2, George Bent Letters, HC; Grinnell, *Fighting Cheyennes*, 12–21, 152, 164–80, 200.

22. Bent to Hyde, November 10, 1915, Box 2, George Bent Letters, HC; Grinnell, *Fighting Cheyennes*, 179, 180–86; Bent to Hyde, September 23, 1913, Folder 24, George Bent Letters, BRBM.

23. George Bent to George Hyde, July 18, 1911, Folder 13, Bent to Hyde, November 17, 1911, Folder 15, and Bent to Hyde, December 21, 1914, Folder 25, all in George Bent Letters, BRBM; Bent to Hyde, September 9, 1913, Folder 3, George Bent Letters, HC; and Bent to Hyde, September 23, 1913, Box 2, Bent Papers, CHS.

24. "Influenza Among American Indians," *Public Health Reports* 34, no. 19 (May 9, 1919): 1008–9; Faller and Bent, "Making Medicine," 85–90.

25. *East Oregonian*, May 16, 1913, 8; Margaret Ann Knox, "Identity, Territory and Place: Insights from the Warm Springs Reservation," Ph.D. diss., University of Oregon, 2005.

26. Nancy Bristow, *American Pandemic: The Lost Worlds of the 1918 Influenza*

Epidemic (Oxford University Press, 2017); Lewis Meriam, *The Problem of Indian Administration* (USGPO, 1928), 3–53.

27. U.S. Census, 1870, 1880, 1900, 1910, Sault Ste. Marie, Mich.; Indian Census Rolls, 1885, Menominee, Wisc.

28. Canadian Census, 1881, District 79, Quebec City, MF C-13211; Canadian Census, 1901, District 178, Quebec City, MF T-6415; Charlotte McMurray Killaly, death certificate, 1928, Registrations of Deaths, Archives of Ontario, Toronto.

29. Indian Census Rolls, 1921, Yankton Sioux; U.S. Census, 1920, 1930, 1940, Sioux City, Ia.; "Projects in South Dakota," *Living New Deal*, https://livingnewdeal.org/us/sd/.

30. Theda Perdue, ed., *Nations Remembered: An Oral History of the Cherokee, Chickasaws, Choctaws, Creeks, and Seminoles in Oklahoma, 1865–1907* (University of Oklahoma Press, 1993), 179–85; Chang, *Color of Land*, 176–80; Jean Dennison, "The Logic of Recognition: Debating Osage Nation Citizenship in the Twenty-First Century," *American Indian Quarterly* 38, no. 1 (2014): 1–35; J. Kirsty Gover, "Genealogy as Continuity: Explaining the Growing Tribal Preference for Descent Rules in Membership Governance in the United States," *American Indian Law Review* 33, no. 1 (2008): 243.

31. "Eastern Oregon Indians Prepare for Their Root Festival," *La Grande Observer*, April 21, 1939; Pendleton High School Yearbook, 1952, 50; Pendleton High School Yearbook, 1953, 43; Joan Burbick, *Rodeo Queens and the American Dream* (PublicAffairs, 2002), 86.

32. Clippings, "Miss Indian America Archive," Box 3, Folder 7, M0810, Special Collections, Stanford University; *La Grande Observer*, August 6, 1954.

33. Gregory Nickerson, "The All-American Indian Days and the Miss Indian America Contest," *Montana: Magazine of Western History* 67, no. 2 (2009): 3–26.

INDEX